LEGAL WRITING FROM THE GROUND UP

ASPEN COURSEBOOK SERIES

LEGAL WRITING FROM THE GROUND UP

Process, Principles, and Possibilities

TRACY TURNER
Director of Legal Analysis, Writing, and Skills
Southwestern Law School

Wolters Kluwer

Published by Wolters Kluwer in New York.

Wolters Kluwer serves customers worldwide with CCH, Aspen Publishers, and Kluwer Law International products. (www.wolterskluwerlb.com)

To contact Customer Service, e-mail customer.service@wolterskluwer.com, call 1-800-234-1660, fax 1-800-901-9075, or mail correspondence to:

Wolters Kluwer
Attn: Order Department
PO Box 990
Frederick, MD 21705

Printed in the United States of America.

1 2 3 4 5 6 7 8 9 0

ISBN 978-1-4548-5216-2

Design and composition by Keithley & Associates, Inc.

Turner, Tracy L., author.
Legal writing from the ground up : process, principles, and possibilities / Tracy Turner, Director of Legal Analysis, Writing, and Skills, Southwestern Law School.
pages cm
Includes bibliographical references and index.
ISBN 978-1-4548-5216-2 (alk. paper)
1. Legal composition. 2. Law--United States--Language I. Title.
KF250.T87 2015
808.06'634--dc23

2014045918

About Wolters Kluwer Law & Business

Wolters Kluwer Law & Business is a leading global provider of intelligent information and digital solutions for legal and business professionals in key specialty areas, and respected educational resources for professors and law students. Wolters Kluwer Law & Business connects legal and business professionals as well as those in the education market with timely, specialized authoritative content and information-enabled solutions to support success through productivity, accuracy and mobility.

Serving customers worldwide, Wolters Kluwer Law & Business products include those under the Aspen Publishers, CCH, Kluwer Law International, Loislaw, ftwilliam.com and MediRegs family of products.

CCH products have been a trusted resource since 1913, and are highly regarded resources for legal, securities, antitrust and trade regulation, government contracting, banking, pension, payroll, employment and labor, and healthcare reimbursement and compliance professionals.

Aspen Publishers products provide essential information to attorneys, business professionals and law students. Written by preeminent authorities, the product line offers analytical and practical information in a range of specialty practice areas from securities law and intellectual property to mergers and acquisitions and pension/benefits. Aspen's trusted legal education resources provide professors and students with high-quality, up-to-date and effective resources for successful instruction and study in all areas of the law.

Kluwer Law International products provide the global business community with reliable international legal information in English. Legal practitioners, corporate counsel and business executives around the world rely on Kluwer Law journals, looseleafs, books, and electronic products for comprehensive information in many areas of international legal practice.

Loislaw is a comprehensive online legal research product providing legal content to law firm practitioners of various specializations. Loislaw provides attorneys with the ability to quickly and efficiently find the necessary legal information they need, when and where they need it, by facilitating access to primary law as well as state-specific law, records, forms and treatises.

ftwilliam.com offers employee benefits professionals the highest quality plan documents (retirement, welfare and non-qualified) and government forms (5500/PBGC, 1099 and IRS) software at highly competitive prices.

MediRegs products provide integrated health care compliance content and software solutions for professionals in healthcare, higher education and life sciences, including professionals in accounting, law and consulting.

Wolters Kluwer Law & Business, a division of Wolters Kluwer, is headquartered in New York. Wolters Kluwer is a market-leading global information services company focused on professionals.

To my husband and children for inspiring me to greet each day with enthusiasm and optimism.

To my legal writing colleagues at Southwestern for generously sharing the ideas that have shaped me as a teacher.

To the legal writing giants for teaching me how to teach.

SUMMARY OF CONTENTS

TABLE OF CONTENTS

PREFACE

The Goals of the Book

"What is in this package in my faculty mailbox? Another legal writing textbook." Legal writing professors are excellent teachers and excellent writers. So, it is no surprise that we have a wealth of textbooks filling up our shelves. Each new book helps move along our evolving pedagogy and improve our ability to reach students. I hope this book makes its own contribution. I wrote it out of love for both my students and my legal writing colleagues around the country.

Specificity. This book is the result of my commitment to reach today's law students and arm them with the skills and mindset they will need to succeed as attorneys. When students first walk into my classroom, many have never faced an academically rigorous program that has challenged them to question and support their assumptions. I have learned that teaching students what to do is insufficient; they need to be shown how at a very basic and specific level. This book follows years of dissecting the processes of legal reasoning and writing for my students with increasing specificity. My goal has been to provide students with something more than, "You need to prove this conclusion." Instead, I offer them a step-by-step process for every topic from complex skills like legal reasoning to more mechanical tasks like citation. The book's pages are full of the helpful tips, strategies, warnings, encouragements, explanations, illustrations, and examples I have given to my students as they sit in my office or ask questions in class.

Awareness of Learning Styles. With the goal of providing specificity, I have tried to carefully balance the importance of readability. The Internet has made our students a demanding audience. They are used to finding answers quickly and in a variety of formats suitable to their individual learning processes. To meet their needs, I have designed the book in a visually pleasing, easy-to-read format and have incorporated a variety of teaching tools including full-text explanations for the verbal learner; charts, diagrams, illustrations, and annotated in-text samples for the visual learner; and integrated exercises and checklists for those who learn best by doing. I have also developed narrated PowerPoint presentations that complement the book for the auditory learner. And to appeal to all learning types, the text of the book is written in a personal, engaging, practical, and occasionally humorous tone that connects with today's law students.

Flexibility. The other risk of specificity is rigidity. In writing this book, I was always mindful of this risk. Writing is ultimately a creative, strategic, and personal endeavor that specific lessons can aid but not direct. I aim for an ideal balance between instruction and flexibility. Whenever possible, I include multiple options for achieving the overall goals of clear writing and logical reasoning. Moreover, because multiple options sometimes confuse rather than enlighten students, I also incorporate decision-making strategies to help them understand why and how each option works in a particular context.

Transferability. Finally, the book aims to create self-directed learners and to increase the transfer of knowledge by incorporating take-away learning tools like mindset toward feedback, critical reading techniques, checklists, charts, and diagrams.

The Organization of the Book

I strongly believe that the fundamentals of good legal writing are universal, regardless of the format of a particular document and even regardless of whether the document is objective or persuasive. The book's organization reflects this belief by devoting Part I to universal lessons regarding legal reasoning and writing. Part II then covers the specific format of the objective legal research memorandum, and Part III covers persuasive briefs. Moreover, because the lessons on persuasion are universal regardless of whether the brief is an appellate or a trial brief, universal lessons are again presented before the specific formats of trial and appellate briefs are covered. For example, persuasive facts sections, persuasive issue statements, and persuasive techniques in the argument section are covered in depth in the early chapters of Part III while formatting differences between appellate briefs and memoranda of points and authorities are covered in the last two chapters. Appendix B includes sample documents of legal research memoranda, appellate briefs, and trial briefs. Multiple samples are included to illustrate different organizational choices. Some samples are annotated while others are left without annotations so that the professor can use in-class exercises to help students dissect the samples on their own. Excerpts from the Appendix B samples are also integrated into the text of every chapter in the book so that students can both focus on the particular lesson covered by a chapter or section of the book and see the document as a whole in Appendix B. Finally, more complex chapters include self-tests with answers in the back of the book so that students can test their grasp of key concepts.

Adapting the Book to Different Programs and Teaching Styles

Selfishly, I wrote this book first for my own students. So, it is geared toward the structure of our legal writing program—predictive writing in the fall and then persuasive writing in the spring. However, because the book covers fundamentals in Part I before introducing the specific formats of predictive and persuasive writing, it adapts well to different structures. A program that teaches persuasive writing first, for example, can cover Part I (universal fundamentals) and then skip over Part II (predictive writing) and move right into Part III (persuasive writing). Any cross-references in Part III refer the reader back to the Part I fundamentals rather than to Part II.

A Note on Chapter 6 (Organizational Paradigms)

Chapter 6 (Organizational Choices) is a unique aspect of the book that I feel I should take some time to explain. For the first few years that I taught legal writing, I stuck religiously to the CREAC format and instructed students to put all of the law on a particular issue or element before any of the application to the facts of the problem case. Chapter 6 labels this the TRRRAAAC format. However, I began to think that although this structure can be stretched to various hypotheticals, it is not always the best fit. I also came to believe that while CREAC was adequate for teaching predictive writing, it did not give students enough flexibility to write persuasively. Therefore, I spent a summer figuring out both how different textbooks teach legal writing and how (quality) legal writers in fact write. I looked both at the text of legal writing textbooks and at the samples they included. Chapter 6 reflects the different organizations that I either read explicitly in the textbooks or mapped out from reviewing the samples in the textbooks. In drafting Chapter 6, I aimed to adequately explain each organizational option through using an adaptation of the CRAC (or TRAC) paradigm along with annotated samples and to provide decision-making strategies to help students understand the strengths and weaknesses of each choice. When I teach Chapter 6, I usually cover only 6.1 (basic TRAC) and 6.2 (TRRRAAAC) for the first fall problem. I introduce 6.3 (Multiple TRAC Structures: TRRRAAAC by Heading) and 6.4.1 (TRARARAC) for the second fall problem. I save all of the remaining structures in Chapter 6 for the spring semester when we transition to persuasive writing. This incremental approach has worked well. I have many students who decide not to vary from TRRRAAAC. However, my stronger writers are willing and able to use the other structures effectively. My best briefs are better than they have ever been. Moreover, I believe that I have at least exposed every student to alternatives rather than suggesting that legal writing is a one-size-fits-all mechanical process.

Nonetheless, I recognize that members of the legal writing community have varied opinions on whether first-year students are ready to be taught flexibility in their writing, particularly with respect to organization. Therefore, I carefully separated different approaches into different section numbers so that professors can easily assign only the approaches they want their students to consider at any given time in the course.

Tracy Turner
December 2014

LEGAL WRITING FROM THE GROUND UP

PART I

THE FUNDAMENTALS

SECTION **A**

THINKING AND READING LIKE A LAWYER

CHAPTER **1**

Tools for Success

Think of this textbook more like a self-help book than a typical college textbook. Its pages do not contain information to memorize and regurgitate. It is not designed to be read once and immediately understood. Instead, it teaches skills that you will learn only through trial and error, reflection, and processing. Ideally, you will refer to your favorite pages so often that the book will quickly become worn and wrinkled. You will fill its margins with highlighting, notes, tags, and questions. And you will use it as only one part of a strategy to learn the craft of legal writing. This first chapter will orient you toward the tasks ahead, arming you with effective learning strategies and the right outlook.

1.1 | UNDERSTANDING THE TASK OF LEGAL WRITING

Some students choose law school because they love the thrill of a face-to-face debate. They envision themselves in the courtroom wowing a jury with their conviction and poise or sealing a deal with their charm and wit. Every courtroom drama and groundbreaking deal, however, follows toil at the computer, researching and writing about the applicable principles of law and their implications for the lawyer's case. Writing is as critical a skill to a lawyer as oration or people smarts. Naturally, we all have our strengths and weaknesses. A lawyer who loves to write may stress over a courtroom appearance, and another who thrives in the courtroom may cower at a blank computer screen. Effective lawyers build on their strengths but simultaneously work to improve their weaknesses. No matter whether you love or fear the task of writing, it is a skill worth improving because it can win (or lose) your client's case, seal (or break) a deal, enhance (or deflate) your reputation, and land (or preclude) a job opportunity.

Often, incoming law students assume that strong legal writing shares the same attributes as strong writing in other disciplines. To some extent, it does. The clarity and precision that mark effective legal writing also serve other disciplines well. However, the task of legal writing requires much more than editing skills. Clear writing requires clear thinking. Perfecting legal writing therefore requires perfecting legal analysis. This textbook is as much about thinking as it is about writing: dissecting a court opinion to find the secret to winning your case, breaking your conclusions into provable statements joined by the power of logic, synthesizing decades of court opinions to enable an accurate prediction about how your client's case will turn out, and disciplining yourself to see all sides of an argument. These skills can be elusive, but the disciplined approach described in the sections to follow can help you master them.

1.2 | USING THE BOOK AS A REFERENCE

Your first read of any particular section of this textbook may be to prepare for class discussion or an in-class exercise. However, you should think of that first read as just an introduction to the lesson. When it is time to start drafting your first assignment, pull the book back out and read the applicable sections again. Break down tasks into specific steps. For example, when you are writing your first rule statement paragraph, reread section 4.2 on rule statement paragraphs and look at all of the sample rule statement paragraphs again. As you start typing, have your favorite sample handy and try to model the content and organization of the rule statement paragraph. Do not blindly copy. Use your common sense and adapt when necessary, but use the sample as a tool as you write.

After you receive comments on your papers, consider opening the textbook again. It may help you understand the comments and resolve the problems they point out.

Keep the book and use it in your first internship, externship, or job in exactly the same specific, careful manner. Depending on how long ago you finished your legal writing course, you may have forgotten some things, most things, or maybe even everything, but the book can help you recall the lessons quickly.

1.3 | LEARNING FROM FEEDBACK

Picture yourself walking into class with this textbook in one hand. What's in the other hand? Perhaps a latte? Put down the latte. Fill the empty hand with your professor's comments on your papers. Now keep that image in your head.

This book's guidance and your professor's instruction will help you develop strong legal writing skills. However, the only way to *really* learn how to write is to do it and to get feedback. Most writers solicit feedback from others. Journalists, novelists, academicians, poets, screenwriters—none are safe from red ink, and most participate in workshops to hone their skills. The more feedback you seek, the better you will become.

Your legal writing professor is not writing comments to torture you, to "put you in your place," to flout her superiority, or for any other ignoble purpose. To the contrary, the comments are designed to help you. Legal writing professors spend hours identifying and diagnosing the weaknesses in your papers and even more hours trying to explain solutions in a manner that you can understand and learn from. Receiving feedback on your writing is not easy; you may feel deflated or disheartened. However, you can choose another response. Conceptualize feedback as opportunity rather than pronouncement. If your legal writing professor thought you could not improve, she would have little reason to comment on your writing. The comments represent her sincere belief that you can improve not just on the one assignment but on all future assignments as well. Welcome feedback. Embrace it. Celebrate it. Act on it.

Learning from feedback is an active process. Use your professor's comments to make a checklist of things you need to fix in that particular paper; then generalize the checklist to help avoid similar issues in your next assignment. Ask your professor about comments you do not understand. Go back to the relevant portions of the textbook for help in improving the identified areas of weakness.

1.4 | DEVELOPING PERSONALIZED CHECKLISTS

The longer chapters in this textbook include a checklist of the chapter's key lessons. Use them!

A wide body of research links checklists to success in various disciplines.[1] Writing is no exception. The words we type on our keyboards are projections of our voices. They are as personal and specific to us as our thumbprints. Often when we sit down to self-edit, we are lulled by the "sound" of our own voices. We gloss over our weaknesses and miss errors. Checklists allow you to depersonalize an otherwise subjective process into an objective list of goals. Checklists also enable you to break down the big task of writing into smaller, more achievable goals.

When you think you are done with a particular piece of your assignment, use the checklists to make sure you did not forget something important. For example, as you finish your rule statement and rule explanation paragraphs, review each item in the Chapter 4 checklist. If you do not recognize one of the items in the checklist, review the relevant portion of the chapter to remind yourself of the lesson.

1. Atul Gawande, *The Checklist Manifesto: How to Get Things Right* (2009).

The checklists in this book are a good start. However, because they attempt to capture every lesson, they are cumbersome. The more cumbersome a checklist, the less effective it becomes. The best approach is to start customizing your checklists as you receive more feedback on your writing. Take out the lessons you are confident you have internalized, leaving those you know you struggle with. Change the language of the checklists to reflect the "aha" moments you have throughout the learning process. Organize them by topic and by priority. Add samples that will help you remember the right fix for a particular challenge. Your checklists should always be a work in progress like your course outlines in Property and Torts. For an example of a smaller, personalized, more manageable checklist, see the Sample Self-Editing Plan in section 7.5.

1.5 | LEARNING THE LANGUAGE OF THE LAW

This chapter's final tip: devote yourself to learning the language of the law.

You are about to become immersed in a foreign language. Legal discourse may have just enough familiarity to mislead you into thinking you understand the gist of what you are reading. But if you devote some time in the beginning to understanding legal terms that are foreign to you, all of the other lessons of law school will come to you much more quickly. The advice is simple: look it up.

To get you started on this disciplined approach to learning the language of the law, here is a small sampling of key legal terms defined.

Affirm. To agree with a lower court (i.e., a higher reviewing court decides that the lower court was correct).

Answer. A document filed by the defendant in response to a complaint.

Appeal. A request that a higher court review a lower court's decision. The losing party in a trial can appeal to the court of appeal on the ground that the court that held the trial made an error or the verdict was blatantly wrong based on the evidence presented at the trial.

Appellate court. A higher court that reviews trial court decisions; also known as a court of appeal.

Civil court. Handles lawsuits that are based on civil law (see definition below).

Civil law. Rules governing wrongful conduct that is not defined as criminal by statute. Civil law consists of both statutes and common law.

Common law. Rules that courts identify from societal customs and precedent, not from statutes.

Complaint. The document filed by a party to initiate a legal proceeding in a civil court.

Court case (or just "case"). A civil lawsuit or a criminal prosecution.

Court opinion. A written decision by a judge or justice in a particular legal proceeding.

Crime. Statutes deem particular wrongs to be crimes. Not every wrong is a crime. Wrongs not defined as crimes by statute are governed by civil law and are addressed in civil courts.

Criminal court. Handles criminal law cases. (See definition below.)

Criminal law. Statutes that define crimes and related legal authority including, for example, prior court opinions interpreting criminal statutes.

Criminal prosecution. A legal proceeding commenced when a law enforcement agency such as the District Attorney's Office charges a person or an entity with a crime.

Defendant. The party against whom a lawsuit or criminal charge is filed.

Dicta. Court statements that are not rules and that do not factor into a court's holding in the case.

Holding (held, hold). *See* Ruling.

Lawsuit. A court case initiated when one party files a complaint against another in civil court.

Legal authority. A legitimate source of law (e.g., prior court opinions, statutes, ordinances, regulations).

Legal proceeding (related terms: criminal proceeding, civil proceeding, court proceeding). A court case.

Litigation. *See* Lawsuit.

Plaintiff. The party who files a complaint (i.e., who initiates a civil case).

Pleading. A complaint or an answer.

Precedent. Prior court opinions and other preexisting law, statutes, ordinances, regulations, and treaties.

Prosecution. (1) The District Attorney's Office or other law enforcement agency that initiates criminal charges against a defendant. (2) The process of bringing and proving criminal charges against a defendant.

Reverse. To undo or erase a lower court's decision (i.e., a higher reviewing court decides that the lower court made an error in the proceedings or that the jury's verdict was not supported by the evidence). Technically, it means to order the opposite of the lower court's decision, but it is often used more loosely.

Rule (as a noun). A principle, test, standard, requirement, or other generalized statement that can be applied to future cases to determine the right outcome of a case. (By "determine," I do not mean to suggest that the right answer is clear from the rule; interpretation of rules is the lifeblood of legal analysis.)

Rule (as a verb). Describes a court's action in making a pronouncement or a decision.

Ruling (as a noun). (1) Any court statement about the law that changes or clarifies existing law (e.g., a new interpretation of existing law, a more specific definition of a term used in preexisting legal authority, or a new exception). (2) The ultimate decision of the court on a particular issue in a particular case.

Statutes. Laws created by state or federal legislatures.

Tort. A wrong done to someone or an injury for which the law permits monetary recovery. This term is not used to refer to crimes but to civil wrongs.

Trial court. The court in which a case is initially filed and adjudicated.

Vacate. To undo a lower court's decision (i.e., a decision by a higher reviewing court that the lower court made some mistake). When the reviewing court "vacates" rather than "reverses," the lower court usually has to hold some new proceedings below. A decision to "vacate" does not mean the court disagreed with the ultimate outcome of the lower court case but only that an error occurred that requires a do-over.

CHAPTER 1 SELF-TEST

Name at least three techniques that you can use to ensure that you are applying the lessons of this text to your writing.

1.

2.

3.

See answers on page 337.

CHAPTER **2**

Lawyerly Logic

As a law student, you are embarking on a course that will change the way you think forever. One of my favorite undergraduate professors taught a course on legal issues in health care. When I shared my professional plans with her, she told me that I would lose all of my creativity by the end of law school. Now, as a legal writing professor, I can happily disagree with her prognosis. After reading hundreds of student papers on identical legal issues that nonetheless offered a rich variety of unique thoughts, decisions, and styles, I am convinced that creativity is not the enemy of good legal writing but its closest ally. Nor is legal writing divorced from emotion. The ability to tell a compelling story often sets apart an excellent piece of legal writing from an adequate one. Still, while bringing creativity and a sense of justice to their practice of law, lawyers do have to master the mathematical precision of logic.

2.1 | LEARNING TO THINK LIKE A LAWYER

Learning to think like a lawyer requires a transformation from cursory analysis to rigorous logic. The transformation looks something like this:

Illustration of a Law Student's Transformation

BEFORE INEZ ATTENDS LAW SCHOOL

Inez: I can't believe you didn't at least rinse this dish before you went to bed. I am never going to get this syrup off.
Mark: You didn't tell me you wanted me to rinse it.
Inez: I am not your mother!
Mark: That's for sure!
Inez: What is that supposed to mean?
Mark: Never mind.

Cont.

AFTER INEZ ATTENDS LAW SCHOOL

Inez: Because you didn't rinse this dish last night, this syrup is stuck. I have been rinsing and scrubbing it for three minutes, and you can see I've made no progress.
Mark: You didn't tell me you wanted me to rinse it.
Inez: I would have expected that at age 23, you would know that food sticks to dishes if you do not rinse them soon after use.
Mark: I didn't think about it.
Inez: I suspect that if you took over the task of loading the dishwasher, you might be more likely to rinse the dishes in the future. I'll put together a schedule of chores so that we both understand our obligations.
Mark: I don't think I want my life so scheduled.
Inez: The alternative seems to be that we fight.
Mark: I'm okay with fighting.
Inez: That's not logical.

Poor Inez. Law school has changed her forever; she is now a logic machine. After attending law school, Inez breaks her thoughts down into more specific and provable statements. She thinks about and expresses cause-and-effect relationships, she uses facts to justify her conclusions, she articulates why Mark's conclusions are flawed, and she seeks fair solutions to problems that will minimize future uncertainty and conflict. Hopefully Mark will forgive her move to the dark side and love her anyway.

You will experience this transformation. Maybe not overnight. Law school is just the beginning of the process. The change will be slow and subtle. I was oblivious to my own transformation until many years after I graduated from law school when my preschool-age daughter pleaded for dessert by enumerating her arguments: "First, I did not have dessert last night. Second, I ate all of my broccoli." I had poisoned her with lawyerly logic.

When you start law school, the process of supporting your conclusions with sound reasoning requires deliberate, structured thought. But with practice, this way of thinking will become second nature. Think back to a skill you once had to master like typing, swimming, driving, or algebra. Remember the effort and attention it took when you first started. Approach your law school classes, including your legal writing course, with the same effort and attention. In law school, the target of the effort and attention is the "why" behind your conclusions. You will learn to ask "why" where others would just accept the truth of a statement.

2.2 | THE ROLE OF PRECEDENT

It is impossible to write about lawyerly logic without addressing the role of precedent, meaning prior court decisions and other preexisting law. Precedent is simultaneously an important limit and an important facilitator of lawyerly logic.

Imagine, for a moment, a society without traffic rules. You step out of your house or apartment and get into your car to go to school. Some people drive on the right side of the street, some on the left, and some in the middle. You have no stop signs, no traffic lights, and no lane markers. No one knows who has the right of way and who has to yield.

Now imagine a society in which traffic rules change on a whim. One week, citizens are told they should drive on the right, and the next week, they are told they should drive on the left. And it changes back and forth every so often. Or, even worse, imagine two equal authorities in the community disagreeing—one telling citizens to drive on the right and the other telling them to drive on the left.

Under these lawless scenarios, driving would be more stressful and dangerous.

You may have heard the term "rule of law": the idea that everyone is subject to the laws of the society. The rule of law is the opposite of an autocratic society in which the powerless are at the mercy of the whims and desires of the powerful. As the traffic hypotheticals above illustrate, predictability is essential to the rule of law.

Predictability, in turn, requires consistency in the development of the law. To achieve consistency and predictability, modern law is governed by the principle of stare decisis. Stare decisis requires courts to base their decisions in each new case on prior court opinions or other preexisting sources of law.

The result of stare decisis is that lawyers have to base every argument they make on precedent. Accordingly, the skills of finding, reading, understanding, and extrapolating principles from prior court opinions are essential components of lawyerly logic. These skills form the backbone of effective legal writing.

2.3 | UNDERSTANDING THE U.S. COURT SYSTEM

As a prelude to discussing how to read court opinions, this section discusses where court opinions come from. The U.S. court system is incredibly complex, and the value that a court opinion carries as precedent depends on the issuing court's place in the judicial hierarchy.

2.3.1 | Federal and State Courts

U.S. courts are divided into two main systems: federal and state. Like a good highway system, they operate separately but cross paths every now and then.

Understanding the parallel systems is essential to making sense out of your law school courses and many of the court opinions you will read.

2.3.1.1 | Federal Courts

In Washington, D.C., the U.S. Congress is busy making federal statutes. Federal statutes are published in a multivolume compendium called the United States Code. Some federal statutes define crimes that can be prosecuted by the United States Attorney's Office; others prohibit or require certain conduct by private individuals, entities, or corporations and can be enforced through litigation by a government agency or even personal lawsuits; others establish special remedies for harm suffered by individuals. A court case that requires application of a federal statute usually lands in a federal court.

2.3.1.2 | State Courts

While the U.S. Congress is busy making federal laws in Washington, D.C., each state's legislature is busy making its own statutes. States publish their statutes in their own sets of codes. State statutes cannot conflict with federal statutes or the U.S. Constitution, but they otherwise can cover a vast array of topics including both criminal and civil law. Usually, a court case that requires application of a state statute lands in one of that state's courts.

The other great contributor to the workload of a state court is common law, which derives from societal customs and precedent rather than statutes.

You might think states' common law would be universal. After all, common law is premised on certain universal customs and unwritten codes of conduct that date to the beginning of modern law. And yet, common law is encumbered by vast complexities, inconsistencies, confusion, and disagreement. As a result, each state has its own version of common law.

2.3.1.3 | Diversity Jurisdiction

Ever meet a New Yorker who thinks Californians are all crazy hippies or a Midwesterner who thinks New Englanders are snobs? Do you have a passion for your local sports team? Would you buy a drink for a stranger simply because he is from your hometown? Recognizing that stereotypes, rivalries, favoritism, or other biases may influence judicial outcomes, our government allows parties from different states to seek a neutral ground in the federal court system. Imagine, for example, two courthouses right next to each other in a city in Kansas. One is staffed by federal judges appointed by the federal government and the other by state judges appointed or elected by Kansans. If you were a Bostonian needing to sue a Kansan, which court would you rather be in? Our court system assumes that the Bostonian should have the option to sue in a neutral federal forum. Similarly, a Bostonian sued by a Kansan has the right to move the case to federal court. Federal courts resolve these "diversity" cases according to the state's statutes and common law.

2.3.2 | Court Hierarchy and the Weight of Court Opinions

2.3.2.1 | Federal Court Hierarchy

Most court cases in the federal court system begin in the federal trial courts, which are called district courts. Their name derives from the numerous districts into which the 50 states are divided in the federal court system. A losing party in the district courts has the right to appeal to a circuit court of appeals. The United States has 11 numbered circuits (First Circuit, Second Circuit, Third Circuit, etc.) and an additional circuit for the District of Columbia. For example, California is in the Ninth Circuit; appeals are heard in the U.S. Court of Appeals for the Ninth Circuit. Finally, a two-time loser in the district court and the circuit court of appeals will sometimes "petition for review" by the U.S. Supreme Court.

Federal Court Structure

A district court's decision can be reversed by a circuit court of appeals, and a circuit court of appeals' decision can be reversed by the U.S. Supreme Court.

2.3.2.2 | State Court Hierarchy

Most states have three levels of judicial hierarchy: (1) trial courts, (2) intermediate appellate courts (most often called "courts of appeal"), and (3) courts of last resort (most often called "supreme courts"). Intermediate appellate courts have the power to reverse decisions by the trial courts, and state courts of last resort have the power to reverse decisions by the intermediate appellate courts.

Typical State Court Structure

A state trial court's decision can be reversed by one of the state's courts of appeal, and a state court of appeal's decision can be reversed by the state's highest court.

2.3.2.3 | The Impact of Hierarchy on Legal Writing

When you commence a legal writing project, you will be looking for precedent. You will need to know which court's precedent matters to your case. If your case is pending in a Texas state court and involves Texas state law, you will be looking for opinions of the Texas state courts. You will stray from Texas only if desperate—that is, if the Texas courts do not have any prior opinions that govern the issues involved in your case. These out-of-state opinions can help persuade Texas courts, but the Texas courts are not required to follow them.

You will also need to know how to handle disagreement between courts. Lower courts in a jurisdiction are required to follow the opinions of higher-level courts in the same jurisdiction. Same-level ("sister") courts *should* listen to each other for the sake of consistency, but they do not have to. For example, a California appellate court cannot disagree with the California Supreme Court, but a court of appeal in Los Angeles can disagree with a court of appeal in San Francisco.

Illustration of Hierarchy

Suppose you are a ten-year-old child with two older twin brothers, Ned and Ted, and one parent. You want to watch television. You turn on the television and Ned comes over and tells you to turn it off. You say, "Ted told me I could watch TV." Ned thinks for a moment and says, "I don't care what he told you. He's wrong. Television is bad for your brain." You then say, "Mom said it was okay too." At this point, Ned should be thinking that if he insists on turning off the television against your mother's wishes, he might get in trouble.

Same-level courts are like Ned and Ted; they can disagree but they cannot cross Mama. On the other hand, sister courts usually try to agree with one another because of the stare decisis doctrine discussed earlier in this chapter. Therefore, a decision of a sister court is highly persuasive, even if not binding.

2.3.2.4 | Federal Courts v. State Courts

Students usually assume that federal courts rank higher than state courts. The truth, however, is not that simple. Federal courts are the highest authority on issues involving federal statutes, but a state's own courts are the highest authority on issues involving its statutes and its common law. Although the federal and state courts generally run on separate tracks, sometimes they intersect. When exercising diversity jurisdiction, for example, a federal court may have to apply the law of a state and will defer to prior opinions of that state's courts. So when a Kansan sues a Bostonian in federal court for a claim that arises out of Kansas state law, the federal court should defer to decisions of the Kansas courts.

COURT HIERARCHY SELF-TEST

Suppose your supervisor asks you to research whether homeowners can sue their neighbors for refusing to chop down a tree on their property that is in danger of falling. There is no applicable federal statute. The issue is governed by state common law.

1. **Scenario #1.** The only relevant cases you find are two state court of appeal decisions that disagree with one another about whether this type of lawsuit should be permitted. What do you tell your supervisor?
2. **Scenario #2.** You find two state court of appeal decisions that disagree with one another about whether this type of lawsuit should be permitted. However, you also find a state supreme court case that permits the lawsuit. What do you tell your supervisor now?
3. **Scenario #3.** The only relevant case you find is a state court of appeal opinion that permits the lawsuit. What do you tell your supervisor?
4. **Scenario #4.** The only relevant cases you find are a federal appellate court opinion decided in 1999 that holds that the state's law supports the lawsuit and a state supreme court opinion decided in 2001 that disagrees with the federal court's 1999 opinion and holds that the lawsuit cannot be brought. What do you tell your supervisor?

See answers on page 337.

2.4 | HOW TO READ A COURT OPINION

2.4.1 | Active Reading

Reading a court opinion is probably unlike any reading you have done before now. You do not read an opinion simply to regurgitate the information you find. Instead, you are trying to extract underlying principles from the opinion and apply them to the context of your own client's case.

One read of a court opinion is *never* sufficient. Reread the opinion. Highlight important parts of it. Write in the margins. Take notes on a separate piece of paper or on your computer. Ask yourself questions about the opinion. Use charts to figure out how one opinion fits in with the others you read. Look back at the opinion when you go to write your lawyerly papers. Look back at the opinion when you go to revise your lawyerly papers. Keep engaging with the court opinion. I find that every time I look at a court opinion with fresh eyes, I find something new and useful. Sometimes that last look gives me the key I need to win an argument.

Reading a court opinion is an active process: stretch it, crumple it, and challenge it until you truly know all of its qualities.

2.4.2 | Reading with a Purpose

In your doctrinal classes, you will read court opinions to learn about the law. In legal writing, you will read court opinions for a narrower purpose. You have a client. Your client has a case. Your client's case involves some question of law about which you are uncertain. You want an answer to that question. And if you cannot find a clear answer, you want to understand all of the possible arguments that both sides could make. If you find yourself reading an opinion without remembering the precise legal issue you are addressing, stop yourself and go back to the assignment memorandum from your supervisor before proceeding to read the opinion.

With your issue in mind, you should have two primary goals as you read the opinion:

1. Identify and understand the legal rules that govern the issue.
2. Identify and understand the reasons why the court concluded that those legal rules justified its decision in the case.

2.4.3 | Identifying Legal Rules

A legal rule is a principle, test, standard, requirement, definition, limitation, exception, prohibition, or other generalizable statement that can be applied to future cases to determine the right outcome in a case.

Example: Rule v. Case-Specific

Not a rule: Mary cannot sue Joe because the accident was entirely her fault.

A rule: Persons are only liable for the proportion of harm caused by their own actions.

Picture the town crier ringing his bell to announce edicts of the king. You are looking for the edicts of the court. The only problem is... no bell. In fact, they may be deceptively hard to find. They may be buried deep in the midst of a long historical dissertation on the development of the law. They may be hidden in a footnote. And an opinion may recite so many rules that you will find it hard to decide which rules are important to your legal issue.

Most legal issues involve a specific starting point—the rule from which all other rules governing the issue are derived. For example, if you are trying to figure out whether your client committed robbery, the starting point would be the statute that defines the crime of robbery. Or if you are considering whether to rely on the insanity defense, the starting-point rule would explain that insanity is a defense to criminal charges.

Examples of Starting-Point Rule

Robbery is the taking of property from the person of another by means of force or fear.

Insanity is a defense to intentional crimes.

After the starting-point rule comes a complex web of tests, definitions, exceptions, limitations, and other pronouncements that help us understand the meaning and scope of the starting-point rule. For example, in the scenario above, you would be interested in any limitations on the insanity defense, any definitions of the defense, any standards that must be met before it can be asserted, and so on. You also would want to look for the reasons behind the various rules you find to the extent the opinion provides them (I will refer to this as "policy"). For example, you would want to know why the insanity defense was created and any societal considerations the courts have weighed in determining its proper scope and application—fairness to the defendant, protection of the public, and so on.

Examples of Other Types of Rules

Insanity includes either an inability to distinguish between right and wrong or an inability to conform one's conduct to the law that is caused by a severe mental disease or defect.

The insanity defense exists because it is unfair to impose criminal penalties on someone who lacks the ability to understand or control wrongdoing.

To be insane, a person's disease or defect must be "settled" but need not be permanent.

Mere intoxication is not a defense to a crime, but long-term drug abuse can cause insanity.

2.4.4 | Identifying Court Reasoning

Identifying court reasoning tends to be even more difficult than finding rules. Most court opinions involve complex issues that cannot be solved simply by stating rules and then announcing, with a big "ta-dah," the conclusion they warrant in the case. Instead, courts use logical reasoning to bridge the gap between the rules and the facts in the case at hand.[1] Do the same when you apply the rules to the facts of your case.

Identifying and understanding the court's reasoning is an extremely important step in reading court opinions. Students often mistake the rules, facts, or holding as reasoning. The following chart illustrates how a court's reasoning bridges the gap between the rules and the facts to support its holding. The court's reasoning explains *why* the rules warrant the court's holding under the particular facts of the case.

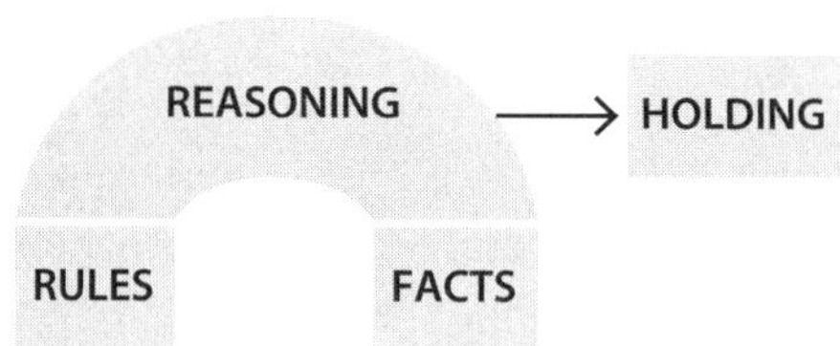

Suppose you are reading a court opinion on the insanity defense. You read that the insanity defense is available when a mental illness results in the inability to distinguish right from wrong. The facts of the case involve a defendant who smashed the victim's car window with an umbrella because mental illness caused her to believe that the victim was trying to run her over. However, no one was in the car at the time. The court's opinion holds that the insanity defense is available to the defendant. Now you want to find the court's reasoning, its explanation as to why the defendant's mental illness satisfies the inability to distinguish right from wrong requirement. The court's reasoning might be as follows:

Example of Court Reasoning

Due to the defendant's mental illness, she was unable to correctly read the circumstances. In her mind, the car was about to run her over. In those fictional circumstances, which were real to the defendant, using her umbrella to defend herself from the approaching car was not "wrong" but was, instead, a necessary act of self-defense. Her mental illness caused an inability to distinguish right from wrong because it created a fiction in which a wrong act was right.

The following diagram illustrates how this reasoning bridges the gap between the facts of the case and the definition of insanity.

1. "The case at hand" is a common phrase that means the case that is being litigated. You might use "the case at hand" to refer to your own client's case. A court might use it to refer to the case it is presiding over.

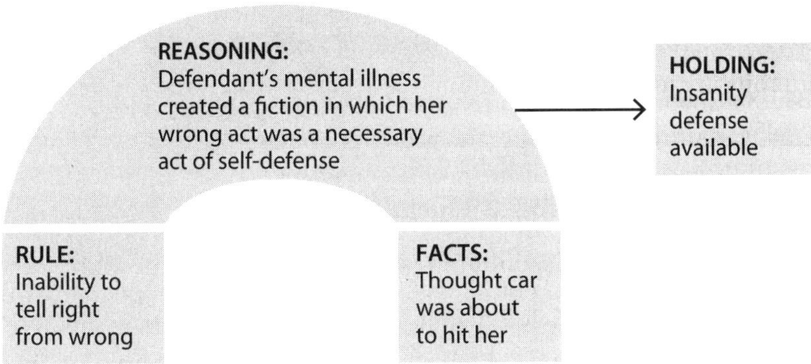

When you read court opinions, you are looking for these bridges between the legal rules and the facts of the case—the court's explanation as to why the rules *as applied to the facts* justify its holding.

EXERCISE 1

Now that you have had some instruction on how to read a court opinion, it is time to try it. Recall that section 2.4 advised to always have your purpose in mind before you read a court opinion. The following hypothetical provides your purpose for this exercise. Read the hypothetical and then read the court opinion that follows (*People v. Valencia*). Identify rules from the court opinion that might be relevant to your client and the court's reasoning as to why the rules warranted its holding in the case.

YOUR HYPOTHETICAL CLIENT SITUATION

You work for a district attorney who asks you to evaluate whether a criminal charge of burglary against a defendant is likely to succeed. If the charge is unlikely to succeed, the district attorney may decide to let the defendant plead to a less serious charge of theft. The issue is whether the defendant entered a building. If he did not enter a building, he cannot be guilty of burglary. The defendant used a stolen ATM card to obtain money from an ATM machine. The ATM machine was located in an enclosed kiosk adjacent to a bank. The kiosk shared one wall with the bank; its three other walls protruded from the shared wall. It had its own ceiling, separate from the bank's ceiling. Its one external door did not have a locking mechanism. The bank built the kiosk to provide protection from theft and believed that it would provide some protection even without a lock on the door. The bank was near a bus stop, and people sometimes waited for the bus in the kiosk. The bank manager usually asked loiterers to leave but sometimes tolerated loitering during off-hours.

THE PEOPLE, Plaintiff and Respondent, v. CUAHUTEMOC SANCHEZ VALENCIA, Defendant and Appellant.

No. S095385.

SUPREME COURT OF CALIFORNIA

28 Cal. 4th 1; 46 P.3d 920; 120 Cal. Rptr. 2d 131; 2002 Cal. LEXIS 3564; 2002 Cal. Daily Op. Service 4794; 2002 Daily Journal DAR 6095

June 3, 2002, Decided
June 3, 2002, Filed

COUNSEL: Chris Truax, under appointment by the Supreme Court, for Defendant and Appellant.

John T. Philipsborn and Cliff Gardner for California Attorneys for Criminal Justice as Amicus Curiae on behalf of Defendant and Appellant.

Bill Lockyer, Attorney General, David P. Druliner and Robert R. Anderson, Chief Assistant Attorneys General, Gary W. Schons, Assistant Attorney General, Megan J. Beale, Racquel M. Gonzalez, Crystal L. Bradley, Peter Quon, Jr., and Quisteen S. Shum, Deputy Attorneys General, for Plaintiff and Respondent.

JUDGES: (Opinion by George, C. J., with Baxter, Werdegar, Chin, Brown, and Moreno, JJ., concurring. Dissenting opinion by Kennard, J.)

OPINION BY: GEORGE

OPINION

GEORGE, [*3] **C.** [***132] **J.**

[**920] Under California law, the crime of burglary is committed when a person "*enters* any [**921] . . . *building*," including a "house," "with intent to commit . . . larceny or any felony." (Pen. Code,[1] § 459, italics added; see § 460.)

1. Unless otherwise specified, all section references are to the Penal Code.

We granted review to determine whether penetration into the area behind a window screen amounts to an entry of a building within the meaning of the [*4] burglary statute when the window itself is closed and is not penetrated. As we shall explain, we conclude that it does. Accordingly, we reverse the judgment of the Court of Appeal, which held to the contrary.

I

The evidence presented at defendant's trial for the crime of burglary, viewed in the light most favorable to the judgment, reveals the following facts pertinent to the issue before us:

On the morning of February 4, 1998, Lee Florea left the house he shared with his wife and children in Santa Ana to go to work, with the doors and windows locked and the window screens secured in their tracks in front of the windows.

About noon, Nicky Nava, who lived across the street from the Floreas, came home for lunch. Looking out through a screen door, Nava saw a person later identified as defendant. As she watched, defendant, who apparently had a screwdriver in his hand, removed a window screen from a bathroom window of the Floreas' house and tried unsuccessfully to open the window itself. Evidently, defendant earlier had pulled a window screen away from a bedroom window of the Floreas' house and had tried unsuccessfully to open that window as well.

Nava called the Santa Ana Police Department and described defendant and his activities. As she continued to watch, moving at some point up to her screen door and then outside, defendant walked from the bathroom window of the Floreas' house and tried unsuccessfully to open the front door. Apparently in anger or frustration, defendant banged on the wall and then sat down for a few minutes. Defendant then got into an automobile, which resembled a gray or brown Monte Carlo or LTD, drove down the street about four houses away, parked, and got out.

[***133] By this time, Santa Ana Police Officer John Douthit had arrived at the scene. Douthit approached defendant, who was standing in the driveway of the house in front of which he had parked. Douthit asked defendant whether he owned the automobile parked in front of the house, and defendant answered he did not; Douthit asked defendant what he was doing, and defendant answered he was looking for a friend he called "Tommy." Douthit then searched defendant's pants pocket and found a pair of black gloves and a screwdriver with a bent blade and shank. Through a police dispatcher, Douthit confirmed that defendant matched the description reported by Nava. Douthit then arrested defendant. Defendant protested that he had not done [*5] anything wrong, and that he merely had been looking for a friend, whom he now called "Tony," to help in locating a stolen bicycle.

Going to the Floreas' house, Officer Douthit found what appeared to be rub marks on the bathroom window that could have been made by defendant's hand or hands as he tried to open the window. Douthit also found several pry marks on the frame of the bedroom window that could have been made by defendant's screwdriver. Florea returned to his house about this time, finding the scene as described above. Douthit later determined that defendant did indeed own the automobile he had denied owning.

After the presentation of evidence, the trial court instructed the jury on the offense of burglary. At the People's request, and over defendant's objection, the court gave the following instruction, drawn directly from *People v. Nible* (1988) 200 Cal.App.3d 838 [247 Cal.Rptr. 396] (*Nible*) and indirectly from *People v. Ravenscroft* (1988) 198 Cal.App.3d 639 [243 Cal.Rptr. 827] (*Ravenscroft*): "Any kind of entry, partial or complete, will satisfy the element of entry. The entry may be made by any part of the body or by use of an instrument or tool. *In order for there to have been an entry, a part of the defendant's body or some instrument, tool or other object* [**922] *under his control must have penetrated the area inside where the screen was normally affixed in the window frame in question.*" (Italics added.) The court refused to give the following instruction, based upon language from *Nible*, which defendant requested and the People objected to: "The test of whether an entry has occurred is whether a reasonable person would believe a window screen provides some protection against unauthorized intrusions."

The jury returned a verdict finding defendant guilty of burglary and determining that the burglary was of the first degree because it involved an inhabited dwelling house (§ 460, subd.

(a)). The trial court rendered a judgment of conviction on the jury's verdict, imposing a sentence of four years in prison.[2]

2. In addition to being found guilty by the jury of first degree burglary, defendant pleaded guilty to possession of heroin (Health & Saf. Code, § 11350, subd. (a)) and admitted an allegation that he committed the crimes in question while released from custody on bail or on his own recognizance (Pen. Code, § 12022.1). Together with the sentence of four years in prison for first degree burglary, the trial court imposed a sentence of two-thirds of a year for possession of heroin plus a two-year enhancement for committing the crimes while released from custody, for a total determinate sentence of six and two-thirds years.

On appeal, the Court of Appeal held that penetration into the area behind a window screen does not amount to an entry of a building within the meaning of the burglary statute, at least when, as in this case, the window itself is closed and is not penetrated. [***134] The Court of Appeal therefore concluded that the trial court erred by instructing the jury as requested by the [*6] People. The Court of Appeal also concluded that the trial court did not err by refusing to instruct as requested by defendant. The Court of Appeal went on to determine that, "[a]s a matter of law," defendant "was guilty only of attempted [first degree] burglary." As a consequence, the Court of Appeal reversed defendant's conviction and sentence for first degree burglary and remanded the case to the trial court with directions to enter a conviction for attempted first degree burglary and to impose sentence accordingly.

We granted the People's petition for review in order to consider the validity of the Court of Appeal's holding. As stated above, we reach a conclusion contrary to that reached by the Court of Appeal and therefore reverse the judgment rendered by that court.

II

The crime of burglary is committed when a person "*enters* any . . . *building*," including a "house," "with intent to commit . . . larceny or any felony." (§ 459, italics added.)[3] [HN2] Burglary may be of the first or second degree,[4] but in either event involves an entry into a building or other specified structure.

3. Section 459 provides: "Every person who enters any house, room, apartment, tenement, shop, warehouse, store, mill, barn, stable, outhouse or other building, tent, vessel, as defined in Section 21 of the Harbors and Navigation Code, floating home, as defined in subdivision (d) of Section 18075.55 of the Health and Safety Code, railroad car, locked or sealed cargo container, whether or not mounted on a vehicle, trailer coach, as defined in Section 635 of the Vehicle Code, any house car, as defined in Section 362 of the Vehicle Code, inhabited camper, as defined in Section 243 of the Vehicle Code, vehicle as defined by the Vehicle Code, when the doors are locked, aircraft as defined by Section 21012 of the Public Utilities Code, or mine or any underground portion thereof, with intent to commit grand or petit larceny or any felony is guilty of burglary. As used [herein], 'inhabited' means currently being used for dwelling purposes, whether occupied or not. A house, trailer, vessel designed for habitation, or portion of a building is currently being used for dwelling purposes if, at the time of the burglary, it was not occupied solely because a natural or other disaster caused the occupants to leave the premises."

4. Section 460 provides in pertinent part: "(a) Every burglary of an inhabited dwelling house, vessel, as defined in the Harbors and Navigation Code, which is inhabited and designed for habitation, floating home, as defined in subdivision (d) of Section 18075.55 of the Health and Safety Code, or trailer coach, as defined by the Vehicle Code, or the inhabited portion of any other building, is burglary of the first degree. [¶] (b) All other kinds of burglary are of the second degree."

The issue before us is whether penetration into the area behind a window screen amounts to an entry of a building within the meaning of the burglary statute when the [**923] window itself is closed and is not penetrated. As we shall explain, we conclude that it does.

In *People v. Davis* (1998) 18 Cal.4th 712 [76 Cal.Rptr. 2d 770, 958 P.2d 1083] (*Davis*), we recently had occasion to discuss the offense of burglary, [*7] including consideration of its historical background and its general contours today. Our discussion provides a useful starting point for addressing the rather narrow question presented in this case.

In *Davis*, we explained that "[t]he interest sought to be protected by the common law crime of burglary was clear. At common law, burglary was the breaking and entering of a dwelling in the nighttime. The law was intended to protect the sanctity of a person's home during the night hours when the resident was most vulnerable. [***135] As one commentator observed: 'The predominant factor underlying common law burglary was the desire to protect the security of the home, and the person within his home. Burglary was not an offense against property, real or personal, but an offense against the habitation, for it could only be committed against the dwelling of another.... The dwelling was sacred, but a duty was imposed on the owner to protect himself as well as looking to the law for protection. The intruder had to break and enter; if the owner left the door open, his carelessness would allow the intruder to go unpunished. The offense had to occur at night; in the daytime home-owners were not asleep, and could detect the intruder and protect their homes.' " (*Davis, supra*, 18 Cal.4th at p. 720.)

We went on to explain in *Davis* that, "[i]n California, as in other states, the scope of the burglary law has been greatly expanded. There is no requirement of a breaking; an entry alone is sufficient. The crime is not limited to dwellings, but includes entry into a wide variety of structures. The crime need not be committed at night." (*Davis, supra*, 18 Cal.4th at pp. 720-721.)

Nonetheless, as we added in *Davis*, the great expansion in the scope of the burglary law has not been unlimited. "In *People* v. *Gauze* (1975) 15 Cal.3d 709 [125 Cal.Rptr. 773, 542 P.2d 1365], we ... observed that '[a] burglary remains an entry which invades a possessory interest in a building.' [Citation.] ... ' "Burglary laws are based primarily upon a recognition of the dangers to personal safety created by the usual burglary situation — the danger that the intruder will harm the occupants in attempting to perpetrate the intended crime or to escape and the danger that the occupants will in anger or panic react violently to the invasion, thereby inviting more violence. The laws are primarily designed, then, not to deter the trespass and the intended crime, which are prohibited by other laws, so much as to forestall the germination of a situation dangerous to personal safety." [The burglary statute], in short, is aimed at the danger caused by the unauthorized entry itself.' " (*Davis, supra*, 18 Cal.4th at p. 721.)

In *Davis*, we further proceeded to note and approve the rule reflected in *People v. Moore* (1994) 31 Cal.App.4th 489, [37 Cal.Rptr.2d 104], [*8] *People v. Walters* (1967) 249 Cal.App.2d 547 [57 Cal.Rptr. 484], and *People v. Osegueda* (1984) 163 Cal.App.3d Supp. 25 [210 Cal.Rptr. 182], that entry may be effected by the intruder or by an instrument employed by the intruder, whether used "solely to effect entry, or to accomplish the intended larceny or felony as well." (*Davis, supra*, 18 Cal.4th at p. 717.)

Accordingly, resolution of the question before us does not depend upon whether penetration into the area behind a window screen is effected by the intruder or by an instrument employed by the intruder. Rather, it turns solely upon whether any such penetration amounts to an entry of a building.

In approaching this question, the People and defendant place considerable reliance, as did the Court of Appeal, on two Court of Appeal decisions — *Ravenscroft* and *Nible* — that preceded our decision in *Davis*.

In *Ravenscroft*, the Court of Appeal held that a defendant's insertion of an automatic teller machine (ATM) card into an ATM that was mounted inside a bank and was secured flush with the bank's exterior wall amounted to an entry of a building within the meaning [**924] of the burglary statute, because the ATM was part of the bank's outer boundary for purposes of burglary. [***136] In so holding, the Court of Appeal rejected a claim by the defendant that "his insertion of an ATM card into" an ATM did "not constitute an entry" of the bank "since he did not violate [its] air space." (*Ravenscroft, supra*, 198 Cal.App.3d at p. 643.) The Court of Appeal stated: "The insertion of an ATM card . . . is no less an entry into the air space of a bank as would be the use of any other tool or instrument. Although the California Penal Code does not define 'entry' for the purpose of burglary, the California courts have found that a burglary is complete upon the slightest partial entry of any kind, with the requisite intent. . . ." (*Ibid.*) In support, the Court of Appeal relied upon *People v. Walters, supra*, 249 Cal.App.2d at page 550, where the intruders simply pried off and removed the lid of a rooftop vent and lowered a rope into a building. The Court of Appeal also relied upon *People v. Osegueda, supra*, 163 Cal.App.3d Supp. at pages 31-32, where the intruders merely sawed a six-inch by four to five-inch hole through the wall of a building.

In *Nible* — which is the California case whose facts are closest to ours, and which we accordingly discuss at some length — the Court of Appeal held that a defendant's penetration into the area behind a window screen amounted to an entry of a building within the meaning of the burglary statute, because the window screen was part of the building's outer boundary for purposes of burglary.

In support of its holding, the Court of Appeal in *Nible* explained: "No California authority has considered whether the penetration of a window [*9] screen, without penetration of . . . the window beyond, constitutes an entry within the meaning of [the burglary statute]. Defendant contends the correct analysis to determine whether a burglarious entry has occurred is whether the 'air space' of a protected structure has been penetrated by a part of the defendant's body or an instrument or tool wielded by him. (See *People v. Ravenscroft* (1988) 198 Cal.App.3d 639, 643-644 [243 Cal.Rptr. 827] . . . .) The 'air space' analysis of *Ravenscroft* . . . does not necessarily lead to the result defendant suggests. Rather, it is reasonable to conclude that a window screen contains the outer boundary of a building's air space, especially when, as here, the window itself was left open. However it might be applied here, in our view the 'air space' test, although useful in some situations, is inadequate as a comprehensive test for determining when a burglarious entry occurs." (*Nible, supra*, 200 Cal.App.3d at pp. 843-844, fn. omitted.)

The Court of Appeal in *Nible* went on to state that "a more comprehensive test is suggested by the California Supreme Court's analysis" (*Nible, supra*, 200 Cal.App.3d at p. 844) in *People v. Gauze* (1975) 15 Cal.3d 709 [125 Cal.Rptr. 773, 542 P.2d 1365], which we have quoted above.

Moving beyond our discussion in *Gauze*, the Court of Appeal in *Nible* reasoned: "As the burglary statute is designed to protect against unauthorized entry and its attendant dangers, the ultimate test of whether a burglarious entry has occurred must focus on the protection the owners or inhabitants of a structure reasonably expect. The proper question is whether the nature of a structure's composition is such that a reasonable person would expect some protection from unauthorized intrusions. A structure with a locked door or window clearly affords a reasonable expectation of protection from invasion. But even an open door or window affords some expectation of protection from unauthorized intrusion because reasonable persons [***137] understand the social convention that portals may not be crossed without permission from the structure's owner." (*Nible*, *supra*, 200 Cal.App.3d at p. 844.)

"Thus," stated the Court of Appeal in *Nible*, "the focus of the question whether the penetration of a window screen constitutes a burglarious entry must be on whether a reasonable person would believe a window screen provides some protection against unauthorized intrusions. The answer is unequivocally in the affirmative. The opening of a screen door or window is deemed a burglarious breaking, . . . In such cases the [**925] screen door [or window] is not to be considered as a mere protection against flies, but rather as a permanent part of the dwelling. The holdings proceed, it would seem, on the grounds that the screen door [or window] is a part of the house on which the occupants rely for protection and that to open such a door [or window] is a violation of the security of the dwelling house which is the peculiar [*10] gravamen of a burglarious breaking.' . . ." (*Nible*, *supra*, 200 Cal.App.3d at p. 845.)

The Court of Appeal in *Nible* concluded: "The purposes of the burglary laws are best served by our holding the penetration of a window screen constitutes entry within the meaning of [the burglary statute]. As noted above, the burglary law protects against the dangers caused by unauthorized entry. The inhabitants of a building are just as likely to react violently to an intruder's penetration of their window screen as to the penetration of the window itself." (*Nible*, *supra*, 200 Cal.App.3d at p. 845.)

In *Davis*, subsequent to the Court of Appeal decisions in *Ravenscroft* and *Nible*, we faced the question whether a defendant's placing of a forged check into a chute in a walk-up window at a check-cashing facility amounted to an entry of a building within the meaning of the burglary statute. We held that it did not. In so holding, we accepted that the chute was part of the building's outer boundary for purposes of burglary. We reasoned, however, that although the placing of the forged check into the chute effected a type of entry, it was not "the type of entry *the burglary statute was intended to prevent*." (*Davis*, *supra*, 18 Cal.4th at p. 720, italics added.) In support, we stated that the act did not "violate[] the occupant's possessory interest in the building" (*id.* at p. 722) or threaten " ' "the germination of a situation dangerous to personal safety" ' " (*id.* at p. 721).

In the course of our discussion in *Davis*, we "disapprove[d]" *Ravenscroft* to the extent it held that a defendant's insertion of an ATM card into an ATM in a bank amounted to an entry of a building within the meaning of the burglary statute. (*Davis*, *supra*, 18 Cal.4th at p. 722, fn. 5.) At the same time, however, we added that we did "not disapprove the other aspects of . . . *Ravenscroft*, including its conclusion that the ATM card in that case was inserted into the air space of the ATM," and on this point we inserted a citation to *Nible*. (*Davis*, *supra*, 18 Cal. 4th at p. 722, fn. 5.)

As we have seen, the Court of Appeal in *Nible* found in *Ravenscroft* what it called a sometimes "useful," but sometimes "inadequate," " 'air space' test." (*Nible*, *supra*, 200 Cal.App.3d at p. 844.) The Court of Appeal in *Nible* proposed as "more comprehensive" a "reasonable belief" or "reasonable expectation" test. (*Id.* at p. 844; see *id.* at pp. 844-845 & fn. 4.)

[***138] Like the Court of Appeal in *Nible*, we have misgivings about the general usefulness of an airspace test to define the outer boundary of a building for purposes of burglary. An airspace test, to be sure, may be helpful when the question is whether there is the "slightest partial entry" of a building [*11] (*Ravenscroft*, *supra*, 198 Cal.App.3d at p. 643), as when an intruder simply lowers a rope into a building through a rooftop vent (see *People v. Walters*, *supra*, 249 Cal.

App.2d at p. 550) or saws a hole through the wall of a building (see *People v. Osegueda, supra,* 163 Cal.App.3d Supp. at pp. 31-32). But an airspace test does not help define the outer boundary of a building when that boundary is not otherwise established. The airspace of a building is not independent of the outer boundary of a building; rather, the airspace of a building simply is that which is surrounded by the building's outer boundary. (See *People v. Elsey* (2000) 81 Cal.App.4th 948, 963, fn. 7 [97 Cal.Rptr.2d 269].)

In most instances, of course, the outer boundary of a building for purposes of burglary is self-evident. Thus, in general, the roof, walls, doors, and windows constitute parts of a building's outer boundary, the penetration of which is sufficient for entry.

[**926] In other instances, in which the outer boundary of a building for purposes of burglary is *not* self-evident, we believe that a reasonable belief test generally may be useful in defining the building's outer boundary. Under such a test, in dealing with items such as a window screen, a building's outer boundary includes any element that encloses an area into which a reasonable person would believe that a member of the general public could not pass without authorization. Thus, whereas decisions treat an "ordinary, unenclosed front porch" of a house (*People v. Brown* (1992) 6 Cal.App.4th 1489, 1497 [8 Cal.Rptr.2d 513] [construing § 198.5, the "Home Protection Bill of Rights," which is similar to § 459]) as not part of the building's outer boundary, because a reasonable person usually would believe that a member of the general public did not need authorization to pass onto such a porch, they treat a screen door to an enclosed porch of a house (see *Bowers v. State* (1982) 164 Ga.App. 462, 462-463 [297 S.E.2d 359]; *State v. Jenkins* (Mo.Ct.App. 1987) 741 S.W.2d 767, 769) and a locked gate covered with iron mesh in front of an enclosed and roofed front stairway of a house (see *People v. Wise* (1994) 25 Cal.App.4th 339, 344-348 [30 Cal. Rptr. 2d 413]) as part of the building's outer boundary, because a reasonable person usually would believe that a member of the general public needed authorization to walk through such a screen door or gate. The test reflects and furthers the occupant's possessory interest in the building and his or her personal interest in freedom from violence that might ensue from unauthorized intrusion.[5]

5. In defining the outer boundary of a building for purposes of burglary, the reasonable belief test focuses on whether a reasonable person would believe that a member of the general public *needed* authorization to pass beyond a given element of the building, not on whether any particular individual *possessed* authorization. It is important to keep in mind that the test is concerned with defining the outer boundary of a building, not with determining whether a particular individual lawfully may pass beyond that boundary. Thus, although the test is generally useful in defining the outer boundary of a building, it is not intended to resolve all other material issues, including the lawfulness of entry (cf., e.g., *People v. Barry* (1892) 94 Cal. 481, 483 [29 P. 1026] [holding that a person who enters a business during business hours when the public is invited nevertheless enters unlawfully if he "enters with the intention to commit a felony": such a person "enters without an invitation," since "[h]e is not one of the public invited, nor is he entitled to enter"]).

Furthermore, in defining the outer boundary of a building for purposes of burglary, the reasonable belief test necessarily refers only to an element of a building that reasonably can be viewed as part of *the building's* outer boundary. The test does not encompass any feature that is not such an element, such as a lawn, courtyard, unenclosed patio, or unenclosed balcony that may be located in front of or behind a building; nor does the test purport to define any such feature as part of a building's outer boundary.

[***139] We note that, at one point in its discussion, the Court of Appeal in *Nible* employed language that might be understood to cast the reasonable belief [*12] test in terms of "whether a reasonable person would believe" that any given element of a building "provides some [physical]

protection against unauthorized intrusions." (*Nible, supra*, 200 Cal.App.3d at p. 845.) The latter quoted language might be appropriate if the offense of burglary continued to require unlawful breaking as well as entering. In that event, an element of a building would have to be something that could protect against breach. But, as we have stated most recently in *Davis*, burglary now entails only unlawful entry. (*Davis, supra*, 18 Cal.4th at p. 722.) In light of that circumstance, we believe that the test properly is phrased in terms of whether a reasonable person would believe that the element of the building in question enclosed an area into which a member of the general public could not pass without authorization. Indeed, as so phrased the test is not inconsistent with what the Court of Appeal in *Nible* seems to have had in mind. As we have noted, that court stated that "even an open door or window affords some expectation of protection from unauthorized intrusion because reasonable persons understand the social convention that portals may not be crossed without permission" (*Nible, supra*, 200 Cal.App.3d at p. 844) — implying that what matters is not whether a reasonable person would believe that a given element of a building provides some physical protection against unauthorized intrusion, but simply whether a reasonable [**927] person would believe that a member of the general public needed authorization to pass beyond it.

Under the reasonable belief test as set forth above, we are of the view that a window screen is clearly part of the outer boundary of a building for purposes of burglary. A reasonable person certainly would believe that a window screen enclosed an area into which a member of the general public could not pass without authorization. As the Court of Appeal in *Nible* implied, window screens, which announce that intrusion is unauthorized, do not limit their message to flies but extend it to burglars as well.

We recognize that penetration into the area behind a window screen without penetration of the window itself usually will effect only a minimal [*13] entry of a building in terms of distance. But it has long been settled that "[a]ny kind of entry, complete or partial, . . . will" suffice. (2 Witkin & Epstein, Cal. Criminal Law (3d ed. 2000) Crimes Against Property, § 120, p. 151.) All that is needed is entry "inside the premises" (*People v. Failla* (1966) 64 Cal.2d 560, 569 [51 Cal.Rptr. 103, 414 P.2d 39]), not entry inside *some inner part of* the premises. Furthermore, there is little doubt that even the minimal entry effected by penetration into the area behind a window screen — without penetration of the window itself — is "the type of entry the burglary statute was intended to prevent." (*Davis, supra*, 18 Cal.4th at p. 720.) [***140] Such an entry "violates the occupant's possessory interest in the building . . . ." (*Id.* at p. 722.) It also threatens " ' "the germination of a situation dangerous to personal safety." ' " (*Id.* at p. 721.) As the Court of Appeal in *Nible* observed, "[t]he inhabitants of a building are just as likely to react violently to an intruder's penetration of their window screen as to the penetration of the window itself." (*Nible, supra*, 200 Cal.App.3d at p. 845.) In *Davis*, we held that the placing of a forged check into a chute in a walk-up window at a check-cashing facility was not "the type of entry the burglary statute was intended to prevent," because it did not violate any occupant's possessory interest in a building or his or her personal interest in freedom from violence that might ensue from unauthorized intrusion. (*Davis, supra*, 18 Cal.4th at p. 720.) By contrast, penetration into the area behind a window screen — even without penetration of the window itself — is just such an entry, because it violates both of these interests.

In view of the foregoing, we conclude that penetration into the area behind a window screen amounts to an entry of a building within the meaning of the burglary statute even when the window itself is closed and is not penetrated.[6]

[Footnote 6 and remainder of opinion omitted]

2.5 | CASE ANALYSIS SHEETS

As Exercise 1 may have convinced you, court opinions typically involve a complex web of rules, difficult and often conflicting facts, couched rulings, and not-so-intuitive reasoning. Especially as a beginner, but even as a seasoned attorney, you need a technique to ensure that you approach court opinions as an active reader. In your doctrinal classes, you have probably been advised to prepare case briefs. Case briefs are also helpful to legal writers but with a twist: you should focus more on the particular issue(s) raised by your client's case.

What follows is a standard, easy-to-read format you can use to tweak case briefing to your needs as a legal writer. Notice its use of headings and the type of information it prompts you to find. Fill out a case analysis sheet for every important court opinion you find on your research issue. Develop a style that works well for you, keeping in mind the following guide.

Case Analysis Sheet

PLAINTIFF v. DEFENDANT (1990)

(Fill in the case name and the year of the court opinion above)

Relevance: How is this case relevant to your research issue?

Outcome: For which side did the court rule?

Issues: What question(s) or issue(s) did the court address? Include only those relevant to your research issue.

Holdings: For each question or issue above, indicate how the court answered it.

Starting-Point Rule: State the starting-point rule that defines the crime, claim, or defense at issue.

Preexisting Rules: List any *preexisting* rules[2] that seem important to the court's opinion or particularly relevant to your issue and/or the facts of your client's case.

New Rules: List any *new* rules[3] created in this opinion.

Reasoning: List all of the reasons the court found that the rules you listed required the result it reached.[4]

---

2. *Preexisting rules* are definitions, tests, or more specific rules or pronouncements that restate or summarize from prior opinions or statutes. These rules may include the policy justifications for particular rules and even the broad purpose of the statute or common law principle at issue.

3. *New rules* are definitions, tests, or more specific rules or pronouncements that expand, limit, further define, interpret, or otherwise adjust or change a preexisting rule.

Hint: I have had students unnecessarily agonize over whether a particular rule is preexisting or new. First, do not stress. Keeping new rules separate from preexisting rules is not absolutely essential. It is merely a technique to help you understand the significance of the particular opinion you are reading and the evolution of the law from opinion to opinion over time. Second, you can tell the difference fairly easily. A rule is preexisting if it is merely restated or summarized from prior opinions or statutes. By contrast, a rule is new if it is an expansion, limitation, further definition, interpretation or otherwise an adjustment or change from prior opinions or statutes.

4. *Hint:* Go to the portion of the opinion where the court states its conclusion about how to resolve the issue in the case at hand. Track and write down each step in its logic, including both key facts and logical reasoning.

EXERCISE 2

Fill out a case analysis sheet for *People v. Valencia,* the case from Exercise 1. Do not look at the sample case analysis sheet shown in this exercise until you have filled in your own. You will learn better if you try this on your own first. *It is worth the time.*

After you fill out the case analysis sheet, compare yours to the sample. Following the sample case analysis sheet is an annotated version of the *Valencia* opinion that decodes the opinion step by step. The annotated court opinion will help you understand where the answers to the sample case analysis sheet came from and some of the judgment calls regarding what information was important to include. More generally, it will help you understand how to read a court opinion efficiently and thoroughly.

Before continuing, reread the hypothetical situation from Exercise 1.

Sample Case Analysis Sheet

PEOPLE v. VALENCIA, **46 P.3D 920 (CAL. 2002)**

Relevance: This case defines what structures constitute the outer boundary of a building under the burglary statute.

Outcome: In favor of the prosecution.

Issue: Did the defendant enter the house when he used a screwdriver to remove a window screen but ultimately failed to get the window open?

Comments 7, 13, and 22 in the annotated court opinion shows where the issue and holding appear.

Holdings: Yes.

Starting-Point Rule: Burglary requires entry of a building with an intent to commit larceny or any felony.

Comments 6 and 11 show where the starting-point rule came from.

Preexisting Rules:

1. Burglary laws are based primarily upon recognition of the dangers to personal safety created by the usual burglary situation—the danger that the intruder will harm the occupants in attempting to perpetrate the crime or to escape and the danger that occupants will in anger or panic react violently, thereby inviting violence.
2. The ultimate test must focus on the protection the owners or inhabitants of a structure reasonably expect from unauthorized intrusions.
3. Even an open door or window affords some expectation of protection from unauthorized intrusion because reasonable persons understand the social convention that portals may not be crossed without permission from the structure's owner.
4. A porch meets the reasonable expectation test but only if it is enclosed.

Comments 13-14, 17, and 19 explain how to find and differentiate between the preexisting and new rules that are pertinent to your issue.

New Rules:

1. An airspace test does not help define the outer boundary of a building: the airspace of a building is simply that which is surrounded by the building's outer boundary
2. A building's outer boundary includes any element that encloses an area into which a reasonable person would believe that a member of the public could not pass without authorization.
3. This test focuses on whether a person needs authorization and not on whether any particular individual possessed authorization. The test does not affect the general rule that a person who enters a business during hours when the public is invited enters unlawfully if he enters with the intent to commit a felony.
4. The structure at issue does not need to provide physical protection against unauthorized entry.

Reasoning:

1. A reasonable person would believe that the public needs authorization to enter a window screen. The window screen announces that authorization is required.
2. Removing the screen violated the occupant's possessory interest.
3. It threatened a situation dangerous to personal safety—inhabitants are likely to react violently.

Comments 23-24 explain where this reasoning came from.

THE PEOPLE, Plaintiff and Respondent, v. CUAHUTEMOC SANCHEZ VALENCIA, Defendant and Appellant. ❶

No. S095385.

SUPREME COURT OF CALIFORNIA ❷

28 Cal. 4th 1; 46 P.3d 920; 120 Cal. Rptr. 2d 131 ❸

June 3, 2002, Decided
June 3, 2002, Filed

COUNSEL: Chris Truax, under appointment by the Supreme Court, for Defendant and Appellant.

John T. Philipsborn and Cliff Gardner for California Attorneys for Criminal Justice as Amicus Curiae on behalf of Defendant and Appellant.

Bill Lockyer, Attorney General, David P. Druliner and Robert R. Anderson, Chief Assistant Attorneys General, Gary W. Schons, Assistant Attorney General, Megan J. Beale, Racquel M. Gonzalez, Crystal L. Bradley, Peter Quon, Jr., and Quisteen S. Shum, Deputy Attorneys General, for Plaintiff and Respondent.

JUDGES: (Opinion by George, C. J., with Baxter, Werdegar, Chin, Brown, and Moreno, JJ., concurring. Dissenting opinion by Kennard, J.)

OPINION BY: GEORGE ❹

OPINION

GEORGE, C.J. ❺

❻ Under California law, the crime of burglary is committed when a person "*enters* any . . . *building*," including a "house," "with intent to commit . . . larceny or any felony." (Pen. Code,[1] § 459, italics added; see § 460.)

1. Unless otherwise specified, all section references are to the Penal Code.

1. This is the "caption" or title of the case. The caption identifies the people or entities involved in the case. This is a criminal case filed by "the People" (i.e., the Attorney General's Office) against an individual named Cuahutemoc Valencia.
2. This is the name of the court that wrote the opinion. In this case, the defendant already lost the trial and lost an appeal to an intermediary level court called the "court of appeal." He is now asking the Supreme Court to disagree with both the trial court and the court of appeal.
3. This is the citation. Chapter 8 will cover citation. For now, just know that this is a reference number for the case.
4. You may see summaries and headnotes after the caption and before the actual start of the opinion. These are not citable portions of the case. Look for the judges' names and words like "Opinion by." This is where the actual opinion begins.
5. This is the last name of the justice who wrote the opinion. "C.J." stands for Chief Justice. The other names listed here are the justices who agree with the opinion.
6. This is the starting-point rule that defines the crime of burglary with a citation to the Penal Code provision that defines burglary. The Penal Code is a volume of enacted statutes. The California legislature enacted a law that specifically defines burglary. Because statutes are rarely self-explanatory, courts must interpret their meaning. The rest of this opinion interprets the word "building" as used in the statute.

We granted review to determine whether penetration into the area behind a window screen amounts to an entry of a building within the meaning of the burglary statute when the window itself is closed and is not penetrated. As we shall explain, we conclude that it does. Accordingly, we reverse the judgment of the Court of Appeal, which held to the contrary. ❼

I ❽

The evidence presented at defendant's trial for the crime of burglary, viewed in the light most favorable to the judgment, reveals the following facts pertinent to the issue before us:

On the morning of February 4, 1998, Lee Florea left the house he shared with his wife and children in Santa Ana to go to work, with the doors and windows locked and the window screens secured in their tracks in front of the windows.

About noon, Nicky Nava, who lived across the street from the Floreas, came home for lunch. Looking out through a screen door, Nava saw a person later identified as defendant. As she watched, defendant, who apparently had a screwdriver in his hand, removed a window screen from a bathroom window of the Floreas' house and tried unsuccessfully to open the window itself. Evidently, defendant earlier had pulled a window screen away from a bedroom window of the Floreas' house and had tried unsuccessfully to open that window as well.

Nava called the Santa Ana Police Department and described defendant and his activities. As she continued to watch, moving at some point up to her screen door and then outside, defendant walked from the bathroom window of the Floreas' house and tried unsuccessfully to open the front door. Apparently in anger or frustration, defendant banged on the wall and then sat down for a few minutes. Defendant then got into an automobile, which resembled a gray or brown Monte Carlo or LTD, drove down the street about four houses away, parked, and got out.

By this time, Santa Ana Police Officer John Douthit had arrived at the scene. Douthit approached defendant, who was standing in the driveway of the house in front of which he had parked. Douthit asked defendant whether he owned the automobile parked in front of the house, and defendant answered he did not; Douthit asked defendant what he was doing, and defendant answered he was looking for a friend he called "Tommy." Douthit then searched defendant's pants pocket and found a pair of black gloves and a screwdriver with a bent blade and shank. Through a police dispatcher, Douthit confirmed that defendant matched the description reported by Nava. Douthit then arrested defendant. Defendant protested that he had not done anything wrong, and that he merely had been looking for a friend, whom he now called "Tony," to help in locating a stolen bicycle.

Going to the Floreas' house, Officer Douthit found what appeared to be rub marks on the bathroom window that could have been made by defendant's hand or hands as he tried to open

7. Here the court previews the question it needs to answer to resolve the appeal, its answer to the question, and the action it will take. The Supreme Court is disagreeing with the court of appeal and requiring that the judgment be changed.
8. Here, the court summarizes the facts of the case. Most court opinions start with a factual summary like this. On your first read of the court opinion, you do not need to pay much attention to the fact summary. It is usually better to just skim or even skip the fact summary until you have read and understood the court's analysis of the law and how it affects the case. Once you have a better feel for the court's analysis, go back and read the facts more carefully. After reading the court's legal analysis, it is usually easier to determine which factual details matter.

the window. Douthit also found several pry marks on the frame of the bedroom window that could have been made by defendant's screwdriver. Florea returned to his house about this time, finding the scene as described above. Douthit later determined that defendant did indeed own the automobile he had denied owning.

After the presentation of evidence, the trial court instructed the jury on the offense of burglary. At the People's request, and over defendant's objection, the court gave the following instruction, drawn directly from *People v. Nible* (1988) 200 Cal.App.3d 838 [247 Cal.Rptr. 396] (*Nible*) and indirectly from *People v. Ravenscroft* (1988) 198 Cal.App.3d 639 [243 Cal.Rptr. 827] (*Ravenscroft*): "Any kind of entry, partial or complete, will satisfy the element of entry. The entry may be made by any part of the body or by use of an instrument or tool. *In order for there to have been an entry, a part of the defendant's body or some instrument, tool or other object under his control must have penetrated the area inside where the screen was normally affixed in the window frame in question.*" (Italics added.) The court refused to give the following instruction, based upon language from *Nible*, which defendant requested and the People objected to: "The test of whether an entry has occurred is whether a reasonable person would believe a window screen provides some protection against unauthorized intrusions." 9

The jury returned a verdict finding defendant guilty of burglary and determining that the burglary was of the first degree because it involved an inhabited dwelling house (§ 460, subd. (a)). The trial court rendered a judgment of conviction on the jury's verdict, imposing a sentence of four years in prison.[2]

2. In addition to being found guilty by the jury of first degree burglary, defendant pleaded guilty to possession of heroin (Health & Saf. Code, § 11350, subd. (a)) and admitted an allegation that he committed the crimes in question while released from custody on bail or on his own recognizance (Pen. Code, § 12022.1). Together with the sentence of four years in prison for first degree burglary, the trial court imposed a sentence of two-thirds of a year for possession of heroin plus a two-year enhancement for committing the crimes while released from custody, for a total determinate sentence of six and two-thirds years.

On appeal, the Court of Appeal held that penetration into the area behind a window screen does not amount to an entry of a building within the meaning of the burglary statute, at least when, as in this case, the window itself is closed and is not penetrated. The Court of Appeal therefore concluded that the trial court erred by instructing the jury as requested by the People. The Court of Appeal also concluded that the trial court did not err by refusing to instruct as requested by defendant. The Court of Appeal went on to determine that, "[a]s a matter of law," defendant "was guilty only of attempted [first degree] burglary." As a consequence, the Court of Appeal reversed defendant's conviction and sentence for first degree burglary and remanded the case to the trial court with directions to enter a conviction for attempted first degree burglary and to impose sentence accordingly.

10 We granted the People's petition for review in order to consider the validity of the Court of Appeal's holding. As stated above, we reach a conclusion contrary to that reached by the Court of Appeal and therefore reverse the judgment rendered by that court.

9. Here, the court explains the "procedural history" of the case. The procedural history includes the events in the case to date. The history of the case consists of a trial and conviction, a sentence, and a prior appeal. The court includes a jury instruction that is relevant to the issues that are raised in the appeal.

10. Procedural history ends here.

II (11)

The crime of burglary is committed when a person *"enters* any . . . *building,"* including a "house," "with intent to commit . . . larceny or any felony." (§ 459, italics added.)[3] Burglary may be of the first or second degree,[4] but in either event involves an entry into a building or other specified structure.

3. Section 459 provides: "Every person who enters any house, room, apartment, tenement, shop, warehouse, store, mill, barn, stable, outhouse or other building, tent, vessel, as defined in Section 21 of the Harbors and Navigation Code, floating home, as defined in subdivision (d) of Section 18075.55 of the Health and Safety Code, railroad car, locked or sealed cargo container, whether or not mounted on a vehicle, trailer coach, as defined in Section 635 of the Vehicle Code, any house car, as defined in Section 362 of the Vehicle Code, inhabited camper, as defined in Section 243 of the Vehicle Code, vehicle as defined by the Vehicle Code, when the doors are locked, aircraft as defined by Section 21012 of the Public Utilities Code, or mine or any underground portion thereof, with intent to commit grand or petit larceny or any felony is guilty of burglary. As used [herein], 'inhabited' means currently being used for dwelling purposes, whether occupied or not. A house, trailer, vessel designed for habitation, or portion of a building is currently being used for dwelling purposes if, at the time of the burglary, it was not occupied solely because a natural or other disaster caused the occupants to leave the premises."
4. Section 460 provides in pertinent part: "(a) Every burglary of an inhabited dwelling house, vessel, as defined in the Harbors and Navigation Code, which is inhabited and designed for habitation, floating home, as defined in subdivision (d) of Section 18075.55 of the Health and Safety Code, or trailer coach, as defined by the Vehicle Code, or the inhabited portion of any other building, is burglary of the first degree. [¶] (b) All other kinds of burglary are of the second degree."

(12) The issue before us is whether penetration into the area behind a window screen amounts to an entry of a building within the meaning of the burglary statute when the window itself is closed and is not penetrated. As we shall explain, we conclude that it does.

In *People v. Davis* (1998) 18 Cal.4th 712 [76 Cal.Rptr. 2d 770, 958 P.2d 1083] (*Davis*), we (13)
recently had occasion to discuss the offense of burglary, including consideration of its historical background and its general contours today. Our discussion provides a useful starting point for addressing the rather narrow question presented in this case.

In *Davis*, we explained that "[t]he interest sought to be protected by the common law crime of burglary was clear. At common law, burglary was the breaking and entering of a dwelling in the nighttime. The law was intended to protect the sanctity of a person's home during the night hours when the resident was most vulnerable. As one commentator observed: 'The predominant factor underlying common law burglary was the desire to protect the security of the home, and the person within his home. Burglary was not an offense against property, real or personal, but an offense against the habitation, for it could only be committed against the dwelling

11. The court repeats the starting-point rule here. Most court opinions will put the starting-point rule at the start of their discussion of the law.

As the annotations proceed, they will provide a thought process that you would go through as you read the opinion. Then you can start to understand how to exercise your own judgment as you read more court opinions. You may not have made the same judgments as the annotations do. You should expect some differences.

12. Here, the court states the issue or question it is answering about how the law applies in this particular case.
13. Here, the court starts discussing precedent. At this point, we do not know whether the court agrees with the quotations and pronouncements it is reciting. The court is just giving us a history. When reading a case, look to see which of the various quotations and pronouncements the court actually ends up applying to the case it is deciding.

of another. . . . The dwelling was sacred, but a duty was imposed on the owner to protect himself as well as looking to the law for protection. The intruder had to break and enter; if the owner left the door open, his carelessness would allow the intruder to go unpunished. The offense had to occur at night; in the daytime home-owners were not asleep, and could detect the intruder and protect their homes.' " (*Davis, supra*, 18 Cal.4th at p. 720.)

We went on to explain in *Davis* that, "[i]n California, as in other states, the scope of the burglary law has been greatly expanded. There is no requirement of a breaking; an entry alone is sufficient. The crime is not limited to dwellings, but includes entry into a wide variety of structures. The crime need not be committed at night." (*Davis, supra*, 18 Cal.4th at pp. 720-721.)

Nonetheless, as we added in Davis, the great expansion in the scope of the burglary law has not been unlimited. "In *People v. Gauze* (1975) 15 Cal.3d 709 [125 Cal.Rptr. 773, 542 P.2d 1365], we . . . observed that '[a] burglary remains an entry which invades a possessory interest in a building.' [Citation.] . . . '"Burglary laws are based primarily upon a recognition of the dangers to personal safety created by the usual burglary situation — the danger that the intruder will harm the (14) occupants in attempting to perpetrate the intended crime or to escape and the danger that the occupants will in anger or panic react violently to the invasion, thereby inviting more violence. The laws are primarily designed, then, not to deter the trespass and the intended crime, which are prohibited by other laws, so much as to forestall the germination of a situation dangerous to personal safety." [The burglary statute], in short, is aimed at the danger caused by the unauthorized entry itself.'" (*Davis, supra*, 18 Cal.4th at p. 721.)

(15) In *Davis*, we further proceeded to note and approve the rule reflected in *People v. Moore* (1994) 31 Cal.App.4th 489, [37 Cal.Rptr.2d 104], [*8] *People v. Walters* (1967) 249 Cal.App.2d 547 [57 Cal.Rptr. 484], and *People v. Osegueda* (1984) 163 Cal.App.3d Supp. 25 [210 Cal.Rptr. 182], that [HN7] entry may be effected by the intruder or by an instrument employed by the intruder, whether used "solely to effect entry, or to accomplish the intended larceny or felony as well." (*Davis, supra*, 18 Cal.4th at p. 717.)

Accordingly, resolution of the question before us does not depend upon whether penetration into the area behind a window screen is effected by the intruder or by an instrument employed by the intruder. Rather, it turns solely upon whether any such penetration amounts to an entry of a building.

(16) In approaching this question, the People and defendant place considerable reliance, as did the Court of Appeal, on two Court of Appeal decisions — *Ravenscroft* and *Nible* — that preceded our decision in *Davis*.

14. This preexisting rule ended up being important because the court later used it to justify its ultimate conclusion. You won't know which preexisting rules are important until you finish the case—another reason why one read is never enough.
15. Now the court applies the precedent to the case. Now you can understand the purpose of the preceding historical discussion: the court is explaining that the defendant's failure to put any part of his body into the area behind the screen is not relevant to the issue. The case analysis sheet did not include this conclusion because it is not relevant to our hypothetical, which involved a defendant who actually walked into the structure at issue.
16. Now the court is going into a new discussion of precedent. Presumably, this discussion will have a somewhat different purpose than the earlier historical discussion. So, again, look to see how the court applies these precedent cases to the issue in the case at hand.

In *Ravenscroft*, the Court of Appeal held that a defendant's insertion of an automatic teller machine (ATM) card into an ATM that was mounted inside a bank and was secured flush with the bank's exterior wall amounted to an entry of a building within the meaning of the burglary statute, because the ATM was part of the bank's outer boundary for purposes of burglary. In so holding, the Court of Appeal rejected a claim by the defendant that "his insertion of an ATM card into" an ATM did "not constitute an entry" of the bank "since he did not violate [its] air space." (*Ravenscroft, supra*, 198 Cal.App.3d at p. 643.) The Court of Appeal stated: "The insertion of an ATM card . . . is no less an entry into the air space of a bank as would be the use of any other tool or instrument. Although the California Penal Code does not define 'entry' for the purpose of burglary, the California courts have found that a burglary is complete upon the slightest partial entry of any kind, with the requisite intent . . . ." (*Ibid.*) In support, the Court of Appeal relied upon *People v. Walters, supra*, 249 Cal.App.2d at page 550, where the intruders simply pried off and removed the lid of a rooftop vent and lowered a rope into a building. The Court of Appeal also relied upon *People v. Osegueda, supra*, 163 Cal.App.3d Supp. at pages 31-32, where the intruders merely sawed a six-inch by four to five-inch hole through the wall of a building.

In *Nible* — which is the California case whose facts are closest to ours, and which we accordingly discuss at some length — the Court of Appeal held that a defendant's penetration into the area behind a window screen amounted to an entry of a building within the meaning of the burglary statute, because the window screen was part of the building's outer boundary for purposes of burglary.

In support of its holding, the Court of Appeal in *Nible* explained: "No California authority has considered whether the penetration of a window screen, without penetration of . . . the window beyond, constitutes an entry within the meaning of [the burglary statute]. Defendant contends the correct analysis to determine whether a burglarious entry has occurred is whether the 'air space' of a protected structure has been penetrated by a part of the defendant's body or an instrument or tool wielded by him. (See *People v. Ravenscroft* (1988) 198 Cal.App.3d 639, 643-644 [243 Cal.Rptr. 827] . . . .) The 'air space' analysis of *Ravenscroft* . . . does not necessarily lead to the result defendant suggests. Rather, it is reasonable to conclude that a window screen contains the outer boundary of a building's air space, especially when, as here, the window itself was left open. However it might be applied here, in our view the 'air space' test, although useful in some situations, is inadequate as a comprehensive test for determining when a burglarious entry occurs." (*Nible, supra*, 200 Cal.App.3d at pp. 843-844, fn. omitted.)

The Court of Appeal in *Nible* went on to state that "a more comprehensive test is suggested by the California Supreme Court's analysis" (*Nible, supra*, 200 Cal.App.3d at p. 844) in *People v. Gauze* (1975) 15 Cal.3d 709 [125 Cal.Rptr. 773, 542 P.2d 1365], which we have quoted above.

Moving beyond our discussion in *Gauze*, the Court of Appeal in *Nible* reasoned: "As the burglary statute is designed to protect against unauthorized entry and its attendant dangers, the ultimate test of whether a burglarious entry has occurred must focus on the protection the owners or inhabitants of a structure reasonably expect. The proper question is whether the nature of 17

17. The court is still in its historical discussion of precedent cases and preexisting rules. The case analysis sheet includes this rule because later in the opinion, the court adopts a more specific test (see Comment 19) that derives from this broad test.

a structure's composition is such that a reasonable person would expect some protection from unauthorized intrusions. A structure with a locked door or window clearly affords a reasonable expectation of protection from invasion. But even an open door or window affords some expectation of protection from unauthorized intrusion because reasonable persons understand the social convention that portals may not be crossed without permission from the structure's owner." (*Nible, supra*, 200 Cal.App.3d at p. 844.)

"Thus," stated the Court of Appeal in *Nible*, "the focus of the question whether the penetration of a window screen constitutes a burglarious entry must be on whether a reasonable person would believe a window screen provides some protection against unauthorized intrusions. The answer is unequivocally in the affirmative. 'The opening of a screen door or window is deemed a burglarious breaking, . . . In such cases the screen door [or window] is not to be considered as a mere protection against flies, but rather as a permanent part of the dwelling. The holdings proceed, it would seem, on the grounds that the screen door [or window] is a part of the house on which the occupants rely for protection and that to open such a door [or window] is a violation of the security of the dwelling house which is the peculiar gravamen of a burglarious breaking.' . . ." (*Nible, supra*, 200 Cal.App.3d at p. 845.)

The Court of Appeal in *Nible* concluded: "The purposes of the burglary laws are best served by our holding the penetration of a window screen constitutes entry within the meaning of [the burglary statute]. As noted above, the burglary law protects against the dangers caused by unauthorized entry. The inhabitants of a building are just as likely to react violently to an intruder's penetration of their window screen as to the penetration of the window itself." (*Nible, supra*, 200 Cal.App.3d at p. 845.)

In *Davis*, subsequent to the Court of Appeal decisions in *Ravenscroft* and *Nible*, we faced the question whether a defendant's placing of a forged check into a chute in a walk-up window at a check-cashing facility amounted to an entry of a building within the meaning of the burglary statute. We held that it did not. In so holding, we accepted that the chute was part of the building's outer boundary for purposes of burglary. We reasoned, however, that although the placing of the forged check into the chute effected a type of entry, it was not "the type of entry *the burglary statute was intended to prevent*." (*Davis, supra*, 18 Cal.4th at p. 720, italics added.) In support, we stated that the act did not "violate[] the occupant's possessory interest in the building" (*id.* at p. 722) or threaten " ' "the germination of a situation dangerous to personal safety" ' " (*id.* at p. 721).

In the course of our discussion in *Davis*, we "disapprove[d]" *Ravenscroft* to the extent it held that a defendant's insertion of an ATM card into an ATM in a bank amounted to an entry of a building within the meaning of the burglary statute. (*Davis, supra*, 18 Cal.4th at p. 722, fn. 5.) At the same time, however, we added that we did "not disapprove the other aspects of . . . *Ravenscroft*, including its conclusion that the ATM card in that case was inserted into the air space of the ATM," and on this point we inserted a citation to *Nible*. (*Davis, supra*, 18 Cal. 4th at p. 722, fn. 5.)

As we have seen, the Court of Appeal in *Nible* found in *Ravenscroft* what it called a sometimes "useful," but sometimes "inadequate," " 'air space' test." (*Nible, supra*, 200 Cal.App.3d at p. 844.) The Court of Appeal in *Nible* proposed as "more comprehensive" a "reasonable belief" or "reasonable expectation" test. (*Id.* at p. 844; see *id.* at pp. 844-845 & fn. 4.)

18 Like the Court of Appeal in *Nible*, we have misgivings about the general usefulness of an airspace test to define the outer boundary of a building for purposes of burglary. An airspace test, to be sure, may be helpful when the question is whether there is the "slightest partial entry" of a building (*Ravenscroft, supra*, 198 Cal.App.3d at p. 643), as when an intruder simply lowers a rope into a building through a rooftop vent (see *People v. Walters, supra*, 249 Cal.App.2d at p. 550) or saws a hole through the wall of a building (see *People v. Osegueda, supra*, 163 Cal.App.3d Supp. at pp. 31-32). But an airspace test does not help define the outer boundary of a building when that boundary is not otherwise established. The airspace of a building is not independent of the outer boundary of a building; rather, the airspace of a building simply is that which is surrounded by the building's outer boundary. (See *People v. Elsey* (2000) 81 Cal.App.4th 948, 963, fn. 7 [97 Cal. Rptr.2d 269].)

In most instances, of course, the outer boundary of a building for purposes of burglary is self-evident. Thus, in general, the roof, walls, doors, and windows constitute parts of a building's outer boundary, the penetration of which is sufficient for entry.

In other instances, in which the outer boundary of a building for purposes of burglary is 19
not self-evident, we believe that a reasonable belief test generally may be useful in defining the building's outer boundary. Under such a test, in dealing with items such as a window screen, a building's outer boundary includes any element that encloses an area into which a reasonable person would believe that a member of the general public could not pass without authorization. Thus, whereas decisions treat an "ordinary, unenclosed front porch" of a house (*People v. Brown* 20
(1992) 6 Cal.App.4th 1489, 1497 [8 Cal.Rptr.2d 513] [construing § 198.5, the "Home Protection Bill of Rights," which is similar to § 459]) as not part of the building's outer boundary, because a reasonable person usually would believe that a member of the general public did not need authorization to pass onto such a porch, they treat a screen door to an enclosed porch of a house (see *Bowers v. State* (1982) 164 Ga.App. 462, 462-463 [297 S.E.2d 359]; *State v. Jenkins* (Mo.Ct.App. 1987) 741 S.W.2d 767, 769) and a locked gate covered with iron mesh in front of an enclosed and roofed front stairway of a house (see *People v. Wise* (1994) 25 Cal.App.4th 339, 344-348 [30 Cal. Rptr. 2d 413]) as part of the building's outer boundary, because a reasonable person usually would believe that a member of the general public needed authorization to walk through such a screen door or

18. Now the historical discussion is done, and the court explains how it is relevant. Your ears should perk up, and you should be reading closely to understand what the court is going to conclude from the historical discussion. Reading this paragraph, you can understand that the court is telling us that the "air space" test is irrelevant to whether a particular structure is part of the building. This is the heart of the opinion. The case analysis sheet includes many of the rules that follow. Some, however, did not seem even arguably applicable to our client's case, so they are not included.
19. This is a very important part of the opinion. The court is announcing what the rule should be for determining the outer boundary of a building. This is exactly the issue that we are researching in our hypothetical, so we do not want to miss this.
20. The court now gives examples of how the test it is announcing should be applied. The case analysis sheet includes these examples in the preexisting rules/pronouncements section because they were important to understanding the test that the court is announcing in this case.

gate. The test reflects and furthers the occupant's possessory interest in the building and his or her personal interest in freedom from violence that might ensue from unauthorized intrusion.[5]

5. In defining the outer boundary of a building for purposes of burglary, the reasonable belief test focuses on whether a reasonable person would believe that a member of the general public *needed* authorization to pass beyond a given element of the building, not on whether any particular individual *possessed* authorization. It is important to keep in mind that the test is concerned with defining the outer boundary of a building, not with determining whether a particular individual lawfully may pass beyond that boundary. Thus, although the test is generally useful in defining the outer boundary of a building, it is not intended to resolve all other material issues, including the lawfulness of entry (cf., e.g., *People v. Barry* (1892) 94 Cal. 481, 483 [29 P. 1026] [holding that a person who enters a business during business hours when the public is invited nevertheless enters unlawfully if he "enters with the intention to commit a felony": such a person "enters without an invitation," since "[h]e is not one of the public invited, nor is he entitled to enter"]). 21

Furthermore, in defining the outer boundary of a building for purposes of burglary, the reasonable belief test necessarily refers only to an element of a building that reasonably can be viewed as part of *the building's* outer boundary. The test does not encompass any feature that is not such an element, such as a lawn, courtyard, unenclosed patio, or unenclosed balcony that may be located in front of or behind a building; nor does the test purport to define any such feature as part of a building's outer boundary.

We note that, at one point in its discussion, the Court of Appeal in *Nible* employed language that might be understood to cast the reasonable belief test in terms of "whether a reasonable person would believe" that any given element of a building "provides some [physical] protection against unauthorized intrusions." (*Nible, supra*, 200 Cal.App.3d at p. 845.) The latter quoted language might be appropriate if the offense of burglary continued to require unlawful breaking as well as entering. In that event, an element of a building would have to be something that could protect against breach. But, as we have stated most recently in *Davis*, burglary now entails only unlawful entry. (*Davis, supra*, 18 Cal.4th at p. 722.) In light of that circumstance, we believe that the test properly is phrased in terms of whether a reasonable person would believe that the element of the building in question enclosed an area into which a member of the general public could not pass without authorization. Indeed, as so phrased the test is not inconsistent with what the Court of Appeal in Nible seems to have had in mind. As we have noted, that court stated that "even an open door or window affords some expectation of protection from unauthorized intrusion because reasonable persons understand the social convention that portals may not be crossed without permission" (*Nible, supra*, 200 Cal.App.3d at p. 844) — implying that what matters is not whether a reasonable person would believe that a given element of a building provides some physical protection against unauthorized intrusion, but simply whether a reasonable person would believe that a member of the general public needed authorization to pass beyond it.

22 Under the reasonable belief test as set forth above, we are of the view that a window screen is clearly part of the outer boundary of a building for purposes of burglary. A reasonable person

21. When reading a court opinion, do not ignore the footnotes. Sometimes, the footnotes will contain the most useful language in the entire opinion. The case analysis sheet included the point of this footnote under new rules/pronouncements because the distinction the court makes here between belief that authorization is needed and actual authorization might be important to our case because our case involves an ATM kiosk in which members of the public were sometimes permitted to wait for the bus in inclement weather.

22. The court now turns to applying the law it has discussed to the case at hand. Whenever you read a case, you should look for this critical transition. You know that here is where you will find the holding and reasoning, which will be important to your ability to apply the law to your case. The word "holding" is often used very loosely and can include both the new rules or pronouncements and the fact-specific finding of the court in the particular case. In this text, think of the "holding" as the fact-specific finding. Here, the holding is that the

certainly would believe that a window screen enclosed an area into which a member of the gen-
23 eral public could not pass without authorization. As the Court of Appeal in *Nible* implied, window screens, which announce that intrusion is unauthorized, do not limit their message to flies but extend it to burglars as well.

We recognize that penetration into the area behind a window screen without penetration of the window itself usually will effect only a minimal entry of a building in terms of distance. But it has long been settled that "[a]ny kind of entry, complete or partial, . . . will" suffice. (2 Witkin & Epstein, Cal. Criminal Law (3d ed. 2000) Crimes Against Property, § 120, p. 151.) All that is needed is entry "inside the premises" (*People v. Failla* (1966) 64 Cal.2d 560, 569 [51 Cal.Rptr. 103, 414 P.2d 39]), not entry *inside some inner part of* the premises. Furthermore, there is little doubt that even the minimal entry effected by penetration into the area behind a window screen — without penetration of the window itself — is "the type of entry the burglary statute was intended to prevent." (*Davis, supra*, 18 Cal.4th at p. 720.) Such an entry "violates the occupant's possessory interest in 24
the building . . . ." (*Id.* at p. 722.) It also threatens " ' "the germination of a situation dangerous to personal safety." ' " (*Id.* at p. 721.) As the Court of Appeal in Nible observed, "[t]he inhabitants of a building are just as likely to react violently to an intruder's penetration of their window screen as to the penetration of the window itself." (*Nible, supra*, 200 Cal.App.3d at p. 845.) In *Davis*, we held that the placing of a forged check into a chute in a walk-up window at a check-cashing facility was not "the type of entry the burglary statute was intended to prevent," because it did not violate any occupant's possessory interest in a building or his or her personal interest in freedom from violence that might ensue from unauthorized intrusion. (*Davis, supra*, 18 Cal.4th at p. 720.) By contrast, penetration into the area behind a window screen — even without penetration of the window itself — is just such an entry, because it violates both of these interests.

In view of the foregoing, we conclude that penetration into the area behind a window screen amounts to an entry of a building within the meaning of the burglary statute even when the window itself is closed and is not penetrated.[6]

[Footnote 6 and remainder of opinion omitted]

window screen was part of the outer boundary of the house (and the defendant entered the house when he removed the screen).

23. Here is where the reasoning of the court begins. All of the remaining text here should be summarized in the case analysis sheet.
24. Here, the court concludes that the purpose of the burglary statute to protect against the potential for violence includes the penetration of the screen. When evaluating this case, you would be asking whether the defendant's conduct carried the potential for violence. Sample B in Appendix B of this text is based on the same hypothetical case. You can take a moment now to look at pages 7-8 of the sample memorandum to see how the potential for violence factored into the analysis of the case.

EXERCISE 2 DEBRIEF

The case analysis sheet is a tool to help you focus on the important information from a court opinion. The sheet is similar to a case brief you would prepare in a doctrinal law school course but reflects the more goal-oriented approach of a practitioner trying to address a specific client's situation (as opposed to a law student trying to learn legal doctrine).

The annotated court opinion demonstrates that reading court opinions is not a linear front-to-back process. As you read further into an opinion, you may begin to see connections you missed at first. In particular, when you get to the court's holding and reasoning, you may realize that a certain rule, policy, or fact in the case was more important than you thought. Stop reading immediately and go back to find the important information you mistakenly skipped or glossed over.

Do not worry too greatly if some of the decisions made in the sample case analysis sheet and the annotated court opinion remain mysterious to you. At this early stage in your learning, you cannot expect yourself to think as an experienced lawyer would think. Progress takes time. Moreover, the sample reflects many judgment calls rather than one correct set of answers. However, do make sure you understand where in the court opinion the key rules and reasoning appear. Understanding the basic structure of a typical court opinion is important to your ability to proceed to the rest of the lessons in this textbook. Understanding the basic structure includes understanding the differences and interconnections between the facts of the case, legal rules, and court reasoning. Keep looking at the annotated court opinion and cross-referencing it with the sample case analysis sheet until you believe you understand these concepts. Return to the annotated court opinion as you read new court opinions until you feel confident that you are reading like a lawyer.

2.6 | RULE CHARTS

The sample case analysis sheet will help you pull and record important information from each court opinion you read. However, the other more challenging tasks ahead are to understand how all of the opinions you read fit together and how they speak to your client's case. The next tool, a rule chart, will help you see the big picture as you read a heavy load of court opinions. A rule chart is probably overkill for a research project that involves only a few cases. However, in more complex research projects, a chart is extremely beneficial.

I recommend that you complete case analysis sheets on all of the important cases you read on your project before filling out the rule chart. Going through all of the sheets first can help you be more selective about which rules and illustrations you include in the chart. As you become more experienced with case reading, you may be able to skip right to the chart without missing anything important. When you are starting out as a novice opinion reader, however, the disciplined approach of the case analysis sheet is necessary to ensure you capture the nuances of each court opinion.

The rule chart has three columns: rule, illustration, and application. It is organized by rule and not by case to reflect the rule-based organization you will use in your writing.

RULE CHART

RULE	ILLUSTRATION	APPLICATION
Keep related rules close to one another and place broad rules before more specific rules.	List the precedent cases that apply the rule and summarize their holdings and reasoning.	What arguments might be made about how the rule applies to the facts of your case? Identify arguments on each side and even possible rebuttals.
Rule 1		
Rule 2		
Rule 3		

Transfer information from the case analysis sheets to the rule chart one case at a time.

Rule column. Look at the preexisting and new rules you listed on the case analysis sheet. List the rules in the rule column using a new box for each rule that you think is important to the legal issue you are addressing. Keep related rules next to one another, and put broader rules above more narrow rules. Next to each rule, put the name of the court opinion where you found it.

Illustration column. This is where you enter the court's reasoning—the bridge between the rule and the facts of the case the court was deciding. Think about which of the rules listed in your rule column directly factored into the court's reasons for its holding, and fill in the illustration column next to each of those rules by indicating how the court applied the rule to the facts of the particular case. Often, a rule column will include broader rules that relate to more specific rules; to avoid repetition, complete the illustration column only for rules that are not broken down into more specific subrules.

Application column. For each entry you make in the illustration column, indicate in the application column how you think the same rule would play out in the facts of your client's case. Try to identify arguments that could be made in each side's favor. Base your application column entries on both the language of the rule and the court's reasoning you identified in the illustration column.

How to handle repeated rules. After you transfer information from a case analysis sheet to the rule chart, move on to the next case. Go through the same process for each case analysis sheet you have completed. You may find that some of the rules on each new case analysis sheet are already on the rule chart because an earlier case already mentioned them. This should happen more frequently as you go through more case analysis sheets. If a rule is repeated, just add the name of the new court opinion as an additional source for the repeated rule. Note, however, that if you are working on a brief rather than an objective research memorandum, you should select the most strategic wording for your client's position. So when you find a repeated rule, replace the old language with the new if the new is better for your client.

When you encounter a repeated rule, fill out the illustration column to indicate how the repeated rule factored into the court's reasoning in the new case. And add to the application column if you have any new ideas about potential arguments in your client's case.

How to handle new rules. If, on the other hand, you find new rules not already on the chart, add them in the rule column and fill in the corresponding columns.

EXERCISE 3

Read the two provided cases, *People v. Davis* and *People v. Franco.* Complete a rule chart that includes the information from the sample case analysis sheet you completed for *People v. Valencia* in Exercise 2 and the new information from these two new cases. Complete the rule chart on your own before looking at the sample.

Assume that you are dealing with the same hypothetical situation as in Exercise 1 (see page 20).

After you complete the rule chart, review the sample rule chart that follows the *Davis* and *Franco* opinions. Flip back and forth between the sample rule chart and Sample B in Appendix B to see how the chart helped determine the organization of the final product.

Supreme Court of California
The PEOPLE, Plaintiff and Respondent,
v.
Michael Wayne DAVIS, Defendant and Appellant.

No. S058743.

July 30, 1998.

George O. Benton, under appointment by the Supreme Court, Santa Rosa, for Defendant and Appellant.

Daniel E. Lungren, Attorney General, George Williamson, Chief Assistant Attorney General, Ronald A. Bass, Assistant Attorney General, Catherine A. Rivlin and Gregg E. Zywicke, Deputy Attorneys General, for Plaintiff and Respondent.

GEORGE, Chief Justice.

Defendant was convicted of forgery, receiving stolen property, and burglary, based upon evidence that he presented a stolen and forged check to the teller at a check-cashing business by placing the check in a chute in a walk-up window. Defendant maintains that the burglary conviction must be reversed because he did not enter the check-cashing facility. For the reasons that follow, we agree.

I

On May 27, 1995, defendant approached the walk-up window of a check-cashing business named the Cash Box and presented a check to the teller by placing the check in a chute in the window. The teller later described the chute as follows: "It has a handle, and it opens out like a flap. It opens out, and they put the check in. They pass the check through." The check was drawn on the account of Robert and Joan Tallman, whose names were imprinted on the check, and was payable in the amount of $274 to Mike Woody, a name defendant sometimes used. The check was signed with the name Robert Tallman.

The teller placed a small, white, oval sticker on the back of the check, passed the check back to defendant, and asked him to place his thumbprint on the sticker and endorse the check. Defendant placed his thumbprint on the sticker, signed the back of the check with the name Michael D. Woody, and passed the check back to the teller, using the chute.

The teller telephoned Robert Tallman, who denied having written the check. Tallman later discovered that a group of checks, including this one, had been stolen from his automobile. The teller placed Tallman on hold and telephoned the police. An officer arrived within minutes and arrested defendant, who still was waiting at the window. At the police station, the police directed defendant to give several examples of his handwriting by repeatedly signing the name "Robert Tallman."

At trial, Tallman testified that neither the signature nor any of the other writing on the check was his.

Defendant was convicted of forgery (Pen.Code, § 470),[FN1] burglary (§ 459), and receiving stolen property (§ 496, subd. (c)). Defendant waived his statutory right to a jury trial

FN1. All further statutory references are to the Penal Code, unless otherwise indicated.

as to the truth of the prior prison term allegation, and after a brief hearing the trial court found true the allegation that defendant previously had been convicted of a felony for which he had served a prison term. (§ 667.5, subd. (b).) Defendant was sentenced on the forgery count to the upper term of three years in prison, plus an additional year for the prior prison term enhancement, for a total term of four years in prison. Defendant was sentenced on the burglary count to a concurrent term of three years in prison, and on the receiving stolen property count to a concurrent term of three years in prison. The Court of Appeal affirmed the judgment. We granted review to determine whether there was sufficient evidence to support the conviction for burglary.

II

Under section 459, a person is guilty of burglary if he or she enters any building (or other listed structure) with the intent to commit larceny or any felony.[FN2] We must determine whether the Legislature intended the term "enter," as used in the burglary statute, to encompass passing a forged check through a chute in a walk-up window of a check-cashing or similar facility.

[text omitted]

The burglary statutes do not define the term "enter." In the present case, the Attorney General conceded at oral argument that no part of defendant's body entered the building, but it long has been established that a burglary also can be committed by using an instrument to enter a building.

[text omitted]

. . . a burglary may be committed by using an instrument to enter a building — whether that instrument is used solely to effect entry, or to accomplish the intended larceny or felony as well. Thus, using a tire iron to pry open a door, using a tool to create a hole in a store wall, or using an auger to bore a hole in a corn crib are sufficient entries to support a conviction of burglary. But it does not necessarily follow that the placement of a forged check in the chute of a walk-up window constitutes entering the building within the meaning of the burglary statute, although that conclusion would be compelled were we to follow the decision in *People v. Ravenscroft* (1988) 198 Cal.App.3d 639, 243 Cal.Rptr. 827, the only California authority to address an analogous question. As we shall explain, we do not find the reasoning in *Ravenscroft* persuasive.

The defendant in that case was convicted of two counts of burglary based upon his conduct of "surreptitiously stealing and inserting the automatic teller machine (ATM) card of his traveling companion, Barbara Ann Lewis, in two ATMs and punching in her personal

FN2. Section 459 states: "Every person who enters any house, room, apartment, tenement, shop, warehouse, store, mill, barn, stable, outhouse or other building, tent, vessel, as defined in Section 21 of the Harbors and Navigation Code, floating home, as defined in subdivision (d) of Section 18075.55 of the Health and Safety Code, railroad car, locked or sealed cargo container, whether or not mounted on a vehicle, trailer coach, as defined in Section 635 of the Vehicle Code, any house car, as defined in Section 362 of the Vehicle Code, inhabited camper, as defined in Section 243 of the Vehicle Code, vehicle as defined by the Vehicle Code, when the doors are locked, aircraft as defined by Section 21012 of the Public Utilities Code, or mine or any underground portion thereof, with intent to commit grand or petit larceny or any felony is guilty of burglary."

identification number, which he had previously noted, on the ATM keypads in order to withdraw funds from her account." (*People v. Ravenscroft, supra,* 198 Cal.App.3d 639, 641, 243 Cal.Rptr. 827.) The Court of Appeal first concluded that an ATM is a structure protected by the burglary statute. The court then turned to the question whether insertion of the ATM card constituted an entry into that structure. The court rejected the defendant's arguments that insertion of the card did not violate the air space of the ATM, and that insertion of the card did not constitute an entry, because the defendant lost control of the card once it entered the ATM: "The insertion of an ATM card to effectuate larcenous intent is no less an entry into the air space of a bank as would be the use of any other tool or instrument. Although the California Penal Code does not define 'entry' for the purpose of burglary, the California courts have found that a burglary is complete upon the slightest partial entry of any kind, with the requisite intent, even if the intended larceny is neither committed nor even attempted. [Citations.] By pushing Lewis's card into an ATM's slot, the defendant completed the crime. Further control of the card is unnecessary." (*Id.* at p. 643, 243 Cal. Rptr. 827.)

The Court of Appeal then rejected the defendant's further contention that he did not commit burglary by inserting the ATM card, because this act differed from other examples of entry by instrument: "Ravenscroft argues that *Walters* and *Osegueda, supra,* should not apply to this case since they involve more traditional violations of air space with more traditional burglars' tools. . . . [¶] . . . [¶] The fact that both *Walters* and *Osegueda* involve more traditional methods of burglary is of no moment. The gravamen of burglary is an act of entry, no matter how partial or slight it may be, with an instrument or tool which is appropriate for the particular instance, accompanied by the proper intent. [Citations.]" (*People v. Ravenscroft, supra,* 198 Cal.App.3d 639, 643-644, 243 Cal.Rptr. 827.)

The appellate court in *Ravenscroft* properly rejected various arguments presented by the defendant, correctly concluding that the card was inserted into the air space of the ATM, that the circumstance that the defendant lost control of the card is not dispositive, and that the rule governing entry by means of an instrument is not limited to traditional burglar tools.[FN3] Instruments other than traditional burglar tools certainly can be used to commit the offense of burglary. A laser could be used to cut an opening in a wall, a robot could be used to enter a building, or an ATM card could be used to "jimmy" a lock. But it does not necessarily follow from these conclusions that insertion of a stolen card into an ATM constitutes burglary.

The Court of Appeal in *Ravenscroft* appeared to reason that because an entry by means of an instrument is not limited to the use of traditional burglar's tools, there are no limitations within the meaning of the burglary statute on what constitutes entry by means of an instrument. It certainly is within the scope of the burglary statute to recognize that using

FN3. In *People v. Montoya* (1994) 7 Cal.4th 1027, 1041-1042, 31 Cal.Rptr.2d 128, 874 P.2d 903, we cited the decision in *Ravenscroft,* along with numerous other decisions, in support of the general proposition that "[o]ne may be liable for burglary upon entry with the requisite intent to commit a felony or a theft (whether felony or misdemeanor), regardless of whether the felony or theft is different from that contemplated at the time of entry, or whether any felony or theft actually is committed." Our decision in *Montoya* had no occasion to consider the specific holding or analysis in *Ravenscroft* that is at issue in the present case.

a cutting tool to breach the walls, doors, or windows of a building constitutes an entry, whether the burglar uses traditional burglar tools or a laser, and that using an instrument to reach into a building and remove property constitutes burglary whether that instrument is a hook or a robot. These are the traditional types of entry prohibited by the burglary statute, even though the entry may be accomplished in new ways.

Inserting a stolen ATM card into the designated opening in an ATM is markedly different from the types of entry traditionally covered by the burglary statute, as is passing a forged check through a chute in a walk-up window. In each situation the defendant causes an object to enter the air space of a building, but it is not apparent that the burglary statute was meant to encompass such conduct. It is important to establish reasonable limits as to what constitutes an entry by means of an instrument for purposes of the burglary statute. Otherwise the scope of the burglary statute could be expanded to absurd proportions. For example, the Attorney General asserted at oral argument that mailing a forged check from New York to a bank in California, or sliding a ransom note under a door, would constitute burglary. A person who mails a forged check to a bank or slides a ransom note under a door causes that forged check or ransom note to enter the building, but it cannot reasonably be argued that these acts constitute burglary. Under the expansive approach to the burglary statute taken by the Attorney General and reflected in the *Ravenscroft* decision, it is difficult to imagine what reasonable limit would be placed upon the scope of the burglary statute. It could be argued similarly that a defendant who, for a fraudulent purpose, accesses a bank's computer from his or her home computer via a modem has electronically entered the bank building and committed burglary.

The crucial issue, not considered by the court in *Ravenscroft*, is whether insertion of the ATM card was the type of entry the burglary statute was intended to prevent. In answering this question, we look to the interest sought to be protected by the burglary statute in general, and the requirement of an entry in particular.

The interest sought to be protected by the common law crime of burglary was clear. At common law, burglary was the breaking and entering of a dwelling in the nighttime. The law was intended to protect the sanctity of a person's home during the night hours when the resident was most vulnerable. As one commentator observed: "The predominant factor underlying common law burglary was the desire to protect the security of the home, and the person within his home. Burglary was not an offense against property, real or personal, but an offense against the habitation, for it could only be committed against the dwelling of another. . . . The dwelling was sacred, but a duty was imposed on the owner to protect himself as well as looking to the law for protection. The intruder had to break and enter; if the owner left the door open, his carelessness would allow the intruder to go unpunished. The offense had to occur at night; in the daytime home-owners were not asleep, and could detect the intruder and protect their homes." (Note, *Statutory Burglary—The Magic of Four Walls and a Roof* (1951) 100 U. Pa. L.Rev. 411, 427, fns. omitted.) The drafters of the Model Penal Code observed: "The notable severity of burglary penalties is accounted for by the fact that the offense was originally confined to violent nighttime assault on a dwelling. The dwelling was and remains each man's castle, the final refuge from which he need not flee even if the alternative is to take the life of an assailant. It is the place of security for his family, as well as his most cherished possessions. Thus it is perhaps understandable that the offense should have been a capital felony at common law. . . ." (Model Pen.Code & Commentaries (1980) com. to § 221.1, p. 67.)[FN4]

More than a century ago, in *People v. Barry* (1892) 94 Cal. 481, 29 P. 1026, this court addressed the subject of what constitutes an entry for purposes of burglary. The defendant in *Barry* entered a grocery store during business hours and attempted to commit larceny. This court, rejecting the contention that a burglary had not occurred because the defendant had entered lawfully as part of the public invited to enter the store, stated: " [A] party who enters with the intention to commit a felony enters without an invitation. He is not one of the public invited, nor is he entitled to enter." (*Id.* at p. 483, 29 P. 1026; *People v. Salemme* (1992) 2 Cal.App.4th 775, 781, 3 Cal.Rptr.2d 398 [entering a residence to sell fraudulent securities is an entry within the meaning of the burglary statute].)

In *People v. Gauze* (1975) 15 Cal.3d 709, 125 Cal.Rptr. 773, 542 P.2d 1365, we clarified our holding in *Barry* and held that a person cannot burglarize his or her own home. We observed that "[a] burglary remains an entry which invades a possessory right in a building." (*Id.* at p. 714, 125 Cal.Rptr. 773, 542 P.2d 1365.) We then discussed the interest protected by the burglary statute: " 'Burglary laws are based primarily upon a recognition of the dangers to personal safety created by the usual burglary situation — the danger that the intruder will harm the occupants in attempting to perpetrate the intended crime or to escape and the danger that the occupants will in anger or panic react violently to the invasion, thereby inviting more violence. The laws are primarily designed, then, not to deter the trespass and the intended crime, which are prohibited by others laws, so much as to forestall the germination of a situation dangerous to personal safety.' Section 459, in short, is aimed at the danger caused by the unauthorized entry itself." (*Id.* at p. 715, 125 Cal.Rptr. 773, 542 P.2d 1365.)

We repeated that sentiment in *People v. Montoya, supra,* 7 Cal.4th 1027, 1045, 31 Cal. Rptr.2d 128, 874 P.2d 903, in which we held that, "for the purpose of assessing the liability of an aider and abettor, a burglary is considered ongoing during the time the perpetrator remains inside the structure." We stated: "The crime of burglary consists of an act-unlawful entry-accompanied by the 'intent to commit grand or petit larceny or any felony.' " (*Id.* at p. 1041, 31 Cal.Rptr.2d 128, 874 P.2d 903, fn. omitted.) We noted that the "underlying basis for the criminal sanction" of burglary is " 'the danger caused by the unauthorized entry itself.' " (*Id.* at p. 1042, 31 Cal.Rptr.2d 128, 874 P.2d 903.) The Model Penal Code echoes this theme by noting that the crime of burglary "reflects a considered judgment that especially severe sanctions are appropriate for criminal invasion of premises under circumstances likely to terrorize occupants." (Model Pen.Code & Commentaries, *supra,* com. to art. 221, p. 59.)

FN4. Blackstone's Commentaries states that burglary "has always been looked upon as a very heinous offense; not only because of the abundant terror that it naturally carries with it, but also as it is a forcible invasion and disturbance of that right of habitation, which every individual might acquire even in a state of nature; an invasion, which in such a state would be sure to be punished with death, unless the assailant were the stronger. But in civil society the laws also come in to the assistance of the weaker party; and, besides that they leave him this natural right of killing the aggressor, if he can . . . , they also protect and avenge him, in case the might of the assailant is too powerful. And the law of England has so particular and tender a regard to the immunity of a man's house, that it styles it his castle, and will never suffer it to be violated with impunity. . . ." (4 Blackstone's Commentaries 223.)

Inserting a stolen ATM card into an ATM, or placing a forged check in a chute in the window of a check-cashing facility, is not using an instrument to effect an entry within the meaning of the burglary statute. Neither act violates the occupant's possessory interest in the building as does using a tool to reach into a building and remove property. It is true that the intended result in each instance is larceny. But the use of a tool to enter a building, whether as a prelude to a physical entry or to remove property or commit a felony, breaches the occupant's possessory interest in the building. Inserting an ATM card or presenting a forged check do not. Such acts are no different, for purposes of the burglary statute, from mailing a forged check to a bank or check-cashing facility.[FN5]

By analogy, a person who returns books to a library by depositing them in a book drop, causing the books to slide down a chute into the library, has not entered the library. It would be unreasonable to characterize the books as "instruments" used to enter the library. But if a person reaches his or her hand into the book drop, or uses a tool, in an attempt to steal books, such an act would constitute burglary.[FN6]

Our conclusion that the limits of the burglary statute should not be stretched beyond recognition does not leave the public without reasonable protection from criminal conduct, for the Legislature has enacted a variety of penal statutes that apply to the criminal activity involved in cases such as *Ravenscroft* or the present case. The use of an ATM card with intent to defraud, for example, specifically is penalized by section 484g and the Legislature, of course, could enact a similar statute pertaining to check-cashing facilities. Unauthorized entry into a computer system is addressed by sections 502 and 502.01. And in the present case, our reversal of defendant's conviction of burglary does not affect his convictions for forgery and receiving stolen property, or his resulting sentence of four years in prison.[FN7]

For the reasons discussed above, we conclude that defendant's placement of a forged check in the chute of the walk-up window of the check-cashing facility at issue cannot reasonably be termed an entry into the building for purposes of the burglary statute. Accordingly, the judgment of the Court of Appeal is reversed to the extent it affirms defendant's conviction for burglary, and affirmed in all other respects.

MOSK, KENNARD and WERDEGAR, JJ., concur.

FN5. [text omitted]

FN6. The record in the present case does not disclose whether, or to what extent, defendant reached into the chute of the walk-up window as he passed the check into the facility. As noted above, the Attorney General conceded at oral argument that no part of defendant's body entered the check-cashing facility. We need not, and therefore do not, consider whether a slight entry of a portion of defendant's body into the chute of the walk-up window would be a sufficient entry under the statute defining the offense of burglary.

FN7. [text omitted] Finally, the dissent asserts that our decision will produce anomalous results, because a person who inserts a stolen ATM card into an ATM affixed to an exterior wall of a bank does not commit burglary, but a person who enters the lobby of a bank to perform the same act does commit burglary. (Dis. opn., *post*, pp. 786-87 of 76 Cal.Rptr.2d, pp. 1099-1100 of 958 P.2d.) There is no anomaly in the circumstance that one who attempts a crime outside a building does not commit burglary, while another person who enters a building in order to attempt the same crime does commit burglary. Burglary is defined as an entry into a specified structure with the intent to commit larceny or any felony. Under the statute, if there is no entry, no burglary has occurred.

District Court of Appeal, First District, Division 1, California.

PEOPLE
v.
FRANCO.

Nov. 10, 1926.

Appeal from Superior Court, Fresno County; Charles R. Barnard, Judge.

Raymond Franco was convicted of burglary in the second degree, and he appeals. Affirmed.

Refusal to permit impeachment of witness for prosecution by quizzing as to felony commission held harmless error, where testimony given was entirely within matters voluntarily admitted by defendant to officers.

Marlowe Bumpus, of Fresno, for appellant.

U. S. Webb, Atty. Gen., and Emery F. Mitchell, of San Francisco, for the People.

TYLER, P. J.

Defendant was charged by information with the crime of burglary. He was tried and convicted. A motion for a new trial was made and denied. This appeal is from the judgment and order.

The evidence established the following facts: One H. R. Schucker was operating a shoe store in the city of Fresno. The store was situated in the basement of the building known as 1047 1/2 Fulton street. In order to enter the store, it was necessary to proceed down some stairs leading from the sidewalk to the store proper. Along the walls and sides of the stairway some five showcases had been installed, in which were displayed numerous pairs of shoes. On the night of February 19, 1926, the lock on one of these showcases was broken open and six pairs of shoes taken therefrom. Early in the morning of the following day, defendant rented a room under an assumed name at a certain hotel in Fresno, at which time he left a box containing the stolen shoes with the proprietor. Later in the morning, accompanied by one Nick Rodriquez, he appeared at the hotel and asked that the box be delivered to him. In the meantime, the police officers of Fresno had ascertained that the box was at the hotel and a detective had stationed himself at the door thereof for the purpose of apprehending defendant. Rodriquez left the hotel with the box in his possession and proceeded to enter an automobile when he was arrested. Immediately afterwards, defendant was also taken into custody. They were brought before the assistant district attorney and questioned. Defendant admitted that Rodriquez was in no manner implicated in the affair and had merely agreed to take the box to the express office for the purpose of having it shipped. Rodriquez was subsequently released from custody. At the time of his arrest, defendant had a tire iron on his person which was capable of being used to commit the offense charged. Defendant offered no evidence in his own behalf. He was convicted of burglary in the second degree. In support of this appeal, it is first urged that, as there was no internal communication between the display cases and the store proper, the cases were not a part of the store, and, consequently, there was no entry of the store proved which would bring the offense within the contemplation of the statute defining burglary. The Penal Code, in defining this offense, provides that:

"Every person who enters any house, room, apartment, tenement, shop, warehouse, store, mill, barn, stable, outhouse or other building, tent, vessel, railroad car, mine, or any underground portion thereof, with intent to commit grand or petit larceny or any felony is guilty of burglary." Section 459.

It is clearly apparent that the statutory crime of burglary is much more comprehensive than the offense at common law. 4 Cal. Jur. 723. [text omitted]. Here the roof of the building covers the showcases. They are, therefore, in legal effect, part of the store proper, and the entry of the place where they are situated must be held a sufficient entry to constitute the statutory offense. It has been uniformly held, under burglary statutes, that the word "house" has the very broadest significance and meaning and is very comprehensive. Williams v. State, 72 Tex. Cr. R. 371, 162 S. W. 838. In this case, a showcase was broken open and certain shoes taken therefrom. The showcase, as here, was outside of the store and there was no entrance to it from the inside of the store proper. It was there held that it was a part of the house so as to constitute a sufficient entry. See, also, Lewis v. State, 72 Tex. Cr. R. 377, 162 S. W. 866.

[text omitted]

There is no merit in the appeal.

The judgment and order are affirmed.

We concur: KNIGHT, J.; CAMPBELL, Justice pro tem.

SAMPLE RULE CHART

RULE	ILLUSTRATION	APPLICATION
Keep related rules close to one another and place broad rules before more specific rules.	List the precedent cases that apply the rule and summarize their holdings and reasoning.	What arguments might be made about how the rule applies to the facts of your case? Identify arguments on each side and even possible rebuttals.
Burglary requires entry of a building with intent to commit larceny or felony. *Valencia*; Penal Code §459.	[Broad rules do not need entries in these columns. Wait until the rules become more specific.]	
The ultimate test of whether a burglarious entry has occurred must focus on the protection the owners or inhabitants of a structure reasonably expect. *Valencia*.		
A building's outer boundary includes any element that encloses an area into which a reasonable person would believe that a member of the general public could not pass without authorization. *Valencia*.	*Valencia*. A reasonable person would believe that she needs authorization to pass through a window screen. Even an open door or window affords protection from unauthorized intrusion because of the social convention that portals may not be crossed without permission.	Plaintiff would argue the ATM kiosk was completely enclosed with walls and a door. Social convention suggests authorization is needed to go through the door. Defendant would argue that members of public would not think permission was needed since the bank tolerated loitering.
Burglary carries a higher penalty because it threatens violence either by the perpetrator to complete the crime or escape or by the occupants of the building. *Valencia*. *Davis*.	*Valencia*. A person is no less likely to react violently to the penetration of the screen than to the penetration of the window itself. *Davis*. Placing a forged check in a chute at a bank window is not entry under the burglary statute. There is no risk of violence.	Plaintiff would argue that bank employees or customers would react violently if they figured out what Defendant was up to. Also, Defendant might resort to violence to escape the kiosk. Defendant would argue that bank employees and customers would have no way of knowing that he was not a valid customer and therefore would not be likely to react. No potential for violence.

RULE	ILLUSTRATION	APPLICATION
An element of a building does not need to offer physical protection. *Valencia*.	*Valencia*. Not applied, but the court mentions that even an unlocked door or window satisfies the reasonable belief test due to the social convention against crossing portals.	Plaintiff would argue that the lack of a lock on the ATM kiosk door is not relevant (because even an unlocked door satisfies the reasonable belief test).
Outer boundary question is separate from the question of whether public had permission to enter the structure. *Valencia*.	*Valencia*. Not applied in the case—just dicta.	Plaintiff would argue that Defendant's argument that the bank permitted loitering is not relevant.
A house is a structure that has walls on all sides and is covered by a roof. *Franco*.	*Franco*. Show cases along stairwell leading down to shoe store were part of the building because they shared the same roof as the store.	Plaintiff would argue that the kiosk was completely enclosed (walls and roof). Defendant would argue that the kiosk did not share a roof with the bank.
Burglary must invade possessory interest of the occupant. *Davis*.	*Davis*. Passing forged check into chute at bank window did not invade bank occupants' possessory interest any more than mailing a forged check would.	Plaintiff would argue possessory interest was invaded since Defendant walked into the kiosk and did not just place an item in a chute. Defendant would argue possessory interest was not invaded since kiosk was not part of the outer boundary of the building.

READING A COURT OPINION SELF-TEST

1. Rereading a case more than once, although helpful, is not enough to ensure that you will understand the case and extract all of the information you need. What two tools does this chapter provide to help you analyze and synthesize cases?

2. One of the most important parts of a case to understand is the reasoning behind the court's decision. Reasoning is more than just the legal rules and the case facts. What else are you looking for?

See answers on page 337.

SECTION **B**

WRITING A LEGAL ANALYSIS

CHAPTER **3**

The Context of Legal Writing

Writing will be a large part of your life as a lawyer. You will write in many different formats: e-mails, contracts, letters, interview summaries, court briefs, pleadings, written interrogatories, proposed legislation, advocacy documents, and countless others. This text covers challenging forms of legal writing: objective legal writing in the form of legal research memoranda and persuasive legal writing in the form of court briefs.

In both legal research memoranda (Part II) and briefs (Part III), lawyers analyze how the law impacts their clients' legal rights and responsibilities. Both genres are typically limited to one or more discrete questions about the law (legal issues) that are relevant to a client's situation. In research memoranda, lawyers assess the strengths and weaknesses of their clients' cases. In briefs, they try to convince courts to resolve cases in their clients' favor.

Research memoranda and briefs have different components and structures, the way book reviews differ from exposés. And, just like two journalists might have slightly different templates for an exposé, two lawyers might make different choices about how to set up a research memorandum or brief. In Parts II and III, this text teaches common templates. For now, in Part I, we need to work on the fundamentals that underlie a written legal analysis regardless of whether it is an objective research memorandum or a persuasive brief and regardless of the particular preferences that a lawyer may apply to create a template of her own.

As Chapter 2 explains, the law that lawyers apply to analyze their clients' cases is a complex web of rules expressed and implied from a variety of sources, including, for example, statutes enacted by governing bodies, regulations promulgated by government agencies, and prior court decisions. Although we like to think of the law as something definite and indisputable, it is more often evasive and subject to different interpretations. Writers of both legal research memoranda and court briefs have to grapple with this uncertainty. They have to first explore existing law and its plausible interpretations. Then they have to analyze the impact of those possible interpretations on their clients' cases given the specific and often unique facts they present.

Before Parts II and III get into the differences between legal research memoranda and briefs, Chapters 4 and 5 ground you in the two core steps these writings share: (1) discussion of the law including legal precedent and (2) application of the law to the particular facts of a client's case. Chapter 4 discusses legal precedent, which includes "rule statement" and "rule explanation" paragraphs. Chapter 5 covers "application" paragraphs.[1]

---

1. Chapters 4 and 5 will refer to rule statement, rule explanation, and application "paragraphs" because these functions are usually separated into their own paragraphs. However, sometimes writers will combine rule explanation and application. See section 6.4.2 for an example of an organization that does not use separate paragraphs for rule explanation and application. Even when you combine rule explanation and application into a shared paragraph, you should think of them as separate functions so that you do not miss any steps.

CHAPTER 4

Writing About the Law

This chapter explains how to construct a thorough discussion of the law. The lessons in this chapter apply equally to legal research memoranda and briefs.

This chapter is one of the most important chapters in the text because a discussion of the law sets the foundation for the entire written analysis. You cannot adequately implement the lessons of Chapter 5 on successfully applying the law unless you first thoroughly and accurately discuss the law in your memorandum or brief.

4.1 | AN ORIENTATION

Your memorandum or brief and, therefore, your discussion of the law, is usually targeted toward one or more specific legal issues that arise in your client's case. A discussion of the law typically involves two components: (1) a "rule statement" paragraph that summarizes and synthesizes the key legal rule(s) on the issue, and (2) several "rule explanation" paragraphs that use specific details from precedent cases or other sources of law to explain and illustrate the rules.

The specifics of rule statement and rule explanation are explained in detail in the coming sections. For now, here is a sample to show you the distinction between the two. Notice that the first paragraph, the rule statement, contains generalized statements of rules whereas the second paragraph, the rule explanation, starts with a couple of rule sentences but then recites the specifics of a precedent case to prove and illustrate the rule.

Sample Rule Statement and Rule Explanation

To establish burglary under California law, the prosecution must establish that the defendant "enter[ed]" a "building" "with the intent to commit...larceny or felony." Cal. Penal Code § 459 (West 2004). The entry requirement distinguishes burglary from other theft crimes by emphasizing interference with the possessory interest of a build- Rule statement

Cont.

ing's occupants. *People v. Davis*, 958 P.2d 1083, 1089 (Cal. 1998). As explained by the California Supreme Court, the higher penalties burglary charges carry "are based primarily upon a recognition of the... danger that the intruder will harm the occupants in attempting to perpetrate the intended crime or to escape and the danger that occupants will in anger or panic react violently to the invasion." *Id.* Because burglary is based on the dangers inherent in an intrusion, "'[t]he ultimate test of whether a burglarious entry has occurred must focus on the protection the owners or inhabitants of a structure reasonably expect.'" *People v. Valencia*, 46 P.3d 920, 924 (Cal. 2002) (quoting *People v. Nible*, 247 Cal. Rptr. 396, 399 (Ct. App. 1988)).

Rule explanation

Even the "slightest partial entry" of the outer boundary of a building constitutes an entry. *Id.* at 925. Consistent with the "ultimate test" that the California Supreme Court adopted in *Valencia*, a building's outer boundary includes any element that encloses an area into which a reasonable person would believe that a member of the general public could not pass without authorization. *Id.* at 926. In *Valencia*, the court found that the defendant had entered a house when he removed a window screen with a screwdriver even though he did not successfully open the window. *Id.* at 927. The court reasoned that a screen window announces that intrusion is unauthorized. *Id.* The court also noted that an element of a structure need not offer physical protection to be considered part of the building's outer boundary. *Id.* at 926. "[W]hat matters is not whether a reasonable person would believe that a given element of a building provides some physical protection against unauthorized intrusion, but simply whether a reasonable person would believe that a member of the general public needed authorization to pass beyond it." *Id.* at 926-27. The court noted with approval a prior holding that "'even an open door... affords some expectation of protection from unauthorized intrusion because reasonable persons understand the social convention that portals may not be crossed without permission.'" *Id.* at 926 (quoting *Nible*, 247 Cal. Rptr. at 399).

At this point, you might also want to know where within a document the rule statement and rule explanation appear. They usually start at the top of the "Analysis" section of a research memorandum and the "Argument" section of a brief after an initial thesis sentence or paragraph (see images below). The choices

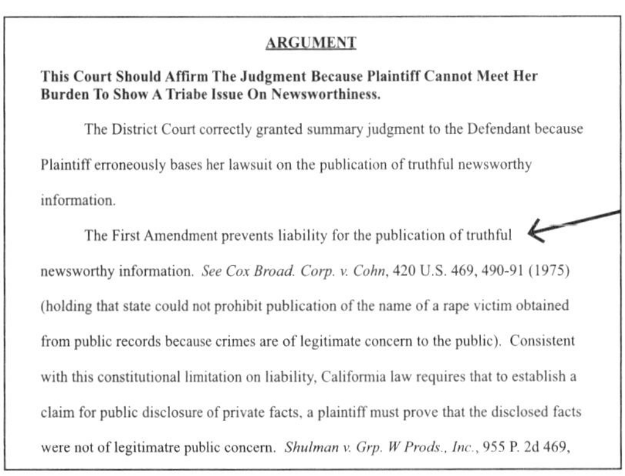

ARGUMENT

This Court Should Affirm The Judgment Because Plaintiff Cannot Meet Her Burden To Show A Triabe Issue On Newsworthiness.

The District Court correctly granted summary judgment to the Defendant because Plaintiff erroneously bases her lawsuit on the publication of truthful newsworthy information.

The First Amendment prevents liability for the publication of truthful newsworthy information. *See Cox Broad. Corp. v. Cohn*, 420 U.S. 469, 490-91 (1975) (holding that state could not prohibit publication of the name of a rape victim obtained from public records because crimes are of legitimate concern to the public). Consistent with this constitutional limitation on liability, California law requires that to establish a claim for public disclosure of private facts, a plaintiff must prove that the disclosed facts were not of legitimatre public concern. *Shulman v. Grp. W Prods., Inc.*, 955 P. 2d 469,

Appellate Brief

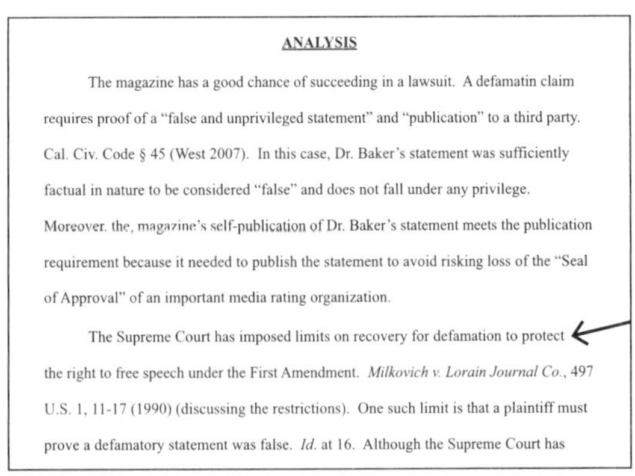

ANALYSIS

The magazine has a good chance of succeeding in a lawsuit. A defamatin claim requires proof of a "false and unprivileged statement" and "publication" to a third party. Cal. Civ. Code § 45 (West 2007). In this case, Dr. Baker's statement was sufficiently factual in nature to be considered "false" and does not fall under any privilege. Moreover, the, magazine's self-publication of Dr. Baker's statement meets the publication requirement because it needed to publish the statement to avoid risking loss of the "Seal of Approval" of an important media rating organization.

The Supreme Court has imposed limits on recovery for defamation to protect the right to free speech under the First Amendment. *Milkovich v. Lorain Journal Co.*, 497 U.S. 1, 11-17 (1990) (discussing the restrictions). One such limit is that a plaintiff must prove a defamatory statement was false. *Id.* at 16. Although the Supreme Court has

Legal Research Memorandum

regarding how to organize multiple rule statement and rule explanation paragraphs are complex and covered in Chapter 6. To keep things simple for now, imagine them all placed together at the start of an analysis before any of the application paragraphs discussed in Chapter 5.

You can also take a moment to look at Appendix B, Sample A (legal research memorandum) or Appendix B, Sample E (appellate brief). The rule statement and explanation paragraphs are labeled for you.

4.2 | THE RULE STATEMENT

"Rule statement" is a common term in legal writing pedagogy, but you could also think of the rule statement as a rule introduction. A rule statement presents an overview of the rules that apply to the legal issue. It serves to introduce the more detailed discussion of the rules and precedent cases that follow in the rule explanation paragraphs. Rule statements are typically contained in a single paragraph, but in complex analyses, they may need to be broken up into multiple paragraphs.

The most important strategy for drafting an effective rule statement is to put yourself in your reader's shoes. Assume your reader is an experienced attorney who is familiar with the legal system and legal terminology but is not familiar with the particular issue of law you are analyzing. When drafting the rule statement paragraph, try to disassociate yourself from all the research you have done. Imagine that you know nothing about the law on your issue. What is the first thing you would need to know? What other essential rules would you need to understand about the issue? For each sentence, ask yourself, "Would I understand that sentence, or is there a term or concept I would need explained?"

4.2.1 | Structuring the Rule Statement Like a Funnel: Broad to Narrow

Think of the rule statement paragraph as a funnel. A funnel is wide at the top and gradually becomes narrow. The function of your rule statement is similar. You are guiding your reader step by step from broad legal principles to the more narrow starting point of your first rule explanation paragraph.

Start your rule statement with the most general principle applicable to your issue (the "starting-point rule" discussed in section 2.4.3). Usually, this rule will require the element or permit the defense your analysis will discuss. For example, if you are analyzing whether your client can assert a defense of entrapment in his trial for drug trafficking offenses, you might start by stating that entrapment is a defense in certain circumstances:

> The defense of entrapment is available when the police lead defendants to commit crimes they would not otherwise have committed.

You can also look at Annotation 12 in Appendix B, Sample A, for another example of a first sentence that identifies the element at issue.

4.2.2 | Determining What to Put in the Funnel

After the first sentence, use your judgment. What does the reader need to know? In our entrapment example, what terms might be vague to the reader? Probably "lead" and "would not otherwise have committed." The reader needs definitions of these terms. For example, your entire rule statement paragraph on entrapment might look like this:

Sample Rule Statement

The defense of entrapment is available when the police lead defendants to commit crimes they would not otherwise have committed. To establish that the police led them to commit a crime, defendants must establish significant police involvement in designing or carrying out the crime. Moreover, defendants will not be able to prove they "would not otherwise have committed" the crime if they have engaged in similar crimes in the recent past.

Now the reader has a better understanding: significant police involvement and the defendant's involvement in similar past crimes are the two key factors in determining when entrapment is a defense.

Of course, questions remain. What does "significant involvement" mean? What does "similar" mean? But these questions are starting to get very specific. To define "significant" and "similar," you are going to need to get into specific factual examples from court opinions. Rule statements should not start getting into any specific factual scenarios from court opinions, so your intuition that specific examples are needed is a pretty good clue that the rule statement is done; save the details for the rule explanation paragraphs.

Determining what should go in the rule statement is an art. Include the main determinative rules, but not so many rules that the reader cannot digest the information. Avoid getting so detailed that the reader is going to want to start seeing some fact-specific examples. Save the specifics for the rule explanation.

4.2.3 | Using Connectors in Your Rule Statement

Your reader needs to understand how the rules you are stating interact with one another. Except for the first sentence, every sentence in the rule statement should connect back to a previous sentence. Below I discuss two effective methods of stating connections between rules: the mobile and the chain method.

The Mobile Here is the sample rule statement again, but this time with the connectors shaded.

> The defense of entrapment is available when the police lead defendants to commit crimes they would not otherwise have committed. To establish that the police led them to commit a crime, defendants must establish significant police involvement in designing or carrying out the crime. Moreover, defendants will not be able to prove they "would not otherwise have committed" a crime if they engaged in similar crimes in the recent past.

Notice how the connectors in this sample tie each sentence back to the starting-point rule stated in the first sentence by using the same terminology: "lead" and "would not otherwise have committed." This rule statement is structured like a mobile: two or more points are tied back to the same string.

The Chain Method Another option is to connect each new sentence to its predecessor, like a chain. The following sample demonstrates the chain model in which the connectors (shaded) tie each sentence to its predecessor.

> The defense of entrapment is available when the police lead defendants to commit crimes they would not otherwise have committed. To meet this standard, defendants must establish significant police involvement in designing or carrying out the crime. However, even if defendants can establish significant involvement, they cannot establish entrapment if they committed similar crimes in the recent past.

The two types of transitions are equally effective and can be used together as well. For example, your second and third sentences might tie back to your starting-point rule, but then you might switch to the chain approach and tie your fourth sentence to the third sentence.

See Annotation 12 in Appendix B, Sample A, for another example of using connecting language in the rule statement paragraph.

In theory, drafting connectors should be easy. Unfortunately, the connections between rules are not always stated explicitly in the case law. Often, you have to put the pieces together yourself, which is called "rule synthesis" or, sometimes, "case synthesis." This is a difficult aspect of legal analysis. Although the involvement of case law complicates the concept of synthesis, the logic of synthesis is not specific to the field of law.

Think back to the following childhood game:

Match each item in the left column to its partner in the right column

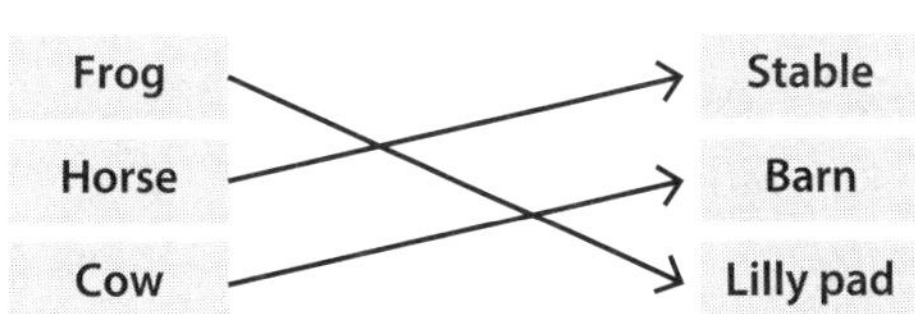

Suppose for a moment that you are a young child who does not know where each animal belongs. What could you do? You could walk around looking for frogs, horses, and cows and observing their habitat.

Rule synthesis is the same process. When court opinions do not expressly state all of the relationships between various rules, you have to be a good investigator and observe how each rule is used in the court's reasoning. Again, you have this skill. You just need to learn to use it in this new context. If you have organized your rule chart (see section 2.6) according to the relationships between the rules (e.g., broad to narrow and with related rules next to one another), you might already have a good framework. Creating a diagram of the rules that show their relationships to one another (see section 7.3.2) or a flow chart (see section 7.3.3) can also help.

Compare the rule statement below to the diagram that follows it. Notice that the "broad rules" box is organized in a broad-to-narrow manner from the existence of the tort at issue, to its limitations, and then to a specific test to determine liability. None of the connectors (in bold) are explicit in the rules; instead, they represent logical choices that reflect the relationships identified in the diagram.

Try following the same process when you write a rule statement—use a rule chart and diagram to map out the relationships, and you will find it easier to select the right connectors. Sometimes, you can look back at the cases to see how the courts have made the connections between the rules. But other times, the cases may not be clear about the connections and you have to think them through on your own.

Corresponding Rule Statement

The First Amendment prevents liability for the publication of truthful newsworthy information. *See Cox Broad. Corp. v. Cohn*, 420 U.S. 469, 490-91 (1975) (holding that state could not prohibit publication of the name of a rape victim obtained from public records because crimes are of legitimate concern to the public). **Consistent with this constitutional limitation on liability,** California law requires that to establish a claim for public disclosure of private facts, a plaintiff must prove that the disclosed facts were not of legitimate public concern. *Shulman v. Grp. W Prods., Inc.*, 955 P.2d 469, 478-79 (Cal. 1998). **To determine whether disclosed facts are of legitimate public concern,** courts consider "the social value of the facts [], the depth of the article's intrusion into ostensibly private affairs, and the extent to which the party voluntarily acceded to a position of public notoriety." *Kapellas v. Kofman*, 459 P.2d 912, 922 (Cal. 1969). Where, as in the instant case, the facts relate to a private person involuntarily caught up in events of public interest, the California Supreme Court **has defined the inquiry as** whether the facts "bear a logical relationship to the newsworthy subject" of the article and "are not intrusive in great disproportion to their relevance." *Shulman*, 955 P.2d at 478 (plurality opinion).

Sample Diagram

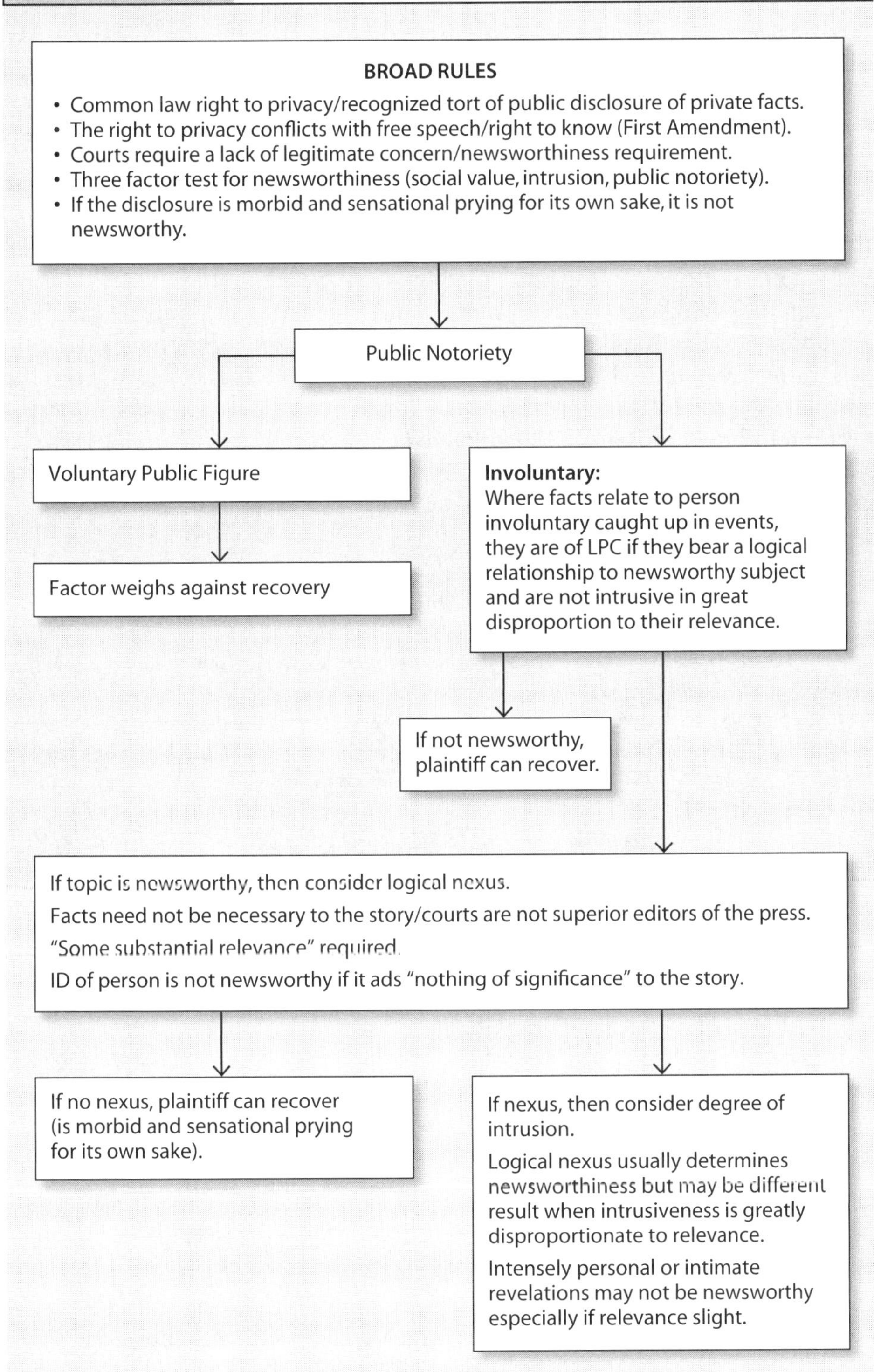

(The voluntary public figure side of the diagram was not included in the rule statement because the plaintiff at issue in the author's case was not a voluntary public figure.)

4.2.4 | Rule Statement in Questions of First Impression

The most common type of legal analysis—and therefore the focus of the preceding discussion of the rule statement—applies settled law to a set of facts. However, lawyers also analyze unsettled law, that is, a novel question of law that has not been resolved in the particular jurisdiction. Such "questions of first impression" might include the interpretation of a vague word or phrase in a statute, a proposed extension of existing law to a novel situation, a proposed exception to existing law required by a novel situation, or even a brand new area of the law. Rule statements in analyses of questions of first impression are still organized from broad to narrow and still need connectors. The difference is that a rule statement on a question of first impression will end by identifying the hole in the law that the analysis will address.

Sample Rule Statement for a Question of First Impression

A plaintiff must ordinarily prove that the defendant caused her injury. *Smith v. Eli Lilly & Co.*, 560 N.E.2d 324, 328 (Ill. 1990). Whether seeking to recover under a negligence or strict liability theory, a plaintiff in a products liability suit must establish a causal relationship between the defendant and the injury-producing agent. *Id.; Zafft v. Eli Lilly & Co.*, 676 S.W.2d 241, 244 (Mo. 1984). In other words, a plaintiff must establish that the defendant "produced, manufactured, sold, or was in some way responsible for" the particular item that caused her injury. *Smith*, 560 N.E.2d at 328. This requirement fairly limits liability to the responsible party. *See id.* at 329 (noting that the identification element of causation assigns blameworthiness to culpable parties). In addition, it avoids exposing manufacturers to excessive liability that might deter the development of new products. *Id.* However, a small number of jurisdictions have relied on the exception that is implicated in the case at hand: market share liability. *See generally Sindell v. Abbott Labs.*, 607 P.2d 924 (Cal. 1980); *Conley v. Boyle Drug Co.*, 570 So. 2d 275 (Fla. 1991); *Smith v. Cutter Biological, Inc.*, 823 P.2d 717 (Haw. 1991); *Hymowitz v. Eli Lilly & Co.*, 539 N.E.2d 1069 (N.Y. 1989); *Martin v. Abbott Labs.*, 689 P.2d 368 (Wash. 1984); *Collins v. Eli Lilly Co.*, 342 N.W.2d 37 (Wis. 1984).

In the above example, the author is going to analyze whether her jurisdiction should adopt the market share liability theory, which presumably would save the plaintiff's case despite an inability to identify the source of the product that caused her injuries. General rules are first laid out in the usual broad-to-narrow fashion with connectors like "in other words," "in addition," and "however." Then the wrinkle in the law is disclosed—the market share liability exception. The rule explanation would then explore the arguments for and against the market share liability theory. Section 4.3.1.6 discusses this next step in the process.

Checklist for the Rule Statement

- ☐ You have taken time to think about how the rules you have pulled from different cases relate to one another.
- ☐ Your first sentence states the starting-point rule on the element or defense, followed by the basic rules that govern your issue.
- ☐ You include key tests and definitions while saving more narrow subrules for your rule explanation.
- ☐ You structure the paragraph with increasing levels of specificity: broader rules are stated before more specific rules.
- ☐ You use connectors to clarify the relationship between the rules you state.

4.3 | RULE EXPLANATION

After the rule statement paragraph, several paragraphs are typically needed to define, explain, and exemplify the rules. This process of "rule explanation" is often the longest part of a legal analysis. Each paragraph of rule explanation[1] should use a transition, a topic sentence that states a subrule relevant to the legal issue, and at least one case example that proves or illustrates the subrule stated in the topic sentence. Each of these three components is explained in more detail in the sections that follow. For now, use the following sample to get a general feel for the placement of these three components within a rule explanation.

Sample Rule Explanation Paragraph

Even the "slightest partial entry" of the outer boundary of a building constitutes an entry. *Id.* at 925. Consistent with the "ultimate test" that the California Supreme Court adopted in *Valencia*, a building's outer boundary includes any element that encloses an area into which a reasonable person would believe that a member of the general public could not pass without authorization. *Id.* at 926. In *Valencia*, the court found that the defendant had entered a house when he removed a window screen with a screwdriver even though he did not successfully open the window. *Id.* at 927. The court reasoned that a screen window announces that intrusion is unauthorized. *Id.* The court also noted that an element of a structure need not offer physical protection to be considered part of the building's outer boundary. *Id.* at 926. "[W]hat matters is not whether a reasonable person would believe that a given element of a building provides some physical protection against unauthorized intrusion, but simply whether a reasonable person would believe that a member of the general public needed authorization to pass beyond it."

Transition

Topic sentence

Case example

Cont.

1. Rule explanation usually occurs in its own paragraph or set of paragraphs. Chapter 6 discusses alternative organizations; but, for now, think of rule explanation as a separate paragraph or set of paragraphs within your legal analysis.

Id. at 926-27. The court noted with approval a prior holding that "'even an open door... affords some expectation of protection from unauthorized intrusion because reasonable persons understand the social convention that portals may not be crossed without permission.'" *Id.* at 926 (quoting *Nible*, 247 Cal. Rptr. at 399).

4.3.1 | Crafting Effective Topic Sentences

Like rule statements, rule explanations require synthesis. One of the main places in a rule explanation to synthesize is the topic sentence. Achieving synthesis through your topic sentences is a critical aspect of your job as a legal writer. Imagine that your professor required 20 textbooks for your legal writing class, and some of these books differed on certain writing principles. This would not be good, right? Instead, you would rely on your professor to synthesize the materials for you. Your reader similarly relies on you to synthesize the case law.

4.3.1.1 | Stating a Subrule

The topic sentence of a rule explanation should state a subsidiary rule, definition, test, factor, or policy consideration ("subrule") that helps edify or expand on the rules you have presented in your rule statement.

Students are often tempted to present descriptions of court opinions in an unsynthesized fashion. They devote each paragraph to describing a court opinion without a topic sentence:

ERROR **Illustration of Undesirable Case-by Case Organization**

Paragraph 1: In Case A, the court held...

Paragraph 2: In Case B, the court held...

Such a case-by-case organization reads like a list of case summaries. The reader gets bored and struggles to identify themes from the cases. To avoid this result, start each rule explanation paragraph with a subrule or lesson you are pulling from the cases that you discuss in the paragraph, as in the following example:

Sample Topic Sentences

The government becomes significantly involved in the commission of a crime where its agents not only supply the materials necessary to the crime but also direct

Cont.

the commission of the crime. [In the rest of this paragraph, you would discuss at least one precedent case that proves and illustrates that supplying the materials and directing the crime constitutes significant involvement.]

By contrast, merely supplying the materials necessary to the crime does not establish entrapment. [In the rest of this paragraph, you would discuss at least one precedent case that proves and illustrates that merely supplying the materials is not sufficient.]

The final consideration is whether the defendant committed similar crimes in the recent past and, therefore, was predisposed to commit the crime. Predisposition is established when the past and current crimes involved the same underlying motivation. [In the rest of this paragraph, you would discuss at least one precedent case that proves and illustrates that crimes involving the same underlying motivation establish predisposition.]

Now, here is a more complete example to illustrate the role of topic sentences in a rule explanation. Notice that each paragraph of the rule explanation is devoted to a subrule. The subrule is identified in the topic sentence (bolded in each paragraph below) and then exemplified with one or more case examples. You might also notice that the topic sentence is not always the first sentence in the paragraph. Sometimes, you may want to include an initial transition sentence or perhaps some more general rules that lead in to the specific subrule to be addressed in the paragraph. You do not have to rigidly force the subrule into the first sentence as long as you identify the subrule before you launch into your case examples.

Sample Rule Explanation

The first part of the test, subjective belief, is satisfied by an employee's professed belief that participation was required. **Indeed, a belief that one *should* participate is sufficient.** In *Ezzy*, for example, a law clerk was injured while playing on her firm's softball team. 194 Cal. Rptr. at 91. She testified that because the team did not have enough female players to satisfy the league's rules, she felt she "should" play when a partner handed her a tee shirt and game schedule and said, "At the next one, we'll see you there." *Id.* at 92. Her statement under oath was sufficient to satisfy the subjective belief requirement. *Id.* at 96.

Transition: "The first part..."

Topic: "should" is sufficient

Case example that proves "should" is sufficient.

Failing the subjective belief requirement seems to be a risk only when the employee did not truly feel obligated to participate. *Compare Smith v. Workers' Comp. Appeals Bd.*, 236 Cal. Rptr. 248, 254-55 (Ct. App. 1987) (holding that deceased teacher's wife's testimony that teacher went to a picnic because his department head asked him to, he felt he had a "responsibility" to go, and he believed he had to participate in a certain number of extracurricular activities satisfied the subjective element of the test to establish coverage for injuries sustained while he was windsurfing during the picnic), *and Wilson v. Workers' Comp. Appeals Bd.*, 239 Cal. Rptr.

Transition: "Failing the subjective belief..."

Topic: feeling obligated is the key

Case examples that prove feeling obligated is the determining factor.

Cont.

719, 721 (Ct. App. 1987) (holding that police officer's testimony that he believed he had to keep in shape to stay on a special emergency unit satisfied the subjective element to establish coverage for an injury sustained while running off-duty), *with City of Stockton v. Workers' Comp. Appeals Bd.*, 38 Cal. Rptr. 3d 474, 483 (Ct. App. 2006) (denying coverage to officer injured while playing basketball when he admitted he could satisfy the job requirement of keeping in shape without playing basketball).

Transition: "Because the subjective . . ."

More general rule (implied pressure) leads into topic of the paragraph (need to participate to remain or advance)

Because the subjective element is easily met, most cases turn on the reasonableness of the employee's belief. Even as to this second element, however, courts have been liberal in their interpretation of "expectancy" and have found it satisfied based merely on "implied pressure" on an employee to participate in the activity at issue. *Smith*, 236 Cal. Rptr. at 254 ("[E]vidence demonstrating and proving express or implied pressure upon the employee serves to establish the objective reasonableness of that employee's belief that he or she was required to participate"). **The need to participate in the activity to remain or advance in employment can establish implied pressure.** *See Wilson*, 239 Cal. Rptr. at 722. In *Wilson*, a police officer claimed coverage for injuries sustained while running on his own time off work premises. *Id.* at 719. Police officers in the plaintiff's special emergency unit were tested four times per year and those in his age group had to run two miles in seventeen minutes. *Id.* at 722. The court found plaintiff reasonably believed he had to keep in shape to remain in the unit and was therefore entitled to coverage. *Id.* It reasoned that it would be "unrealistic" to think that such a requirement could be met without off-duty exercise. *Id.* The court similarly found implied pressure satisfied in *Kidwell v. Workers' Comp. Appeals Bd.*, 39 Cal. Rptr. 2d 540, 545-46 (Ct. App. 1995), where a police officer was injured while practicing long jumps at home, because testimony established that promotion and benefits were contingent on passing a long jump test that required practice.

Case examples that prove the need to participate to remain or advance establishes implied pressure

Transition: "Implied pressure may be exacerbated . . ."

Topic: vulnerable position

Case examples that prove relevance of vulnerable position

Implied pressure may be exacerbated when an employee is in a vulnerable position. *See Smith*, 236 Cal. Rptr. at 257 (noting that the employee was more vulnerable to pressure because as a temporary instructor, he needed to participate in extracurricular activities to better his chances of being rehired); *Ezzy*, 194 Cal. Rptr. at 95 (finding that a law clerk's belief that her participation in a softball game was expected was reasonable based in part on the pressure a law clerk would naturally feel when urged to participate in a softball game by a partner at the firm).

Look back at the above example one more time. Notice that some of the cases are mentioned in more than one paragraph. With the preferred organization by subrule (rather than by case), you may discuss different aspects of the same case in different paragraphs.

4.3.1.2 | Connecting Two Subrules

Topic sentences may include more than a single subrule. In fact, topic sentences that logically relate two subrules can be extremely helpful to the reader. Just make sure that you are combining *related* subrules and that your topic sentence explains the relationship.

ERROR **Irrational Relationship—Confuses the Reader**

Similarities between past crimes and the current crime indicate a defendant was predisposed to commit the current crime, but reluctance to commit the current crime suggests the defendant was not predisposed to commit the current crime.

Contrast the next example, which explains the relationship between the subrules (past crimes and reluctance). Note that even though the writer is combining related subrules into one sentence, she avoids the hazard of making the sentence too wordy.

Rational Relationship—Helps the Reader

A defendant who has committed similar past crimes was most likely predisposed to commit the current crime unless he can prove his reluctance.

The sentence would be followed by discussion of cases to prove the synthesis—e.g., that reluctance can counter the similarity between crimes.

Alternatively, the two synthesized subrules can be placed in separate sentences, each with its own proof, as in the following sample (the two subrules are bolded).

Sample Synthesis of Related Subrules

"Unwarranted physical, or perhaps mental, coercion" may shock the conscience. *Bogart*, 783 F.2d at 1438; *see also Greene*, 454 F.2d at 786 (finding that veiled threat by agent to pressure defendants into production of bootleg alcohol supported dismissal of the indictment). **However, the courts have recognized that undercover agents often must engage in "unsavory conduct," including language that could be construed as threatening, to maintain their cover.** *United States v. Emmert*, 829 F.2d 805, 812 (9th Cir. 1987). In *Emmert*, two government agents negotiated a drug deal with the defendant and some other accomplices. *Id.* at 807. When the deal failed to go through, one of the accomplices asked the undercover agents for some money up front and expressed concern that one of the agents was a policeman. *Id.* In response, one of the agents said, "Maybe we'll do the deal in an airplane and if something goes wrong, we'd have one parachute and guess who'd come down without one." *Id.* And the other agent said she had three words for the defendant's accomplice, "R.I.P." *Id.* A few months later, the defendant was able to put the deal together and was arrested at the scene. *Id.* In rejecting the threats as a reason to dismiss the indictment, the court stated that "[e]xpress or implied threats may be warranted under certain circumstances" and "may not always constitute outrageous conduct." *Id.* at 811. The court concluded that the

Cont.

threats aimed at Emmert were "scarcely more than bluster" and were "ordinary bargaining tactics in drug deals." *Id.* at 812. It further explained that "government agents may need to engage in such "unsavory conduct to maintain their cover." *Id.* The court concluded that the threats were necessary to allay suspicions about the undercover agents. *Id.*

4.3.1.3 | Express Subrules: Where Does Rule Statement Stop and Rule Explanation Begin?

As mentioned at the start of section 4.3, your rule explanation topic sentences pick up where your rule statement left off. They should provide more specific definitions, factors, limitations, or other types of subrules, to clarify the rules that you included in your rule statement. In your rule chart (see section 2.6), these rules would be somewhere toward the bottom on the scale of broad-to-narrow: broad enough to state a general principle but more specific than the rules that you included in rule statement. Consider the following example.

Suppose that you want to know whether your uncle is liable for stopping to help someone in a car crash. He wrapped the victim's leg in a shirt to stop it from bleeding but did not put on a tourniquet. He was too scared to use a tourniquet because he knew it would require amputation of the leg. The victim died.

You ask me for advice, and I tell you that Good Samaritans are not liable unless they are grossly negligent. (A Good Samaritan is someone who stops to offer help to others.)

You would wonder, "What is gross negligence?" This rule is pretty vague.

What if I next tell you that gross negligence is more than just the lack of care; it is deliberate neglect. "Deliberate neglect" is still vague, and you probably remain unsure about your uncle's innocence under the law.

Now, how about this rule? Deliberate neglect requires awareness by the Good Samaritan that he is withholding necessary care.

At this point, you have a rule that you can really work with. You need to figure out whether your uncle knew the tourniquet was necessary. You can look at the facts to answer this question: Did your uncle know that the victim would die without the tourniquet, or was he hoping the shirt would be enough?

When you are deciding which rules are sufficiently specific to serve as a rule explanation topic sentence, you are looking for rules like "withholding necessary care" that are more easily proven true or false with cold, hard facts. More general rules can be placed in the rule statement or perhaps used as lead-ins to the rule explanation topic sentence as illustrated in the sample rule explanation at the end of section 4.3.1.1.

4.3.1.4 | Inferred Subrules

Sometimes, the rules expressed in the court cases may not tell the whole story. You may need to craft your own subrules based on observations of patterns in the case law or logical connections you can draw between the cases.

To infer subrules, you have to ask yourself some hard questions:

- Can you come up with a general statement that would be consistent with all of the cases?
- What factors seem important and under what circumstances?
- Can you reconcile seemingly conflicting results by identifying guiding principles that make the conflict seem more logical and less arbitrary?

Here is an example to illustrate the process of inferring rules.

Background for Inferred Rules Illustration

Suppose that you ask some lawyers how you should choose a law school, and you hear the following three stories.

Story 1. Mary works in a large law firm. Her law firm does not even consider candidates unless they have graduated from a first-tier law school. Mary explains that to be competitive, a large law firm needs to have lawyers with universally recognized credentials.

Story 2. Jose works as a public defender. He was hired over a Harvard Law graduate because his employer knows that Jose's school provides its students with a practical education.

Story 3. Sally works for a nonprofit organization. Before she found her current job, she worked for a large law firm and was unhappy. If she had been exposed to a wider range of legal work during law school, Sally tells you, she would have gone right into her current position. She recommends choosing a law school that has a wide range of course options and clinical programs.

Now compare the following paragraph that synthesizes the three stories above. The example assumes that the stories represent the experiences of similarly situated individuals and infers a rule that fairly accounts for all three stories (in bold).

Inferred Rules Illustration

Law school applicants should select their schools according to their career interests if they know what careers they want to pursue. Legal employers will select employees based on organizational needs. Large law firms need lawyers with univer-

Cont.

sally recognized credentials. They will hire only from first-tier schools. A public defender's office, by contrast, prioritizes the ability of its new hires to handle a case on their own and, as a result, wants graduates from schools that are known to provide good practical training. Applicants who do not know what career they want to pursue may want to select a law school based on the breadth of the curriculum so that they are exposed to as many options as possible.

From the first two stories, it seems that career interests are the determinative factor. However, the third story about Sally, who did not know her career interests, throws in a monkey wrench. The starting sentence in the above discussion of the three stories reconciles the conflict by explaining that career interests are determinative *if* they are known. As in this illustration, cases might seem inconsistent at first but can often be put together in a way that makes sense. Making sense out of the various court cases on your issue is one of your primary jobs in crafting an effective legal analysis.

4.3.1.5 | Crafting Result-Oriented Topic Sentences

Legal writing is goal-oriented. Whether you are writing an objective or persuasive analysis, you are aiding a decision in the case. A topic sentence that does not help the reader make a decision is ineffective. The topic sentence must state a subrule that helps predict legal outcomes.

ERROR Example of an Ineffective Topic Sentence

The final consideration is whether the defendant committed similar crimes in the recent past and, therefore, was predisposed to commit the crime at issue.

This sentence states a factor but does not help the reader make a decision. The sentence would be fine as a transition or lead-in to a topic sentence, but a more results-oriented statement is needed.

Sample Results-Oriented Topic Sentence

Predisposition is established when the past and current crimes involved the same underlying motivation.

In contrast to the "whether" sentence, the sample results-oriented topic sentence provides a firm rule that can help predict the outcome of future cases.

4.3.1.6 | Crafting Topic Sentences in Questions of First Impression Analyses

Rule explanation topic sentences might look somewhat different in a question of first impression to the extent the lawyer is arguing about what the law *should be* as opposed to establishing the existing law that governs the legal issue.

A topic sentence in a rule explanation paragraph in an analysis of a question of first impression can (1) make a statement about existing law in other jurisdictions; (2) state a reason to adopt a specific interpretation of the law; or (3) state a reason to reject a specific interpretation of the law. A sample of each follows. The first option should seem very familiar because it is identical to the rule explanation topic sentence that states a subrule discussed in section 4.3.1.1; the only difference is that it discusses the law of other jurisdictions because no law within the correct jurisdiction is available.

Sample Topic Sentence That States a Rule from Other Jurisdictions

Courts in other jurisdictions with anti-baby-selling statutes similar to section 7680, subdivision (b), have found that surrogacy contracts are unlawful. In *In re Baby M.*, 537 A.2d 1227, 1228 (N.J. 1988), the court held that a surrogate mother could not be contractually compelled to forfeit her parental rights pursuant to a surrogacy contract because the contract is "for the sale of a child, or, at the very least, the sale of a mother's right to her child." *Id.* The court reasoned that "almost every evil that prompted the prohibition on the payment of money in connection with adoptions exists here." *Id.*; *see also In re Adoption of Paul*, 550 N.Y.S.2d 815, 817 (Fam. Ct. 1990) (holding that adoption of a child born through traditional surrogacy would be approved only if the surrogate agreed not to accept compensation because "[i]t is clear . . . that compensation direct to the mother for her 'services' in conceiving, carrying and giving birth to the child is not permitted" under an anti-baby-selling statute similar to section 7680, subdivision (b)).

In the above sample, the author is analyzing whether her jurisdiction should find that surrogacy contracts are unlawful under section 7680(b) of her jurisdiction's Family Code. The topic sentence (in bold) states an observation that other jurisdictions have found them to be unlawful and then cites two supportive cases as examples to prove the statement.

Sample Topic Sentence That Gives a Reason to Adopt an Interpretation

The purpose of anti-baby-selling statutes compels their interpretation to prohibit surrogacy. The court in *In re Baby M.* concluded that all of the evils inherent in baby-selling are equally posed by surrogacy including the lack of any determination whether the purchasing parties are suitable parents, the absence of any counseling for the mother in making her life-changing decision, the possibility that the mother's financial circumstances may make her decision less than voluntary, and the likelihood that the child will not be adequately informed of his natural parents' medical history. 537 A.2d at 1241.

In this second example, the author is giving a reason that the court should follow the jurisdictions that have invalidated surrogacy contracts. The analysis of this issue would have included many more rule explanation paragraphs like this one—each paragraph starting with a topic sentence that states a reason to adopt the proposed rule, followed by details from cases that support the argument.

Sample Topic Sentence That Gives a Reason to Reject an Interpretation

Allowing surrogacy contracts to govern parental rights would harm children because surrogacy contracts ignore the best interests of the child. *Id.* ("The negative consequences of baby-buying are potentially present in the surrogacy context, especially the potential for placing and adopting a child without regard to the interest of the child or the natural mother."). As explained in *Baby M.*, surrogacy contracts do not typically involve a determination of the fitness of the intended parents or the effect on the child of not living with the birth mother. 537 A.2d at 1242.

In this example from the same analysis, the author states a reason to reject a contrary interpretation of the statute that would permit surrogacy contracts to govern parental rights. You might notice that the difference between the second and third sample topic sentences is very slight—a minor change in emphasis and wording. Sometimes, the difference might be more pronounced. Let's say, for example, that you are analyzing whether the use of cell phones by a driver should be banned. One possible rule would be that drivers could never use their phones. An alternative might be that a driver could use a cell phone with the use of a hands-free device. If you wanted to argue for the first rule, then you would want to explain the safety reasons for banning phones (to support your rule) and then explain why hands-free devices do not adequately prevent accidents (to convince the court to reject the alternative rule).

The bottom line is that rule explanation topic sentences in analyses of a question of first impression are not very different except that they cannot state a subrule within the jurisdiction because no subrules exist. Instead, they will either explore the status of relevant law in other jurisdictions or expound reasons to adopt or reject a particular interpretation of the law.

4.3.2 | Including Transitions

Each rule explanation paragraph should use transitional language to link it to the prior paragraph. To illustrate this, here is our sample rule explanation again but with the transitional language in bold. The sample begins with the rule statement to show how the first rule explanation paragraph transitions by further defining the significant involvement test introduced in the rule statement.

Sample Transitions

The defense of entrapment is available when the police led the defendant to commit a crime he would not otherwise have committed. To establish that the police "led" him to commit the crime, the defendant must establish significant police involvement in designing or carrying out the crime. Moreover, the defendant will not be able to prove he "would not otherwise have committed the crime" if he has engaged in similar crimes in the recent past.

The government becomes significantly involved in the commission of a crime where its agents not only supply the materials necessary to the crime but also direct the commission of the crime. [In the rest of this paragraph, you would discuss at least one precedent case that proves and illustrates that supplying the materials and directing the crime constitutes significant involvement.]

By contrast, merely supplying the materials necessary to the crime does not establish entrapment. [In the rest of this paragraph, you would discuss at least one precedent case that proves and illustrates that merely supplying the materials is not sufficient.]

The final consideration is whether the defendant committed similar crimes in the recent past and, therefore, was predisposed to commit the crime. Predisposition is established when the past and current crimes involved the same underlying motivation. [In the rest of this paragraph, you would discuss at least one precedent case that proves and illustrates that crimes involving the same underlying motivation establish predisposition.]

Chapter 12 instructs on drafting effective transitions. Refer to Chapter 12 as you draft your rule explanation. To check for transitions, you might want to copy the first two sentences of each rule explanation paragraph and paste them into a separate document. If the beginnings of the paragraphs do not connect well to one another, you should work on your transitions. Sometimes this exercise will help you see that you need to put some more time into thinking about how the subrules fit together before you can draft better transitions.

4.3.3 | Case Examples

After stating a subrule in each topic sentence, legal writers typically use case examples to explain and exemplify the subrule. This section discusses two types of case examples: full and parenthetical. Both types present the facts, holding, and reasoning of the case that the writer is using to support the topic sentence but with different levels of detail.

4.3.3.1 | Full Case Examples

A full case example is a narrative summary of the relevant facts, holding, and reasoning of a case to prove the subrule stated in the topic sentence of the paragraph. And usually this exact order works best. The facts set the stage for the holding, so they come first. And the reasoning comes last because reasoning does not usually make sense to the reader until the writer has stated the holding. Putting the reasoning first would be kind of like giving someone written instructions on how to assemble a desk without first telling them what they are building. The example below illustrates the recommended organization of a rule explanation paragraph.

Full Case Example

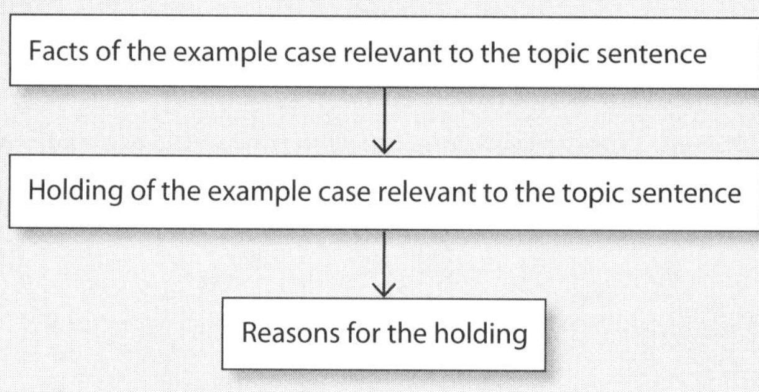

Sample Full Case Example

Topic sentence | Facts from case example | Holding | Reasoning

The need to participate in the activity to remain or advance in employment can establish implied pressure. In *Wilson*, a police officer claimed coverage for injuries sustained while running on his own time off work premises. Testimony established that the police officers in the plaintiff's special emergency unit were tested four times per year and those in his age group had to run two miles in seventeen minutes. The court found he reasonably believed he had to keep in shape to remain in the unit and was therefore entitled to coverage. It reasoned that it would be "unrealistic" to think that such a requirement could be met without off-duty exercise.

See Annotation 27 in Sample A in Appendix B for an additional example of a full case explanation that follows this structure.

Deciding Which Facts to Include A case example usually needs to include the basic facts of who did what to whom. What did the defendant allegedly do? What happened to the plaintiff (in a civil case) or the victim (in a criminal case)? If the case involves multiple parties or claims, include only the parties and claims related to your issue.

After this background information, include factual details about the case that are relevant to your topic sentence. For example, if you are analyzing whether your client can establish an entrapment defense, you would want to include factual details that relate to the government's involvement in planning or encouraging the crime, but you would not need to include details about the harm the victim of the crime suffered. Students often either fail to include enough information about the precedent case or include extraneous information about the case that is not relevant to the topic sentence.

Illustration of Focusing on Relevant Information

Imagine you are interviewing for a job as a lawyer. The interviewer asks you to name and explain one personality trait that you feel best identifies you. You decide to choose your creativity. You then want to give some examples of your creativity. You would probably not choose to talk about how you decorated your bedroom to look like a fairyland or your role as Annie in kindergarten. The interviewer does not care about these examples of your creativity—they are irrelevant to the job of a lawyer. Approach each paragraph of your rule explanation in a similar manner. In discussing each case example, include only details that are relevant to the topic sentence.

Describing the Holding After the facts of the precedent case, indicate the court's holding. The term "holding" is mercilessly confusing. Here, think of the "holding" as the court's announcement regarding how the pertinent rule plays out in the case. For example, if your paragraph is discussing predisposition as a factor in an entrapment defense, then you want to tell the reader whether the court found the defendant in the case was predisposed to commit the crime.

Describing the Court's Reasoning After the facts and holding of the precedent case, describe the court's reasoning. The reasoning consists of the connections the court makes between the relevant rules, the facts of the case, and the holding. For example, if the holding you are using in the paragraph is the court's holding that the defendant was predisposed to commit the crime, the reasoning is going to be all the reasons why the court found he was predisposed.

The most common mistake students make at this point is to repeat the relevant facts because they think the facts are the reasoning. Facts are not reasoning. Reasoning connects the facts to the holding. The reasoning is the explanation or proof the court offers to explain why the facts of the case and the legal rules it has identified in the opinion warrant the holding it reaches.

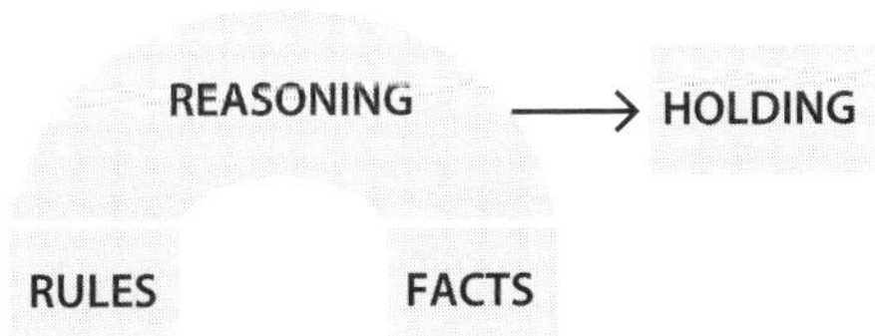

The following poor case example provides only the facts that led to the court's holding and does not indicate the reasons why the court found those facts proved that the victim was reasonably afraid. Including detailed reasoning is the key to an effective case example. Without it, you cannot predict an outcome in a case with different facts because you cannot determine which factual differences matter and which do not.

ERROR **Example of an Incomplete Case Example That Omits Reasoning**

In *People v. Flynn*, the court upheld a robbery conviction even in the absence of any overt threats by the defendant. The court concluded that the victim was reasonably afraid of the defendant where the crime occurred at night in a bad neighborhood, the victim was a female, the defendant grabbed her bag as she passed by him and his fellow gang members, and, after taking her bag, the defendant showed a gun that had been in the bag to his friends and yelled at the victim to get away from his car.

How do you avoid imitating the poor example? You first must find the reasoning from the court opinion and then regurgitate the reasoning in your rule explanation. When you describe the court's reasoning, consider using quotations. This is not a time to fear plagiarism. As long as you cite properly (see Chapter 8), you will not be plagiarizing the court. Nor is it time for creativity. Restrain yourself from butchering the court's intended meaning; even minor variations in language can have significant ramifications in legal analysis.

When deciding whether to quote the court's exact language, consider the following. First, avoid huge block quotes. Some readers may skip block quotations, and others will read them but with annoyance. Instead, quote only the core of the court's sentences. Second, do not use quotation marks for mundane information from the case like procedural history, basic terminology, or common phrases such as "summary judgment should be granted." Instead, save your quotation marks for the heart of the court's reasoning.

To illustrate how to carry over language from a court opinion into a case example in a rule explanation, below is an excerpt from a court opinion with the key reasoning in bold and then a corresponding rule explanation with the carried-over language also in bold. Notice how the key reasoning is incorporated into the rule explanation. Notice also how quotations are used selectively to capture just the heart of the court's reasoning and are woven into sentences of the author's own creation.

Illustration: Finding Reasoning in a Court Opinion *(Flynn)*

EXCERPT FROM *PEOPLE v. FLYNN*, 91 Cal. Rptr. 2d 902, 906-07 (Ct. App. 2000)

The facts of the present case substantially support this theory of robbery. Although defendant did nothing designed to instill fear prior to the taking, **he chose the moment**

Cont.

and location of the crime knowing the likely effect on the lone, female victim. He also chose to remain at the scene. Defendant is taller and bigger than the victim. Although in her own neighborhood, the victim was outnumbered six to one by a group of male gang members located in their own territory. **Defendant's brazen behavior once he was armed with the stolen gun revealed his confidence in the powerlessness of the victim.** After defendant yelled at the victim to stay away from his car, she ran from the scene and was afraid to report the crime until her mother convinced her to do so ten days later.

On these facts, defendant used fear to accomplish the robbery just as surely as if he had verbalized the threats inherent in the surrounding circumstances. Defendant's argument concerning his passivity and all the things he did not do ignores the fact that **his snatching of the bag, not to mention his subsequent display of the stolen weapon, immediately changed what might have been an innocuous set of circumstances into one of significant fear for the victim.**

To the extent that it was the victim's perceptions of her circumstances that directly caused the fear, **those perceptions were reasonable and a reasonable jury could have found that defendant took advantage of them in a calculated fashion.**

Sample Full Case Example to Match the Reasoning *(Flynn)*

The force or fear element of robbery does not require any overt acts by the defendant designed to instill fear in the victim. The use of fear can be established where the defendant **took advantage of surrounding circumstances** that reasonably instilled fear in the victim. *People v. Flynn*, 91 Cal. Rptr. 2d 902, 907 (Ct. App. 2000). In *Flynn*, the defendant was charged with robbery but claimed that the force or fear element could not be met because he had not engaged in any overt act designed to instill fear in the victim. *Id.* at 905. The defendant snatched the victim's bag as she walked by him and his fellow gang members in a bad neighborhood at night. *Id.* at 904. After taking the bag, he took out its contents, including a gun, and showed them to his friends. *Id.* When the victim tried to get a good look at the defendant, he yelled at her to get away from his car. *Id.* She fled and was too scared to report the crime for several days. *Id.* The court upheld the robbery conviction. *Id.* at 906. The court concluded that the defendant's snatching of her bag and display of the stolen gun **"immediately turned what might have been an innocuous set of circumstances into one of significant fear for the victim."** *Id.* at 907. Moreover, because the defendant chose the moment and location of the crime **"knowing its likely effect on the lone, female victim,"** the jury could have found that the defendant purposefully **took advantage of circumstances** that reasonably caused the victim to be afraid. *Id.*

Topic sentence states surrounding circumstances subrule

Background facts

Facts relevant to surrounding circumstances subrule

Holding

Reasoning relevant to surrounding circumstances subrule

4.3.3.2 | Parenthetical Case Examples

Additional case examples can help prove and illustrate the subrule stated in your topic sentence. However, your reader may become bored by multiple case narratives. Enter the parenthetical. A parenthetical is a snapshot of the aspect of a case that is relevant to your point. To illustrate, the sample below adds a parenthetical to the discussion of *Flynn* that was included as a sample in section 4.3.3.1. Notice how the bolded language from the topic sentence matches the bolded language in the parenthetical. The parenthetical should help prove or illustrate the subrule in your topic sentence.

Sample Rule Explanation with a Parenthetical

Topic sentence

The force or fear element of robbery does not require any overt acts by the defendant designed to instill fear in the victim. The use of fear can be established where the **defendant took advantage of surrounding circumstances that reasonably instilled**

Full case example

fear in the victim. *People v. Flynn*, 91 Cal. Rptr. 2d 902, 907 (Ct. App. 2000). In *Flynn*, the defendant was charged with robbery but claimed that the force or fear element could not be met because he had not engaged in any overt act designed to instill fear in the victim. *Id.* at 905. The defendant snatched the victim's bag as she walked by him and his fellow gang members in a bad neighborhood at night. *Id.* at 904. After taking the bag, he took out its contents, including a gun, and showed them to his friends. *Id.* When the victim tried to get a good look at the defendant, he yelled at her to get away from his car. *Id.* She fled and was too scared to report the crime for several days. *Id.* The court upheld the robbery conviction. *Id.* at 906. The court concluded that the defendant's snatching of her bag and display of the stolen gun "immediately turned what might have been an innocuous set of circumstances into one of significant fear for the victim." *Id.* at 907. Moreover, because the defendant chose the moment and location of the crime "knowing its likely effect on the lone, female victim," the jury could have found that the defendant purposefully took advantage of circumstances that reason-

Parenthetical

ably caused the victim to be afraid. *Id.*; *see also People v. Brew*, 2 Cal. Rptr. 2d 851, 853-54 (Ct. App. 1991) (finding that defendant used fear to commit robbery because when he stepped within two or three feet of the store clerk to demand money, **he was taking advantage of** the absence of a counter or other protective shield).

A parenthetical should include, at a minimum, the relevant holding and related facts of the case. In addition, sometimes, the court's reasoning is necessary to prove your topic sentence and to help your evaluation of your client's case. Here is a breakdown of the components of the parenthetical in the sample:

"see also"	This is an introductory signal. Introductory signals are an aspect of case citation. Explanatory parentheticals nearly always need an introductory signal. Chapter 8 discusses how to choose the right signal.
People v. Brew, 2 Cal. Rptr. 2d 851, 853-54 (Ct. App. 2011)	This is the case citation. Case citation is covered in Chapter Eight.

(finding that defendant used fear…	The first several words in the parenthetical state the key holding relevant to the point of the paragraph. Notice that the parenthetical does not start with a capital letter and is not in complete sentence format. Parentheticals usually start with an "ing" action by the court (finding, holding, stating, etc.).
because when he stepped within two or three feet of the store clerk to demand money	The next several words of the parenthetical give the key facts relevant to the stated holding.
he was taking advantage of the absence of a…shield).	This part of the parenthetical provides the portion of the court's reasoning that is relevant to the topic sentence.

4.3.3.3 | Bridging Full Case Examples and Parentheticals

Sometimes, you will need a sentence to bridge the gap between your parenthetical(s) and the prior case example. In the sample in section 4.3.3.2, repeated below, no bridge is needed because the parenthetical logically relates to the preceding sentence. The bolded language in the "moreover" sentence matches the bolded language in the parenthetical.

Sample Where No Bridge Is Needed

Moreover, because the defendant chose the moment and location of the crime "knowing its effect on the lone, female victim," the jury could have found that the defendant purposefully **took advantage** of circumstances that reasonably caused the victim to be afraid. *Id.*; *see also People v. Brew*, 2 Cal. Rptr. 2d 851, 853-54 (Ct. App. 1991) (finding that defendant used fear to commit robbery because when he stepped within two or three feet of the store clerk to demand money, he was **taking advantage** of the absence of a counter or other protective shield).

By contrast, the following sample includes a sentence to bridge the gap because the *Smith*, *Wilson*, and *Stockton* parentheticals do not logically connect to the last sentence of the discussion of *Ezzy*. The bridge is in bold below.

Sample Rule Explanation with a Full Sentence Bridge

The first part of the test, subjective belief, is satisfied by an employee's professed belief that participation was required. Indeed, a belief that one *should* participate is suf-

Cont.

ficient. In *Ezzy*, for example, a law clerk was injured while playing on her firm's softball team. *Ezzy*, 194 Cal. Rptr. at 91. She testified that because the team did not have enough female players to satisfy the league's rules, she felt she "should" play when a partner handed her a tee shirt and game schedule and said, "At the next one, we'll see you there." *Id.* at 92. The court found her statement under oath was sufficient to establish her subjective belief of expectancy. *Id.* at 96. Bridge **Failing the subjective belief requirement seems to be a risk only when the employee did not truly feel obligated to participate.** *Compare Smith v. Workers' Comp. Appeals Bd.*, 236 Cal. Rptr. 248, 254-55 (Ct. App. 1987) (holding that deceased teacher's wife's testimony that teacher went to a picnic because his department head asked him to, he felt he had a "responsibility" to go, and he believed he had to participate in a certain number of extracurricular activities satisfied the subjective element of the test to establish coverage for injuries sustained while he was windsurfing during the picnic), *and Wilson v. Workers' Comp. Appeals Bd.*, 239 Cal. Rptr. 719, 721 (Ct. App. 1987) (holding that police officer's testimony that he believed he had to keep in shape stay on a special emergency unit satisfied the subjective element to establish coverage for an injury sustained while running off-duty), *with City of Stockton v. Workers' Comp. Appeals Bd.*, 38 Cal. Rptr. 3d 474, 483 (Ct. App. 2006) (denying coverage to officer injured while playing basketball when he admitted he could satisfy the job requirement of keeping in shape without playing basketball).

One alternative to a full-text sentence bridge is a hybrid text and parenthetical bridge, as in the sample below.

Sample Hybrid Bridge

In addition to evidence of pressure on an employee to participate in an activity, evidence that the employer sponsored or encouraged participation and benefited from the activity can establish reasonable expectancy. Employer involvement and benefit can establish indirect encouragement by the employer that changes the voluntary nature of the activity and, therefore, requires coverage of resulting injuries. *Ezzy*, 194 Cal. Rptr. at 95. For example, in finding reasonable expectancy in *Ezzy*, the court pointed to evidence that the firm provided tee shirts and refreshments at the games and held a special banquet for participants. *Id.* The court also noted the benefit to the firm from increased morale. *Id.* Bridge **Employer encouragement and benefit similarly played a large role in securing coverage in** *Smith*, 236 Cal. Rptr. at 257-58 (relying on the school's role in planning the picnic at which the employee was injured including its collection of permission slips, advertisement of planning meetings, and payment for refreshments; the benefit of the picnic to the school through improved teacher-student relationships; and the school's general encouragement of teacher participation in extracurricular activities) and *Wilson*, 239 Cal. Rptr. at 722 (relying on the benefit to the police department from the ability of the employee's specially trained unit to handle situations too extreme for its standard force).

Another option, illustrated below, is to provide a parenthetical-like snippet but in a text sentence, like the bolded part of the following example.

Sample One-Sentence Case Example

The need to participate in the activity to remain or advance in employment can establish implied pressure. *See Wilson*, 239 Cal. Rptr. at 722. In *Wilson*, a police officer claimed coverage for injuries sustained while running on his own time off work premises. *Id.* at 719. Police officers in the plaintiff's special emergency unit were tested four times per year and those in his age group had to run two miles in seventeen minutes. *Id.* at 722. The court found he reasonably believed he had to keep in shape to remain in the unit and was therefore entitled to coverage. *Id.* It reasoned that it would be "unrealistic" to think that such a requirement could be met without off-duty exercise. *Id.* **The court similarly found implied pressure satisfied in *Kidwell v. Workers' Comp. Appeals Bd.*, 39 Cal. Rptr. 2d 540, 545-46 (Ct. App. 1995), where a police officer was injured while practicing long jumps at home, because testimony established that promotion and benefits were contingent on passing a long jump test and passing the test required practice.**

4.3.3.4 | Deciding Whether You Need a Full Case Example

As mentioned at the start of section 4.3.3, including both a full case example and parentheticals is the safest approach for a novice legal writer. However, readers do not always need a full case example to understand a subrule. Sometimes, a point can be made sufficiently clear with parentheticals only. Once you have a little experience under your belt, you can start thinking about whether you need to include a full case example in every rule explanation paragraph. Here are some considerations to help you decide when you can forgo a full case example.

Use a full case example when the subrule stated in your topic sentence is critical to the analysis of your case. The more important a subrule is to the outcome of your case, the more careful you should be in explaining and illustrating its meaning.

Use a full case example when application of the subrule relies heavily on an examination of the specific facts involved in the case. The surrounding circumstances rule in the sample rule explanation paragraph regarding *Flynn* is a great example of a subrule that relies heavily on specifics. Stating that the circumstances surrounding a crime can amount to the use of fear to accomplish robbery would be meaningless without at least one detailed explanation of the facts of a case in which the required circumstances were present.

Consider using only parentheticals when the subrule stated in your topic sentence merely states that a particular consideration is either not relevant or not determinative of your issue. Suppose you are analyzing a landlord's liability for his tenant's dog's attack on another person. Case law establishes that liability depends on the landlord's knowledge that the dog was dangerous. One of your rule explanation paragraphs starts by stating a subrule that the breed of a dog is not evidence of its viciousness. Since your subrule is merely dismissing breed as a relevant consideration, a full case example describing details about the attack or other traits of the dog would be unnecessary and even distracting. Instead, a simple parenthetical could prove and illustrate the subrule:

Sample Parenthetical-Only Rule Explanation

The breed of a dog is not evidence of its viciousness. *See Lundy v. California Realty*, 216 Cal. Rptr. 575, 580 (Ct. App. 1985) (declining to find that a German shepherd's breed could be evidence of its viciousness).

Consider using only parentheticals when the courts apply the subrule without a detailed examination of the specific facts of the case. In the following example, the parenthetical tells us all we need to know to understand the role of age in sentencing. A full case example would be unnecessary.

Sample Parenthetical-Only Rule Explanation

The age of a defendant is relevant to the likelihood that he will re-offend and, therefore, to the determination of his sentence. *See People v. Bishop*, 66 Cal. Rptr. 2d 348, 350 (Ct. App. 1997) (noting that age was relevant to sentencing where a reduced sentence of 12 years would keep defendant in prison until he was more than 60 years old, an age at which recidivism was unlikely).

Sometimes, a parenthetical may not even be needed. When a topic sentence is so specific that the parenthetical would merely repeat the information in the topic sentence, a citation alone is sufficient. For example, what would be the purpose of including the parenthetical below?

ERROR Example of an Unnecessary Parenthetical

A four-year-old child cannot be found negligent because he lacks the ability to foresee and understand danger. *Greene v. Watts*, 26 Cal. Rptr. 334, 336 (Ct. App. 1962) (finding that a four-year-old child cannot be guilty of negligence because he lacks the ability to foresee and understand danger).

4.3.4 | Checking for Paragraph Coherence

The case examples and parentheticals in a rule explanation are devoted to proving and explaining the subrule stated in the topic sentence of each paragraph. Double-check that you have explained how the subrule was applied in the cases you cite in the paragraph. Review the below "force or fear" sample rule explanation paragraph again. This time, focus on how the discussion of *Flynn* and the parenthetical at the end explain the court's application of the subrule regarding surrounding circumstances that was stated in the topic sentence. Notice the coherence created by the bolded parts of the paragraph.

Sample Rule Explanation Paragraph Coherence

The force or fear element of robbery does not require any overt acts by the defendant designed to instill fear in the victim. The use of fear can be established where the **defendant took advantage of surrounding circumstances that reasonably instilled fear in the victim**. *People v. Flynn*, 91 Cal. Rptr. 2d 902, 907 (Ct. App. 2000). In *Flynn*, the defendant was charged with robbery but claimed that the force or fear element could not be met because he had not engaged in any overt act designed to instill fear in the victim. *Id.* at 905. The defendant snatched the victim's bag as she walked by him and his fellow gang members in a bad neighborhood at night. *Id.* at 904. After taking the bag, he took out its contents, including a gun, and showed them to his friends. *Id.* When the victim tried to get a good look at the defendant, he yelled at her to get away from his car. *Id.* She fled and was too scared to report the crime for several days. *Id.* The court upheld the robbery conviction. *Id.* at 906. The court concluded that the defendant's snatching of her bag and display of the stolen gun "immediately turned what might have been an innocuous set of circumstances into one of significant fear for the victim." *Id.* at 907. Moreover, because the defendant chose the moment and location of the crime "knowing its likely effect on the lone, female victim," the jury could have found that **the defendant purposefully took advantage of circumstances that reasonably caused the victim to be afraid**. *Id.*; *see also People v. Brew*, 2 Cal. Rptr. 2d 851, 853-54 (Ct. App. 1991) (finding that defendant used fear to commit robbery because when he stepped within two or three feet of the store clerk to demand money, he was **taking advantage of** the absence of a counter or other protective shield).

The rule about taking advantage of surrounding circumstances to cause fear is stated here in the topic sentence.

Then, as the author explains *Flynn*, she states what the court concluded about how the subrule played out in the case—i.e., the defendant did take advantage of the circumstances to cause fear.

And the parenthetical similarly focuses on the defendant's decision to take advantage of the circumstances to cause fear.

Students often fail to revisit the subrule in their case examples and parentheticals. They sometimes think that since they have already stated the subrule (e.g., the surrounding circumstances rule in the above example) in the topic sentence, they do not need to repeat it again. However, the purpose of the case example and parentheticals is to show how the subrule was applied in the cases. This goal cannot be accomplished without repeating the key language of the subrule and clarifying how that language was found to be satisfied (or not satisfied) under the facts of the precedent case. The goal is not to repeat the subrule ("the use of fear can be established where the defendant took advantage of . . .") but to explain how the court used the subrule to support its holding ("the jury could have found that the defendant purposefully took advantage . . ."). Therefore, the statements are not repetitive.

Checklist for Rule Explanation

- ☐ Synthesis of the cases is critical. You can synthesize through your topic sentences and transitions. Use your rule chart to help you figure out how the cases fit together before you start writing.
- ☐ Each rule explanation paragraph should start with a topic sentence that states a subrule that helps the reader understand how the broader rules that you stated in your rule statement have been applied by the courts. Sometimes, you may be able to synthesize two subrules in a topic sentence.
- ☐ Use transitional language at the beginning of each new paragraph of rule explanation to connect the topic of the new paragraph to the topic of its predecessor.
- ☐ Follow the transitional language and topic sentence with a description of the precedent case(s) that support and exemplify the subrule that you stated in the topic sentence.
- ☐ Usually, you will want to provide at least one full case example (facts + holding + reasoning) and one or more parentheticals for each subrule. However, in some instances, parentheticals alone may suffice.
- ☐ The most important information to provide in rule explanation is the court's reasoning. Reasoning is not the same thing as key facts. Reasoning connects the key facts to the rules. Dig for the reasoning in the cases and carry it over into your rule explanation. Use quotes for the heart of the court's reasoning.
- ☐ Make sure you have explicitly described how the subrule was applied by the court in the case example and parentheticals you provide.
- ☐ A rule explanation requires a citation after nearly every sentence. The only possible exceptions are transitional and topic sentences.
- ☐ When you use parentheticals after a full case example, you may need to use one of the bridging techniques discussed in this chapter to logically connect the parenthetical to the end of the full case example.
- ☐ Some special considerations for parentheticals:
    - ☐ Use a signal like "see also."
    - ☐ Start with an "-ing" action by the court (holding, stating, finding, etc.).
    - ☐ Include at least the holding and key facts of the case; include the reasoning also if necessary to prove your topic sentence or set up the points you want to make in the corresponding application paragraph.
    - ☐ Keep the parenthetical short, and do not use more than one partial sentence.

CHAPTER 4 SELF-TEST

1. What is the purpose of the rule statement?
2. What does it mean to say that the rule statement should be organized like a funnel?
3. What is a good clue that a rule is too specific to put in the rule statement and should be saved for rule explanation?
4. What are connectors?
5. What are the typical components of a rule explanation paragraph?
6. What should the topic sentence of a rule explanation paragraph do?
7. What does it mean to say that the topic sentence should be result-oriented?
8. What are the components of a full case example in a rule explanation paragraph, and what order is usually best?
9. What can you do to ensure that your case example includes an adequate summary of the court's reasoning?
10. What is a parenthetical, and what does it typically include?
11. If your rule explanation paragraph has a full case example, where does the parenthetical go?
12. What is a bridge, and when do you need it?

See answers on page 337.

CHAPTER **5**

Writing About Your Case

So far we have covered the discussion of the law (rule statement and rule explanation), the first step in a legal analysis. We now turn to the second main component of a legal analysis, the application of the law to your client's case.

The application uses the rules, subrules, and case examples from the rule statement and rule explanation to support your prediction about how the issue you are analyzing will play out in your case. It does not repeat the information from the rule statement and rule explanation but applies the rules to the facts of your client's case. The application uses four key tools: (1) comparisons between the facts of your client's case and the facts in the precedent cases; (2) application of the courts' reasoning in the precedent cases to the facts of your client's case; (3) factual details from your client's case; and (4) commonsense logic to back up your conclusions. These tools are discussed in detail in section 5.3. For now, compare the rule explanation with the rule application shown in the following sample.

Sample to Illustrate Rule Explanation v. Application

Rule explanation

Subjective belief is satisfied by an employee's professed belief that participation was required. Indeed, a belief that one *should* participate is sufficient. In *Ezzy*, for example, a law clerk was injured while playing on her firm's softball team. 194 Cal. Rptr. at 91. She testified that because the team did not have enough female players to satisfy the league's rules, she felt she "should" play when a partner handed her a tee shirt and game schedule and said, "At the next one, we'll see you there." *Id.* at 92. The court found her statement under oath was sufficient to establish her subjective belief of expectancy. *Id.* at 96.

Rule explanation

Failing the subjective belief requirement seems to be a risk only when the employee did not truly feel obligated to participate. *Compare Smith v. Workers' Comp. Appeals Bd.*, 236 Cal. Rptr. 248, 254-55 (Ct. App. 1987) (holding that deceased teacher's wife's testimony that teacher went to a picnic because his department head asked him to, he felt he had a "responsibility" to go, and he believed he had to participate in a certain number of extracurricular activities satisfied the subjective element of the test to establish

Cont.

coverage for injuries sustained while he was windsurfing during the picnic), *and Wilson v. Workers' Comp. Appeals Bd.*, 239 Cal. Rptr. 719, 721 (Ct. App. 1987) (holding that police officer's testimony that he believed he had to keep in shape to stay on a special emergency unit satisfied the subjective element to establish coverage for an injury sustained while running off-duty), *with City of Stockton v. Workers' Comp. Appeals Bd.*, 38 Cal. Rptr. 3d 474, 483 (Ct. App. 2006) (denying coverage to officer injured while playing basketball when he admitted he could satisfy the job requirement of keeping in shape without playing basketball).

Application

Based on the case law explained above, Gator's subjective belief that he was expected to play paddleball can be established by his testimony that he thought he needed to play to advance in the company. His use of the word "needed" even more clearly demonstrates a belief in expectancy than did Ezzy's use of the word "should." Moreover, unlike the employee in *City of Stockton*, Gator never admitted that paddleball was optional. Therefore, Gator should be able to establish the requisite subjective belief.

In a more complex analysis, the application would be much longer, consisting of several paragraphs and addressing counterarguments. To see a more complex application, refer to Appendix B, Sample A, Annotations 29-37. The application paragraphs are labeled in the margin.

5.1 | MATCHING THE APPLICATION TO THE RULE EXPLANATION

The organization of the application follows that of the rule explanation. Just as each rule explanation paragraph is devoted to *explaining* a subrule, each application paragraph should *apply* one of those subrules to the facts of your case. Think of this like a picnic. In your rule explanation, you lay out the picnic spread. Now, you get to eat it. But, you have to be civilized. Do not put the apple and the sandwich in your mouth at the same time. Maybe you have a friend or family member who eats food in a linear fashion—first the apple, then the sandwich, and last the drink. Let's call this person Grandma Dora. The approach to applying the rules in your application paragraphs is like the Grandma Dora dining style—finish one thing before moving on to the next. Finish applying one subrule before moving on to the next.

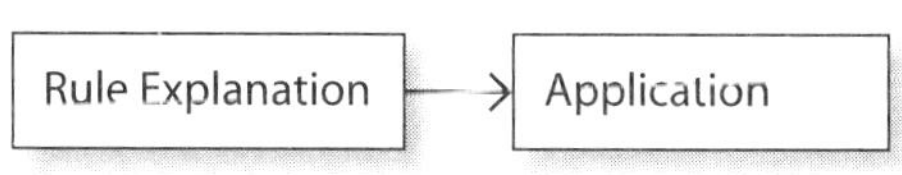

The application paragraphs should closely match the rule explanation paragraphs. Use all of the subrules you took the time to explain in the rule explanation, but do not introduce new information about the law. This includes specific details like a fact from the case or a particular quote. Place the fact or quotation in the matching rule explanation paragraph first before referencing it in an application paragraph. When you introduce new information about the law in your application section, it loses its force because it is divorced from its context. For example, if you insert a new quotation from a case in application, the reader does not know how that quote played into the outcome of the case and therefore may view the quote with suspicion or may not understand the significance of the quotation. To help yourself remember this, think about the following analogy: if you forget to pack water in your picnic basket, you will have nothing to drink at your picnic.

5.2 | CRAFTING APPLICATION TOPIC SENTENCES

Each application paragraph should start with a topic sentence that clearly states the conclusion you are reaching about how a subrule plays out in your case. For examples, look at the topic sentences of each application paragraph in Appendix B, Sample A. They are copied below, but you should also flip back to the full sample to see how they fit into the overall organization.

Sample Application Topic Sentences

Gator's subjective belief that he was expected to play paddleball can be established by his testimony that he thought he needed to play to advance in the company.

Gator can also establish his belief was reasonable. Evidence of implied pressure is strong.

In addition, Fitness Functions sponsored and benefitted from the paddleball games.

The pressure to play paddleball does not rise to the level of expectancy.

Randolph's use of paddleball as an opportunity to discuss business with her employees transformed a recreational activity into a work-related activity.

Application topic sentences should not sound like pronouncements of rules (e.g., To satisfy the subjective belief requirement, a plaintiff must show...). Instead, phrase them as conclusions about your case (e.g., Plaintiff can satisfy the subjective belief requirement in this case because...).

Incorrect v. Correct Application Topic Sentences

Incorrect:

Sting operations are not a form of entrapment.

Correct:

The government's conduct in this case does not establish entrapment because it was a sting operation that did not target Defendant specifically.

Cont.

Incorrect:

A landlord's knowledge of prior attacks by a tenant's dog can justify liability for an attack on a third person.

Correct:

Mr. Johnston's knowledge that Cujo had attacked a small child three years ago is sufficient to warrant imposing liability on him for failing to ensure his tenant kept Cujo restrained.

The incorrect topic sentences sound more like subrules, which belong in the rule explanation. By contrast, the correct topic sentences state a conclusion about the case the author is analyzing. Take a moment to look back at Annotations 30-34 of Appendix B, Sample A. Notice that the topic sentences of the application match the topic sentences of the earlier rule explanation in terms of the subrules they apply, but each is phrased as a conclusion about the case at hand rather than as a rule.

5.3 | THE FOUR TOOLS OF EFFECTIVE APPLICATION PARAGRAPHS

The next step is to prove the conclusion you have stated in each application paragraph's topic sentence. This is undoubtedly the most challenging task you will face as your legal writing skills progress. It requires you to consolidate all of the skills you are learning in law school: logical reasoning, rule-based analysis, and use of precedent.

To help demystify this process, this text introduces four tools you can use in your application paragraphs to prove your conclusions: (1) case comparison sentences; (2) use of court reasoning carried over into the application paragraph from the corresponding rule explanation paragraph; (3) use of specific factual details from your case file; and (4) commonsense inferences. Before we explore each of these tools, here is a sample to show how they work together in a paragraph.

Sample of Four Tools

Gator can also establish his belief was reasonable. Evidence of implied pressure is strong. Playing paddleball with Randolph was necessary to advance in the job. Randolph invited Gator to play while complimenting his job performance and expressing a desire to see continued successes. The coupling of a discussion of job performance with an invitation to play paddleball justifies Gator's impression that paddleball and advancement in the company were related. Indeed, Randolph admitted that she uses paddleball games as an opportunity to discuss business with employees. Therefore,

Topic sentence

Factual details

Commonsense inference

Factual details

Cont.

Commonsense inference

Case comparison sentence and use of court reasoning carried over from rule explanation

by turning down paddleball, an employee would necessarily be turning down an opportunity to discuss business with the Director. No ambitious employee would refuse such an invitation. Just like it would have been unrealistic to think that the police officers in *Wilson* and *Kidwell* could have passed their employers' fitness tests without training, it would be unrealistic to think that Gator would have the same opportunity to advance in the company if he turned down the opportunity for one-on-one time with Randolph on the paddleball court. The possible adverse effect of a refusal on Gator's advancement justifies his sense of pressure.

5.3.1 | Case Comparison Sentences

The case examples used to explain the rules in your rule explanation should serve as tools to build your thesis into a well-supported conclusion. Prove each of your topic sentences in the application by drawing comparisons between the case examples and the case at hand. Take a moment to refer to Annotations 31, 33, and 36 in Appendix B, Sample A, to see how comparisons to precedent cases are used to prove the topic sentences in the application.

5.3.1.1 | Crafting Relevant Comparisons

A case comparison sentence can either analogize to or distinguish your case from a precedent case. To analogize means to state a similarity; to distinguish means to state a difference. Of course, the point is not to choose some random fact to compare to precedent cases but to carefully consider which similarities or differences are relevant to the conclusion you state in your topic sentence. It would be easy to list all of the ways a frog is similar to a snake. But it would be a meaningless exercise unless we had some reason to care about the similarities. What matters is the *relevance* of the similarities.

5.3.1.2 | Tying Comparisons to the Rules

Therefore, in drawing analogies between a precedent case and your case, the goal is to explain the significance of the similarity to the application of the rules: why does the factual similarity require the same result as in the precedent case in light of the rules you have discussed in your rule explanation section? The analogies to precedent are a tool, but the real focus is on the *application* of the rules.

Sample Comparison Sentences

Gator's use of the word "needed" **even more clearly demonstrates a belief in expectancy** than did Ezzy's use of the word "should."

Like the vulnerable positions of the employees in *Ezzy* and *Smith*, Gator's probationary status **made him particularly susceptible to pressure.**

Cont.

In addition, like the *Ezzy* employer, Fitness Functions **benefitted from employee participation in the recreational activity.**

Notice that these samples do not merely state a factual similarity (e.g., Gator's use of the word "needed" is similar to Ezzy's use of the word "should"). They also tie the similarity to the subrule the author is applying (in the bolded portions of the samples).

5.3.1.3 | Making Comparisons Grammatically Parallel

The classic construction of a case comparison sentence follows the following formula.

Formula for a Comparison Sentence

Like [specific fact] in *Precedent Case A*, [specific fact from your case].

Like the *Ezzy* employer, Fitness Functions benefitted from employee participation in the recreational activity.

In crafting these sentences, ensure that the facts on either side of the comparison are in the same grammatical form and are comparable.

Example 1

Incorrect:

Like in *Ezzy*, Fitness Functions benefitted from employee participation in the recreational activity.

Explanation:

In this example, the sentence lacks a subject to match "Fitness Functions." Notice how the bolded subjects match in the revised version below.

Revised version:

Like the *Ezzy* **employer, Fitness Functions** benefitted from employee participation in the recreational activity.

Example 2

Incorrect:

Like Ezzy and Smith, Gator's probationary status made him particularly susceptible to pressure.

Cont.

Explanation:

In this example, the sentence compares probationary status to two plaintiffs. These are not comparable subjects. Notice the comparable subjects in the revised version below.

Revised version:

Like the **vulnerable positions** of the employees in *Ezzy* and *Smith*, Gator's **probationary status** made him particularly susceptible to pressure.

Example 3

Incorrect:

Gator's use of the word "needed" even more clearly demonstrates a belief in expectancy than did the word "should" in *Ezzy*.

Explanation:

In this example, the sentence compares "the word 'should'" to Gator's "use." These are not comparable subjects. Notice the matching of the subjects in the revised version below.

Revised version:

Gator's **use** of the word "needed" even more clearly demonstrates a belief in expectancy than did Ezzy's **use** of the word "should."

Grammatical parallelism in comparison sentences does not come naturally. You may miss the errors unless you carefully examine each comparison sentence to check for parallelism. Make parallelism in your comparison sentences a component of your self-editing checklist.

On the other hand, grammatical parallelism does not require strict rigidity to the formula described above. You can use a variety of techniques to state a comparison without getting into parallelism problems. Here are two common alternatives.

Alternative 1: The "here as in *Precedent Case A*" construction One alternative to the case comparison formula is the "here as in *Precedent Case A*" construction. The key to successfully using this alternative is to ensure that what comes after "here as in *Precedent Case A*" is sufficiently generic to apply both to the precedent case and to your case.

Example

Incorrect:

Here, as in *Williams*, agent Morlandia did not sanction any actual crimes

Cont.

Explanation:

Morlandia is the name of the agent in the author's case but was not the name of the agent in *Williams*. Therefore the "as in *Williams*" clause does not make sense in this sentence. It is too specific to the author's case. The revised version below replaces Morlandia with the generic subject, "the government." Both cases involve the government, so the "here, as in *Williams*" clause makes sense.

Revised version:

Here, as in *Williams*, the government did not sanction any actual crimes.

Alternative 2: The Two-Sentence Construction Another alternative is to use a first sentence to repeat the relevant point from your rule explanation and a second sentence to apply it to your case.

Example

Incorrect:

In *Williams*, the court found that past similar crimes can prove predisposition. 547 F.3d at 1201. Similarly, here, Defendant's prior acts of terrorism prove predisposition.

Explanation:

The point pulled from *Williams* is too general. As a result, the two sentences sound repetitive and do not enlighten the reader. In the revised version, a more nuanced point about the degree of similarity between prior acts and the current crime is pulled from *Williams*. Because the point is more specific, its application to the author's case is more compelling.

Revised version:

In *Williams*, the court found that a difference in degree does not detract from the similar nature of crimes. 547 F.3d at 1201. Similarly, here, the increased danger posed by the bombing does not make it dissimilar from Defendant's prior acts of terrorism.

A few things to keep in mind about this technique:

1. Use it sparingly because it is inherently repetitive.
2. Make the repeated point short and specific to avoid making it sound like another rule explanation paragraph.
3. Make sure the point is worth repeating. Do not use this construction, for example, to repeat your rule explanation topic sentence. Your reader will notice the repetition. By contrast, this construction works well when your reader might otherwise miss the nuance from the precedent case that you want to use in your comparison.
4. Include a citation after the first sentence since it is stating a conclusion reached by the court.

5.3.1.4 | Comparing Cases as a Group

Often, rule explanations will cite more than one case. There is little point in including multiple cases in the rule explanation only to ignore them in the application. Therefore, you will often want to compare multiple precedent cases in a single application paragraph. It is usually better to compare the cases together than to try to compare each case one at a time. Comparing each case to yours one at a time departs from the rule-based organization that is the hallmark of legal writing and results in repetition.

Sample Bulk Case Comparisons

Like the vulnerable positions of the employees in *Ezzy* and *Smith*, Gator's probationary status made him particularly susceptible to pressure.

The company can distinguish *Wilson* and *Kidwell* because in those cases, employees had to train to pass required fitness tests.

5.3.2 | Carrying Over Court Reasoning

The case comparison sentence is merely one piece of an effective application paragraph. The relevance of a case comparison must be not only stated but also proved. To prove the significance of similarities or differences between a precedent case and your case, you can use the court's logic from the precedent case. A similarity is significant only if it implicates the reasoning that led to the holding of the precedent case.

Illustration Ineffective Analogy

I bet Mary likes oranges. I know she likes apples. Oranges, like apples, have peels. Therefore, because Mary likes apples, she must like oranges too.

Why is this sample ineffective? We do not know that Mary likes apples *because* they have peels. Therefore, she would not necessarily like another fruit just because it has peels too. To make this convincing, we need to establish why peels are important. Once we understand why peels are important, then we can use those reasons to assess whether Mary likes oranges.

In the Illustration that follows, think of the first paragraph as the equivalent of a rule explanation. It states specific reasons that Mary likes fruits with peels. The foundation of a good application is a good rule explanation that provides the reasoning behind court decisions. Think of the last two paragraphs in the illustration as the equivalent of an application. They use the reasons that Mary likes fruits with peels to justify the conclusion that she will also like oranges.

Illustration Effective Analogy

Mary likes fruits that have peels. For example, she loves apples. She explained to me once that peels are nutritious and that fruits with peels can be cleaned more thoroughly than those without peels. Mary will not eat fruits that do not have peels because she is afraid they may have harmful chemicals on them that cannot be completely washed away. She also told me that she loves fruits with peels because they tend to be juicier than other fruits.

Mary would like oranges. Like apple peels, orange peels protect the fruit from chemicals. In fact, whereas people sometimes eat apple peels, people do not usually eat orange peels. Therefore, orange peels provide even better protection from harmful chemicals than do apple peels.

Oranges would also satisfy Mary's desire for juicy fruits. Oranges are even juicier than apples, and, therefore, Mary is likely to enjoy oranges as much as apples.

The court reasoning you include in your rule explanation becomes the ammunition for an effective application. Recall from section 4.3.3.1 that court reasoning consists of the justifications the court offers for its holding under the applicable legal rules and the facts of the case. In the following paragraphs, notice how the reasoning carries over from the rule explanation to the application. Shared language is bold.

Sample Rule Explanation

The need to participate in the activity to remain or advance in employment can establish implied pressure. *See Wilson*, 239 Cal. Rptr. at 722. In *Wilson*, a police officer claimed coverage for injuries sustained while running on his own time off work premises. *Id.* at 719. The police officers in the plaintiff's special emergency unit were tested four times per year, and those in his age group had to run two miles in seventeen minutes. *Id.* at 722. The court found he reasonably believed he had to keep in shape to remain in the unit and was therefore entitled to coverage. *Id.* **It reasoned that it would be "unrealistic" to think that such a requirement could be met without off-duty exercise.** *Id.* The court similarly found implied pressure satisfied in *Kidwell v. Workers' Comp. Appeals Bd.*, 39 Cal. Rptr. 2d 540, 545-46 (Ct. App. 1995), where a police officer was injured while practicing long jumps at home, because testimony established that **promotion and benefits were contingent on passing a long jump test and that passing the test required practice.**

Sample Application Paragraph

Gator can establish his belief was reasonable. Evidence of implied pressure is strong. Playing paddleball with Randolph was necessary to advance in the job. Randolph

Cont.

invited Gator to play while complimenting his job performance and expressing a desire to see continued successes. The coupling of a discussion of job performance with an invitation to play paddleball justifies Gator's impression that paddleball and advancement in the company were related. Indeed, Randolph admitted that she uses paddleball games as an opportunity to discuss business with employees. Therefore, by turning down paddleball, an employee would necessarily be turning down an opportunity to discuss business with the Director. No ambitious employee would refuse such an invitation. **Just like it would have been unrealistic to think that the police officers in *Wilson* and *Kidwell* could have passed their employers' fitness tests without training, it would be unrealistic to think that Gator would have the same opportunity to advance in the company if he turned down the opportunity for one-on-one time with Randolph on the paddleball court.** The possible adverse effect of a refusal on Gator's advancement justifies his sense of pressure.

To maximize the effectiveness of your analysis, look for and include the reasoning from the relevant precedent cases in your rule explanation and then use that reasoning to support your arguments in the application. Using court reasoning skillfully to support your arguments requires practice and effort. The connections will not jump out at you—discipline yourself to look for them.

5.3.3 | Using Specific Facts from the Case File

In addition to case comparison sentences and court reasoning, an effective application should include specific facts, even quotations, from your client's case file that help prove your conclusions. Case outcomes often turn on such factual nuances. Therefore, sifting through pleadings, transcripts, discovery responses, and other case file documents to find the most important details is an essential skill. The factual details are necessary to prove your legal conclusions. In the next sample, the underlined conclusion would be unsupported without the bolded factual detail that proves it.

Sample Use of Facts

Gator can also establish his belief was reasonable. Evidence of implied pressure is strong. <u>Playing paddleball with Randolph was necessary to advance in the job.</u> **Randolph invited Gator to play while complimenting his job performance and expressing a desire to see continued successes.** The coupling of a discussion of job performance with an invitation to play paddleball justifies Gator's impression that paddleball and advancement in the company were related. **Indeed, Randolph admitted that she uses paddleball games as an opportunity to discuss business with employees.** Therefore, by turning down paddleball, an employee would necessarily be turning down an opportunity to discuss business with the Director. No ambitious employee

Cont.

would refuse such an invitation. Just like it would have been unrealistic to think that the police officers in *Wilson* and *Kidwell* could have passed their employers' fitness tests without training, it would be unrealistic to think that Gator would have the same opportunity to advance in the company if he turned down the opportunity for one-on-one time with Randolph on the paddleball court. The possible adverse effect of a refusal on Gator's advancement justifies his sense of pressure.

When you are preparing your application, go back to your client's case file and pull out all of the specific details that help prove your points. If you find some compelling quotations from a witness, include them. Carefully scrutinize your application to determine whether you have offered sufficient factual details to prove each conclusion. One trick is to look at each sentence and determine whether someone could ask "why?" after reading it. For example, someone could ask "why?" after reading the statement that playing paddleball was necessary to advance in the job. Therefore some proof was necessary.

5.3.4 | Using Commonsense Inferences

Finally, commonsense inferences are often needed to fill in any gaps between the factual details and the conclusions stated in an application. Compare the following two versions of an application paragraph. The sentences in bold in the second version justify the underlined conclusion that playing paddleball was necessary to advance in the job.

ERROR Example of Gaps in Reasoning

Gator can also establish his belief was reasonable. Evidence of implied pressure is strong. Playing paddleball with Randolph was necessary to advance in the job. Randolph invited Gator to play while complimenting his job performance and expressing a desire to see continued successes. Indeed, Randolph admitted that she uses paddleball games as an opportunity to discuss business with employees. The possible adverse effect of a refusal on Gator's advancement justifies his sense of pressure.

Sample Use of Common Sense to Fill Gaps

Gator can also establish his belief was reasonable. Evidence of implied pressure is strong. <u>Playing paddleball with Randolph was necessary to advance in the job.</u> Randolph invited Gator to play while complimenting his job performance and expressing a desire to see continued successes. **The coupling of a discussion of job**

Cont.

performance with an invitation to play paddleball justifies Gator's impression that paddleball and advancement in the company were related. Indeed, Randolph admitted that she uses paddleball games as an opportunity to discuss business with employees. **Therefore, by turning down paddleball, an employee would necessarily be turning down an opportunity to discuss business with the Director. No ambitious employee would refuse such an invitation.** Just like it would have been unrealistic to think that the police officers in *Wilson* and *Kidwell* could have passed their employers' fitness tests without training, **it would be unrealistic to think that Gator would have the same opportunity to advance in the company if he turned down the opportunity for one-on-one time with Randolph on the paddleball court.** The possible adverse effect of a refusal on Gator's advancement justifies his sense of pressure.

Students are often afraid to state these inferences because they are not based on any express statements in the precedent cases. However, common sense plays a vital role in applying the law to new factual scenarios. No one can be a successful lawyer without using common sense.

Common sense, of course, is an amorphous concept. A lawyer has to use and trust her instincts. My daughter is only seven, but I can see the look in her eyes when she knows she is not making sense in the middle of a negotiation for something she wants. I call it the "B.S. Look."

My Daughter: Tonight should be movie night. I did not watch any T.V. this morning, and I am tired after soccer practice.

Me: Monday is too early in the week for movie night, and you have to practice violin tonight.

My Daughter: I don't have to practice. I already know how to play. [The B.S. Look.]

Me: Really?

My Daughter: Anyway I can't practice because... Baby Shane is making too much noise right now. I can't concentrate. [The B.S. Look again.]

If a seven year old has these instincts, so do you. You just need to turn on your B.S. radar and listen to yourself.

5.3.5 | Proving a Positive with a Negative: Analysis Pitfall

Merely distinguishing a case does not prove anything affirmative about your case. Distinguishing adverse cases (cases that had a result that was the opposite of the result you are predicting in your case) can be an effective way to bolster your conclusion, but you should also analogize your case to favorable precedent cases whenever possible. For example, suppose I want to prove that I am a nice person, and I offer the following argument:

Example of the Pitfall

Janice is mean because she yells at people. I do not yell at people. Therefore, I am nice.

I have not proven that I am nice. At most, I have proven that I am not mean. The following would be a better argument because it compares me to an analogous case rather than just distinguishing me from Janice:

Sample with a Positive Comparison

Peter is a nice person because he helps people in need and never yells. I also help people in need and never yell. Therefore, I am a nice person too.

After comparing myself to Peter, I could also distinguish myself from Janice as *additional* proof. Use of adverse cases in legal analysis should be similar. Distinguishing adverse cases is a secondary form of proof.

5.3.6 | Applications in Analyses of Questions of First Impression

Recall from section 4.3.1.6 that rule explanation on a question of first impression might start by discussing the status of the law in other jurisdictions, but it ultimately needs to provide reasons to adopt one possible interpretation or rule over other alternatives. The application paragraphs that follow these rule explanations can sometimes serve different functions.

Once you finish arguing for a particular interpretation or rule, you will need to address how that interpretation or rule applies to your case. This is the standard form of application discussed in sections 5.3.1 through 5.3.5. Depending on whether your initial rule explanations address a very broad rule (e.g., whether to enforce surrogacy contracts) or propose a specific standard (e.g., whether it should adopt one jurisdiction's three-factor test or another jurisdiction's five-factor test), you may need additional rule explanation paragraphs to explore the specific criteria that the court should use to apply your proposed rule before getting into application. If you merely argue that the court should enforce surrogacy contracts, you would probably need to identify criteria for enforcement before analyzing whether your client's contract should be enforced. However, if you argue for a specific three-factor test, you could probably move right into applying the three factors. For an example of an analysis that first argues in favor of a general rule and then provides additional rule explanation exploring the specific criteria used to apply the general rule, see the sample in section 6.3.5.

In addition to the traditional form of application—applying a specific rule to a set of facts—you can also use application to bolster your arguments in favor of a proposed interpretation or rule. In this other form of application paragraph, you can still use all of the four tools of application paragraphs, but the purpose of the paragraph is to support your argument about the law.

Rule Explanation on a Question of First Impression

Surrogacy contracts are not exploitive or coercive; they are made prior to conception and require voluntary active participation by the surrogate in order to become pregnant. In *Johnson*, the court stated that "[a]lthough common sense suggests that women of lesser means serve as surrogate mothers more often than do wealthy women, there has been no proof that surrogacy contracts exploit poor women to any greater degree than economic necessity in general exploits them by inducing them to accept lower-paid or otherwise undesirable employment." *Johnson*, 851 P.2d at 785. Agreeing to be a compensated surrogate might be a reasonable choice for a woman. Assuming that a woman cannot enter into a surrogacy contract "knowingly and intelligently" "carries overtones of the reasoning that for centuries prevented women from attaining equal economic rights and professional status under the law" and forecloses a "personal and economic choice on the part of the surrogate mother." *Id.* Because women are presumably capable of making rational choices, the court should enforce the legal consequences of their choices.

Application Paragraph to Bolster the Rule Explanation Paragraph

The surrogacy contract in this case was entered into voluntarily and was a reasonable economic choice for Ms. Binsky. Her mother was in need of a kidney transplant that she could not afford. Mr. Mackey wanted to help her, but he needed his savings to pay for either surrogacy or private adoption. He explained that if Ms. Binsky agreed to serve as a surrogate for him, he would be able to afford to help her mother. Mr. Mackey did not pressure Ms. Binsky to agree to carry his child. Ms. Binsky carefully weighed her cultural aversion to surrogacy against the benefits her service as a surrogate would provide and ultimately decided the benefits were too great to pass up. Her testimony does not suggest that her decision to serve as a surrogate was in any way influenced by her employment relationship with Mr. Mackey. Indeed, Ms. Binsky had previously declined to be a surrogate for Mr. Mackey with no adverse effects on her employment. Mr. Mackey did not exploit his superior knowledge of adoption law. He offered to call an attorney to represent Ms. Binsky, but she said that was not necessary. Although Mr. Mackey drafted the agreement, Ms. Binsky understood its terms, and no one has contended that the agreement was drafted in an unethical manner. In sum, Ms. Binsky was not the victim of exploitation; she voluntarily agreed to act as a surrogate after considering the benefits of the agreement. Failure to enforce this contract would dishonor Ms. Binksy's rational decision to act as a surrogate to secure financing for her mother's surgery.

In this example, the rule explanation gives a reason to enforce surrogacy contracts—they are not exploitative—and the matching application uses the specific facts of the author's case to drive the point home by proving that Ms. Binsky's decision to act as a surrogate was not coerced but rather deliberate and rational. In addition to this type of application paragraph to help bolster the arguments in favor of allowing surrogacy in general, a later section of the analysis would need to include rule explanation on the criteria for enforcement of a surrogacy contract and then additional application paragraphs to apply the criteria to Ms. Binsky's case. Section B in the sample in section 6.3.5 models how to establish and apply criteria after arguing a question of first impression, in that case whether the court should adopt the market share liability theory.

5.3.7 | The Four Tools Revisited

Here are some more examples from Appendix B, Sample A, to illustrate the four tools for application paragraphs: (1) case comparison sentences, (2) court reasoning, (3) factual details, and (4) commonsense inferences. Notice that the four tools can be used in different combinations and do not appear in any set order.

Sample Application Using the Four Tools

❶ Fitness Functions sponsored and benefitted from the paddleball games. ❷ Fitness Functions went beyond the *Ezzy* employer's provision of shirts and refreshments at softball games. ❸ Fitness Functions built a court on the premises and provided all necessary supplies — even sneakers and exercise clothes. ❹ This sponsorship of paddleball supports Gator's belief that his participation was expected. ❺ In addition, like the *Ezzy* employer, Fitness Functions benefitted from employee participation in the recreational activity. ❻ Randolph believed that paddleball increased morale. ❼ It also enabled Randolph to foster her relationships with her employees much like the picnic improved teacher-student relationships in *Smith*. ❽ Fitness Functions' sponsorship of and benefit from paddleball distinguish this case from *City of Stockton* and *Taylor*, where the employers encouraged physical fitness in general but not the specific injury-causing activities, and from *Todd* and *Tensfeldt*, where the employers merely condoned the injury-causing activities.

1. Topic sentence
2. Comparison sentence
3. Factual details
4. Conclusion
5. Comparison sentence
6. Use of court reasoning from Ezzy (increased morale)
7. Comparison sentence and use of reasoning from *Smith*
8. Comparison sentence and use of reasoning from multiple cases

Sample Application Using the Four Tools

❶ Fitness Functions will need to argue that the pressure to play paddleball does not rise to the level of expectancy. ❷ The company can distinguish *Wilson* and *Kidwell* because in those cases, employees had to train to pass required fitness tests. ❸ Fitness Functions employees did not need to play paddleball to satisfy an express job requirement. ❹ *Ezzy* can also be distinguished because in that case, a partner directly urged the law clerk to play by telling her "we'll see you" at the next game. *Ezzy*, 194 Cal. Rptr. at 92. ❺ In this case, by contrast, Randolph merely invited Gator to play. ❻ Moreover, no one with supervisory authority, including Randolph, ever suggested that employees should play paddleball. ❼ Although a coworker once advised Gator that he should play, she did not have supervisory authority and therefore cannot be considered to have been speaking as a representative of the company. ❽ Finally, Fitness Functions can argue that unlike participation in extracurricular activities in *Smith*, paddleball was not an overt aspect of employee evaluations. ❾ In sum, Fitness Functions can argue that expectancy should require more than a mere sense that participating in the activity will help get an "in" with the supervisor. ❿ Personal one-on-one time always helps advance a career. ⓫ If the mere desire to become closer with a supervisor were sufficient, a supervisor could never invite an employee to play golf without worrying that a resulting injury would be subject to workers' compensation coverage.

1. Topic sentence
2. Comparison sentence (distinguishing) and use of court reasoning from *Wilson* and *Kidwell*
3. Factual details
4. Comparison sentence (distinguishing)
5. Factual detail
6. Factual detail
7. Factual detail and commonsense inference
8. Comparison sentence (distinguishing) and use of court reasoning from *Smith*
9. Commonsense inference
10. Commonsense inference
11. Commonsense inference

Checklist for Application Paragraphs

- ☐ Draft topic sentences for each paragraph in your application section that state a conclusion about your case based on one of the subrules in your rule explanation topic sentences. Phrase the topic sentences as specific conclusions about your case (e.g, "Here, Thompson was not involved in any prior crimes . . .") rather than as rules (e.g., "Prior crimes weigh heavily against leniency in sentencing.").
- ☐ Match your application paragraphs to your rule explanation paragraphs.
- ☐ Prove the topic sentences using the four tools: case comparisons, court reasoning carried over from your rule explanation, factual details from your case file, and commonsense inferences.
  - ☐ Case comparisons should be relevant and tied to the rules you discussed in your rule explanation.

Cont.

- ☐ Comparison sentences should be in parallel grammatical form and should compare the right subjects.
- ☐ Refer back to your rule explanation while drafting your application to look for and incorporate court reasoning into your application paragraphs.
- ☐ Refer back to the case file to find helpful factual details to support your points in the application paragraphs.
- ☐ Use commonsense inferences to bridge gaps between factual details and your conclusions.

☐ Avoid relying solely on distinguishing adverse cases; include supportive cases unless none exist.

CHAPTER 5 SELF-TEST

1. What is the purpose of an application paragraph?
2. What is the relationship between an application paragraph and a rule explanation paragraph?
3. What should a topic sentence of an application paragraph do?
4. What is wrong with this comparison sentence: "Like in *Smith*, our client was not performing her work duties as a waitress when she left the restaurant to meet her friend for a quick smoke."?
5. What does it mean to carry over reasoning from your rule explanation to your application?
6. How can you prepare for drafting your application to ensure that you include sufficiently specific factual details?

See answers on page 338.

CHAPTER 6

Organizational Choices

Chapters 4 and 5 teach the core components of a written legal analysis: discussion of the law (rule statement and rule explanation) and discussion of your client's case (application). This chapter explains the organizational choices that lawyers make when they decide where to put these two components within a legal research memorandum or brief. This chapter addresses structure in a manner that is not specific to either objective or persuasive legal writing. Some of the samples will be legal research memoranda, and others will be persuasive briefs. When you review the samples, focus on the organization of the paragraphs. Do not become distracted by whether the headings are topical or persuasive or the extent to which counterarguments are addressed, lessons that are covered in Part II (objective writing) and Part III (persuasive writing).

6.1 | THE TRAC PARADIGM

Usually, legal writers discuss the law (Chapter 4) before they apply the law to the client's case (Chapter 5). You already use this deductive method of analysis in your daily life. Suppose you are playing Scrabble with a friend. Your friend puts down letters to spell "Zoinks." Your conversation might be as follows:

Illustration of Deductive Reasoning

You: You can't do that.
Your friend: Why not?
The law — **You:** The directions say the word has to be in the dictionary.
Your friend: Okay. So?
Application of the law to your case — **You:** "Zoinks" is not in the dictionary. Therefore, you cannot use it.

This text uses the "TRAC" acronym to structure legal analysis paragraphs. You might also encounter alternatives such as "CRAC," "IRAC," and "CREAC." Each acronym represents the same basic principles of organization discussed in this text.

A MOTTO FOR LEGAL WRITING: DO NOT LOSE "TRAC" OF YOUR ORGANIZATION

T	First, state your **thesis** (i.e., should your client prevail on the legal issue you are analyzing?).
R	Next, state, explain, and exemplify the applicable **rules** you can discern from the statutes and/or cases you have read that govern the legal issue you are analyzing. This is the discussion of the law including both rule statement and rule explanation (Chapter 4).
A	Then, **apply** the applicable rules to your case (i.e., explain how you think those rules play out in your case and why). Here, you support your thesis using the rules and cases discussed in your rules sections. The application discusses your client's case using the four tools of effective application paragraphs (Chapter 5).
C	State your **conclusion.**

Here is the Scrabble example again but with a full TRAC this time.

Illustration of TRAC

You cannot get points for "Zoinks." T

The directions say the word has to be in the dictionary. R

"Zoinks" is not in the dictionary. A

Therefore, "Zoinks" violates the rules of the game. C

Now you can transfer the same principles to a legal analysis. In the following sample, modified from Appendix B, Sample A, the lawyer analyzes whether his client, Mark Gator, can receive workers' compensation benefits for an injury he sustained while playing a game of paddleball against his supervisor at work. Notice how the standards that govern benefits are established before any detailed evaluation of whether the client can obtain benefits in his particular situation.

Sample TRAC

Mark Gator's testimony that he felt he needed to play paddleball with Randolph satisfies the subjective belief requirement. T Thesis

Subjective belief is satisfied by an employee's professed belief that participation was required. *Ezzy v. Workers' Comp. Appeals Bd.*, 194 Cal. Rptr. 90, 96 (Ct. App. 1983). Indeed, a belief that one *should* participate is sufficient. *Id.* In *Ezzy*, for example, a law clerk was injured while playing on her firm's softball team. *Id.* at 91. She testified that R Rules and cases

Cont.

because the team did not have enough female players to satisfy the league's rules, she felt she "should" play when a partner handed her a tee shirt and game schedule and said, "At the next one, we'll see you there." *Id.* at 92. The court found her statement under oath was sufficient to establish her subjective belief of expectancy. *Id.* at 96. Failing the subjective belief requirement seems to be a risk only when the employee did not truly feel obligated to participate. *See City of Stockton v. Workers' Comp. Appeals Bd.*, 38 Cal. Rptr. 3d 474, 483 (Ct. App. 2006) (denying coverage to officer injured while playing basketball when he admitted he could satisfy the job requirement of keeping in shape without playing basketball).

A
Application of the rules and cases to your case

Based on the case law explained above, Gator's subjective belief that he was expected to play paddleball can be established by his testimony that he thought he needed to play to advance in the company. His use of the word "needed" even more clearly demonstrates a belief in expectancy than did Ezzy's use of the word "should." Moreover, unlike the employee in *City of Stockton*, Gator never admitted that paddleball was optional. Therefore, Gator should be able to establish the requisite subjective belief.

C
Conclusion

The TRAC structure is easy to follow when you need only one paragraph to discuss the law and another to apply the law. However, most legal issues will require more analysis. Instead of one R paragraph and one A paragraph, you will need several R paragraphs to adequately explain the law and several A paragraphs to apply the law to your case. A question then arises: Do you alternate between R paragraphs and A paragraphs (i.e., TRARARAC) or finish all of your R paragraphs before starting your first A paragraph (i.e., TRRRAAAC)? A host of other questions arise as you begin to work through various legal writing assignments. Can you ever combine R and A into one paragraph? Is there any way to make the structure less monotonous? This chapter attempts to answer these questions in a manner that provides guidance but allows flexibility. For consistency, the sections that follow use three Rs and three As, but, of course, the number of Rs and As you need may vary. You might have three Rs but only one A or two Rs but three As.

6.2 | A ONE-TRAC STRUCTURE USING TRRRAAAC

T
R^1
R^2
R^3
A^1
A^2
A^3
C

One approach to organizing an analysis that will include multiple R paragraphs and multiple A paragraphs is to keep all of the R paragraphs together in the first part of the analysis and all of the A paragraphs together in the second part of the analysis. Imagine a line drawn in the sand with all of the Rs above the line and all of the As below the line. This organization does not use headings.

The TRRRAAAC approach offers a few advantages. First, it is usually the easiest for novice writers to understand. Second, the grouping of the R paragraphs helps remind novice writers to synthesize the law on the issue. Third, it is a very adaptable model—one that can work in any situation.

Sample TRRRAAAC

The prosecution can establish that Savonarola entered a building and therefore committed burglary when he entered the bank kiosk and used a stolen ATM card to withdraw money. Thesis

To establish burglary under California law, the prosecution must establish that the defendant "enter[ed]" a "building" "with the intent to commit . . . larceny or felony." Cal. Penal Code § 459 (West 2004). The entry requirement distinguishes burglary from other theft crimes by emphasizing interference with the possessory interest of a building's occupants. *People v. Davis*, 958 P.2d 1083, 1089 (Cal. 1998). As explained by the California Supreme Court, the higher penalties burglary charges carry "are based primarily upon a recognition of the . . . danger that the intruder will harm the occupants in attempting to perpetrate the intended crime or to escape and the danger that occupants will in anger or panic react violently to the invasion." *Id.* Because burglary is based on the dangers inherent in an intrusion, "'[t]he ultimate test of whether a burglarious entry has occurred must focus on the protection the owners or inhabitants of a structure reasonably expect.'" *People v. Valencia*, 46 P.3d 920, 924 (Cal. 2002) (quoting *People v. Nible*, 247 Cal. Rptr. 396, 399 (Ct. App. 1988)). Rule statement

Even the "slightest partial entry" of the outer boundary of a building constitutes an entry. *Id.* at 925. Consistent with the "ultimate test" that the California Supreme Court adopted in *Valencia*, a building's outer boundary includes any element that encloses an area into which a reasonable person would believe that a member of the general public could not pass without authorization. *Id.* at 926. In *Valencia*, the court found that the defendant had entered a house when he removed a window screen with a screwdriver even though he did not successfully open the window. *Id.* at 927. The court reasoned that a screen window announces that intrusion is unauthorized. *Id.* The court also noted that an element of a structure need not offer physical protection to be considered part of the building's outer boundary. *Id.* at 926. "[W]hat matters is not whether a reasonable person would believe that a given element of a building provides some physical protection against unauthorized intrusion, but simply whether a reasonable person would believe that a member of the general public needed authorization to pass beyond it." *Id.* at 926-27. The court noted with approval a prior holding that "'even an open door . . . affords some expectation of protection from unauthorized intrusion because reasonable persons understand the social convention that portals may not be crossed without permission.'" *Id.* at 926 (quoting *Nible*, 247 Cal. Rptr. at 399). Rule explanation 1

The outer boundary of a building also includes any integral part of the structure of the building. *People v. Franco*, 250 P. 698, 699 (Cal. Ct. App. 1926). In *Franco*, the defendant stole shoes from showcases that were located on the external walls of a shoe store along a stairway that led from the sidewalk down to the store. *Id.* at 698. The court stated that with respect to the types of structures it covers, the burglary statute "has the very broadest significance and meaning and is very comprehensive." *Id.* at 699. The court noted that the roof of the building covered the showcases and therefore concluded that the showcases were "part of the store proper." *Id.* Rule explanation 2

On the other hand, if the defendant's act does not invade the possessory interest of a building's occupants, then the stiffer penalties under the burglary statute are not Rule explanation 3

Cont.

justified. *Davis*, 958 P.2d at 1089. In *Davis*, the defendant submitted a forged check to a drive-up check-cashing facility by inserting it into a chute in the window of the facility. *Id.* at 1084. Although previous cases had found entry based upon the slightest intrusion into the air space of a building, the court stated that courts must "establish reasonable limits as to what constitutes an entry...for the purposes of the burglary statute" to avoid expanding the statute to "absurd proportions." *Id.* at 1087. In determining the appropriate limits, the court considered the interest sought to be protected by the burglary statute. *Id.* at 1088. The statute was originally intended to protect the sanctity of a person's home. *Id.* Although it has since been expanded by the legislature to cover other buildings, it is still "based primarily upon a recognition of...the danger the intruder will harm the occupants in attempting to perpetrate the intended crime or to escape and the danger that the occupants will in anger or panic react violently to the invasion." *Id.* at 1089. These dangers exist only when the defendant has invaded the possessory interest of a building's occupants. *Id.* The court analogized the insertion of the forged check into the window chute to mailing a forged check to a bank, inserting a stolen ATM card into an ATM, and returning library books through a chute and concluded that none of these acts violate an occupant's possessory interest. *Id.* at 1089-90. Therefore, they do not constitute entry under the burglary statute. *Id.* at 1090. By contrast, in *Valencia*, the court concluded that removing the window screen did carry the potential for violence because a homeowner would be just as likely to react violently to removal of the screen as to penetration of the window itself. *Valencia*, 46 P.3d at 927.

Application 1 Consistent with the case law discussed above, Savonarola should be found guilty of burglary. Under *Valencia*, the bank's outer boundary included the ATM kiosk because it was an enclosed area into which a reasonable person would believe that a member of the public could not pass without permission. Like a door or window, the kiosk affords protection from unauthorized intrusions. Indeed, the bank representative stated that the reason the bank built the kiosk was to protect customers from theft. It does not matter that the external door of the kiosk does not lock. As the court explained in *Valencia*, even an unlocked door prompts an expectation of protection because social norms preclude crossing such portals without permission. *Valencia*, 46 P.3d at 926. The bank representative confirmed that the bank did have this expectation. Specifically, he stated, "We figured that even without a lock, the doors are a deterrent." Because the bank reasonably expected the kiosk to offer protection from unauthorized intrusion, the "ultimate test" for entry is satisfied.

Application 2 Moreover, the kiosk was an integral part of the structure of the bank. Just as the casements in *Franco* were part of the store proper, the kiosk was part of the bank proper. Like the casements, the kiosk was attached to one of the exterior walls of the building. Giving the statute its broadest interpretation, as directed by the court in *Franco*, the court should conclude that when Savonarola entered the kiosk, he entered the bank.

Application 3 Savonarola may argue that *Valencia* is distinguishable because members of the public reasonably believed they *could* enter the kiosk without permission. The bank representative stated that he has occasionally permitted noncustomers to wait for the bus in the kiosk. The bank's failure to assert a possessory interest over the kiosk by asking loiterers to leave arguably removes any expectation of protection from

Cont.

intrusion the bank and its customers could otherwise reasonably expect. The absence of such an expectation is significant under *Davis*. *Davis* explained that the limits of the burglary statute should be based on the underlying rationale for the criminal sanction it imposes—the danger posed by the entry into an area reserved for only certain occupants. 958 P.2d at 1089. Because the kiosk was not reserved for customers, neither Savonarola nor the bank's representatives and customers would be likely to resort to violence in connection with his entry. Therefore, the underlying rationale for the high penalty associated with burglary arguably does not apply.

Savonarola may also argue that the kiosk was not an integral part of the bank's structure because unlike the casements in *Franco*, the kiosk did not share a roof with the bank. Application 4

Savonarola's arguments are likely to fail. Although the bank's efforts to reserve the kiosk for customers were not consistent, the bank representative stated that he "usually" asks loiterers to leave. Therefore, the bank did assert its possessory interest in the kiosk. Moreover, no court has suggested that a building's owner forfeits his possessory interest merely by tolerating uninvited guests. Application 5

The court should also reject the argument that Savonarola's entry into the kiosk did not carry a risk of violence. *Davis* is distinguishable because the defendant did not enter any part of the building; he merely inserted a check in a window chute. Here, Savonarola walked into the kiosk. Unlike the check, Savonarola's entry into the kiosk implicates the rationale behind the criminal sanction for burglary. Once Savonarola passed through the kiosk door, he was in a confined space. Had someone guessed that Savonarola was using a stolen card and confronted him, he might have resorted to violence to escape. The potential for violence was the same as if he entered the bank lobby and used the ATM card to withdraw money at the teller's window, an act that would clearly fall within the burglary statute. Therefore, the purpose behind the burglary penalties does not warrant a different result in this case. Application 6

Finally, the attempt to distinguish *Franco* should also fail. Although the casements happened to share a roof with the shoe store in that case, the court's focus was on the physical and functional connection between the casements and the store. Here, the kiosk shared a wall with the bank; it was no less integral to the bank than were the casements to the shoe store in *Franco*. Application 7

For the foregoing reasons, the prosecution should be able to meet the entry requirement to sustain the burglary charge against Savonarola. Conclusion

As Chapter 5 explains, application paragraphs should apply the subrules stated in the topic sentences of the rule explanation paragraphs. Ideally, the organization of the application paragraphs should match the organization of the rule explanation paragraphs: the first application paragraph matches the first rule explanation paragraph, the second application paragraph matches the second rule explanation paragraph, and so on. Consistency always benefits the reader. If you find yourself tempted to use a different order in your application paragraphs, take some time to look back at your rule explanation paragraphs and consider whether you could reorder them to match the order of your application paragraphs.

However, if you can articulate good reasons to use a different order in your rule explanation and application paragraphs, give yourself the flexibility to follow your intuition. For example, you may need two rule explanation paragraphs to explain how two contrary lines of cases fit together but only one application paragraph to apply the synthesized rule you derived from the conflicting cases. And sometimes the application of a subrule that took only one rule explanation paragraph to explain will take three application paragraphs to apply (this is illustrated in the sample above, which includes three rule explanation paragraphs and seven application paragraphs). So, while an exact TRRRAAAC is ideal, it may not always be possible, and you may end up with a TRRRAAC or a TRAAAC or some other adaptation. Do not stick rigidly to TRRRAAAC when it would result in unnecessary repetition of points, awkward transitions, or other organizational oddities that your common sense tells you are undesirable.

6.3 | MULTIPLE TRAC STRUCTURES: TRRRAAAC BY HEADING

So far, we have covered the most basic TRAC structure and the more complex TRRRAAAC structure. Now we have to address another typical situation you will face as a practicing lawyer: an analysis that is so complex and lengthy that TRRRAAAC cannot handle its own weight.

Using a single TRRRAAAC organization for a legal analysis works well when the issue you are addressing involves an easily manageable number of subrules. However, you will frequently encounter issues that involve multiple elements, factors, or tests. Each element, factor, or test may then have its own set of subrules. A one-TRRRAAAC structure for such a complex analysis is not workable. The reader would struggle to member all of the details of your rule explanation paragraphs when she gets to your application paragraphs. Follow your instincts and break up the huge TRRRRRRRRAAAAAAAAC block.

Heading A.
T
R
A
C
Heading B.
T
R
A
C
Heading C.
T
R
A
C

One option is to divide your analysis into multiple TRRRAAAC sequences. For example, the analysis of workers' compensation coverage in Appendix B, Sample A, identifies two requirements: the employee's subjective belief that his participation in the activity was expected and the objective reasonableness of his belief. The annotated sample uses a single TRRRAAAC, handling both requirements at the same time. However, stop here for a moment and go to Appendix B to compare Sample A to Sample C. The latter sample demonstrates an alternative organization that creates one heading for subjective belief and another for objective reasonableness. Each requirement is separately analyzed under its respective heading with its own TRRRAAAC. The TRRRAAAC by heading sample is easier for the reader to follow because it divides the analysis into more digestible pieces.

The TRRRAAAC by heading organization is an easy adaptation of the organization described in section 6.2. It involves only two new skills: (1) use of headings and (2) use of umbrella paragraphs to set the stage for the headings.

6.3.1 | Adding Headings to Create Separate TRAC Sequences

When you decide to subdivide your analysis into multiple TRRRAAACs, each TRRRAAAC needs its own heading. Headings in objective writing are simple subject indications like "Subjective Belief" and "Objective Reasonableness," as in the sample at the end of this section. Headings in persuasive writing are much more of an art and are discussed in Part III. Regardless of whether you are writing an objective or a persuasive piece, however, your first task in creating headings is to ensure that the heading accurately reflects the analysis that it introduces. The text that appears under the heading "Subjective Belief" should cover only whether the employee subjectively believed his participation was expected and no other issues. You will also have an umbrella paragraph that states your overall thesis and includes the rule statement.

Illustration

Before heading A., include an umbrella paragraph to introduce your thesis, general rules, and the headings.

A. Subjective Belief
   Thesis on Subjective Belief
   Rule Statement on Subjective Belief, if needed
   Rule Explanation on Subjective Belief
   Application on Subjective Belief
   Conclusion on Subjective Belief
B. Objective Reasonableness
   Thesis on Objective Reasonableness
   Rule Statement on Objective Reasonableness, if needed
   Rule Explanation on Objective Reasonableness
   Application on Objective Reasonableness
   Conclusion on Objective Reasonableness

This illustration shows only one entry for rule explanation and application, but you might have several rule explanation paragraphs and several application paragraphs. In this organization, within section A, all of the rule explanation paragraphs on subjective belief would precede the first application paragraph on subjective belief; within section B, all of the rule explanation paragraphs on objective reasonableness would precede the first application paragraph on objective reasonableness. The components of the initial umbrella paragraph and the placement of rule statement paragraphs are discussed in more detail in the sections to follow.

6.3.2 | Adding Umbrella Paragraphs

One of the challenges in using a TRRRAAAC by heading organization is that the law is more than just the sum of its parts. Inevitably, any legal issue will involve general overarching principles that do not fit naturally under any one subpart. One solution to this problem is to create an initial paragraph (an "umbrella" paragraph) before your first heading. The umbrella paragraph is the first paragraph of an analysis. At a minimum, the umbrella paragraph should (1) state your overall thesis on the issue, (2) provide any broad rules necessary to set up your two headings (an umbrella rule statement), and (3) preview the conclusions you will reach under each heading.

Sample Umbrella Paragraph

Overall thesis

Broad rules that would not fit under the headings

Introduction of the two requirements that set up the subjective belief and objective reasonableness headings

Preview of the conclusions that will be reached under each heading

Gator is entitled to coverage. Labor Code section 3600, subdivision (a)(9), excludes from workers' compensation coverage injuries arising from "voluntary participation in any off-duty recreational, social, or athletic activity not constituting part of the employee's work-related duties, except where these activities are a reasonable expectancy of, or are expressly or impliedly required by, the employment." Cal. Labor Code, § 3600(a)(9) (West 2003). The exception for activities that are a reasonable expectancy of employment applies when (1) the employee subjectively believes participation in the activity is expected; and (2) the employee's belief is objectively reasonable. *Ezzy v. Workers' Comp. Appeals Bd.*, 194 Cal. Rptr. 90, 93 (Ct. App. 1983). Gator's paddleball game with his supervisor meets this standard for two reasons. First, Gator believed that participation was expected by his boss. Second, his belief was reasonable because Fitness Functions created implied pressure for its employees to play paddleball and encouraged and benefitted from its employees' participation.

I have called this an umbrella paragraph, but in some cases, it may take a few paragraphs to complete these steps. The following sample demonstrates how the components of the umbrella could be spread out into multiple paragraphs.

Sample Multiparagraph Umbrella

Overall thesis

The trial court's denial of Ms. Forrest's motion to dismiss the indictment was erroneous because the government's conduct in this case exceeded due process limits.

Broad rules that would not fit under the headings

The United States Supreme Court has recognized that the Due Process Clause of the Constitution imposes limits on the methods law enforcement may use to obtain convictions, and, accordingly, convictions obtained through improper means are barred. *United States v. Russell*, 411 U.S. 423, 431 (1973) ("we may someday be presented with a situation in which the conduct of law enforcement agents is so outrageous that due process principles would absolutely bar the government from invoking judicial processes to obtain a conviction"). Unlike the defense of entrapment, a claim of outrageous government conduct may be successful even when the

Cont.

defendant was predisposed to commit the crime. *Hampton v. United States*, 425 U.S. 484, 495 (1976) (Powell, J., concurring), 497 (Brennan, J., dissenting); *see also United States v. Bogart*, 783 F.2d 1428, 1432 (9th Cir. 1986) (explaining that the concurring and dissenting justices in *Hampton* comprised a majority to support the availability of an outrageous government conduct claim regardless of the defendant's criminal predisposition).

The availability of a dismissal based on outrageous government conduct is necessary to guard against "'the dangers of overzealous law enforcement.'" *United States v. Twigg*, 588 F.2d 373, 380 (3d Cir. 1978) (quoting *Sherman v. United States*, 356 U.S. 369, 381 (1958) (Frankfurter, J., concurring)). This overzealousness is not merely theoretical but has warranted dismissals of indictments in several federal cases. *Id.*; *United States v. West*, 511 F.2d 1083, 1086 (3d Cir. 1975); *Greene v. United States*, 454 F.2d 783, 786-87 (9th Cir. 1971); *United States v. Gardner*, 658 F. Supp. 1573, 1577 (W.D. Pa. 1987); *United States v. Batres-Santolino*, 521 F. Supp. 744, 752 (N.D. Cal. 1981); *see also United States v. Luttrell*, 889 F.2d 806, 813-814 (9th Cir. 1989) (finding that indictment should be dismissed if government did not have reason to investigate defendants prior to presenting them with an opportunity to engage in criminal conduct and remanding for factual determination of whether such a reason existed); *United States v. Archer*, 486 F.2d 670, 677 (2d Cir. 1973) (dismissing indictment on other grounds but stating it might have found government's authorization of crimes by government agents to be sufficiently outrageous to warrant dismissal on due process grounds).

The dangers of overzealous law enforcement that underlie the outrageous conduct theory are evident in this case. Ms. Forrest was a nonviolent environmental activist who had participated in only two minor acts of vandalism prior to becoming caught up in the criminal plan devised by the government's informant. The informant first coerced her into committing the crime by threatening her life and then directed every aspect of the plan. This case thus presents both of the main factual circumstances that have warranted dismissals of indictments on due process grounds: overinvolvement in criminal activity and coercive tactics. Moreover, the government's conduct was improper even under the five factor test on which the government relies to justify its tactics.

Preview of the conclusions that will be reached under each heading. To see how the three points introduced here (overinvolvement, coercive tactics, and the five-factor test) match the headings that follow, see Sample F in Appendix B.

Placement of Rule Statement The umbrella should include an initial rule statement that funnels down to the elements, factors, or tests that will divide your analysis (i.e., that mirror your headings). Sometimes, you will need another rule statement under one of your headings to provide rules specific to the element, factor, or test addressed in that section before the first rule explanation paragraph in the section. In the sample shown in section 6.3.3, compare section A (which does not include an additional rule statement) with section B (which does include an additional rule statement). Section B needed an additional rule statement to introduce the implied pressure and indirect encouragement tests before the rule explanation paragraphs could dissect the meaning of implied pressure and indirect encouragement in more detail. Section A's discussion of subjective belief, however, had no gap to fill between its first rule explanation and the rule statement in the umbrella paragraph.

6.3.3 | Using Tiered Levels of Headings

Dividing an analysis into multiple TRRRAACs by heading is not always as simple as dividing it by element or factor. Sometimes, one or more of the elements or factors will be so complex that you will want to subdivide it into smaller sections, each with its own TRRRAAAC.

When using tiered divisions, create a special formatting convention for each tier's headings. The samples in this text use A., B., C., etc. to label first-tier headings and 1., 2., 3., etc. to label second-tier headings. Your law office may have its own formatting preferences for the type of document you are creating.

Also, each tier needs its own umbrella paragraph. For example, if your first-tier headings are designated by letters A., B., C., etc. and your second-tier headings are designated by numbers 1., 2., 3., etc., you would have an initial umbrella paragraph before heading A. that introduces headings A. and B. You would have another umbrella paragraph under heading B. if section B. was going to be further subdivided into headings 1. and 2. The illustration demonstrates the inclusion of umbrella paragraphs to introduce each new tier of headings. A more complete sample follows.

Illustration

Before heading A, include an umbrella paragraph to introduce headings A and B.

Heading A

T
R
A
C

Heading B

Before heading 1, include an umbrella paragraph to introduce headings 1 and 2.

Heading 1

T
R
A
C

Heading 2

T
R
A
C

A complete sample analysis using the TRRRAAAC by heading structure follows.

Sample TRRRAAAC by Heading

This is the main umbrella paragraph that introduces subdivisions A and B.

Gator is entitled to coverage because paddleball was a reasonable expectancy of his employment with Fitness Functions. Labor Code section 3600, subdivision (a)(9) excludes from workers' compensation coverage injuries arising from "voluntary participation in any off-duty recreational, social, or athletic activity not constituting part of the employee's work-related duties, except where these activities are a reasonable expectancy of, or are expressly or impliedly required by, the employment." Cal. Labor Code, § 3600 (a)(9) (West 2003). The exception for activities that are a reasonable expectancy of employment applies when (1) the employee subjectively believes participation in the activity is expected; and (2) the employee's belief is objectively reasonable. *Ezzy v. Workers' Comp. Appeals Bd.*, 194 Cal. Rptr. 90, 93 (Ct. App. 1983). Gator's paddleball game with his supervisor meets this standard for two reasons. First, Gator believed that participation was expected by his boss. Second, his belief was reasonable because Fitness Functions created implied pressure for its employees to play paddleball and encouraged and benefitted from its employees' participation.

Overall thesis

Broad rules (initial rule statement)

Introduction of the two requirements that will be covered under headings A and B

Preview of the conclusions that will be reached under headings A and B

A. Subjective Belief

Gator's testimony that he felt he needed to play paddleball with Randolph satisfies the subjective belief requirement.

Thesis for section A

Subjective belief is satisfied by an employee's professed belief that participation was required. Indeed, a belief that one *should* participate is sufficient. In *Ezzy*, for example, a law clerk was injured while playing on her firm's softball team. 194 Cal. Rptr. at 91. She testified that because the team did not have enough female players to satisfy the league's rules, she felt she "should" play when a partner handed her a tee shirt and game schedule and said, "At the next one, we'll see you there." *Id.* at 92. Her statement under oath was sufficient to establish her subjective belief of expectancy. *Id.* at 96.

Rule explanation 1 for section A

Failing the subjective belief requirement seems to be a risk only when the employee did not truly feel obligated to participate. *Compare Smith v. Workers' Comp. Appeals Bd.*, 236 Cal. Rptr. 248, 254-55 (Ct. App. 1987) (holding that deceased teacher's wife's testimony that teacher went to a picnic because his department head asked him to, he felt he had a "responsibility" to go, and he believed he had to participate in a certain number of extracurricular activities satisfied the subjective element of the test to establish coverage for injuries sustained while he was windsurfing during the picnic), *and Wilson v. Workers' Comp. Appeals Bd.*, 239 Cal. Rptr. 719, 721 (Ct. App. 1987) (holding that police officer's testimony that he believed he had to keep in shape to stay on a special emergency unit satisfied the subjective element to establish coverage for an injury sustained while running off-duty), *with City of Stockton v. Workers' Comp. Appeals Bd.*, 38 Cal. Rptr. 3d 474, 483 (Ct. App. 2006) (denying coverage to officer injured while playing basketball when he admitted he could satisfy the job requirement of keeping in shape without playing basketball).

Rule explanation 2 for section A

Based on the case law explained above, Gator's subjective belief that he was expected to play paddleball can be established by his testimony that he thought he needed to play to advance in the company. His use of the word "needed" even more

Application for section A

Cont.

clearly demonstrates a belief in expectancy than did Ezzy's use of the word "should." Moreover, unlike the employee in *City of Stockton*, Gator never admitted that paddleball was optional. Therefore, Gator should be able to establish the requisite subjective belief.

Conclusion for section A

B. Reasonableness of the Belief

This is the umbrella paragraph for section B that introduces subdivisions 1 and 2.

Thesis for section B

Introduction of the two methods of proving expectancy to set up subheadings 1 and 2 (a second rule statement)

Preview of conclusions reached in sections 1 and 2

Gator can also establish that his belief that his participation was expected was reasonable. Courts have been liberal in their interpretation of "expectancy" and have found it satisfied based merely on "implied pressure" on an employee to participate in the activity at issue. *Smith*, 236 Cal. Rptr. at 254 ("[E]vidence demonstrating and proving express or implied pressure upon the employee serves to establish the objective reasonableness of that employee's belief that he or she was required to participate."). In addition, an employer's indirect encouragement of the activity may change the voluntary nature of the activity and therefore may warrant coverage of the resulting injuries. *Ezzy*, 194 Cal. Rptr. at 95. In this case, Gator has enough evidence to support both implied pressure and indirect encouragement and, therefore, can satisfy the reasonableness requirement.

1. Implied Pressure to Participate

Thesis for section 1

Gator can establish implied pressure to play paddleball based on his vulnerable status as a probationary employee and the strong connection between paddleball and job advancement at Fitness Functions.

Rule explanation 1 for section 1

A need to participate in the activity to remain or advance in employment may establish implied pressure. *See Wilson*, 239 Cal. Rptr. at 722. In *Wilson*, a police officer claimed coverage for injuries sustained while running on his own time off work premises. *Id.* at 719. Police officers in the plaintiff's special emergency unit were tested four times per year, and those in his age group had to run two miles in seventeen minutes. *Id.* at 722. The court found he reasonably believed he had to keep in shape to remain in the unit and was therefore entitled to coverage. *Id.* It reasoned that it would be "unrealistic" to think that such a requirement could be met without off-duty exercise. *Id.* The court similarly found implied pressure satisfied in *Kidwell v. Workers' Comp. Appeals Bd.*, 39 Cal. Rptr. 2d 540, 545-46 (Ct. App. 1995), where a police officer was injured while practicing a long jump at home, because testimony established that promotion and benefits were contingent on passing a long jump test and that passing the test required practice.

Rule explanation 2 for section 1

Implied pressure may be exacerbated when an employee is in a vulnerable position. *See Smith*, 236 Cal. Rptr. at 257 (noting that the employee was more vulnerable to pressure because as a temporary instructor, he needed to participate in extracurricular activities to better his chances of being rehired); *Ezzy*, 194 Cal. Rptr. at 95 (finding that a law clerk's belief that her participation at the softball game was expected was reasonable based in part on the pressure a law clerk would naturally feel when urged to participate in a softball game by a partner at the firm).

Application 1 for section 1

Evidence of implied pressure is strong in Gator's case. Like the vulnerable positions of the employees in *Ezzy* and *Smith*, Gator's probationary status made him particularly

Cont.

susceptible to pressure. Moreover, playing paddleball with Randolph was necessary to advance in the job. Randolph invited Gator to play while complimenting his job performance and expressing a desire to see continued successes. The coupling of a discussion of job performance with an invitation to play paddleball justifies Gator's impression that paddleball and advancement in the company were related. Indeed, Randolph admitted that she uses paddleball games as an opportunity to discuss business with employees. Therefore, by turning down paddleball, an employee would necessarily be turning down an opportunity to discuss business with the Director. No ambitious employee would refuse such an invitation. Just like it would have been unrealistic to think that the police officers in *Wilson* and *Kidwell* could have passed their employers' fitness tests without training, it would be unrealistic to think that Gator would have the same opportunity to advance in the company if he turned down the opportunity for one-on-one time with Randolph on the paddleball court. The possible adverse effect of a refusal on Gator's advancement justifies his sense of pressure.

Fitness Functions will need to argue that the pressure to play paddleball does not rise to the level of expectancy. The company can distinguish *Wilson* and *Kidwell* because in those cases, employees had to train to pass required fitness tests. Fitness Functions employees did not need to play paddleball to satisfy an express job requirement. *Ezzy* can also be distinguished because in that case, a partner directly urged the law clerk to play by telling her "we'll see you" at the next game. In this case, by contrast, Randolph merely invited Gator to play. Moreover, no one with supervisory authority, including Randolph, ever suggested that employees should play paddleball. Although a coworker once advised Gator he should play, she did not have supervisory authority and therefore cannot be considered to have been speaking as a representative of the company. Finally, Fitness Functions can argue that unlike participation in extracurriculars in *Smith*, paddleball was not an overt aspect of employee evaluations. In sum, Fitness Functions can argue that expectancy should require more than a mere sense that participating in the activity will help get an "in" with the supervisor. Personal one-on-one time always helps advance a career. If the mere desire to become closer with a supervisor were sufficient, a supervisor could never invite an employee to play golf without worrying that a resulting injury would be subject to workers' compensation coverage. Application 2 for section 1

The response to these arguments is that more is present in this case than a mere desire to get an "in" with the supervisor. Randolph's use of paddleball as an opportunity to discuss business with her employees transformed a recreational activity into a work-related activity. Paddleball was a necessary step towards advancing in the company and, therefore, a reasonable expectancy of the job. If Gator had any doubt that paddleball and advancement are connected at Fitness Functions, that doubt would have been erased by the coupling of Randolph's invitation with comments about his job performance. These facts demonstrate a substantial connection between participation in paddleball and employment at Fitness Functions and, therefore, should entitle Gator to coverage. Application 3 for section 1 Conclusion for section 1

2. Indirect Encouragement of the Activity

Gator can also establish indirect encouragement of paddleball by Fitness Functions in light of the company's involvement in and benefit from the activity. Thesis for section 2

Cont.

Rule explanation 1 for section 2

Employer involvement and benefit can establish indirect encouragement by the employer that changes the voluntary nature of the activity and, therefore, requires coverage of resulting injuries. *Ezzy*, 194 Cal. Rptr. at 95. For example, in finding reasonable expectancy in *Ezzy*, the court pointed to evidence that the firm provided tee shirts and refreshments at the games and held a special banquet for participants. *Id.* Employer encouragement and benefit similarly played a large role in securing coverage in *Smith*, 236 Cal. Rptr. at 257-58 (relying on the school's role in planning the picnic at which the employee was injured including its collection of permission slips, advertisement of planning meetings, and payment for refreshments; the benefit of the picnic to the school through improved teacher-student relationships; and the school's general encouragement of teacher participation in extracurricular activities), and *Wilson*, 239 Cal. Rptr. at 722 (relying on the benefit to the police department from the ability of the employee's specially trained unit to handle situations too extreme for its standard force).

Rule explanation 2 for section 2

Sponsorship or encouragement, however, must be linked to the specific activity at issue. An employer's encouragement of general fitness, without any encouragement of the specific activity at issue, does not establish reasonable expectancy. For example, in *City of Stockton*, the employer required employees to remain fit but did not undergo any specific fitness tests. *City of Stockton*, 38 Cal. Rptr. 3d at 483. The basketball game that caused the employee's injuries was off-premises, impromptu, and not known to, much less encouraged by, the employer. *Id.* The court held that the employee could not reasonably believe his participation in such a game was expected. *Id.* at 483-84. The court explained that a general expectation of fitness does not lead to coverage for any activity the employee chooses to fulfill that expectation. *Id.* at 483. To allow such broad coverage would be contrary to the intent of the legislature to exclude coverage for injuries that are only remotely connected to employment. *Id.* at 479, 483; *see also Taylor v. Workers' Comp. Appeals Bd.*, 244 Cal. Rptr. 643, 645 (Ct. App. 1988) (finding no reasonable expectancy where employer informed employees that only approved fitness regimens would be entitled to coverage and employee's basketball game was not part of an approved regimen).

Rule explanation 3 for section 2

Moreover, merely condoning an activity does not create a sufficient connection to employment to warrant liability. *See Tensfeldt v. Workers' Comp. Appeals Bd.*, 77 Cal. Rptr. 2d 691, 698 (Ct. App. 1998) (denying coverage for city employee's basketball injury when employees were allowed but not encouraged to play basketball at a city gym); *Todd v. Workers' Comp. Appeals Bd.*, 243 Cal. Rptr. 925, 927 (Ct. App. 1988) (denying coverage for employee's basketball injury when employer did nothing to encourage the game other than allow employees to install a hoop on the premises using some of the employer's material).

Application for section 2

The evidence in this case demonstrates company sponsorship of and benefit from the paddleball games. Fitness Functions went beyond the *Ezzy* employer's provision of tee shirts and refreshments at softball games. Fitness Functions built a court on the premises and provided all necessary supplies—even sneakers and exercise clothes. This sponsorship of paddleball supports Gator's belief that his participation was expected. In addition, like the *Ezzy* employer, Fitness Functions benefitted from employee participation in the recreational activity. Randolph believed that paddleball increased morale. It also enabled Randolph to foster her relationships with her employees much like the picnic improved teacher-student relationships in *Smith*.

Cont.

Fitness Functions' sponsorship of and benefit from paddleball distinguish this case from *City of Stockton* and *Taylor*, where the employers encouraged physical fitness in general but not the specific injury-causing activities, and from *Todd* and *Tensfeldt*, where the employers merely condoned the activity at issue. Based on Fitness Functions' involvement in and benefit from the paddleball games on its property, Gator's injuries from the paddleball game fall within the scope of workers' compensation coverage. Conclusion for section 2

For the reasons explained above, Gator has a good claim for coverage and should therefore submit an application for adjudication with the Workers' Compensation Appeals Board. Overall conclusion

6.3.4 | Deciding How to Subdivide Your Analysis

The first-tier divisions of the analysis (e.g., sections A., B., C.) are often easy to determine. If you are analyzing three elements of a crime, it is logical to have a section for each element. If your issue is governed by a two-prong test, it makes sense to create a section for each prong. If your issue is governed by a list of factors, you may want to have a section for each factor.

Second-tier divisions (e.g., sections 1., 2., 3. under section A.) can sometimes be less obvious. The governing rules may not be as clear; the factors may not be as discrete. The right organization will depend on the relationship between your points. Independent points can have their own subdivisions; interdependent points need to stay together. Suppose you have just drafted or outlined two rule explanation paragraphs and two application paragraphs. If the two rule explanation paragraphs concern separable subrules that make sense independently of one another and the two application paragraphs do not rely on the same facts from the case file, then you know you have two independent points that can be separated by headings into two separate TRACs. Keep in mind that factors can be separable even if courts ultimately weigh them together.

Illustration

I am deciding whether to go to the beach or the museum tomorrow. You want to help me decide. I tell you that I will weigh three factors: the weather, the amount of time I have available, and the price of gasoline. The application of each factor is completely separate. You can tell me whether the weather is going to be better for the beach or the museum without discussing the other two factors. Therefore, if this were a legal analysis, each factor could have its own heading and its own TRAC. This is true even though my decision will ultimately require weighing the factors. For example, suppose it is going to be a sunny day but gas prices just shot through the roof, and the beach is farther from my house than the museum. The weather would suggest I should go to the beach, but gas prices would suggest I should go to the museum. The analysis of the weather can still have its own section even though my decision may end up being different because of the price of gas.

In a factor-balancing analysis, the factors can be separately TRAC-ed under their respective headings and then balanced at the end of the analysis as in the following sample.

Sample TRRRAAAC by Heading Involving Factor Balancing

ANALYSIS

Umbrella The Three Strikes Law requires a mandatory sentence of twenty-five years to life in prison for any person who commits three serious felonies. Cal. Penal Code § 667(e)(2)(A) (Deerings 2008). The statute's purpose is to take repeat offenders off the streets. *People v. Superior Court (Romero)*, 917 P.2d 628, 630 (Cal. 1996). Courts may dismiss a prior strike only when the "nature and circumstances of [the defendant's] present felonies and prior serious and/or violent felony convictions, and the particulars of his background, character, and prospects" bring the defendant "outside the scheme's spirit, in whole or in part." *People v. Williams*, 948 P.2d 429, 437 (Cal. 1998); *see also* Cal. Penal Code § 1385(a) (Deerings 2008) (giving courts discretion to dismiss an action); *Romero*, 917 P.2d at 647 (holding that under section 1385(a), a court can dismiss a prior conviction to avoid the mandatory sentence under the Three Strikes Law). In applying this standard, courts must carefully consider the interests of society in the "fair prosecution of properly charged crimes." *Romero*, 917 P.2d at 648. By definition, a defendant who commits a third strike is in the class of those with "a long and continuous criminal record," and, therefore, a court should dismiss a prior strike only in "extraordinary circumstances." *People v. Carmony*, 92 P.3d 369, 378 (Cal. 2004).

The trial court's dismissal of a prior strike in this case is unsupported by any "extraordinary circumstances." To the contrary, the record demonstrates the strong likelihood that Romano will continue to be a danger to society unless he receives the mandatory life sentence. He falls squarely within the spirit of the Three Strikes Law for the following reasons: (1) he has failed to learn any lesson from his prior theft crimes; (2) he has not refrained from crime since his prior strikes; (3) he has failed to overcome the drug addiction that underlies his criminal record; and (4) his robbery carried the potential for violence.

A. Romano's third theft felony shows he has not iearned any lessons from his previous time in jail.

T Romano's decision to resort to theft again reveals that he is incapable of change. Accordingly, he falls squarely within the spirit of the Three Strikes Law.

R A criminal who commits the same serious felony three times deserves a Three Strikes sentence. In *Williams*, the court found that the trial court had abused its discretion in striking one of the defendant's prior strikes. *Williams*, 948 P.2d at 439. Williams had been convicted of driving under the influence three times prior to his most recent conviction for the same crime. *Id.* at 438. The court explained that the existence of three prior incidents of the same crime "'reveal[ed] that [he] had been taught, through the application of formal sanction, that [such] criminal conduct was unacceptable—but had failed or refused to learn his lesson.'" *Id.* The court found that the trial court's

Cont.

dismissal of one of the defendant's two prior strikes was an abuse of discretion even though the strikes were both committed thirteen years prior to his third strike. *Id.* at 431; *see also Carmony*, 92 P.3d at 379 (holding that where prior strikes were ten years old but defendant's most recent conviction was his third failure to register as a sex offender, defendant was "an exemplar of the revolving door career criminal" targeted by the Three Strikes statute).

Romano has similarly failed to learn his lesson after his two 1988 burglaries. Although A
his most recent theft was motivated by a need to obtain medicine for his grandmother, his motives are irrelevant. This third theft proves that he will continue to resort to stealing when he needs to. Accordingly, he is precisely the type of "revolving door criminal" the Three Strikes Law addresses. Moreover, *Williams* demonstrates that when the defendant's third strike is a repeat offense, neither the amount of time that has passed since the prior strikes nor the closeness of time within which they occurred warrants their dismissal. Therefore, the weight the defense gives to the amount of time that has passed since Romano's prior burglaries and the closeness in time between them is misplaced. Because Romano has failed to learn his lesson from his prior theft crimes, C
the dismissal of his prior strike was an abuse of discretion.

B. Romano's criminal history shows he Is unable to refrain from crime.

To counterbalance Romano's continuing inability to stop stealing, the defense T
heavily emphasizes Romano's family life and trade to suggest that he has good prospects for the future. However, neither his family nor his trade has prevented him from continuing to break the law. Because he is unable or unwilling to obey the law, he falls squarely within the spirit of the Three Strikes scheme.

Although no one factor is determinative, courts have repeatedly declined to dis- R
miss a prior strike when a defendant's criminal history reveals a continued propensity to break the law. In *People v. Humphrey*, 68 Cal. Rptr. 2d 269, 270 (Ct. App. 1997), the trial court had dismissed one of the defendant's prior strikes because it had occurred approximately twenty years before the defendant's third strike. The Court of Appeal reversed. *Id.* at 271. The court explained that in exercising its discretion, a court should not "simply consult the Gregorian calendar with blinders on." *Id.* The remoteness of a prior conviction is only relevant if there has been a "crime-free cleansing period of rehabilitation" after the prior strikes. *Id.* Because the defendant had failed to live a "legally blameless life" since his prior strikes, the trial court's reliance on the remoteness of the strike was an abuse of discretion. *Id.*; *see also Williams*, 948 P.2d at 438 (holding that dismissal was improper where the defendant did not refrain from criminal activity since his prior strikes); *People v. Philpot*, 19 Cal. Rptr. 3d 280, 290 (Ct. App. 2004) (affirming denial of dismissal where priors were remote but defendant committed crimes thereafter that revealed "an unwillingness or inability to comply with the law").

Like the defendants in *Humphrey*, *Williams*, and *Philpot*, Romano has failed to live A
a legally blameless life since his prior strikes. Only seven years after his release from prison, Romano was arrested for possessing narcotics. He could have been charged with felony possession but plea bargained his way down to a misdemeanor. Instead of serving jail time, he was sentenced to community service and drug counseling. He completed this sentence only six years prior to his current robbery. Further, he broke

Cont.

the law on two more occasions in 2003 and 2005 when, according to the testimony of his drug counselor, he relapsed and ingested narcotics. These frequent relapses and the intervening possession conviction in 2000 make the date of his prior strikes irrelevant. Romano has shown the same inability to comply with the law as the defendants in *Humphrey*, *Williams,* and *Philpot*. In light of his recidivist history, Romano is not
C worthy of leniency under the Three Strikes Law. This Court should, therefore, reverse the judgment and require the trial court to enter the mandatory life sentence.

C. Romano has been unable to overcome the drug addiction that underlies his criminal record.

T Romano is likely to continue his criminal tendencies because his life of crime has been related to an underlying addiction to meth, which he has been unable to overcome.

R An underlying addiction may be a mitigating circumstance. *See, e.g., People v. Garcia*, 976 P.2d 831, 839 (Cal. 1999) (affirming trial court's determination that the link between drug addiction and the defendant's crimes was a mitigating factor). However, when a defendant shows little hope of overcoming his addiction, his prospects for avoiding crime in the future are dismal and therefore weigh heavily against dismissal of a prior strike. In *Williams*, for example, the court noted that the defendant had suffered from a substance abuse problem since he was nine years old. *Williams*, 948 P.2d at 433. The court concluded that although the defendant expressed a desire to overcome his addiction, "he did not follow through in efforts to bring the situation under control." *Id.* at 433. His inability to control his substance abuse was one of the reasons the court held that "there [was] little favorable about Williams's . . . prospects." *Id.* at 438; *see also Carmony*, 92 P.3d at 372, 378 (finding that trial court properly declined to dismiss a prior strike where it concluded that defendant had "done little to address his substance problems" because although defendant had attended Alcoholics Anonymous meetings, he had never participated in a substance abuse treatment program); *Philpot*, 19 Cal. Rptr. 3d at 290 (finding that the defendant's underlying drug addiction revealed poor prospects for the future); *People v. Gaston*, 87 Cal. Rptr. 2d 829, 838 (Ct. App. 1999) (holding that drug dependency is not mitigating where the defendant has failed to address it).

A Although Romano has sought drug counseling over the years, he remains unable to overcome his addiction. He has had at least three relapses since completing the drug treatment program—one in 2003, one in 2005, and one in connection with his current offense. Moreover, only six percent of those addicted to meth ever succeed in avoiding relapses. If released from prison in fifteen years, he is likely to relapse again. And since his addiction has been connected to all four of his prior crimes—the two burglaries in 1998, the possession offense in 2000, and the current robbery—his continuing addiction is strong evidence that he is likely to commit future crimes if given the chance. While his earnest efforts to overcome his addiction make him more sympathetic than the defendants in the above-cited cases, the bottom line is that he is no less likely to relapse and reoffend than were they. His poor prospects for the future
C bring him squarely within the spirit of the Three Strikes scheme and, therefore, provide another reason to reverse the trial court's dismissal.

Cont.

D. Romano's current offense is far from petty.

In addition to his recidivist tendencies, Romano's willingness to provoke fear and endanger the public in the commission of his crimes also requires the mandatory life sentence. Although Romano did not use violence or explicit threats, his crime carried the potential for violence. T

Courts have been more willing to strike priors where the third strike is a nonviolent crime. *See, e.g., People v. Bishop*, 66 Cal. Rptr. 2d 347, 350 (Ct. App. 1997) (affirming dismissal of a prior strike for purposes of sentencing the defendant for a petty theft). However, if a nonviolent crime carries the potential for violence, the fortuitous ability to accomplish the crime without having to resort to violence carries little weight as a factor supporting dismissal. In *People v. Strong*, 104 Cal. Rptr. 2d 490, 502 (Ct. App. 2001), the appellate court reversed a trial court's dismissal of a prior strike. Although the trial court had looked favorably on the absence of any violence in the defendant's third strike for attempting to sell fake drugs, the court of appeal noted that the defendant had threatened that he was armed and the crime carried the potential for violence if arguments over the sale had ensued. *Id.* at 501-02. The court therefore concluded that *Strong* was not a case in which the circumstances surrounding the felony took the defendant outside the spirit of the statute. *Id.* at 502. R

Similar to the defendant's crime in *Strong*, Romano's robbery carried a potential for violence. Although Romano did not verbalize any threats, he sufficiently intimidated the drug store staff to obtain the two bottles of prescription drugs with which he was caught. Moreover, just as the crime in *Strong* could have escalated into violence if one of the potential buyers discovered the defendant's deceit, Romano's robbery could have escalated into violence if a staff member or customer had decided to take action to prevent his theft. Therefore, the instant case is not the type of felony that falls outside the spirit of the statute. Romano remains a danger to society, and the trial court's decision to strike a prior was an abuse of discretion. A C

CONCLUSION

As explained above, the main factors upon which the defense relies, including Romano's drug addiction, his reason for stealing the medicine, the remoteness of his prior strikes, and the absence of violence in the commission of the current robbery, do not support the trial court's decision. Although Romano can point to the love of his family and his ability to find work, these factors are greatly outweighed by the evidence that Romano is likely to commit future crimes if given the chance. He is exactly the type of revolving door criminal for which the statute was enacted. Accordingly, the Court should reverse the judgment. Balancing of the factors

Although a factor-balancing analysis can be presented in a TRRRAAAC by heading structure, it is not always the best fit. In TRRRAAAC by heading, the reader expects to see each section come to a conclusion. However, in some analyses, not every factor will lead to a conclusion on its own. It may be codependent on another factor or perhaps outweighed by another factor. TRRRAAAC by heading does not highlight such relationships since it separates factors. Section 6.4 discusses an alternative structure that offers an advantage over TRRRAAAC by heading for a factor-balancing analysis in some circumstances.

6.3.5 | Using Separate R and A Headings

Occasionally, you may face a legal issue that requires such an extensive analysis to reach the applicable criteria that you want to separate the rule statement/explanation and application under their own headings. Give yourself permission to bend the format to fit your needs. Here is a sample analysis that has a heading A. for arguments in favor of a particular rule (market share liability) and a heading B. for the application of the proposed rule to the case at hand. The analysis under heading B. is not purely application because it contains some new rule explanations, but put that aside for now and just notice the relationship between the analysis under heading A. and that under heading B.

Sample Analysis Using Separate Headings for Discussion of the Law and Application

The Court should reverse the judgment because Plaintiff can proceed against Defendants under a market share liability theory without identifying which manufacturer produced her dose of GFV 12-A.

Thesis and roadmap

Ms. Bay suffered permanent paralysis of her hands as the result of a vaccine manufactured by Defendants. Although she cannot trace her particular dose to any single Defendant, Defendants collectively comprised 85% of the United States market and 90% of the local market. The judgment against her for failing to prove causation should be reversed for the following reasons. First, the Court should permit persons injured by a drug to recover against any manufacturer of the drug in proportion to its share of the market when identification of the manufacturer that produced the injury-causing dose is impossible due to the manufacturers' mass, generic marketing of a fungible product. Second, this case is appropriate for application of the market share theory of liability because Plaintiff's inability to identify the responsible manufacturer is the result of the GFV 12-A manufacturers' decision to mass market the drug in a generic, fungible form.

Section A. convinces the court to adopt the market share liability theory. It contains only rule statement and rule explanation.

A. The Court should permit persons injured by a drug to recover against any manufacturer of the drug In proportion to its share of the market when identification of the manufacturer that produced the injury-causing dose is impossible due to the manufacturers' mass, generic marketing of a fungible product.

Section 1 provides background law

1. Market share liability is a natural extension of existing tort law that relaxes the identification requirement when identification is impossible due to circumstances outside the plaintiff's control.

Several jurisdictions have permitted plaintiffs to recover damages when they are injured by a pharmaceutical product that cannot be traced to a specific manufacturer

Cont.

due to the fungible nature of the product and the mass, generic marketing employed by the companies that made and distributed the product. *See generally Sindell v. Abbott Labs.*, 607 P.2d 924 (Cal. 1980); *Conley v. Boyle Drug Co.*, 570 So. 2d 275 (Fla. 1991); *Smith v. Cutter Biological, Inc.*, 823 P.2d 717 (Haw. 1991); *Hymowitz v. Eli Lilly & Co.*, 539 N.E.2d 1069 (N.Y. 1989); *Martin v. Abbott Labs.*, 689 P.2d 368 (Wash. 1984); *Collins v. Eli Lilly Co.*, 342 N.W.2d 37 (Wis. 1984). The doctrine they have employed to permit such recovery, "market share liability," is a logical extension of existing tort law.

Although a plaintiff is ordinarily required to prove that the defendant caused her injury, tort law has allowed relaxation of this requirement under certain circumstances. *Sindell*, 607 P.2d at 928. One example of a relaxation of the causation requirement is res ipsa loquitur, a doctrine that permits a plaintiff to recover from multiple wrongdoers when she has been injured by an instrumentality or agency under their exclusive management or control. *Id.*

Under another exception to the causation requirement, "alternative liability," courts have shifted the burden of proof on causation from the plaintiff to the defendants where each defendant has been negligent toward the plaintiff but the plaintiff cannot prove which defendant's negligence caused her harm. *Id.*; Restatement (Second) of Torts § 433B(3) (1965). *Summers v. Tice*, 199 P.2d 1, 4 (Cal. 1948) is the most frequently cited example of alternative liability. In *Summers*, the plaintiff was injured after two hunters fired in his direction. *Id.* at 2. The plaintiff was unable to determine which hunter fired the shot that caused his injuries. *Id.* The court allowed the claim to proceed despite the plaintiff's inability to identify the injury-causing tortfeasor. *Id.* The court placed the burden of proof on the defendants to demonstrate that they did not cause the injury. *Id.* at 4. The court reasoned that this burden shifting was justifiable because the defendants were both negligent toward the plaintiff. *Id.* In addition, it held that the defendants were in a better position to supply the evidence to identify which defendant was actually responsible. *Id.*

Market share liability is a logical extension of res ipsa loquitur and alternative liability. *Sindell*, 607 P.2d at 928-29; *Conley*, 570 So. 2d at 283. In *Sindell*, 607 P.2d at 925, the court found that just as the causation requirement is relaxed under these well-accepted doctrines, it should similarly be relaxed when a plaintiff injured by a drug cannot identify which manufacturer produced the dose(s) that caused her injury due to the fungible nature of the drug and the generic marketing methods employed by the manufacturers. The plaintiff in *Sindell* was injured in utero by diethylstilbestrol (DES) ingested by her mother. *Id.* at 926.[1] The court then held that "[w]here...all defendants produced a drug from an identical formula and the manufacturer of the DES which caused plaintiff's injuries cannot be identified through no fault of plaintiff, a modification of the rule in *Summers* is warranted." *Id.* at 937. Provided that a "substantial share" of the market is joined in the action, *Sindell* shifts the burden of proof to the defendants to prove that they could not have made the substance that injured the plaintiff. *Id.* The jury then apportions liability among defendants according to their market share. *Id.* With some modifications regarding how to apportion liability, several other jurisdictions have adopted the market share theory of liability. *Conley*, 570 So. 2d at 285; *Smith*, 823 P.2d at 729; *Hymowitz*, 539 N.E.2d at 1078; *Martin*, 689 P.2d at 383; *Collins*, 342 N.W.2d at 50-54.

1. Portions of this case example are deleted for efficiency.

Cont.

For the reasons discussed below, this Court should follow the jurisdictions that have embraced market share liability as an important and logical extension of doctrines like res ipsa loquitur and alternative liability that relax the identification requirement when necessary to enable a just result.

Section 2 gives one argument in favor of market share liability to convince the court to adopt the theory and permit Plaintiff to proceed with her lawsuit

2. Market share liability appropriately shifts the cost of injury from the innocent plaintiff to the manufacturers that caused the inability to identify the proper defendant by marketing the drug in a generic, fungible form.

As in the situations that led courts to adopt res ipsa loquitur and alternative liability, it would be unfair to require an innocent plaintiff to bear the cost of injuries caused by a manufacturer's design, production, and distribution of a defective pharmaceutical product. *Sindell*, 607 P.2d at 936. Instead, where the plaintiff is unable to identify the responsible manufacturer through no fault of her own and all manufacturers of the product produced a fungible, generically marketed product according to a uniform formula, the cost of any defect in the product should be borne by the manufacturers in proportion to their share of the relevant market. *See Collins*, 342 N.W.2d at 49 (adopting market share liability because "as between the plaintiff, who is probably not at fault, and the defendants, who may have provided the product which caused the injury, the interests of justice demand that the latter should bear the cost of injury"); *accord Martin*, 689 P.2d at 382. The manufacturers in this situation share culpability both in producing and marketing the defective product and in causing the inability to identify the manufacturer that produced the injury-causing dose(s).[2]

Because leaving the cost of injury on the innocent plaintiff would be unjust, market share liability is an appropriate and necessary modification of common law. Courts have a responsibility to "modernize traditional principles of tort law when such becomes necessary 'to ensure that the law remains both fair and realistic as society and technology change.'" *Conley*, 570 So. 2d at 284 (quoting *Ins. Co. of N. Am. v. Pasakarnis*, 451 So. 2d 447, 451 (Fla. 1984)); *see also Collins*, 342 N.W.2d at 52 n.12 (adopting market share liability because it is the function of the courts to modify existing common law when necessary to promote justice).[3]

Section B applies market share liability to determine the outcome of the case

B. The instant case is appropriate for application of the market share theory of liability.

Ms. Bay's lawsuit is appropriate for application of market share liability. It meets all of the requirements that appear in the case law: (1) Plaintiff is unable to identify the responsible manufacturer through no fault of her own due to the fungible nature of GFV 12-A and the generic marketing employed by Defendants; and (2) Plaintiff has named a substantial share of the market. Moreover, none of the Defendants have attempted to exculpate themselves by proving they did not sell GFV 12-A in the relevant market.

2. Remainder of this rule explanation has been omitted.

3. Remainder of this rule explanation has been omitted. Additional arguments were made in favor of market share liability in additional subsections but are omitted here for the sake of efficiency.

Cont.

1. **Plaintiff's inability to identify the responsible manufacturer is the result of the manufacturers' mass marketing of GFV 12-A in a generic, fungible form.**

The principle requirement of market share liability is that the plaintiff is unable to identify the responsible manufacturer through no fault of her own due to the fungible nature of the product and the generic marketing employed by the manufacturers. *Sindell*, 607 P.2d at 937. One jurisdiction has also required the plaintiff show due diligence prior to asserting an inability to identify the responsible manufacturer. *Conley*, 570 So. 2d at 285. *But see McCormack*, 617 F. Supp. at 1528-29 (rejecting a due diligence requirement as unnecessary due to other incentives for plaintiffs to identify the manufacturer if possible and as unworkable because plaintiffs may often be in no better position than a defendant to discover identification evidence). Plaintiff's lawsuit meets the requirements even with the additional burden of showing due diligence.

Rule explanation to establish the first criterion to be applied in market share liability

First, Plaintiff is unable to identify the responsible manufacturer despite due diligence. Prior to filing her lawsuit, Ms. Bay contacted the medical clinic to determine which manufacturer made the dose that caused her injuries. She looked through her medical records to determine the date of her vaccination. She then met with the Director of the clinic and asked which manufacturer supplied the dose she received in 1998. The Director, however, told her it was "impossible" to answer her question because the clinic had recently discarded all records from 1998.

Application of the first criterion

Second, her inability to identify the responsible manufacturer is through no fault of her own. She was never given any information about which manufacturer made the vaccine she received. The only source of evidence on this would have been the medical clinic, which discarded the pertinent records, or the manufacturers. Although Plaintiff's attempt to identify the responsible manufacturer occurred many years after her illness developed, the delay was not due to any fault on her part. She did not know that her illness was possibly linked to the vaccine until she watched the television exposé. The trial court's denial of Defendants' motion to dismiss on statute of limitations grounds, which has not been challenged by Defendants, deflates any argument that she is at fault in the timing of her investigation.

Third, GFV 12-A is an appropriate product for market share liability. The doctrine is not limited to DES litigation and, indeed, has been applied outside the context of DES litigation to lawsuits involving other fungible, generically marketed products. *See Ray v. Cutter Labs.*, 754 F. Supp. 193, 195-96 (M.D. Fla. 1991) (finding that market share liability is not limited to DES litigation and could be applied to litigation against manufacturers of a blood protein product, Factor VIII, that was used interchangeably without regard to source); *accord Morris v. Parke, Davis & Co.*, 573 F. Supp. 1324, 1328-30 (C.D. Cal. 1983) (denying a motion to strike punitive damages where plaintiff relied on market share liability to sue multiple manufacturers of the diphtheria, pertussis, and tetanus (DPT) vaccine); *Wheeler v. Raybestos-Manhattan*, 11 Cal. Rptr. 2d 109, 111-13 (Ct. App. 1992) (applying market share liability in a lawsuit against manufacturers of brake pads that contained identical amounts of asbestos); *Smith*, 823 P.2d at 723-24. Fungibility can be demonstrated where the drug is produced according to a set formula with no variation in the manufacturing process and is administered without regard to the supplier. *See, e.g., Collins*, 342 N.W.2d at 44 (finding that DES was a "fungible" product because it

Cont.

was produced with a chemically identical formula and pharmacists would fill DES prescriptions from whatever stock they had on hand). Generic marketing has been found where the manufacturers do not label the product with their company name and the product has no individualized aesthetic characteristics to distinguish it by manufacturer. *See, e.g., id.* (finding that DES was "generic" because it did not contain any clearly identifiable shape, color, or markings). Similar to DES, GFV 12-A was produced according to a uniform formula with no variation in the manufacturing process. In addition, manufacturers labeled the product identically and without any brand names or other characteristics that could distinguish one manufacturer's product from the others. Moreover, the Director of Plaintiff's medical clinic told Plaintiff that the clinic received GFV 12-A from multiple suppliers and did not record which company supplied a dose given to a particular patient. There is, therefore, no basis to distinguish GFV 12-A from DES and other products to which market share liability has been applied.

Rule explanation and application for a second criterion

2. Plaintiff has named a substantial share of the market.

The only other possible requirement Plaintiff must meet is California's requirement that a plaintiff join a substantial share of the market. *Sindell*, 607 P.2d at 937. Other jurisdictions have rejected this requirement. *Conley*, 570 So. 2d at 286 (adopting *Martin*); *Martin*, 689 P.2d at 382; *Collins*, 342 N.W.2d at 50. In these jurisdictions, a plaintiff can sue any or all manufacturers. *Martin*, 689 P.2d at 383; *Collins*, 342 N.W.2d at 50. In any event, Defendants have not disputed the allegations in the Complaint that they represent 85% of the national market and 90% of the market in Westmoreland during the relevant time. Although *Sindell* did not clarify what it meant by "substantial share," it suggested that 75-80% would be sufficient. *Sindell*, 607 P.2d at 937.

Rule explanation on a third criterion

3. Defendants marketed GFV 12-A during the relevant time period.

Finally, some courts exculpate defendants that can show they did not market the drug during the relevant market or time period. *Sindell*, 607 P.2d at 936 (providing merely for a shifting of the burden of proof on causation to defendants under market share liability); *Conley*, 570 So. 2d at 286 (adopting *Martin*); *Martin*, 689 P.2d at 382; *Collins*, 342 N.W.2d at 52. *But see Hymowitz*, 539 N.E.2d at 1078 (basing liability on each manufacturer's contribution to the overall risk created to the public by the product and therefore declining to exculpate defendants who can prove they did not cause the particular plaintiff's injury).

Application of third criterion

In this case, Defendants have not attempted to present any such evidence. Therefore, Plaintiff can recover against each Defendant. How the jury will apportion damages among Defendants will depend upon which approach to apportionment the Court adopts. Under *Martin*, 689 P.2d at 383, each Defendant would be liable for an equal share of the damages unless it could prove it had a lower share of the market than the other Defendants. If a Defendant can prove it had a lower share of the market than the other Defendants, its liability would be limited to the percentage of the damages that corresponds to its market share. *Id.* The remaining Defendants' shares of the damages would then be increased to ensure Plaintiff recovers all of her damages. *Id.* Under *Collins*, 342 N.W.2d at 50-54, damages would be apportioned according to each Defendant's contribution to the risk as measured by various factors including safety measures, share of the market, role in developing and marketing the

Cont.

drug, and adequacy of warnings to consumers. Finally, under *Hymowitz*, 539 N.E.2d at 1077-78 and *Brown*, 751 P.2d at 486, each Defendant's liability would be limited to a percentage of the damages that corresponds to its share of the national market.

Because market share liability is a necessary extension of existing exceptions to the causation requirement and Plaintiff's lawsuit meets all of the requirements for application of the doctrine, the judgment should be reversed. Wrap-up conclusion

Notice in the above sample that section B. is devoted to applying market share liability but also includes additional rule explanation paragraphs to set forth the specific criteria that should govern the application of market share liability. In other cases, if the rule that section A. works to establish is a very specific test or set of factors, you might not need additional rule explanation paragraphs and might have a section B. that truly contains only application paragraphs.

6.4 | TRARARAC AND ITS SISTER TRATRATRAC

The TRRRAAAC structure described in sections 6.2 and 6.3 is always a safe choice, but it is not necessarily the best choice for every type of analysis. Another option is to alternate between rule explanation and application (TRARARAC). This chapter will discuss when the TRARARAC structure can be beneficial. It will also introduce the option of combining rule explanation and application into the same paragraph with a thesis sentence to provide paragraph unity: TRA-TRA-TRA-C.

This text uses a three-sequence structure to create the TRAC variations (TRRRAAAC, TRARARAC, etc.). This is just to enable an easy visual to distinguish the variations. As section 6.2 mentions, you might have any number of rule explanations and applications, and the number will not always match. Also, once we start getting into these alternative structures, the R represents rule explanation more than rule statement. In multiple-TRAC structures, the rule statement ends up splintered into the umbrella and mini-umbrellas and even lead ins to rule explanation topic sentences.

6.4.1 | TRARARAC

Review the following sample of the TRARARAC structure. Notice that instead of placing all of the Rs before any of the As (TRRRAAAC), it alternates between paragraphs of rule explanation and paragraphs of application. After the sample, the text will discuss how to select between TRRRAAAC and TRARARAC.

TRARARAC Sample

T The court is unlikely to strike one of Romano's prior convictions because Romano's criminal history falls within the spirit of the Three Strikes scheme.

R1 When the nature and circumstances of a defendant's present felony are identical to his prior felonies, the priors should not be stricken because the defendant has failed to "learn his lesson." *Compare Williams*, 948 P.2d at 438 (affirming the appellate court's finding that where defendant's current conviction for driving under the influence mirrored his prior convictions of the same offense, the trial court's decision to strike the priors was an abuse of discretion), *with People v. Cluff*, 105 Cal. Rptr. 2d 80, 87 (Ct. App. 2001) (stating that the defendant's present felony of failing to update his sex offender registration did not prove recidivist tendencies toward child molestation and, therefore, did not prevent the striking of a prior).

A1 In the instant case, all of Romano's previous thefts were committed while he was high on meth. Now he has once again committed a theft while high. Romano has not "learned his lesson," but instead is continuing both his willingness to steal and the addiction that underlies his criminal activity. He is exactly the type of recidivist the Three Strikes law targets.

R2 Another consideration is the seriousness of the present felony. *Compare People v. Burgos*, 12 Cal. Rptr. 3d 566, 572 (Ct. App. 2004) (finding dismissal of a prior was required where two of the defendant's three strikes—using fear to obtain shoes from one fellow detainee and kicking another—were not "the worst of crimes"), *and In re Saldana*, 67 Cal. Rptr. 2d 183, 185 (Ct. App. 1997) (finding trial court properly dismissed a prior conviction where the most recent felony for possession of heroin was "relatively minor"), *with People v. Myers*, 81 Cal. Rptr. 2d 564, 566 (Ct. App. 1999) (holding that the trial court did not abuse its discretion when it declined to strike priors that involved arson and armed robbery). In general, non-violent crimes are less serious than violent crimes. *Compare People v. Bishop*, 66 Cal. Rptr. 2d 347, 349-50 (Ct. App. 1997) (noting that the defendant's petty theft conviction operated as a mitigating factor), *with People v. McGlothin*, 79 Cal. Rptr. 2d 83, 87 (Ct. App. 1998) (holding that trial court erred in striking a prior when defendant's most recent crime involved a physical attack ontwo elderly individuals). However, the non-violent nature of a felony does not necessarily warrant saving the defendant from a Three Strikes sentence. *See People v. Strong*, 104 Cal. Rptr. 2d 490, 501 (Ct. App. 2001) (stating that the intent of the Three Strikes law is "to ensure longer prison sentences" for defendants who have a qualifying strike and subsequently commit "*any felony,*" whether violent or not). Moreover, a crime that poses a potential for violence should be considered a violent crime even if no violence actually ensued. *See id.* at 501-02 (finding that the defendant's fraudulent sale of fake illicit drugs fell within the spirit of the Three Strikes law because it could have led to violence if arguments with the buyers had ensued).

A2 Here, Romano did not commit any violence in carrying out the robbery and did not have a weapon. At first blush, his current crime may not seem any more serious than the crimes in *Burgos*. However, Romano sufficiently intimidated the drug store staff to obtain the two bottles of prescription drugs he intended to steal. Moreover, just as the crime in *Strong* could have escalated into violence if one of the potential buyers

Cont.

discovered the defendant's deceit, Romano's robbery could have escalated into violence if one of the staff members or a customer had decided to take action to prevent his theft.

In light of the recidivist nature of his drug-induced theft crimes and the risk of C
violence associated with his current crime, Romano remains a danger to society. The court is unlikely to conclude that he is worthy of a lesser sentence.

6.4.1.1 | Limitations on TRARARAC

The TRARARAC structure often works well when the analysis involves separate factors or elements that can be discussed independently of one another. If, however, the issue involves interrelated factors or elements, TRARARAC may fail to capture the relationship between the factors or elements and may result in repetitive application paragraphs. For example, suppose you are analyzing whether the court has the ability to disregard a prior conviction to avoid imposing a required life sentence under the Three Strikes statute. You find that two of the relevant factors are the seriousness of the prior crimes and the seriousness of the most recent crime. You further realize that when you evaluate the seriousness of the defendant's most recent crime, you will be applying the same case law and making many of the same points you plan to make when you evaluate the seriousness of his past crimes. In this scenario, TRRRAAAC would be a better option because you could synthesize the case law in your rule explanation and then apply the law to both the past and recent crimes without any repetition.

TRARARAC also requires that factors or elements are sufficiently straightforward that they can each be explained in one paragraph and applied in another. If some of the factors or elements require multiple rule explanation or application paragraphs, you would end up with an unruly TRRRARARAAAC structure. As each RA sequence becomes longer (e.g., RRRA), the reader becomes less able to change gears to a new factor or element. Headings then become important to separate the factors or elements, leading you back to a TRRRAAAC by heading organization (see section 6.2).

6.4.1.2 | Benefits of TRARARAC

TRARARAC is appealing because it applies a subrule from a rule explanation paragraph while the rule explanation paragraph is still fresh in the reader's mind. TRRRAAAC by heading can offer the same benefit, however, by breaking TRAC sequences into more manageable blocks. The primary benefits of TRARARAC are specific to factor-balancing analyses.

First, TRARARAC allows you to connect factors at the end of a section. In the sample above, the last sentence (the C in TRARARAC) brings both factors together for a powerful end to this section of the analysis: "In light of the recidivist nature of his drug-induced theft crimes and the risk of violence associated with his current crime, Romano remains a danger to society." Separate TRACs with separate headings would have left each supporting factor isolated in its respective section. The punch would be lost.

Second, TRARARAC avoids the conflicting conclusions that TRRRAAAC by heading might cause when factors disagree with one another. For example, suppose that in the Three Strikes sample above, Romano's current crime was *not* similar to the past crimes. If the author had separate TRACs with separate headings for similarity and severity, the section on similarity would conclude in favor of leniency while the section on severity would conclude against leniency. This anomaly could confuse the reader. Moreover, highlighting an adverse point by giving it its own heading is particularly undesirable in persuasive writing. To avoid these problems, the TRARARAC structure would permit the author to immediately connect and weigh the two opposing conclusions, as illustrated next in the bolded sentence.

Illustration of Factor-Balancing Using TRARARAC

When the nature and circumstances of a defendant's present felony are identical to his prior felonies, the priors should not be stricken because the defendant has failed to "learn his lesson..."

In the instant case, Romano's current crime is not similar to his past crimes...

However, another factor against striking a prior is the seriousness of the present felony...

Here, Romano's robbery may not have involved a weapon but was, nonetheless, a serious crime because it posed a potential for violence...

Because Romano's crimes are becoming more dangerous, the lack of similarity between them is hardly a reason for leniency.

6.4.2 | TRATRATRAC

One of the questions posed at the start of this chapter was whether rule explanation and application can ever be combined into one paragraph. This section will present a "yes, but" answer: yes, but you have to make some adjustments. If you want to combine rule explanation and application into one paragraph, the topic sentence should state a thesis about the case at hand. Otherwise, the paragraph will lack cohesion: the topic sentence needs to unite the rule explanation and application in the paragraph. The best fit is a TRA-TRA-TRA-C structure in which each paragraph contains a thesis, a rule explanation, and an application.

ERROR Illustration of Incorrect Paragraph Structure

When the nature and circumstances of a defendant's present felony are identical to his prior felonies, the priors should not be stricken because the defendant has failed to "learn his lesson." *Compare Williams*, 948 P.2d at 438 (affirming the appellate court's finding that where defendant's current conviction for driving under the influence mirrored his prior convictions of the same offense, the trial court's decision to strike the priors was an abuse of discretion), *with People v. Cluff*, 105 Cal. Rptr. 2d 80, 87 (Ct. App. 2001) (stating that the defendant's present felony of failing to update his sex offender registration did not prove recidivist tendencies toward child molestation and therefore, did not prevent the striking of a prior). In the instant case, all of Romano's previous thefts were committed while he was high on meth. Now he has once again committed a theft while high. Romano has not "learned his lesson," but instead is continuing both his willingness to steal and the addiction that underlies his criminal activity. He is exactly the type of recidivist defendant the Three Strikes law targets.

The above illustration lacks a topic sentence to unite the paragraph. The first sentence states a subrule that could serve as a topic sentence for the *Williams* and *Cluff* case examples. However, the later sentences about Romano do not fit under the topic sentence. Compare the revised version below. The first sentence states a thesis about the case at hand. The thesis unifies the rule explanation and application in the paragraph because they both operate as its proof.

Revised Version

The similarities between Romano's prior convictions and his most recent robbery T
weigh heavily against striking one of the priors. When the nature and circumstances of a defendant's present felony are identical to his prior felonies, the priors should not R
be stricken because the defendant has failed to "learn his lesson." *Compare Williams*, 948 P.2d at 438 (affirming the appellate court's finding that where defendant's current conviction for driving under the influence mirrored his prior convictions of the same offense, the trial court's decision to strike the priors was an abuse of discretion), *with People v. Cluff*, 105 Cal. Rptr. 2d 80, 87 (Ct. App. 2001) (stating that the defendant's present felony of failing to update his sex offender registration did not prove recidivist tendencies toward child molestation and therefore, did not prevent the striking of a prior). In the instant case, all of Romano's previous thefts were committed while he was A
high on meth. Now he has once again committed a theft while high. Romano has not "learned his lesson," but instead is continuing both his willingness to steal and the addiction that underlies his criminal activity. He is exactly the type of recidivist defendant the Three Strikes law targets.

When using TRATRATRAC, you need an initial umbrella thesis to state your overall conclusion before the first TRA sequence. The sample below converts our TRARARAC sample to TRATRATRAC.

TRATRATRAC Sample

Umbrella Thesis The court is unlikely to strike one of Romano's prior convictions because Romano's criminal history falls within the spirit of the Three Strikes scheme.

T1 The similarities between Romano's prior convictions and his most recent robbery R1 weigh heavily against striking one of the priors. When the nature and circumstances of a defendant's present felony are identical to his prior felonies, the priors should not be stricken because the defendant has failed to "learn his lesson." *Compare Williams*, 948 P.2d at 438 (affirming the appellate court's finding that where defendant's current conviction for driving under the influence mirrored his prior convictions of the same offense, the trial court's decision to strike the priors was an abuse of discretion), *with People v. Cluff*, 105 Cal. Rptr. 2d 80, 87 (Ct. App. 2001) (stating that the defendant's present felony of failing to update his sex offender registration did not prove recidivist tendencies toward child molestation and, therefore, did not prevent the striking of a A1 prior). In the instant case, all of Romano's previous thefts were committed while he was high on meth. Now he has once again committed a theft while high. Romano has not "learned his lesson," but instead is continuing both his willingness to steal and the addiction that underlies his criminal activity. He is exactly the type of recidivist defendant the Three Strikes law targets.

T2 The seriousness of Romano's most recent robbery also weighs against leniency. R2 *Compare People v. Burgos*, 12 Cal. Rptr. 3d 566, 572 (Ct. App. 2004) (finding dismissal of a prior was required where two of the defendant's three strikes—using fear to obtain shoes from one fellow detainee and kicking another—were not "the worst of crimes"), *and In re Saldana*, 67 Cal. Rptr. 2d 183, 185 (Ct. App. 1997) (finding trial court properly dismissed a prior conviction where the most recent felony for possession of heroin was "relatively minor"), *with People v. Myers*, 81 Cal. Rptr. 2d 564, 566 (Ct. App. 1999) (holding that the trial court did not abuse its discretion when it declined to strike priors that involved arson and armed robbery). In general, non-violent crimes are less serious than violent crimes. *Compare People v. Bishop*, 66 Cal. Rptr. 2d 347, 349-50 (Ct. App. 1997) (noting that the defendant's petty theft conviction operated as a mitigating factor), *with People v. McGlothin*, 79 Cal. Rptr. 2d 83, 87 (Ct. App. 1998) (holding that trial court erred in striking a prior when defendant's most recent crime involved a physical attack on two elderly individuals). However, the absence of violence in the commission of a felony does not necessarily warrant saving the defendant from a Three Strikes sentence. *See People v. Strong*, 104 Cal. Rptr. 2d 490, 501 (Ct. App. 2001) (stating that the intent of the Three Strikes law is "to ensure longer prison sentences" for defendants who have a qualifying strike and subsequently commit "*any felony*," whether violent or not). Moreover, a crime that poses a potential for violence should be considered a violent crime even if no violence actually ensued. *See id.* at 501-02 (finding that the defendant's fraudulent sale of fake illicit drugs fell within the spirit of the Three Strikes A2 law because it could have led to violence if arguments with the buyers had ensued). Here, Romano did not commit any violence in carrying out the robbery and did not have a weapon. At first blush, his current crime may not seem any more serious than the crimes in *Burgos*. However, Romano sufficiently intimidated the drug store staff to obtain the two bottles of prescription drugs he intended to steal. Moreover, just as the crime in *Strong* could have escalated into violence if one of the potential buyers discov-

Cont.

ered the defendant's deceit, Romano's robbery could have escalated into violence if one of the staff members or a customer had decided to take action to prevent his theft.

In light of the recidivist nature of his drug-induced theft crimes and the risk of C
violence associated with his current crime, Romano remains a danger to society. The court is unlikely to conclude that he is worthy of a lesser sentence.

6.4.3 | Choosing Between TRARARAC and TRATRATRAC

Selection between TRARARAC and TRATRATRAC is mostly a matter of choice. One consideration is the length of the resulting paragraphs: TRARARAC avoids overly long paragraphs, and TRATRATRAC avoids overly short paragraphs. Consider the complexity of each point you plan to include. If each point is fairly straightforward, TRATRATRAC may be the right choice. If the paragraphs end up too long, however, switch to TRARARAC. You can also alternate between the two structures as discussed in section 6.7.

6.4.4 | Transferring Your Skills to TRARARAC and TRATRATRAC

Notice from the samples in sections 6.4.1 and 6.4.3 that none of the lessons regarding how to build effective rule statements, rule explanations, and applications have changed. The R sections in the above samples still use topic sentences that pull and synthesize lessons from the cases. The subrule topic sentences and transitions you learned about in the TRRRAAAC structure are still there. So too are the four tools of effective application paragraphs. TRARARAC and TRATRATRAC merely change the order of tasks, not their nature.

6.5 | ADDING NARRATIVES

6.5.1 | Narratives in General

TRAC, in any of its forms, can be robotic, even boring.[1] To make your writing more engaging, you can use some of the facts of your case to introduce and set the stage for your arguments. I will refer to these factual introductions as narratives.[2] Narratives are especially helpful in persuasive writing because they can help judges see the legal issue from your client's point of view. Umbrella and thesis paragraphs are well suited for the addition of narratives.

---

1. Kenneth D. Chestek, *The Plot Thickens: The Appellate Brief as Story*, 14 Leg. Writing 127 (2008).
2. I am using the term "narrative" very narrowly to refer to factual details regarding the client's case. In many respects, the entire analysis is a narrative—a story about the law's development and its application to your case.

Two cautions in using narratives. First, be wary of repeating the same facts in your application paragraphs. Second, keep the narratives brief to avoid reader impatience to get to the legal analysis of the issue.

Below is a sample that adds a narrative to a thesis sentence. This would be the first paragraph of the analysis. The original thesis is bolded.

Sample Addition of Narratives to a Thesis

Defendant Romano has committed three serious theft crimes. He broke into an elderly woman's home and an electronics store, and, most recently, he intimidated a pharmacy clerk into giving him prescription drugs. He has shown no regard for the property rights of his victims and very little regard for their physical and emotional well-being. Despite jail time and compulsory counseling for his drug addiction, Romano has continued both his drug habit and the life of crime it has led him to embrace. **The trial court's decision to strike one of Romano's prior convictions was an abuse of discretion because Romano's criminal history falls within the spirit of the Three Strikes scheme.**

6.5.2 | Narratives in the TRATRATRAC Structure

Narratives can also be added at the start of each TRA sequence in the TRATRATRAC structure introduced in section 6.4.2. Below is the TRATRATRAC sample from section 6.4.2 with narratives added in the first thesis paragraph and at the start of each TRA sequence.

Sample Narrative TRAC

Added narrative

Defendant Romano has committed three serious theft crimes. He broke into an elderly woman's home and an electronics store and, most recently, he intimidated a pharmacy clerk into giving him prescription drugs. He has shown no regard for the property rights of his victims and very little regard for their physical and emotional well-being. Despite jail time and compulsory counseling for his drug addiction, Romano has continued both his drug habit and the life of crime it has led him to embrace.

Umbrella thesis

The trial court's decision to strike one of Romano's prior convictions was an abuse of discretion because Romano's criminal history falls within the spirit of the Three Strikes scheme.

T1

Romano's repeat offenses do not deserve leniency.

Added narrative

Romano's prior and current crimes share the same fact pattern: he needs money, he gets high, and then he invades a home or business to steal. In his most recent crime, Romano needed medicine he claimed he could not afford. So, he intentionally became high to give himself the "guts"

Cont.

he said he needed to invade the pharmacy during business hours and demand the medicine. Similarities between multiple felonies reveal that the defendant has failed R1
to "learn his lesson" and therefore should not be spared the Three Strikes sentence. *Compare Williams*, 948 P.2d at 438 (affirming the appellate court's finding that where defendant's current conviction for driving under the influence mirrored his prior convictions of the same offense, the trial court's decision to strike the priors was an abuse of discretion), *with People v. Cluff*, 105 Cal. Rptr. 2d 80, 87 (Ct. App. 2001) (stating that the defendant's present felony of failing to update his sex offender registration did not prove recidivist tendencies toward child molestation and, therefore, did not prevent the striking of a prior). Romano has not "learned his lesson," but instead is continuing A1
both his willingness to steal and the addiction that underlies his criminal activity. He is exactly the type of recidivist the Three Strikes law targets.

The severity of Romano's crimes also weighs heavily against leniency. Although he T2
has yet to harm an occupant, his willingness to invade and intimidate show little regard Added narrative
for the safety of his victims. The pharmacy clerk on duty during Romano's most recent theft suffered nightmares as a result of the incident and was too fearful to return to his job. The severity of a defendant's prior and current felonies should play a large role in a court's decision to strike a prior felony. *Compare People v. Burgos*, 12 Cal. Rptr. 3d R2
566, 572 (Ct. App. 2004) (finding dismissal of a prior was required where two of the defendant's three strikes—using fear to obtain shoes from one fellow detainee and kicking another—were not "the worst of crimes"), *and In re Saldana*, 67 Cal. Rptr. 2d 183, 185 (Ct. App. 1997) (finding trial court properly dismissed a prior conviction where the most recent felony for possession of heroin was "relatively minor"), *with People v. Myers*, 81 Cal. Rptr. 2d 564, 566 (Ct. App. 1999) (holding that the trial court did not abuse its discretion when it declined to strike priors that involved arson and armed robbery). In general, non-violent crimes are less serious than violent crimes. *Compare People v. Bishop*, 66 Cal. Rptr. 2d 347, 349-50 (Ct. App. 1997) (noting that the defendant's petty theft conviction operated as a mitigating factor), *with People v. MGlothin*, 79 Cal. Rptr. 2d 83, 87 (Ct. App. 1998) (holding that trial court erred in striking a prior when defendant's most recent crime involved a physical attack on two elderly individuals). However, a crime that poses a potential for violence should be considered a violent crime even if no violence actually ensued. *See People v. Strong*, 104 Cal. Rptr. 2d 490, 501 (Ct. App. 2001) (finding that the defendant's fraudulent sale of fake illicit drugs fell within the spirit of the Three Strikes law because it could have led to violence if arguments with the buyers had ensued). At first blush, Romano's thefts may not seem any A2
more serious than the crimes in *Burgos*. However, in his most recent crime, Romano sufficiently intimidated the drug store staff to obtain the two bottles of prescription drugs he intended to steal. He was convicted of robbery, a crime that requires at least a threat of force. Moreover, just as the crime in *Strong* could have escalated into violence if one of the potential buyers discovered the defendant's deceit, Romano's robbery could have escalated into violence if one of the staff members or a customer had decided to take action to prevent his theft.

In light of the recidivist nature of his drug-induced theft crimes and the risk of C
violence associated with his current crime, Romano remains a danger to society. The court is unlikely to conclude that he is worthy of a lesser sentence.

6.5.3 | Using Narratives in Other Structures

Use of factual narratives in other structures is more limited. TRRRAAAC and TRARARAC do not have a natural home for these narratives apart from umbrella and thesis paragraphs. They do not fit in the rule explanation paragraphs, which are devoted to discussion of the law (see discussion of paragraph unity in section 6.4). And putting them in the application paragraphs would defeat the purpose of the narratives because they would no longer serve as an introduction to your point. They would simply become part of the application. An illustration of the problem follows with the added narrative bolded.

ERROR Illustration of Misplaced Narrative

This rule explanation paragraph adds a narrative at the beginning and loses paragraph cohesion as a result. The narrative is not connected to the point of law. The narrative could be moved into the application paragraph that follows but then it would just become part of the application.

Romano's prior and current crimes share the same fact pattern: he needs money, he gets high, and then he invades a home or business to steal. In his most recent crime, Romano needed medicine he claimed he could not afford. So, he intentionally became high to give himself the "guts" he said he needed to invade the pharmacy during business hours and demand the medicine. When the nature and circumstances of a defendant's present felony are identical to his prior felonies, the priors should not be stricken because the defendant has failed to "learn his lesson." *Compare Williams*, 948 P.2d at 438 (affirming the appellate court's finding that where defendant's current conviction for driving under the influence mirrored his prior convictions of the same offense, the trial court's decision to strike the priors was an abuse of discretion), *with People v. Cluff*, 105 Cal. Rptr. 2d 80, 87 (Ct. App. 2001) (stating that the defendant's present felony of failing to update his sex offender registration did not prove recidivist tendencies toward child molestation and therefore, did not prevent the striking of a prior).

Moving the narrative into the A paragraph here would turn the narrative into part of an ordinary application paragraph. It would not serve its purpose of providing a punchy introduction to your point.

In the instant case, all of Romano's previous thefts were committed while he was high on meth. Now he has once again committed a theft while high. Romano has not "learned his lesson," but instead is continuing both his willingness to steal and the addiction that underlies his criminal activity. He is exactly the type of recidivist the Three Strikes law targets.

6.6 | THE ONE-SENTENCE TRAC

Sometimes an analysis calls for a point so specific and incontrovertible that the entire TRAC sequence on the point can be accomplished in a sentence. This sort of sentence is like a power serve in tennis. It hits so hard and so fast that a rally is impossible. The one-sentence TRAC consists of an assertion about the legal impact of a fact of the case at hand followed by a parenthetical citation that proves the asserted impact.

Sample One-Sentence TRAC

Because only three women at the police department have ever completed the required exam, Plaintiffs cannot use a statistical analysis to prove the exam had a disparate impact on women. *See Mayor of Philadelphia v. Educ. Equal. League*, 415 U.S. 605, 621 (1974) (sample size of thirteen was too small to permit a disparate impact claim); *Morita v. S. Cal. Permanente Med. Grp.*, 541 F.2d 217, 220 (9th Cir. 1976) ("'statistical evidence derived from an extremely small universe...has little predictive value and must be disregarded'").

A one-sentence TRAC is appropriate only when neither the facts nor the point of law require explanation or proof. In the sample above, the record presumably established that only three women took the exam; therefore, there were no facts to dispute or explain. Moreover, the parentheticals are sufficiently specific and targeted to prove the assertion without further explanation. If, for example, the two cited cases had included any limitations or caveats on their pronouncements regarding the impact of a small sample size, then a one-sentence TRAC would not have worked. The nuances would have required a full case explanation and a more elaborate application of the point of law to the facts of the case at hand.

One-sentence TRACs are particularly useful in persuasive writing where, as Part III will explain, you do not want to draw undue attention to your adversary's points. If you can find a sufficiently specific and targeted point with which to take down one of your adversary's arguments, a one-sentence TRAC can be the perfect tool. Again, however, the one-sentence TRAC must be fool-proof. Any limitations or caveats will greatly weaken its effectiveness and may damage your credibility with the court.

6.7 | INTEGRATING STRUCTURES FOR A SOPHISTICATED ORGANIZATION

Armed with some reasonable modifications of TRAC, you can liberate yourself from the traditional TRRRAAAC structure. You can combine the techniques discussed throughout this chapter to escape the monotony of a universal structure and to strengthen strategic effect. An easy way to diversify your organizational structure is to choose your organizational structure by heading. For example, under one heading you can use TRRRAAAC and under another TRARA-

RAC. Narratives and one-sentence TRACs can then be worked in wherever they fit. The sample below incorporates TRRRAAAC, TRATRATRAC, narratives, and one-sentence TRACs.

When you read the sample, notice that despite the variety in its structure, some basic rules are not compromised. Discrete subissues are still divided by headings. Each paragraph is still devoted to a single point, which is stated in the topic sentence of the paragraph. Transitions are still used at the start of each paragraph to link the topic of the new paragraph to its predecessor. And, with the exception of the one-sentence TRAC, the author always states a point or detail from a precedent case before applying it to the facts of the case at hand.

Notice also that the sample matches the strategies identified in sections 6.1 to 6.6 regarding when to use the various techniques. The narrative is added only when the facts help build sympathy for the legal argument. The one-sentence TRAC is used for a very specific point that does not require elaboration either with the details of the cited precedent or with the facts of the case at hand. TRRRAAAC is used in section B. because that section addresses a more complex legal issue that requires a lengthier and well-synthesized discussion of the law. By contrast, TRARARAC is used in section C. because each point is fairly straightforward and is sufficiently independent that it can be applied without repetition.

Integrated Sample

Umbrella The lawsuit against Defendant for expressing his opinions as the leader of his neighborhood association should be dismissed. Defendant's speech was protected by the First Amendment for three reasons. First, it was quintessential political speech that should be afforded the highest level of protection. Second, Plaintiffs' contention that his speech was not protected because he was acting as a city official is contrary to the established right of public officials to engage in public debate. Third, the trial court's conclusion that the commercial speech doctrine permits this lawsuit was erroneous.

A. The First Amendment protected Defendant's right to freely express his opinions on how to improve the neighborhood, even if his opinions were discriminatory.

Narrative At a neighborhood association meeting in the midst of a discussion about the causes and cures for crime in the neighborhood, Defendant blurted out an ignorant opinion that blacks were to blame. No doubt his opinion was hurtful to minorities in attendance. He also advocated some solutions that the Plaintiffs claim were discriminatory. It is not clear whether his proposed solutions were truly discriminatory, but we
T will assume for the purposes of this brief that they were. Nonetheless, Plaintiffs' theory of the case strikes at the heart of the First Amendment. Defendant's efforts to persuade other members of his neighborhood association to follow his ideas for improving the neighborhood were protected by the First Amendment. The First Amendment does not discriminate between good and bad ideas. All are protected.

Cont.

Defendant's opinions on crime and safety in his neighborhood, matters of public concern offered in the course of a public debate, must be afforded the highest level of protection. *See NAACP v. Claiborne Hardware Co.*, 458 U.S. 886, 913 (1982) (stating that "expression on public issues 'has always rested on the highest rung of the hierarchy of First Amendment values' because 'debate on public issues should be uninhibited, robust, and wide-open'"); *Mich. Prot. & Advocacy Serv., Inc.*, 799 F. Supp. 695, 719 (E.D. Mich. 1992) (holding that neighbors' protests against a planned group home were the "purest form of protected First Amendment activity"). One-sentence TRAC (R1 and A1 combined)

Moreover, the First Amendment protects both desirable and undesirable speech. *See Virginia v. Black*, 538 U.S. 343, 365-67 (2003) (holding that a cross-burning statute was unconstitutional because its presumption that cross-burning is intended to intimidate and therefore is unlawful created too great a risk of suppressing political expression); *FCC v. Pacifica Found.*, 438 U.S. 726, 745-46 (1978) ("[I]f it is the speaker's opinion that gives offense, that consequence is a reason for according it constitutional protection" because "it is a central tenet of the First Amendment that the government must remain neutral in the marketplace of ideas"); *Brandenberg v. Ohio*, 395 U.S. 444, 448 (1969) (striking down a statute that prohibited advocating crime and violence). R2

Therefore, even assuming section 1983 and the federal and state housing laws could be construed to ban the expression of discriminatory opinions, the First Amendment would not countenance such content-based regulation of speech. *See White v. Lee*, 227 F.3d 1214 (9th Cir. 2000). In *White*, the plaintiffs had distributed written materials in opposition to the proposed use of property in their neighborhood as a multifamily housing unit. *Id.* at 1220. The Department of Housing and Urban Development (HUD) believed the plaintiffs were opposed to multifamily housing because it would attract mentally disabled residents and substance abusers, a purpose that HUD concluded was discriminatory. *Id.* HUD subjected the plaintiffs to an investigation for violation of the Fair Housing Act and ordered them to cease distribution of "discriminatory" flyers and newsletters. *Id.* The plaintiffs sued HUD officials, arguing that HUD had violated their First Amendment rights. *Id.* This court agreed. *Id.* It found that the plaintiffs' flyers and newsletters were "the advocacy of a politically controversial viewpoint—'the essence of First Amendment protection.'" *Id.* at 1226. More specifically, "The right to expressive association includes the right to pursue, as a group, discriminatory policies that are antithetical to the concept of equality for all persons." *Id.* at 1227. The First Amendment even protects the advocacy of an unlawful act as long as it is not "directed to inciting or producing imminent lawless action and is likely to incite or produce such action." *Id.* (quoting *Brandenberg*, 395 U.S. at 447). The court thus concluded that "a speaker's advocacy of his views, however 'ill-advised, uninformed, and even distasteful,'" can amount to a violation of the Fair Housing Act only if the *Brandenberg* standard is met. *Id.* at 1230. R3

Under the above precedent, the Defendant was free to participate in his neighborhood association, to express his views at the meetings, and to advocate for his desired policies in the newsletters he prepared as chair of the association. He cannot now be punished under the Fair Housing Act or any other law for such political speech merely because his views were offensive or discriminatory. A2 and A3 C

Cont.

B. Defendant did not lose his First Amendment right merely because the city was involved in the neighborhood association. Government officials have a First Amendment right to debate public policy.

T The trial court's ruling that Defendant had no First Amendment right because he was a government agent was erroneous.

R1 The right of government officials to express their opinions on matters of public importance is fundamental and has been accorded the highest level of First Amendment protection. *See Bond v. Floyd*, 385 U.S. 116, 132-33 (1966). In *Bond*, the Court rejected an argument by the Georgia House of Representatives that an individual's right to dissent as a private citizen is limited by his decision to seek membership in the state legislature. *Id.* The plaintiff had been refused membership because he made comments deemed to be disloyal to the United States. *Id.* In finding that the plaintiff's free speech right had been violated, the Court reasoned, "The manifest function of the First Amendment... requires that legislators be given the widest latitude to express their views on issues of policy." *Id.* at 135-36. The Court's conclusion in *Bond* applies to both appointed and elected officials. *See Stella v. Kelley*, 63 F.3d 71, 76 (1st Cir. 1995) (holding that the distinction between elected and appointed officials "is a distinction without a difference" and rejecting an argument that "the First Amendment right...applies less broadly to appointed officials as contrasted with elected officials"); *Schroeder v. Irvine City Council*, 118 Cal. Rptr. 2d 330, 337 n.3 (Ct. App. 2002) (rejecting an argument that city council members do not have rights of speech or petition under the First Amendment). It also extends to the efforts of government agents to espouse and lobby their viewpoints. *See Fischer Sand & Aggregate Co. v. City of Lakeville*, 874 F. Supp. 957, 958-59 (D. Minn. 1994) (holding that city officials could not be sued for exercising their First Amendment right to oppose the plaintiff's mine in rezoning and permit proceedings); *Chambers Dev. Co.*, 617 F. Supp. 820, 823 (W.D. Pa. 1985) (holding that a city councilman's efforts to persuade his colleagues were protected); *Nadel v. Regents of the Univ. of Cal.*, 34 Cal. Rptr. 2d 188, 197 (Ct. App. 1994) (stating that a government employee "should not be treated as having relinquished the protection of the First Amendment by virtue of government employment").

R2 That government agents retain their First Amendment rights is also clear from case law that restricts the government's ability, as an employer, to punish its employees for speaking on matters of public concern. *See Pickering v. Bd. of Educ.*, 391 U.S. 563, 568 (1968) (finding that the idea that a public employee relinquishes the First Amendment right to comment on matters of public interest "has been unequivocally rejected").

A Defendant's alleged comments at the neighborhood association meeting were an expression of opinion in the course of debating how to improve the neighborhood. Defendant did not command, "You must stop renting to blacks." Rather, he argued, "If we don't rent to blacks, we don't have the problem." (1 R. at 99.) He was attempting to convince the other members of the association of his opinion, and his words are not reasonably susceptible to any other interpretation. Defendant's mailings espousing the policies that plaintiffs claim were discriminatory (1 R. at 4-6) were similarly persuasive in nature. For example, he writes, "If you have any kids under 18, you should tell them about the curfew...There are kids that are not in school, and the parents don't seem to care. We must correct this problem for the kids [*sic*] sake." (1 R. at 110.) Similarly,

Cont.

in other instances, he used words that suggest argumentation and persuasion rather
than a directive, including "propose" (1 R. at 115), "desire" (*id.*), and "recommend" (1 R.
at 120). As held in the above precedent, Defendant did not lose his right to advocate for C
solutions to the crime and sanitation issues facing his neighborhood merely because
he held a leadership role in the association.

C. Defendant's speech cannot be regulated as commercial speech because his comments were not connected to a commercial transaction.

The trial court's alternative ruling that Defendant's speech was properly regulated Umbrella thesis
as commercial was also erroneous. The trial court found Defendant's speech was com-
mercial because he "made the[]statements as the owner of investment or income- Narrative
producing properties to other such owners in a meeting of an association that was
founded to advance the owners' interests as owners." (2 ER at 300.) An economic One-sentence TRAC (R1 and A1 combined)
motive, however, is "clearly insufficient" to establish speech as commercial. *Bolger v.
Youngs Drug Prods. Corp.*, 463 U.S. 60, 67 (1983).

Defendant's speech does not fall within the core definition of commercial speech. T2
To fall within the core definition, the speech must have the sole purpose of proposing
a transaction. *Id.* at 66-67. Defendant's speech was not made to prospective tenants R2
but, rather, was made to other landlords with whom he had no interest in transacting. A2
Further, neither Defendant's comments at the October 1998 meeting nor the mailings
related to a specific commercial transaction. Instead, the comments and mailings were
made in the course of a debate on how to improve the neighborhood. They do not,
therefore, fit within the core definition of commercial speech.

Nor do any other factors bring his speech within the commercial speech doctrine. T3
Where speech does not fit the core definition of commercial speech, economic mo-
tivation *together with other factors*, including whether the speech is in the form of an R3
advertisement and whether it references a specific product, can nonetheless charac-
terize it as commercial. *Id.* at 66-67. However, neither of these other factors applies to A3
Defendant's speech. Defendant was not advertising his property and did not make any
representations about it. There is, therefore, no support for the trial court's conclusion
that his right to free speech was diminished because his speech was commercial.

The trial court's reliance on *Harris v. Itzhaki*, 183 F.3d 1043 (9th Cir. 1999) (1 ER T4
at 188), was misplaced. True, *Harris* did allow a Fair Housing Act claim based on the
comments of a property manager. 183 F.3d at 1054. However, the Defendants in R4
Harris did not raise a First Amendment privilege. Their speech was clearly commercial.
In *Harris*, the property manager's statement that the apartment owners "don't want to rent to blacks" was made in the context of a conversation between the manager and the groundskeeper regarding a particular vacancy in the building. *Id.* at 1048. *Harris* does not, therefore, contradict the conclusions of other courts that the Fair Housing Act cannot reach noncommercial political speech. *See United States v. Bob Lawrence Realty, Inc.*, 474 F.2d 115, 122 (5th Cir. 1973) (noting that section 3604(c) does not prohibit noncommercial speech and if it did reach "a non-commercial statement, a political statement, or a purely informational statement, it would naturally be subject to First Amendment attack"); *United States v. Hunter*, 459 F.2d 205, 211 (4th Cir. 1972) (upholding the district court's conclusion that section 3604(c) applies only to com-

Cont.

ments made "in a commercial context and not...to the dissemination of ideas"); *Mich. Prot. & Advocacy Serv.*, 799 F. Supp. at 722 (holding that section 3604(c) of the Fair Housing Act does not prohibit property owners in a community from organizing to oppose establishment of a group home even if their opposition is motivated by discriminatory
A4 animus). Because Defendant's comments were not made in connection with a particular vacancy, *Harris* is inapplicable.

T5 Instead, Defendant's participation in his neighborhood community association was a quintessentially political activity that is deeply rooted in American history. *See* Paul
R5 Rich, *American Voluntarism, Social Capital, and Political Culture*, 565 Annals Am. Acad. Pol. & Soc. Sci. 15, 16 (1999) (discussing the role of volunteer associations in American democracy). Community organizers like Defendant must be free to exchange their ideas with one another without government censorship. *See id.* ("[V]oluntary associations provide[] a source of new opinions independent of the state and a means of
A5 communicating these new suggestions to a large section of the citizenry."). Defendant lawfully exercised his First Amendment right to express his thoughts on how to improve the neighborhood and cannot now be sued merely because his opinions were offensive or unpopular.

One-sentence TRAC The manner in which Plaintiffs seek to invoke the Fair Housing Act directly violates the bedrock principle that all citizens have a right to engage in public debate on po-
Conclusion litical questions. *See Bond*, 385 U.S. at 135-36 (government agents must be given the "widest latitude" to express their views). The trial court's order should be reversed.

Checklist on Organizational Structure

☐ Step 1: Decide whether you will subdivide.
- If your analysis is under 5 pages, you probably do not need to subdivide into headings.
- From 5-10 pages could probably go either way.
- Over 10 pages, subdivide if possible.

If you are subdividing

☐ Step 2: Determine your divisions and draft your umbrella paragraph(s).
- Keep dependent subrules together in a section (section 6.3.4 helps determine whether subrules are separable or dependent).
- Include an initial main umbrella to introduce your first tier of headings (e.g., A., B., and C.). Include secondary umbrellas to introduce each lower tier of headings (e.g., to introduce subsections 1. and 2. under heading A.).
- Initial main umbrellas include your overall thesis, a rule statement, and a preview of your first-tier headings.
- Secondary umbrellas include a thesis for the section, possibly a rule statement, and a preview of your second-tier headings.

☐ Step 3: For each section, determine which structure you will choose (TRRRAAAC, TRARARAC, or TRATRATRAC).
- If the section will address subrules that are separable, you can choose between TRRRAAAC and TRARARAC/TRATRATRAC (section 6.3.4 helps determine whether subrules are separable or dependent).

Cont.

- If the section will address subrules that are dependent, use TRRRAAAC.
- If the section will address law that is evolving or complex, TRRRAAAC may be the best choice.
- If your analysis involves balancing factors, TRARARAC or TRATRATRAC may be the best choice, particularly if the factors conflict.
- If choosing between TRARARAC and TRATRATRAC, consider paragraph length. TRATRATRAC can sometimes lead to overly long paragraphs, and TRARARAC can sometimes lead to overly short paragraphs. Your choice should therefore depend on the complexity of your rule explanations.

☐ Step 4: Start drafting.

- If you are subdividing, ensure that each section fits under its heading (e.g., you should not be analyzing objective reasonableness under a subjective belief heading).
- Look for opportunities to incorporate narratives (especially if writing a brief for the court).
- Remember the one-sentence TRAC option if you have a nondebatable issue you need to quickly dispose of.
- If you are using TRRRAAAC by heading, your conclusion section should discuss how your various conclusions on each factor or element fit together (e.g., it should weigh any conflicting factors).
- If you are using TRATRATRAC, remember to keep each TRA sequence together in a paragraph to avoid paragraph cohesion problems.

CHAPTER 6 SELF-TEST

1. What is the key characteristic of the TRRRAAAC structure?
2. When using TRRRAAAC by heading, does each section (i.e., each heading) have its own TRRRAAAC sequence?
3. What does an umbrella paragraph include?
4. Will you have only one umbrella paragraph or multiple umbrellas?
5. Where does/do the umbrella(s) go?
6. What is the best type of analysis to use TRARARAC for?
7. What is the difference between TRARARAC and TRATRATRAC?
8. What is the main qualifier in deciding between TRARARAC and TRATRATRAC?
9. To what part of TRAC are narratives usually tied?
10. Can you use TRRRAAAC under one heading and TRARARAC under another?

See answers on page 338.

CHAPTER 7

The Pre-Writing Process

You cannot implement the lessons of this textbook without using a layered, effective writing process that includes extensive prewriting work and disciplined self-editing after the first draft. Your legal writing audience — judges, supervising attorneys, and clients—will have little patience for disorganized writing. You must present your material in a logical, easy-to-follow structure, or it may not be read.

Banging out a first draft without careful planning is a mistake. You might tell yourself that you will go back and reorganize later. But the reality is that a finished first draft is likely to inhibit your ability to consider a completely different and perhaps better organization. You may end up merely moving phrases and paragraphs around without stepping back and laying out the structure in a coherent manner. The result may be even worse than the first draft. Prewriting planning is thus absolutely essential to producing an effective written product.

7.1 | TIME MANAGEMENT

The first step in the process of writing should begin before you even pick up the case file. You need to plan to write. For example, sit down with your calendar and your writing course's syllabus. Have all of your syllabi for your other courses handy too. Put all of the key dates into your calendar—assignment due dates, midterms, final exams, review sessions. Next, enter important personal events that you know are going to require some time away from your studies—your cousin's wedding, Thanksgiving Day, March Madness, your significant other's birthday. Finally, start setting weekly goals for yourself. When do you think you should have finished searching for cases? When do you think you should have finished reading the cases? When do you think you should have an outline finished? Break the draft into pieces, each with its own self-imposed deadline. Keep in mind those other calendared events. If you know you will be irresistibly drawn to the television during March Madness, move up those self-imposed deadlines to free up some time to enjoy the games.

Self-imposed deadlines will help keep you on track. First, the process of creating them will show you how tight the schedule is and may give you the insight that falling behind on one piece will sacrifice your ability to meet later deadlines. Second, if you do fall behind, hopefully you will have the discipline to reconfigure the later deadlines so that you can appreciate the accelerated time schedule necessary to meet the due date of the final paper. Third, the process may lead you to reassess your priorities early on. Maybe you have to reduce your work hours, cancel a trip, or rely more on sports recap shows rather than watching March Madness live. Better to figure this out sooner rather than later.

If you cannot force yourself to create a comprehensive calendar, at least consider creating tiered weekly to-do lists. Sit down on Sunday night and think about every major task you have for the week both in law school and out. Prioritize them in the order you think you need to follow. Include the same self-imposed deadlines discussed above.

These time management skills can help you in law school. In your professional career as a lawyer, they will become ten times as important. Imagine yourself handling several cases at once, responding to constant e-mails and calls from clients and other attorneys, making court appearances, attending important networking events, coordinating with fellow members of professional associations, accommodating your children's important school events, and trying to remain knowledgeable about your field as case law continues to evolve. No one can keep so many balls in the air without devoting some time to organizing his or her days. You might as well start developing the skill now while you are in law school.

7.2 | ORGANIZING DURING RESEARCH

The extent of organization required during a research project is proportional to its complexity. If you are writing on a legal issue that has only four on-point cases, preparing case analysis sheets may be sufficient. If, however, you are facing a more typical research project that requires you to sift through a more daunting number of cases, you will likely need a more detailed organizational process.

7.2.1 | Rule Chart

The rule chart described in Chapter 2 is a highly effective method of organizing your research. It forces you to extract the important rules from the cases you read and, significantly, to think about how the rules relate to one another. As you encounter a new rule that is not on your chart, the rule chart encourages you to think about where it fits in. Is it broader or more specific? Does it limit another rule on your chart or further define it? Is it another factor that relates back to some more general test? The rule chart also gets you to record the key facts from each case and to think about the possible arguments the case may support on behalf of or against your client.

If you really do not like the rule chart method, then find another way to record the same information and undergo the same thought process. Here are some possible methods you could use.

7.2.2 | Organized Case Notes

Develop organized notes on the cases you read. For each case, include the case name and the important rules and statements you glean from the case. State the basic fact pattern and, if applicable, some special facts that you think either help analogize the case to yours or distinguish it. When you have gone through a good chunk of cases (maybe 10 to 15), start organizing the notes.

You could use a highlighting system. If, for example, your issue involves the consideration of three main factors, you could use a different color for each factor. When highlighting, keep in mind that any given case might have rules or statements important to more than one factor. You would need different color highlighting within the same case note for the different aspects of the case.

Instead of highlighting, you could also cut and paste your case notes to organize by topic. For example, you could create a heading for each factor and then copy all of the case notes that address a particular factor and paste them under the applicable heading. Keep in mind that just as you might need two or more colors of highlighting for a particular case when using the previous method, you might also need to paste a case note under more than one heading when using this alternative method.

When organizing case notes, you might also want to write in the margin whether the case is helpful to the defendant or the plaintiff/prosecution.

7.2.3 | Case Folders

A less effective but better-than-nothing approach is to record the same information on the front page of case printouts and then organize the cases into folders. You can use hard copies or electronic copies. Online legal research programs allow you to create folders and subfolders and to add notes at the top of any case you save into a folder. If using hard copies, remember that some cases may be relevant to more than one factor and therefore belong in more than one folder. You could make a copy of the case for the other folder(s) or place a note in the other folder(s) to remind yourself to look at the case again on the other factors.

7.2.4 | Genius Notes

In addition to using one (or more) of the above note-taking methods to organize your cases, you should also develop a system for keeping track of your research process. For example, you will often be reading a case and some stroke of genius occurs to you — a new idea, a new argument, a new question. Record these immediately. Do not wait. You could keep these insights as a list on a separate document. You could write them in the margins of the cases that triggered them or in your case notes document or rule chart. My notes typically contain messages to myself like, "Read *Smith v. Jones* on the relevance of prior convictions" or "Does it matter that our client was in jail for three years? *Bogart v. Lewis* suggests it might. Need to follow up."

In summary, whichever methods you use, be sure to take the time to record key rules and statements from the cases, think about how the rules and statements relate to one another, record key facts from the cases, think about how the cases impact the arguments in your case, and record your insights as they emerge. It is impossible to emphasize this enough. Whether novice or expert, a legal writer *cannot* generate a strong paper without going through this prewriting thought process. I have seen so many students skip it and start drowning in their first draft, unable to recover even when they eventually realize the significance of the mistake. Save yourself from this fate. Take the time!

7.3 | OUTLINING

The outline should be an intermediary step between the note-taking process discussed in section 7.2 and the first draft. Trying to create an outline without first going through the note-taking process is a futile endeavor, likely to make you pull out your hair and maybe even cry or scream in frustration. Or worse, it could make you completely oblivious to the difficult aspects of your client's case.

Even if you have followed a thorough note-taking process, the outline will not be easy. You still have to go back to the chart or the highlighting or the notes and figure out a logical structure for your document. This will take more thought, more time. You may even have to reread some of the cases.

An outline should match your style of thinking. For some, a standard outline format with tiered levels works well (whether organized with numbers or letters or even just bullets). Other students, however, may work better with flow charts or diagrams. Follow your instincts; do not be rigid about the form of your outline.

The content of the outline is more important than its form. At a minimum, an outline should include the following: (1) the points you want to make about the law listed in a logical order; (2) the cases you will use for each point; and (3) the arguments, using the facts of your client's case, that you will discuss on each point.

Three sample outlines follow: a standard linear outline, a diagram (in two parts for rules and application), and a flow chart. Each format requires preparatory thinking about how the rules pulled from the cases relate to one another and to the client's case.

7.3.1 | Standard Outline

A standard outline can be an effective method for planning the organization and content of your paper. The sample below presents one possible format.

Sample Linear Outline

Umbrella Paragraph: (1)

- Exclusion for recreational activities unless reasonable expectancy
- Two prongs of reasonable expectancy: objective and subjective

A. Subjective Belief

RE 1: Belief one should participate is sufficient. (2)

Ezzy v. Smith, 194 Cal. Rptr. 90 (law clerk said she felt she "should" play softball when partner handed her a tee shirt and said he would see her at the game).

RE 2: Employee must truly feel obligated.

Smith v. Workers' Comp., 236 Cal. Rptr. 248 (teacher felt he had a "responsibility" to attend picnic and extracurriculars were required)

Wilson, 239 Cal. Rptr. 719 (police officer believed he had to keep in shape to stay on his special unit)

v.

City of Stockton, 38 Cal. Rptr. 3d 474 (officer admitted he could keep in shape without playing basketball)

Application: Gator had a subjective belief

- He said he thought he needed to play paddleball to advance in the company
- He never admitted that paddleball was optional

B. Objective Reasonableness (3)

Mini-umbrella: Implied pressure or indirect encouragement

1. Implied pressure

RE 1: A need to participate to remain or advance in employment is implied pressure.

Wilson, 239 Cal. Rptr. 719 (unrealistic to think officer could pass fitness test without off-duty training)

Kidwell, 39 Cal. Rptr. 2d 540 (officer could not pass long jump test without practicing)

---

1. It is helpful to plan out which rules will be in your umbrella or first rule statement paragraph. Here, the starting-point rule and two prongs lead to the two major divisions of the memo. Section 6.3 discusses when to subdivide.
2. The two RE rules in this outline were not expressed in the cases. The author had to look at the holdings and reasoning of the cases to figure out what sort of facts satisfied subjective belief and what sort of facts led to a holding that it was not satisfied. A mental comparison of cases on each side is essential to developing good RE topic sentences that will flow well and connect to each other logically. See section 4.3 on topic sentences that synthesize the law.
3. The outline plans two subdivisions under objective reasonableness because there are two relevant factors (implied pressure and indirect encouragement), each independent of one another and each fairly complex. A mini-umbrella is planned because of the additional subdivisions. See section 6.3 for more on subdivisions.

Cont.

RE 2: Pressure increases if employee is vulnerable

Ezzy, 194 Cal. Rptr. 90 (law clerk would naturally feel pressure to play when urged by partner)

Smith, 236 Cal. Rptr. 248 (teacher was vulnerable to pressure as a temporary instructor)

Application: Implied pressure was present

- Gator was a probationary employee particularly susceptible to pressure
- Paddleball was necessary to advance
  - Boss invited him while complimenting his job performance and saying she wanted to see continued success
  - Boss testified she uses games as an opportunity to discuss business with employees
  - Unrealistic to think he would have the same chance to advance if he turned down this one-on-one time with boss
- 4 Counterargument:
  - No express job requirement
  - Mere invitation by boss, no expression of pressure
  - No one ever said they had to play (except a coworker with no supervisory authority)
  - 5 Mere desire to connect with boss is insufficient
- Rebuttal:
  - Use of paddleball to discuss business made it work-related
  - Coupling of invitation with comment on job performance increased pressure

2. Indirect encouragement

RE 1: Indirect encouragement that changes the voluntary nature of the activity requires workers' comp. coverage

Ezzy, 194 Cal. Rptr. 90 (firm provided tee shirts and refreshments and held a special banquet for softball team members)

Smith, 236 Cal. Rptr. 248 (school planned the picnic and provided permission slips, advertisements, and refreshments; school benefitted through improved teacher-student relationships; school encouraged teacher participation in extracurricular activities)

Wilson, 239 Cal. Rptr. 719 (police department benefitted from ability of specially trained unit to handle extreme situations)

RE 2: Sponsorship or encouragement must be linked to the specific activity; general fitness requirement not enough

City of Stockton, 38 Cal. Rptr. 3d 474 (employer encouraged general fitness but the basketball game was off-premises, impromptu, and not even known by employer; no coverage for any activity an employee chooses—too broad)

Taylor, 244 Cal. Rptr. 643 (only approved fitness regimens were covered)

---

4. In objective writing (legal research memos), lawyers both explain and rebut counterarguments to their conclusions. Briefs do not include counterarguments, but it might help to note them in the outline anyway because briefs do need to rebut the counterarguments.

5. Not every subsection needs a counterargument; some points may not have a plausible counterargument. Here, subdivision B.1. has a counterargument but subdivision B.2. does not.

Cont.

RE 3: Merely condoning an activity is not pressure

Todd, 243 Cal. Rptr. 925 (employer did nothing to encourage basketball other than install a hoop and allow use of some materials)

Tensfeldt, 77 Cal. Rptr. 2d 691 (city employees allowed but not encouraged to play basketball at city gym)

Application: Sponsorship and benefit present

- Employer built a paddleball court at the workplace and provided nearly all supplies, even sneakers and exercise clothes
- Employer benefitted through increased morale—fostered relationships between boss and employees
- Encouragement was specifically directed at paddleball, not just general fitness

7.3.2 | Diagramming

If a standard outline like the sample above does not come naturally to you or does not help you make connections between concepts, you could try diagramming. A sample diagram outline follows. When you create a diagram, you want to select a language or set of symbols to represent relationships and stay consistent. It does not matter what system you choose, as long as it makes sense to you and as long as you are consistent. The sample below uses single arrows to illustrate broad-to-specific relationships: the more specific concept at the tip of the arrow is necessary to establish the more broad concept at the base of the arrow. The sample uses a plus sign to indicate concepts that work *together* to support a conclusion. A plus sign means that the result depends on both concepts. For example, assume that I need two points to convince my friend to come to a movie with me: (1) I am going to pay for her ticket, and (2) the movie is great. I would join these two different considerations with a plus sign because they work together to support the result that she will join me for the movie. By contrast, divergent arrows (like an upside down "v") represent "or" relationships—either consideration can independently support the result. I would use a "v" instead of the plus sign in the movie example if I knew that either paying for the movie or choosing a great movie would be alone sufficient to convince her to come with me.

For a diagram to function as a full outline, it needs to include both the rules (with cases) and the possible arguments about the writer's case; you may want to create two separate diagrams, one for the rules and the other for the application as in the samples below.

Sample Diagram for Rules

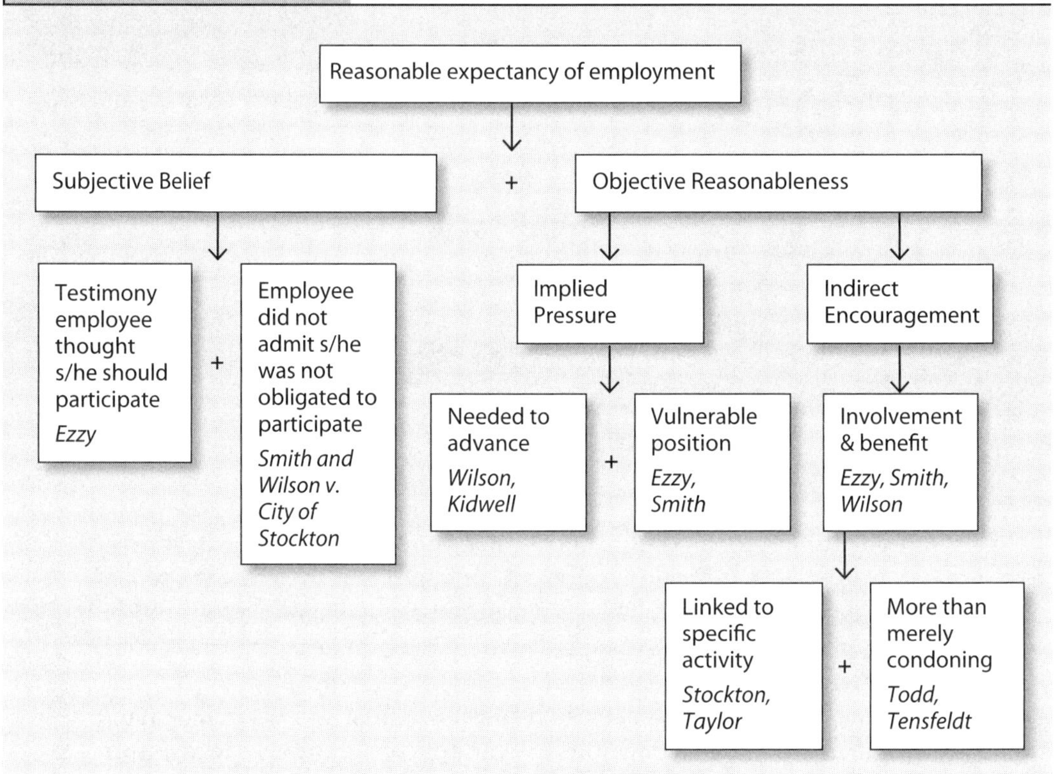

Sample Diagram for Application

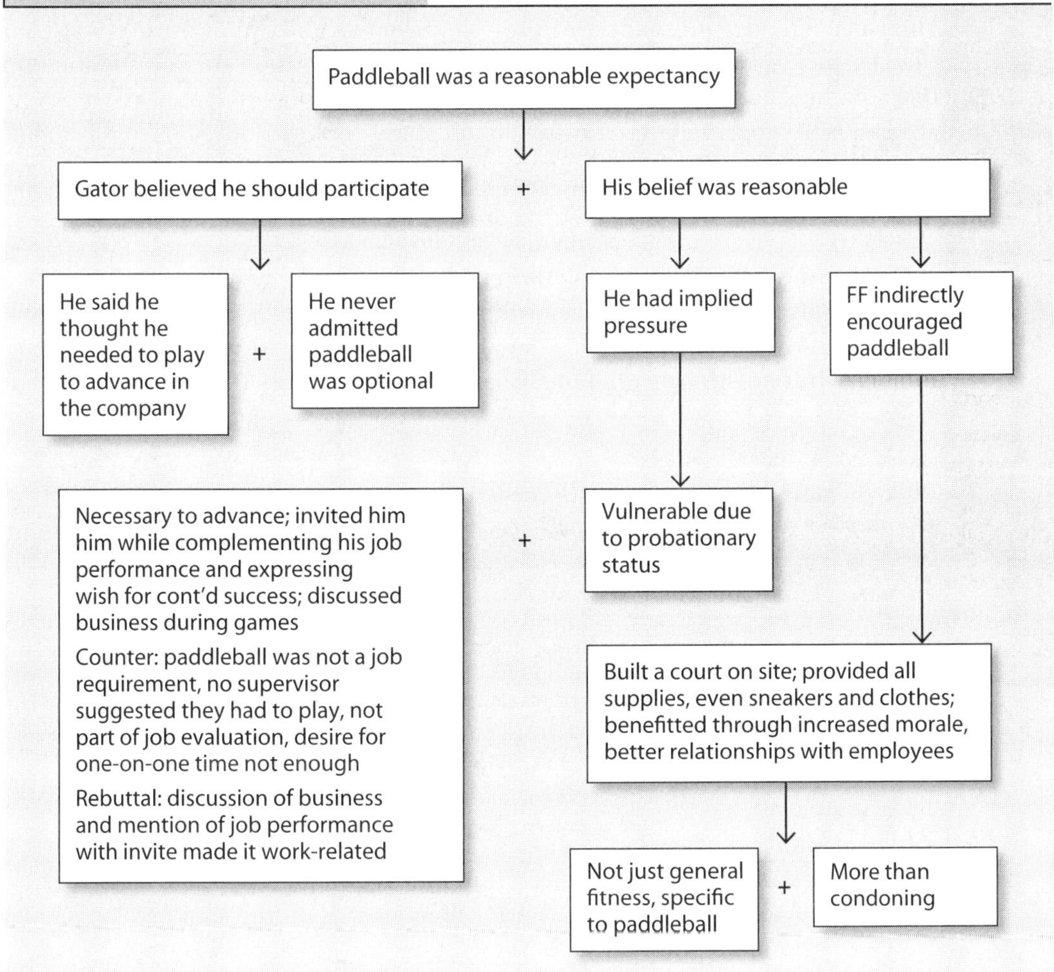

7.3.3 | Flow Charts

Another helpful method is the flow chart. The flow chart is similar to the diagram except that it maps out the legal issue to model your decision-making process rather than focusing on the relationships between rules or concepts. The sample below puts relevant facts from the client's case in brackets near the related steps in the flow chart. Another option would be to use a separate flow chart for the application, like the diagrams in section 7.3.2.

Sample Flow Chart

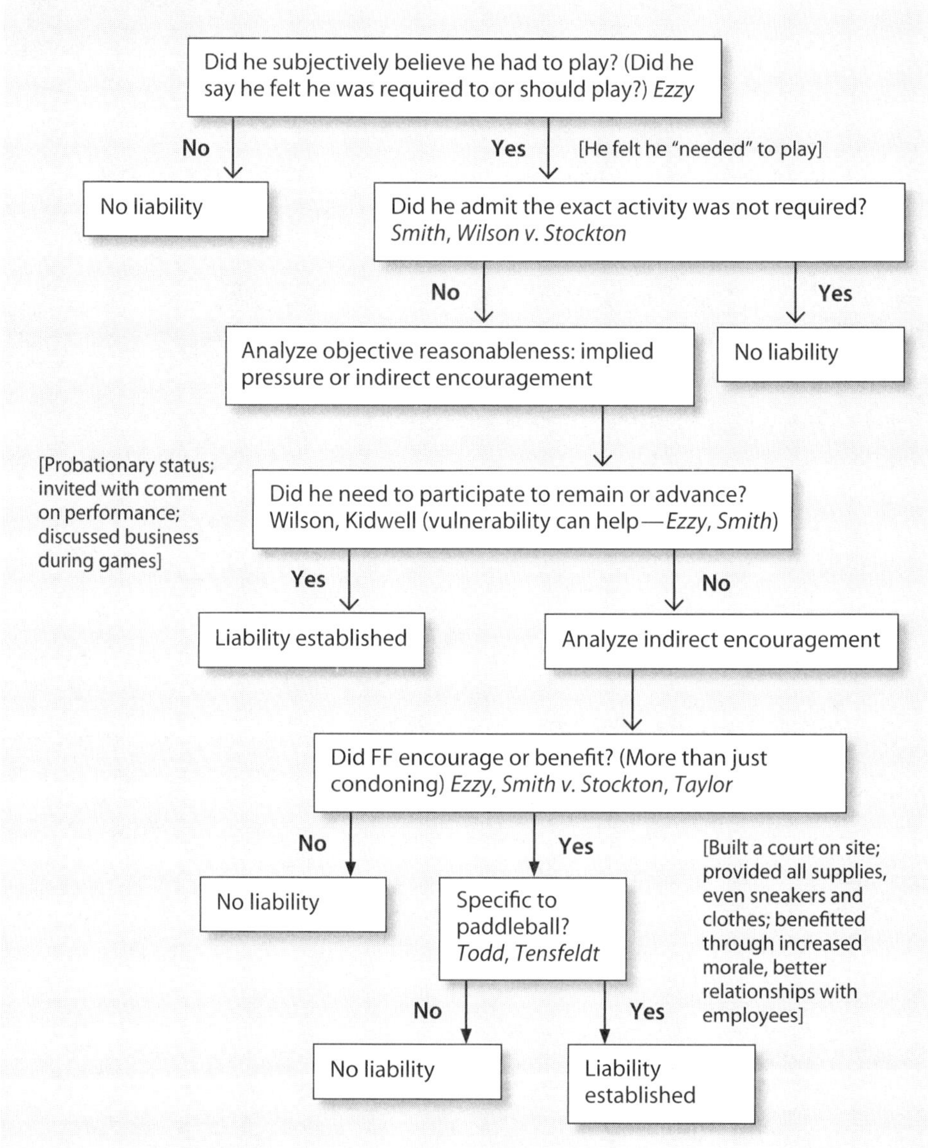

7.4 | THE FIRST DRAFT

Even if you have undertaken the note-taking and outlining steps recommended in sections 7.2 and 7.3, the draft will not write itself. Much more work is ahead.

If your outline did not already include topic sentences, this will be a critical step in moving from the outlining stage to the first draft. The topic sentences of the rule explanation paragraphs are the organizational anchors of your paper. As you draft them, return to the lessons on topic sentences in Chapter 4. Decide whether you want a particular subrule to be in its own topic sentence or whether you want to synthesize it with a related subrule. Decide on some transitional language to link each topic sentence to its predecessor.

Another important step will be to fill in the details about the precedent cases. Returning to the text of the cases themselves is a critical step in this process. Do not rely on your notes or charts. As you start to write in details about a case, get it out and track the court's reasoning very closely without skipping a step in its logic. Decide whether you want to quote any language directly from the case. Do not skip the step of indicating the jump page for your citation (see Chapter 8 on citation). If you skip the jump page as you are drafting, you will need to go back to the cases yet again to find the right references.

When you are ready to draft the application paragraphs, remember that they should match your rule explanation paragraphs by using the same language from the rule explanation topic sentences and some of the court's reasoning. In addition, get out your factual record as you write. Read through the record to find the helpful factual details and quotes to support the points in your application paragraphs. Return to the lessons of Chapter 5 as you write to remind yourself of how to organize an application paragraph and the four tools of effective application paragraphs.

Once you have your rule statement and/or umbrella paragraphs, rule explanation paragraphs, and application paragraphs done, you have a document you can consider a first draft of a legal analysis. However, this first draft should not be the one you show to your professor (or your boss). Any draft you show to another human being should have been through at least three rounds of self-editing, our next topic.

Before we move onto self editing, a word on writer's block. The task of putting your first legal memorandum or brief together can be extremely daunting. You have to pull together all of the cases, all of the facts from the record, and all of your professor's instructions. Outlining is a key tool to avoid writer's block because it breaks down the huge task into segments that you can work on one at a time. As you start to draft, focus on discrete tasks. For example, work on the topic sentences first. Then work on filling in each rule explanation paragraph using the cases you included in your outline. Then move on to each application paragraph, one by one. If you encounter a snag in your planned organization, re-outline. Otherwise, let yourself put the first draft together without second-guessing yourself and without getting bogged down in self-editing. Save self-editing for the next stage to avoid running out of time to complete the other portions of the assignment. Let yourself write! And it is okay to start with the easiest tasks. So if the legal analysis feels too overwhelming, start with the factual narrative (factual background/statement of facts) or issue identification (issue statement/question presented).

7.5 | SELF-EDITING

When you finish your first draft, take a break and do something else for a while. Give yourself as long a break as possible without falling behind on your schedule for the paper. The break can give you mental and emotional separation from the draft that will improve your ability to self-edit objectively.

Hopefully you have developed some effective checklists as discussed in section 1.4. Self-editing without checklists tends to be haphazard and ineffective. Assuming you have checklists, start reviewing the draft in a structured manner. First tackle big-picture issues that could affect the organization and information you have included in your paper. Save grammar, writing style, and citation for later. Otherwise, you may waste your time perfecting a sentence or citation that you later realize you need to delete.

The more you can break down your checklists into smaller tasks, the better the result is likely to be. Your self-editing plan should be particular to your learning style and strengths and weaknesses, but the following sample illustrates the structure of an effective plan. Each numbered step and each bullet represents a separate read-through of the paper; do not try to check for multiple items at the same time. If you already have checklists, you do not need to create a new document like the sample below. Instead, you can just organize your checklists in the order you want to follow.

Sample Self-Editing Plan

1. Review topic sentences
   - Do they state a specific lesson from the cases that further clarifies the rules in my rule statement?
   - Do they flow well (does each connect logically to its predecessor)?
   - Do they accurately reflect the discussion of cases that follows in the paragraph?
   - Do they use firm language rather than "determine whether" and "consider"?
2. Review case discussions
   - Do they focus on the lesson stated in the respective topic sentence?
   - Do they include the facts, holding, and reasoning from the cases?
   - Have they skipped any important steps in the court's logic?
3. Review application paragraphs
   - Do they match one of the rule explanation paragraphs (i.e., do they use language from the rule explanation topic sentences and the court's reasoning)?
   - Do they use details and quotations from the record?
   - Do they use case comparisons?
   - Are the case comparisons stated in grammatically parallel form?
   - Are there any gaps in logic from one sentence to the next?
4. Review writing style
   - Are there any long sentences to trim?

Cont.

- Is there any wordy or filler language (e.g., "the fact that," "it is significant that")?
- Do all sentence subjects and verbs reflect the true heart of each sentence?

5. Review grammar
   - Are all verb tenses correct?
   - Are plural pronouns (e.g., "they," "their") used to refer to singular nouns (e.g., "the court")?
   - Are there any dangling modifiers to correct (e.g., "To find actual malice, a plaintiff must prove" should be changed to "To prove actual malice, a plaintiff must establish").
6. Review citation
   - Are case names abbreviated according to Bluebook or ALWD style?
   - Do case citations use the correct reporters?
   - Do citations include pinpoint cites or jump pages?
   - Are any sentences in the rule statement and rule explanation missing citations?
   - Are signals used where necessary?
   - Are string cites punctuated correctly?
   - Do case citations include courts and jurisdictions in the date parentheticals when necessary?

A thorough self-editor will go through a checklist more than once. For example, if your first run through for wordy sentences revealed errors that you corrected, read through the paper again for wordy sentences until you find none. However, do not give up on self-editing merely because you know you will not have time to be sufficiently thorough. Self-editing is like practicing a sport: every additional hour you put in will improve your performance incrementally. Self-editing is never a waste of time!

CHAPTER **8**

Citation Basics

This chapter explains those strange numbers and "*id.*"s that appear in the sample memoranda and briefs you have seen so far. These mysterious notations are citations, samples of which appear in bold in the following illustration.

Sample Rule Explanation with Citations

"Unwarranted physical, or perhaps mental, coercion" may shock the conscience. ***Bogart*, 783 F.2d at 1438; *see also Greene*, 454 F.2d at 786** (finding that veiled threat by agent to pressure defendants into production of bootleg alcohol supported dismissal of the indictment). However, the courts have recognized that undercover agents often must engage in "unsavory conduct," including language that could be construed as threatening, to maintain their cover. ***United States v. Emmert*, 829 F.2d 805, 812 (9th Cir. 1987).** In *Emmert*, two government agents negotiated a drug deal with the defendant and some other accomplices. ***Id.* at 807.** When the deal failed to go through, one of the accomplices asked the undercover agents for some money up front and expressed concern that one of the agents was a policeman. ***Id.*** In response, one of the agents said, "Maybe we'll do the deal in an airplane and if something goes wrong, we'd have one parachute and guess who'd come down without one." ***Id.*** And the other agent said she had three words for the defendant's accomplice, "R.I.P." ***Id.*** A few months later, the defendant was able to put the deal together and was arrested at the scene. ***Id.*** In rejecting the threats as a reason to dismiss the indictment, the court stated that "[e]xpress or implied threats may be warranted under certain circumstances" and "may not always constitute outrageous conduct." ***Id.* at 811.** The court concluded that the threats aimed at Emmert were "scarcely more than bluster" and were "ordinary bargaining tactics in drug deals." ***Id.* at 812.** It further explained that "government agents may need to engage in such "unsavory conduct to maintain their cover." ***Id.*** The court concluded that the threats were necessary to allay suspicions about the undercover agents. ***Id.***

The functions of citation in legal writing are similar to the functions of citation in other disciplines: attribution of others' ideas and words to avoid plagiarism and proof that your statement is true. However, citation in legal writing has a very specific format, different from the style you might have learned from the *Chicago Manual of Style* or the *MLA Handbook*. The legal profession expects precise adherence to the required format for legal citations. The precision serves several important goals.

First, a citation indicates detailed information about the source, including court name, date of decision, and subsequent decisions. From this information, the reader can evaluate the persuasiveness of the law the writer is relying on. Recall from Chapter 2 that case law follows a hierarchy: trial, appellate, and supreme or last-resort courts, in both federal and state jurisdictions. A legal citation tells the reader where in the hierarchy a case falls, as well as how recent it is. For example, an opinion of a sister court in the same state will be more persuasive than an opinion of a court in another state. In the sample rule explanation paragraph above, the citation to *Emmert* tells the reader that the opinion was rendered by the Ninth Circuit in 1987.

Second, a citation enables the reader to find and verify the sources on which the writer relies. Citations typically include a "jump page" or "pinpoint cite"—the exact page of the source that supports the writer's contention. The reader can use the jump page to verify the writer's contention.

Third, because citation enables the reader to verify sources, it serves another important function—keeping lawyers honest about the law. Lawyers are not likely to misstate the law when they know that their citations can be used to quickly verify the truth of their statements.

Fourth, accurate citation earns the reader's trust. Accurate citation is one of the easiest ways to build your reputation as an honest lawyer.

8.1 | SYSTEMS OF CITATION

With the focus on precision in citation, we might expect to have one single system of legal citation. The *Bluebook* sets forth in excruciating detail a widely used method of citation. The federal courts and some state jurisdictions use the *Bluebook* rules. However, other states have their own special rules of citations that do not necessarily match the *Bluebook* rules. And, in the hope of creating a more intuitive method of citation, the Association of Legal Writing Directors publishes its own suggested rules of citation in the *ALWD Citation Manual*.

Despite variety in citation details, the basic components of a citation remain uniform. Case citations include the name of the case; the volume number, series, and page number of at least one published version of the case; and the date of the opinion and jurisdiction. Statutory citations include the volume number or code name, section number, year, and sometimes publisher information. The use of short forms like "*id.*" is fairly standard across jurisdictions. You will also often need to use "introductory signals" like "*see*" and "*see also*" before a citation, as explained in more detail in section 8.5.

8.2 | WHEN TO CITE

Cite constantly in rule statements and rule explanations and occasionally cite in applications. Citations are needed for nearly every sentence in the rule statement and rule explanation paragraphs. As a general rule, a legal writer cannot make any statement about the law without citing a source. Because rule statements and rule explanations are all about the law, they require constant citation. Application paragraphs, however, rarely introduce information about the law and therefore do not usually need citations. Applications require citations only if they repeat a quotation or rule or holding from a case or other source. In a court brief, citations to supporting documents such as the trial record or interrogatories are also needed for specific factual assertions.

Do not cite only at the ends of paragraphs. Every sentence in the paragraph needs its own citation with the correct jump page. This is necessary even when each sentence relies on the same page of a source. Notice how both the first and the second sentences in the following paragraph (from Appendix B, Sample A) have their own citations. The first cite refers the reader to page 95 of the *Ezzy* case to support the statement about indirect encouragement, and the second cite, *Id.*, is a shorthand method to tell the reader that the same page also supports the summary of the facts that the second sentence provides.

Example of Citing for Every Sentence

Employer involvement and benefit can establish indirect encouragement by the employer that changes the voluntary nature of the activity and, therefore, requires coverage of resulting injuries. *Ezzy*, 194 Cal. Rptr. at 95. For example, in finding reasonable expectancy in *Ezzy*, the court pointed to evidence that the firm provided tee shirts and refreshments at the games and held a special banquet for participants. *Id.*

A case citation usually appears as a separate sentence following the sentence that it supports. In the example above, page 95 of the *Ezzy* opinion supports the preceding statement about employer involvement and benefit.

There are some exceptions, however. The citation manual required by your jurisdiction may require, as the *Bluebook* and *ALWD* do, that citations be split up when different sources support different statements within the sentence.

Sample Citation Split

Although public figures must sacrifice more of their privacy than the average person, *O'Hilderbrandt v. CBS*, 114 Cal. Rptr. 826, 830 (Ct. App. 1974), an individual does not become a public figure merely by engaging in civic life, *Kinsey v. Macur*, 165 Cal. Rptr. 608, 612, 613 (Ct. App. 1980).

Sometimes you will mention a case that has not previously been cited. In this circumstance, the *Bluebook* and *ALWD* require placement of the citation within the sentence.

Sample In-Text Cite

In *People v. Wright*, 59 Cal. Rptr. 2d 316, 322 (Ct. App. 1996), the court held that threats may constitute force. The *Wright* court blurred the line between fear and force. *Id.*

8.3 | CITING STATUTES

A citation to a statute should contain the volume number of the code (if applicable), the title (if applicable), a section symbol (if applicable), the section or other subdivision number, the publisher of the code, and the date of the code. Punctuation of a statutory citation varies, so you will need to consult the citation manual required by your jurisdiction. The following sample is consistent with the *Bluebook* and *ALWD*.

Sample Statutory Citation for Codes with Titles

Title ↓ | Section # ↓ | Date ↓

Cal. Veh. Code § 11506 (West 1987).

Section Symbol ↑ | Publisher ↑

Sample Statutory Citation for Codes Without Titles

Vol. # ↓ | Section Symbol ↓

42 U.S.C. § 1983 (1994).

Name ↑ | Section # ↑ | Date ↑

This example does not have a publisher because the U.S. government publishes the code.

Surprisingly, the rules regarding the correct date to include in a statutory citation are complex. Citations do not use the date the statute was enacted, but rather the date that the compilation of statutes was published. Finding this date can be complicated, especially when accessing statutes online or when the published code volumes are reissued from time to time. Amendments to statutes further complicate this process. Consult the citation manual required by your jurisdiction for guidance.

8.4 | CITING CASES

8.4.1 | Using Case Captions to Derive Citations

Most of the information in a citation to a case comes from the caption page of the published decision. Case citations have four main components, usually appearing in this order:

1. the case name,
2. the location information (volume number, reporter name, reporter series, and first page of the case within the volume),
3. the date parenthetical (court name and date), and
4. the jump page or pinpoint cite.

Here is a citation in the *Bluebook* and *ALWD* format derived from the case caption that follows:

Reporter Name ↓ First Page ↓ Court Name ↓

Hinman v. Westinghouse Elec. Co., 471 P.2d 988, 991 (Cal. 1970).

↑ Case Name ↑ Vol. # ↑ Series # ↑ Jump Page ↑ Year

Sample Caption from a Court Opinion

471 P.2d 988

2 Cal.3d 956, 471 P.2d 988, 88 Cal.Rptr. 188

(Cite as: 2 Cal.3d 956, 471 P.2d 988, 88 Cal.Rptr. 188)

Supreme Court of California,

Eugene C. HINMAN, Plaintiff and Appellant,

v.

WESTINGHOUSE ELECTRIC COMPANY, Defendant and Respondent;

CITY OF LOS ANGELES, Intervener and Appellant.

L.A. 29740.

July 30, 1970.

Case name. The sample case caption shows three named parties: Eugene C. Hinman, Westinghouse Electric Company, and the City of Los Angeles. Include in your citation the first party on each side of the "v.," which stands for "versus." So, in this sample, you would not include the City of Los Angeles. After identifying the right parties to include in your citation, a host of other questions may arise regarding abbreviation, inclusion or exclusion of geographic terms and prepositional phrases, and a host of other ticky-tacky details. To answer these questions, you need to know the rules about case names in the system of citation required by your jurisdiction. The *Bluebook*, for example, has very specific rules about when and how you can abbreviate entity names like Westinghouse Electric Company. *ALWD* is more flexible and merely provides a list of suggested abbreviations.

Reporter information. Court opinions are published in volumes and series, like an encyclopedia. Different publishers may also publish separate compilations of court opinions. The numbers bolded in the sample caption indicate the location of the *Hinman* opinion in three different compilations published by three different publishers: (1) the *Pacific Reporter* (P.2d), (2) the *California Reporter* (Cal. Rptr.), and (3) the *California Reports* (Cal.). For example, "471 P.2d 988" refers to the second series of volume 471 of the *Pacific Reporter.* Citation manuals and sometimes local court rules specify which reporter you should cite to in your legal documents: you have to look it up!

Date parenthetical. The date parenthetical includes an abbreviation of the court that issued the opinion and the year that the opinion was rendered. In the *Hinman* example, notice that the abbreviation in the parentheses ("Cal.") does not much resemble the name of the deciding court indicated in the caption ("Supreme Court of California"). You will need to look up the right abbreviation in your citation manual. The date of the decision is usually obvious. In the *Hinman* caption, we see only one date to use. Sometimes, there may be a few dates in the caption of the court opinion. You might see a "Modified" date or a "Hearing" date. You are looking for the date the opinion was entered. The correct date is usually the one that does not have any description like "modified" or "hearing."

8.4.2 | Finding Jump Pages

A key component of any citation is the jump page or pinpoint cite. This is the exact page of the opinion, statute, or other source that supports your statement. If, during your research, you use the print versions of reporters, the page numbers you need are obvious. However, if you cite using electronic services such as Westlaw or Lexis, you need to figure out the right jump page. Because Westlaw and Lexis include pagination for all relevant reporters, finding the jump page is not a straightforward task. Consider the following excerpt from an electronic service.

Sample Case Excerpt

JOHNSON v. LEWIS,
120 Cal. App. 4th 443, 15 Cal. Rptr. 3d 507 (Ct. App. 2004)

Lewis first noticed plaintiff when she drove to within a few feet of his van, cut in front of him nearly hitting the van, and sped off down the crowded highway before ****513** he could catch up with her. By her own admission, plaintiff was driving at 70 to 75

Cont.

> miles an hour when she first noticed Lewis behind her. When asked if that was exceeding the speed limit, she said, "Sure." Driving in excess of the speed limit establishes a prima facie case of a speeding violation.... That subjected plaintiff to arrest and citation with a notice to appear...for a crime that under the circumstances of this case posed an immediate danger to persons or property. While Lewis was behind plaintiff in traffic, he activated his red light and siren. Plaintiff was thereby obligated to "immediately drive to the right-hand edge or curb of the highway, clear of any intersection, and ***453** thereupon shall stop and remain stopped." (Veh.Code, § 21806, subd. (a)(1).) Her failure to do so, speeding off instead, was an infraction that subjected her to arrest and citation (Veh.Code, §§ 40000.1, 40500) for a crime that posed an immediate danger to persons or property.

Suppose that the citation manual required by your jurisdiction requires you to cite to the *California Reporter* for this case. The header at the top of this entry tells you that this case was published in 15 Cal. Rptr. 3d at page 507. However, the excerpt is not from page 507. It is from the middle of the opinion.

Suppose you have a sentence in your memo that states, "Driving in excess of the speed limit establishes a prima facie case of a speeding violation." You need a citation, with a jump page, for this statement. This language is underlined in the excerpt. On what page of the *California Reporter* does this information appear?

The bolded, starred numbers in the printout represent the beginning of a new page in the reporters. In the excerpt, there are two page numbers, 513 and 453. The text you are relying on appears after the 513 and before the 453. That means it appears on page 513 of one of the reporters and page 452 of the other reporter. Which do you choose? You know that the case begins on page 507 of the *California Reporter*, so the only logical choice is page 513.

So, your citation would look like this:

> Driving in excess of the speed limit establishes a prima facie case of a speeding violation. *Johnson v. Lewis*, 15 Cal. Rptr. 3d 507, 513 (Ct. App. 2004).

8.4.3 | Adding Subsequent History for Full Disclosure

Certain citations also need to include subsequent history. Subsequent history consists of events occurring after the rendering of the opinion you are citing that affect the binding or persuasive force of the opinion. If the opinion you are citing was overruled by a higher court or superseded by a statute, subsequent history must be included in the citation.

Place the subsequent history at the end of the citation after any explanatory parenthetical. Subsequent history notations include a phrase that identifies the nature of the subsequent history (e.g., overruled, abrogated) and a full citation to the subsequent authority. The phrase and the case name should be italicized or underlined:

Case You Are Citing
↓
See Briscoe v. Reader's Digest Ass'n, 483 P.2d 34, 40 (Cal. 1971) (stating that exposing the identity of a long-reformed criminal who had not "reattracted the public eye to himself in some independent fashion" would serve "little...public purpose"), *overruled on other grounds by Gates v. Discovery Commc'ns, Inc.*, 101 P.3d 552, 559-60 (Cal. 2004).
↑ Citation to the Later Case ↑ Phrase

An opinion is overruled by a higher court when the higher court finds that some aspect of the opinion was incorrect. Normally, a lawyer would not cite an opinion as support for a point of law on which the opinion was overruled. That aspect of the opinion would be erased by the higher court's decision. However, you can cite an opinion for one point even if it was overruled on a different point. It should be a completely different aspect of the case. For example, if an opinion discusses both whether a defendant used force or fear as required for a robbery conviction and whether the defendant took the property off of the victim's person, you could cite the opinion on the point about force or fear even if the opinion was overruled on the point about the victim's person.

An opinion is superseded by statute when the legislature passes a statute that changes the rule(s) applied in the opinion.

8.5 | USING SIGNALS

In addition to the basic case citation format discussed above, you will also often need to add an introductory signal. Rules regarding the use of introductory signals are fairly uniform across different systems of citation. An introductory signal communicates to the reader the type and degree of support the cited source provides for your statement. Introductory signals, as you might expect, appear at the beginning of the citation; they are italicized or underlined consistent with the font type of your case name:

Introductory Signal
↓
See People v. Wright, 59 Cal. Rptr. 2d 316, 322 (Ct. App. 1996) (finding that use of fear can be implied by the circumstances surrounding the crime).

Most citations use an introductory signal. Omit a signal only when (1) you are directly quoting the source or (2) when the source says essentially the same thing as your statement without any necessary inferential steps by the reader (i.e., the source "directly states the proposition" you are asserting).

The most common introductory signal is "*see*." *See* tells the reader that the source clearly supports but does not directly state the proposition you are asserting. In other words, *see* alerts the reader that some inferential steps are necessary to understand how the source supports your statement.

Certain signals require explanatory parentheticals at the end of their citations. (Chapter 4 discusses explanatory parentheticals in depth.) For example:

> *See People v. Wright*, 59 Cal. Rptr. 2d 316, 322 (Ct. App. 1996) (finding that use of fear can be implied by the circumstances surrounding the crime).
>
> ↑ Explanatory parenthetical

The following chart can help you figure out which signal to choose and whether you need to include an explanatory parenthetical. The chart omits the formal citations to focus you on the signals and parentheticals.

INTRODUCTORY SIGNALS

SIGNAL	USE, WITH EXAMPLES	NEEDS AN EXPLANATORY PARENTHETICAL?
No signal	Direct quotation or your proposition is directly stated by the cited authority. *Example:* The therapist will not be liable absent an actual belief in the seriousness of the patient's threat. *Ewing v. Northridge.* (To warrant omission of a signal, *Ewing* must state exactly this, though possibly in different words.)	No
See	The proposition is not directly stated by the cited authority but obviously follows from it (i.e., there is an inferential step between the cited authority and the proposition it supports). *Example:* The presence or absence of prior violent behavior by the patient may be relevant to determining whether the therapist believed in the seriousness of the threat. *See Ewing v. Northridge* (finding sufficient evidence of the therapist's belief in the seriousness of the patient's threat and pointing to, among other facts, the patient's worsening depression and recent physical aggression toward his father).	Yes
See also	Same uses as "see" but following a quotation from another source. A plaintiff must prove "the therapist's actual belief or prediction that the patient poses a serious risk of inflicting	Yes

Cont.

SIGNAL	USE, WITH EXAMPLES	NEEDS AN EXPLANATORY PARENTHETICAL?
See also	grave bodily injury." *Ewing v. Northridge; see also Barry v. Turek* (explaining that section 43.92 aimed to eliminate therapist liability for failing to predict harm).	Yes
Accord	For additional authorities that say the same thing as the source you just cited. *Example:* A therapist will not be held liable for failing to warn in the absence of a communicated threat. Cal. Civ. Code § 43.92 (West 2009); *accord Calderon v. Glick.* (For accord to be correct, *Calderon* must say exactly this, though possibly in different words.)	No
Cf.	Cited authority supports a proposition different from the main proposition but sufficiently analogous to lend support. *Example:* A therapist is only liable for failure to warn a reasonably identifiable victim or victims. Cal. Civ. Code § 43.92 (West 2009); *cf. Tarasoff v. Regents of Univ. of Cal.* (noting that a therapist should warn victims that can be identified "on a moment's reflection").	Yes
Compare... with...	Comparison of the authorities supports your proposition. *Example:* The presence or absence of prior violent behavior by the patient may be relevant to the therapist's belief in the seriousness of a threat. *Compare Ewing v. Northridge* (finding sufficient evidence of the therapist's belief in the seriousness of the patient's threat based on the patient's recent physical aggression), *with Barry v. Turek* (finding therapist was not liable because the patient had never been violent).	Yes
But see	Cited authority disagrees with your proposition but with an inferential step needed. Used as the antithesis of *see.* *Example:* Despite the language in section 43.92, a communication directly from the patient to the therapist is not always required. A communication of the patient's threat by a family member offered to the therapist to facilitate the patient's treatment is sufficient. *Ewing v. Goldstein. But see Calderon v. Glick* (stating that a communication by the patient is usually required).	Yes

Cont.

SIGNAL	USE, WITH EXAMPLES	NEEDS AN EXPLANATORY PARENTHETICAL?
See generally	Cited authority gives helpful background information related to your proposition. *Example:* Therapist liability for failing to warn of a patient's threat is an exception to the general rule that no one has a duty to protect from others. *See generally Tarasoff v. Regents of Univ. of Cal.* (basing therapist liability for failure to warn of a patient's threat on analogous exceptions to general rule).	Yes

8.6 | STRING CITATIONS

Already in this text, you have seen multiple citations appear within a single citation sentence. These are called string citations. Punctuation of string citations varies, so you will need to consult the rules of the citation manual that your jurisdiction requires. Most commonly, each citation is separated by a semicolon, as in the following sample.

Sample String Citation

Merely condoning an activity does not create a sufficient connection to employment to warrant liability. *See Tensfeldt v. Workers' Comp. Appeals Bd.*, 77 Cal. Rptr. 2d 691, 698 (Ct. App. 1998) (denying coverage for city employee's basketball injury when employees were allowed but not encouraged to play basketball at a city gym); *Todd v. Workers' Comp. Appeals Bd.*, 243 Cal. Rptr. 925, 927 (Ct. App. 1988) (denying coverage for employee's basketball injury when employer did nothing to encourage the game other than allow employees to install a hoop on the premises using some of the employer's materials).

ALWD permits use of semicolons for all string citations, but the *Bluebook* requires a new citation sentence when you introduce a new signal of a different "type." Rule 1.3 of the *Bluebook* identifies the following types of signals:

- Supportive: no signal, *see, see also, accord*
- Comparative: *compare . . . with . . .*
- Contradictory: *contra, but see*
- Background: *see generally*

So, for example, *see* and *but see* are not the same type of signal: *see* is used for supportive citations and *but see* is used for contrary authority. Therefore, a *but see* cannot follow a *see* in the same citation sentence. Some simplified examples showing *Bluebook*-style string citations follow.

EXAMPLES OF SIGNAL USE AND STRING CITATIONS

ILLUSTRATION	DESCRIPTION / EXAMPLE
Snow is cold. *See Case B* (stating that snow can cause frostbite); *Case C* (finding that snow is colder than water).	Use see for both citations because Cases B and C do not directly state that snow is cold—an inferential step is required to see how they support the statement. Both citations appear in the same citation sentence, separated by a semicolon, because they share the same signal. *Example:* The absence of a plaintiff's role in creating the newsworthy event, therefore, is a significant factor weighing against early dismissal of a public disclosure claim. *See Capra v. Thoroughbred Racing Ass'n of N. Am.*, 787 F.2d 463, 465 (9th Cir. 1986) (recognizing that in balancing a family's privacy interests against the social value of an article that uncovered their government-protected identities, the plaintiff whose participation in organized crime led his family to enter the witness protection program was not "similarly situated" to his innocent wife and son); *Gill v. Curtis Publ'g Co.*, 239 P.2d 630, 634 (Cal. 1952) (reversing dismissal of a public disclosure claim brought by a married couple against a magazine for publishing a photograph of them in a romantic embrace).
Snow is cold. *Case A*; *Case B*; *Case C*.	In this example, Cases A, B, and C all directly support the statement. No signals are needed, and each citation is separated by a semicolon. *Example:* Under California law, three factors determine when the media has gone too far: the social value of the facts published, the depth of the article's intrusion into ostensibly private affairs, and the extent to which the party voluntarily acceded to a position of public notoriety. *Shulman v. Grp. W Prods., Inc.*, 955 P.2d 469, 482 (Cal. 1998); *Kapellas v. Kofman*, 459 P.2d 912, 922 (Cal. 1969).
Snow is cold. *Case A*; *see also Case B* (stating that snow can cause frostbite).	Here, because Case B does not directly support the statement, a see signal and a parenthetical are needed. Case A is cited first because it directly supports the statement, and then Case B is introduced with *see also*. Because *see also* is the same type of signal as no signal, both citations are placed in the same citation sentence and are separated by a semicolon. *Example:* Public figures must sacrifice more of their privacy than the average person. *O'Hilderbrandt v. CBS*, 114 Cal. Rptr. 826, 830 (Ct. App. 1974); *see also Kapellas*, 459 P.2d at 923 (stating that political candidates knowingly subject themselves to "a searching beam of public interest and attention"); *Matson v. Dvorak*, 46 Cal. Rptr. 2d 880, 887 (Ct. App. 1995) (holding that the public had a legitimate interest in a candidate's traffic citations).

Cont.

ILLUSTRATION	DESCRIPTION / EXAMPLE
Snow is cold. *See Case A* (stating that snow can cause frostbite). *But see Case B* (holding that snow is not as cold as ice).	Here, you are disclosing an adverse case. Because a *but see* is a different type of signal than see, it begins a separate citation sentence per Rule 1.3 of the *Bluebook*. *Example:* Once a reasonable purpose for the disclosure has been asserted, it follows that the disclosure was not "morbid and sensational prying *for its own sake.*" *See Virgil*, 424 F. Supp. at 1289-90 (emphasis added) (holding that personal stories regarding surfer's reckless lifestyle were relevant to the article's attempt to explain the surfer's daring approach to the sport and therefore were not "disclosed for their own sake"). *But see M.G. v. Time Warner, Inc.*, 107 Cal. Rptr. 2d 504, 514 (Ct. App. 2001) (finding that defendants' assertion that the use of a photograph of sexual abuse victims strengthened the impact of the story "r[a]ng[] hollow" because the defendants had obscured the victims' faces and protected their identities in other portions of the same broadcast).

8.7 | SHORT FORMS OF CITATION

The full citation forms for cases and statutes described above apply to the first time you cite a case or statute. The second time you cite to the same case or statute, you can use one of two shorter citation forms, depending on the circumstances. These two shorter citation forms are referred to as (1) the "*id.*" form and (2) the "short form."

8.7.1 | The *Id.* Form

The *id.* form consists of the word "*id.*" in italics, most often followed by the word "at" in regular font and a jump page. Its use is limited. You can use *id.* only when citing to the same case that you cited most recently in the document. You cannot use *id.* if you cited a different case more recently or if the cite was in a citation string.

Sample Use of *Id.* with New Page Reference

Plaintiff can prevail on the newsworthiness element only if she can show that the disclosure was "intrusive in great disproportion to [its] relevance." *Shulman v. Grp. W Prods., Inc.*, 955 P.2d 469, 478-79 (Cal. 1998). In most cases, a logical nexus between the disclosed facts and the newsworthy topic entitles the defendant to summary judgment.

Cont.

See id. at 486 (stating that "in the ordinary case," the logical nexus analysis determines newsworthiness).

In this example, *id.* indicates that the second sentence is supported by the same source as the first sentence (*Shulman*), but at page 486 rather than at pages 478 through 479. The use of *id.* is proper since *Shulman* is the most recently cited source (i.e., no intervening citations appear between these two citations to *Shulman*). Also, *Shulman* is the only source cited in the first sentence.

ERROR Example of Incorrect Use of *Id.*

Consistent with this constitutional limitation on liability, California law requires that to establish a claim for public disclosure of private facts, a plaintiff must prove that the disclosed facts were not of legitimate public concern. *Shulman v. Grp. W Prods., Inc.*, 955 P.2d 469, 478-79 (Cal. 1998); *Kapellas v. Kofman*, 459 P.2d 912, 922 (Cal. 1969). The lack of legitimate public concern or "newsworthiness" is a required element of the claim on which the plaintiff carries the burden of proof. *Id.*

The use of *id.* in the above example is incorrect because the prior citation to *Shulman* is accompanied by a citation to another case (*Kofman*). Use *id.* only when the prior cite to the case appears alone. The rationale for this rule is that the presence of a second source can make the *id.* reference unclear to the reader.

The use of *id.* without a jump page indicates that both sentences are supported by the same page(s).

Sample Use of *Id.* with Same Page Reference

Consistent with this constitutional limitation on liability, California law requires that to establish a claim for public disclosure of private facts, a plaintiff must prove that the disclosed facts were not of legitimate public concern. *Shulman v. Grp. W Prods., Inc.*, 955 P.2d 469, 478-79 (Cal. 1998). The lack of legitimate public concern or "newsworthiness" is a required element of the claim on which the plaintiff carries the burden of proof. *Id.*

Id. can be used for statutes too. You can use *id.* for statutes when you are citing the same volume of the same code or the same title as in the previous cite; just insert the new section number.

Sample Use of *Id.* for Statutory Cites

The federal district courts have original jurisdiction over all civil actions arising under the Constitution and laws of the United States. 28 U.S.C. § 1331 (2000). They also have

Cont.

jurisdiction over cases in which the amount of controversy exceeds $75,000 and the parties are citizens of different states. *Id.* § 1332.

To refer to the same section number, use *id.* by itself, as in the case citation example.

8.7.2 | The Short Form

Contrary to its name, the "short form" is not the shortest citation form. *Id.* is the shortest citation form. However, the short form is a bit shorter than the full citation form. The short form of a case citation typically consists of a shortened version of the case name, the volume number, the reporter, and the jump page. Consult your jurisdiction's required citation manual to determine the exact components and format.

The short form does not share *id.*'s limitations. You can use the short form any time you have already cited a case in the same general discussion. In a short 10-page memo, most likely the entire document is the same discussion. In a longer document, you might need to use the full cite again whenever your discussion changes gears (e.g., in a 20-page document, when you move from section I. to section II.). The following sample is consistent with the *Bluebook* and *ALWD*.

Sample Short-Form Case Citation

Private facts about individuals who, like Plaintiff, are "involuntarily involved in an event or activity of legitimate public concern" carry social value only if they "bear a logical relationship to [a] newsworthy subject." *Shulman*, 955 P.2d at 484.

The use of the short form in the above sample would be correct if the writer had included an earlier full cite to the *Shulman* case but *Shulman* was not the most recently cited source and, therefore, the writer could not use *id.* The sample below labels the components of the short form.

Sample Short-Form Case Citation

Shortened version of the case name ↓ | Reporter ↓ | Jump page ↓

Shulman, 955 P.2d at 484.

↑ Vol. # | ↑ "at"

The short form can be used for statutes too. The sample below illustrates one common format: volume number, name of the code, and section number.

Sample Short-Form Statute Citation

The federal district courts have original jurisdiction over all civil actions arising under the Constitution and laws of the United States. 28 U.S.C. § 1331 (2000); *United States Corr. Servs. Corp. v. Malesko*, 534 U.S. 61, 66 (2001). They also have jurisdiction over cases in which the amount of controversy exceeds $75,000 and the parties are citizens of different states. 28 U.S.C. § 1332.

8.8 | FORMATTING QUOTATIONS

8.8.1 | When to Use Quotation Marks

In legal writing, lawyers use many exact phrases from case law and statutes to ensure they are not accidentally misrepresenting the applicable rules. However, if every legally relevant phrase is in quotation marks, the document ends up looking like one big quotation. The first time you state a rule, it is a good idea to use quotation marks around any key phrases so that the reader knows you are using the exact language provided by the court. However, thereafter, you can use the phrases without putting quotation marks around them.

Of course, if you are quoting more than just a key phrase (e.g., if you are quoting some of the court's reasoning), you should use quotation marks to properly attribute the source. For example, if you are analyzing entrapment and the key standard is whether the government was significantly involved in the crime, you would want to put quotation marks around "significantly involved" when you first identify this as the applicable test. Thereafter, you can use the phrase without using quotation marks. In the following excerpt from Appendix B, Sample A, notice that the first mention of the reasonable expectancy test appears in a longer quotation, but thereafter the term is used without quotation marks.

Sample Use of Key Legal Phrase

Labor Code section 3600, subdivision (a)(9), excludes from workers' compensation coverage injuries arising from "voluntary participation in any off-duty recreational, social, or athletic activity not constituting part of the employee's work-related duties, except where these activities are a reasonable expectancy of, or are expressly or impliedly required by, the employment." Cal. Labor Code § 3600(a)(9) (West 2003). The exception for activities that are a reasonable expectancy of employment applies when...

Recall from Chapter 4 that commonly used, mundane terms can be used without quotation marks. For example, the sample above does not put the term "workers' compensation" in quotation marks. Similarly, procedural terms and phrases such as "summary judgment," "judgment as a matter of law," and "triable issue of fact" should not be placed in quotation marks. And facts from a precedent case should not be placed in quotation marks unless the exact wording is significant. For example, the following excerpt from Appendix B, Sample A, uses quotations only for testimony that is relevant to the evaluation of reasonable expectancy—the plaintiff's testimony that she "should" play and the partner's exact words of encouragement.

Sample Use of Quotation Marks

In *Ezzy*, for example, a law clerk was injured while playing on her firm's softball team. 194 Cal. Rptr. at 91. She testified that because the team did not have enough female players to satisfy the league's rules, she felt she "should" play when a partner handed her a tee shirt and game schedule and said, "At the next one, we'll see you there." *Id.* at 92.

8.8.2 | When to Use Block Quotes

A block quote is a long quotation, 50 or more words according to the *Bluebook*. *ALWD* requires block quotes also for quotes that are longer than four lines. Block quotations are indicated by left and right indentation and single spacing rather than by quotation marks.

The citation that follows a block quote should be part of the normal text and not part of the block.

Sample Block Quotation

> This quotation is more than 50 words long. Therefore, I am going to put it in a block quote rather than in quotation marks. To create a block quote, I have indented my left and right margins one-half inch and converted my line spacing to single spacing. This is the proper format for a block quote. I am now going to put my citation for this quote below as part of the normal text and not as part of this block. In other words, unlike this block quote, the citation will not be indented or single spaced.

Turner v. Class, 50 Cal. Rptr. 5th 13, 14 (Ct. App. 2014).

8.8.3 | Quoting a Case That Quotes a Prior Case

Sometimes you will want to quote language from a court opinion that originally came from some prior source. You should

- use internal quotation marks to indicate that your source took the language from a preexisting source, and
- include a "quoting" notation in your citation (if required by your citation manual) (this is required by the *Bluebook* and *ALWD*).

These requirements apply only to direct quotations. If you are paraphrasing, you do not need to worry about this rule. Also, these requirements apply only when the case you are citing was directly quoting, and not paraphrasing, the original source.

8.8.3.1 | Using Internal Quotation Marks

The typical external quotation marks around quoted language represent the writer's quotation of the source in which she found the quote. The sample below quotes language from the *Kapellas* case.

Sample Use of External Quotation Marks

Under California law, three factors determine when the media has gone too far: "the social value of the facts published, the depth of the article's intrusion into ostensibly private affairs, and the extent to which the party voluntarily acceded to a position of public notoriety." *Kapellas v. Kofman*, 459 P.2d 912, 922 (Cal. 1969).

Internal quotation marks appear inside external quotation marks and represent the source's quotation of an earlier source. In the following sample, external and internal quotes are used. The external (double) quotation marks represent the author's quote of the *Shulman* case, and the internal (single) quotation marks represent the *Shulman* case's quotation of the *Gilbert* case.

Sample Use of External and Internal Quotation Marks

Moreover, a logical relationship requires that the specific fact at issue has "'some substantial relevance'" to the topic. *Shulman*, 955 P.2d at 484 (plurality opinion) (quoting *Gilbert v. Med. Econ. Co.*, 665 F.2d 305, 308 (10th Cir. 1981)).

This seems simple enough, but using internal quotation marks gets tricky when the source quotes a preexisting source, which in turn quotes an original source. This happens quite frequently in court opinions. When you face this situation, start with the external quotation marks that represent your quotation of the source that you read, followed by internal quotation marks that represent that source's quotation of a preexisting source, followed by a new set of external quotation marks that represent the preexisting source's quotation of the original source. In other words, keep alternating between external and internal quotation marks.

Illustration of Two-Level Quote

Today my daughter came home from school and told me that a boy in her class was teasing her. She said, "Mommy, James called me a 'sissy.' I didn't like that."

In the above sample, I use external quotation marks to indicate what my daughter said and then internal quotation marks to indicate what she reported that James said. Now suppose that you want to tell a friend about my story.

Illustration of Three-Level Quote

A boy teased Professor Turner's daughter today. He called her a "'"sissy,"'" and she "'didn't like that.'"

In this three-level quote, the word "sissy" has an external quotation mark, an internal quotation mark, and then another external quotation mark on one side of it and then an external quotation mark, an internal quotation mark, and another external quotation mark on the other side of it. The first set of external marks represent your quotation of me. The internal marks represent my quotation of my daughter. And the second set of external marks represent my daughter's quotation of the boy. The "didn't like that" language has only one set of external marks and one set of internal marks because you are quoting me quoting my daughter, but my daughter was not quoting the boy.

If you had even more levels of sources for the quoted language, you would keep alternating between external and internal marks. So far, the sample has external, internal, external. You would resort to a second set of internal marks next.

For example, if the boy was not actually calling my daughter a sissy but was telling her what he overheard someone else say, your description of the event would look like the following example.

Illustration of Four-Level Quote

Someone teased Professor Turner's daughter today. A boy told her daughter that someone called her a "'"'sissy,'"'" but he did not say who it was.

8.8.3.2 | "Quoting" Notations

In addition to the alternation of external and internal quotation marks, the *Bluebook* and *ALWD* require indication of the preexisting source that the source you read was quoting. Here is an example of a quoting notation using the *Bluebook* and *ALWD* styles.

Sample Use of Quoting Notation

"'"[T]he coercive effect of fear...is itself a form of force."'" *People v. Wright*, 59 Cal. Rptr. 2d 316, 322 (Ct. App. 1996) (quoting *People v. Brookins*, 264 Cal. Rptr. 240, 246 (Ct. App. 1989)).

In this example, *Wright* is quoting *Brookins*, which is quoting another case. The second set of external quotes (external-internal-external) indicate that *Brookins* is citing some other source. Notice that the quoting notation goes back only one level to *Brookins*. You do not have to state the name of the case that *Brookins* was quoting.

8.8.4 | Altering Quoted Text

Sometimes, you may want to include only part of a quote. Other times, you may need to change the quote slightly to make it fit into your sentence grammatically. Indicate such changes as follows.

Adding emphasis. If you want to emphasize language in the quotation that is not emphasized in the original, put the language in italics and include the notation "(emphasis added)" in your citation.

Sample Emphasis-Added Notation

"'"[T]he coercive effect of fear...is *itself* a form of force."'" *People v. Wright*, 59 Cal. Rptr. 2d 316, 322 (Ct. App. 1996) (quoting *People v. Brookins*, 264 Cal. Rptr. 240, 246 (Ct. App. 1989)) (emphasis added).

Deleting unnecessary language from a quotation. If you want to delete part of a quotation, use an ellipsis: "..."

Sample Use of Ellipsis

"'"[T]he coercive effect of fear...is itself a form of force."'" *People v. Wright*, 59 Cal. Rptr. 2d 316, 322 (Ct. App. 1996) (quoting *People v. Brookins*, 264 Cal. Rptr. 240, 246 (Ct. App. 1989)).

The three dots in the above sample indicate that there was some language between "fear" and "is itself" in the original source that has now been left out.

If you want to substitute language in a quote to make it fit your sentence grammatically, use brackets [].

Sample Use of Brackets

Her intimidation of the victim constituted robbery because its "'"coercive effect... [was] itself a form of force."'" *People v. Wright*, 59 Cal. Rptr. 2d 316, 322 (Ct. App. 1996) (quoting *People v. Brookins*, 264 Cal. Rptr. 240 (Ct. App. 1989)).

The brackets around "was" in the above sample indicate that *Brookins* did not use the word "was." The author of this sample changed the tense of the verb to make it fit her sentence. The original text in *Brookins* was: "the coercive effect of fear induced by threats to a victim's person or property is in itself a form of force."

8.9 | CAPITALIZATION RULES

This section may not seem like it belongs in the citation chapter, but some citation manuals, including the *Bluebook* and *ALWD*, address capitalization. Capitalization rules are fairly standard across jurisdictions.

Capitalize the word "court" only if you are using the full, formal name of a court (e.g., the Superior Court of Los Angeles, the Court of Appeals for the First Circuit) or are referring to

- the court that is hearing your case, or
- the U.S. Supreme Court.

So, if you are describing a precedent case, do not capitalize the word "court" unless the case was decided by the United States Supreme Court.

Capitalize the words "defendant" or "plaintiff" only when referring to the parties in your case.

Sample 1

Moreover, "substantial relevance" requires more than a minor benefit to the message of a piece. *See M.G.*, 107 Cal. Rptr. 2d at 514. In *M.G.*, the defendants published a photograph of a Little League team with an article that disclosed the coach's sexual abuse of the team members. *Id.* at 507. The defendants argued that the faces of the

Cont.

team members "underscore[d]" the message of the article and broadcast by "showing visually that any child who plays sports could be placed in harm's way." *Id.* at 514. The court found that this asserted justification "[ra]ng[] hollow." *Id.*

In Sample 1, "defendants" and "court" are not capitalized because the author is referring to the defendants and the court in the *M.G.* case and not in her own case.

Sample 2

In this case, Defendant's asserted reasons for including Plaintiff's name in the article fall short of establishing substantial relevance.... First, any minor benefit to the tone of the piece is similar to the visual impact asserted by the defendants in *M.G.* Like the use of the photograph in *M.G.* might have given the sex abuse story more force, the use of Plaintiff's name in Defendant's article might have helped the readers identify with the piece, but such a minor "journalistic impact" or benefit to "credibility" is not sufficient to establish substantial relevance.

In Sample 2, "Defendant's" and "Plaintiff's" are capitalized because the author is referring to the defendant and plaintiff in her own case.

Sample 3

The California Supreme Court has preserved the public disclosure tort to protect an individual's anonymity against media intrusion into her "most intimate activities" and "most personal characteristics." *Briscoe*, 483 P.2d at 37.

In Sample 3, "California Supreme Court" is capitalized because the author is using the full title of the court.

Sample 4

The Court should affirm the judgment in the Defendant's favor because Plaintiff erroneously bases her lawsuit on the publication of truthful newsworthy information.

In Sample 4, "Court," "Defendant's," and "Plaintiff" are capitalized because the author is referring to the court deciding her case and to the parties in her case.

Citation Checklist

Considerations for Citations of Statutes

- ☐ Consult your jurisdiction's required citation manual for the proper format.
- ☐ Rules regarding what date to include can be complex: do not merely assume the correct date to use is that of enactment.

Considerations for First-Time Citations of Cases

- ☐ Get the case name correct by looking up all pertinent rules in your jurisdiction's required citation manual regarding which parties' names to include and when to abbreviate.
- ☐ Cite to the right reporter. Consult your citation manual's rules regarding which reporter to cite.
- ☐ Include the jump page: *Ezzy v. Workers' Comp. Appeals Bd.*, 194 Cal. Rptr. 90, **93** (Ct. App. 1983)).
- ☐ Use a signal if needed and italicize or underline it. Also, include a parenthetical if needed: *See Cox Broad. Corp. v. Cohn*, 420 U.S. 469, 490-91 (1975) (holding that state could not prohibit publication of the name of a rape victim obtained from public records because crimes are of legitimate concern to the public).
- ☐ Refer to the chart on introductory signals in deciding when you need a signal, which signal to use, and when to include a parenthetical. Here are some highlights:
  - Do not use *see* for direct quotes, for summaries of the facts of a case, or for paraphrasing that does not involve "artistic licensing."
  - Do use *see* for statements that are not directly supported by the case (i.e., that require some interpretation to see how they are supported by the case).
  - Use explanatory parentheticals whenever you use *see.*
  - Use *see also* when adding parentheticals after a full case example.

Considerations for Subsequent Citation of a Case

- ☐ Use *id.* if and only if these two elements are true:
  - You are citing to the same case as in your most recent citation.

    Plaintiff can prevail on the newsworthiness element only if she can show that the disclosure was "intrusive in great disproportion to [its] relevance." *Shulman v. Grp. W Prods., Inc.*, 955 P.2d 469, 478-79 (Cal. 1998). In most cases, a logical nexus between the disclosed facts and the newsworthy topic entitles the defendant to summary judgment. *See id.* at 486 (stating that "in the ordinary case," the logical nexus analysis determines newsworthiness).

  - Your most recent citation contains only one source. If the sentence above about intrusiveness had cited an additional case, you could not have used *id.* for the sentence about logical nexus. You would have to use the short form.
- ☐ Considerations when using *id.*:
  - Include the jump page unless you are referring to the exact same page in the most recent cite.
  - Italicize or underline *id.*
  - Include signals and parentheticals when needed.

Cont.

- ☐ When you cannot use *id.*, use the short form. The short form consists of: *Shortened case name*, volume + reporter + "at" + jump cite. *Briscoe*, 483 P.2d at 37.

Things to Recheck After Inputting Your Case Citations

- ☐ Check every case cite to see whether case names, signals, and *id.* are all italicized or underlined.
- ☐ Check every case cite to see whether the volume numbers are indicated (for example, 15 Cal. Rptr. 201).
- ☐ Check every case cite to see whether you include the jump page.
- ☐ Check every case cite to see whether you include the proper court abbreviation and date in parentheses at the end of the citation and before any parenthetical.
- ☐ Check every case cite in a string citation to see whether you use the right signal and properly punctuate the string.

Check Your Quotations

- ☐ Identify changes from the original text by using brackets and ellipses.
- ☐ Use internal (single) quotation marks when quoting a statement that is already in quotation marks in the cited case. Use quotation marks in alternating order, starting with external (double) marks. Use a "quoting" parenthetical if required by your jurisdiction's citation manual.
- ☐ Use block quotes only for 50+ words.

CHAPTER 8 SELF-TEST

1. In a case cite, how do you know which reporter to cite to?
2. What is a jump page or pinpoint cite?
3. What are the two circumstances when your citation does not need a signal?
4. Is the signal italicized/underlined?
5. When do you need to include subsequent history?
6. What punctuation usually separates sources cited in a string citation?
7. When can you use *id.*?
8. When will *id.* include a jump page or pinpoint cite?
9. Do you have to cite the case in full when you cannot use *id.*?
10. When do you capitalize "court" and "defendant"?

See answers on page 339.

SECTION **C**

SETTING THE STAGE FOR A LEGAL ANALYSIS

CHAPTER **9**

Factual Narratives

Factual Background and Statement of Facts

In addition to the analysis or argument section discussed in Section B of Part I, legal documents often also include a factual narrative that provides the details of the client's case. This section is typically referred to as a "factual background" or a "statement of facts."

The basic considerations in drafting an effective factual narrative common to both legal research memoranda and briefs are discussed in this chapter. Section 13.5 explains that the only additional consideration in a legal research memorandum is that the factual narrative must be written in a neutral and objective manner while Chapter 18 provides special techniques that lawyers use to put a persuasive bent on the factual narrative in court briefs.

The factual narrative is usually the easiest section for students to conquer. It is not much different from other styles of writing you may be used to. It needs to be thorough, well organized, clear, accurate, and free of grammatical errors. Some more specific tips follow.

9.1 | USING AN INTRODUCTORY PARAGRAPH

The start of a factual narrative is a bit like a newspaper article. Journalism students learn to put the who, what, where, and when at the start of an article. Lawyers do the same.

Who: Who is suing who? Or, in a criminal case, who is the defendant?

What: What is the defendant being sued for? Or, in a criminal case, with what crime is the defendant charged? You may also want to identify the claim or defense that your analysis will focus on.

Where: Location may or may not be important to include. Include the location of the event(s) involved in the case only if it is relevant to the legal issue(s) you will be analyzing.

When: Timing also may or may not be important to include. Include the date of the event(s) involved in the case only if it is relevant to the legal issue(s) you will be analyzing.

Sample Introductory Paragraph 1

Defendant Nora Roberts has been charged with selling narcotics. She is seeking to establish an entrapment defense based on the involvement of an undercover agent.

Sample Introductory Paragraph 2

Mark Gator is seeking workers' compensation coverage of an injury he sustained while playing paddleball with his supervisor after work on a court in his employer's parking lot.

Sample Introductory Paragraph 3

This office has charged Geraldo Savonarola with burglary for his use of a stolen ATM card to obtain cash from an ATM kiosk adjacent to the victim's bank.

As the samples illustrate, the introductory paragraph at the start of the narrative should provide just enough information to establish a context for the more detailed facts to follow.

9.2 | SELECTING THE RIGHT FACTS

Exclude irrelevant facts. A legal document might address only one small facet of a case. A case file will typically include both information that will factor into your analysis and information that is completely irrelevant to the issue your document will address. You will need to decide which information is relevant to the issue you are addressing. For example, if you are analyzing whether a juvenile defendant's parents could be held responsible for the car crash he caused, you would want to include all information about the parents' actions leading up to the accident, but you would exclude details from your client's medical records about the nature of the injuries your client sustained. Details about the injuries would not help you analyze the parents' degree of fault.

Search the case file. The first time you draft your narrative, take an educated guess about which factual details will be important. Comb through your case file and make a list of key facts you think you should include. As you write the narrative, pull helpful quotes from the case file to help give the narrative greater specificity and clarity.

Crosscheck with your legal analysis. Return to the narrative again after you finish your legal analysis (discussed in Part I, Section B). For each fact you mention in your analysis, whether in connection with your main points or a counterargument, refer to your narrative to ensure the fact is included. Come up with a system. For example, you could place a check mark next to each fact referenced in the analysis after you have checked that it is included in your narrative.

When double-checking your narrative section, be very specific. For example, a quotation from someone's testimony that is included in the analysis should be included verbatim in your narrative.

You may think repeating the same facts and quotations in both the narrative and the legal analysis is repetitive and unnecessary. However, lawyers do not always read a memorandum in a linear fashion. Each section has to independently meet the expectations of your reader without depending on another section. Moreover, including all factual details in the narrative ensures that each detail and quotation will be in its proper context in the overall story of the case.

9.3 | TELLING A GOOD STORY

Here is a life skill that most law students already have and can bring to bear in legal writing. Use your narrative to tell an interesting story for your reader. Do not just list fact after fact like entries in a diary. Instead, weave the facts together. Consider your reader. She would much rather read something fun and interesting than something that reads like an obituary.

A good storyteller uses character building, perspective, plot development, and narrative details. You can use the same techniques in your narrative.

ERROR Example of a Boring Narrative

Pullo was on his way to a therapy session. The bus driver reprimanded Pullo for practicing Tai Chi while the bus was in motion. Pullo refused to comply with the driver's instructions and instead grabbed and twisted the driver's shirt. Later, while in the therapy session, Pullo told Athena he was "going to beat the living hell out of the next rude bus driver he met." Furthermore, since they live close to each other and on certain occasions have ended up on the same bus, Pullo warned Athena not to take the bus home that day so she would not see "one of his episodes." Later, during this same therapy session, Pullo stormed out of the office. Shortly after, Pullo encountered Mr. Curio and attacked him when he requested Pullo get off of the bus after an argument over the bus fare. Mr. Curio is now attempting to sue therapist Athena for damages resulting in her breach of failing to warn him of her patient's threat.

The above example makes no attempt to introduce the characters involved in the case and does not focus on any one person's perspective. It also does not take time to carefully develop the plot. Details are jammed together in monstrously long sentences instead. The paragraph includes few narrative details. Contrast the following revised version.

Sample Narrative Revised

Curio had been a bus driver on the same line for 12 years. **Then, one day, he picked up Spartacus Pullo**. As Pullo and other passengers entered the bus, Curio said, "Move along folks, we've got places to go, people to meet, T.V. to watch, and dinner to eat." **While others chuckled, Pullo was "insulted by his condescension." Pullo then** gave Curio a $10 bill for the $1 bus fare, expecting Curio to make change. Curio told Pullo he needed to either pay the exact fare or get off at the next stop. Pullo then erupted, "That's bull. Bull. Just take my money and give me some change." When Curio refused, Pullo pulled him off his seat and beat him severely.

Earlier the same day, Pullo had a **similar** encounter with another bus driver. **On his way to his therapist's office**, Pullo had grabbed a bus driver's shirt when the driver told Pullo to sit down. Pullo had told his therapist about this incident and stated he was "going to beat the living hell out of the next rude bus driver he met." He even warned his therapist not to take the bus home that day because he did not want her to see him "in one of his episodes." He then stormed out of her office **and, as it turned out, did exactly as he promised—"beat the living hell out of" Curio.**

The revised version tells the story from Curio's perspective. The events are described as Curio experienced them. The revised version also spends a little time building Curio's character by describing his years of service and illustrating his sense of humor. The main improvement, however, is in plot development and use of narrative details. Rather than cramming facts together, the revised version takes the time to lay out the events in a step-by-step fashion. As a result, the reader can more easily follow the story. In addition, the revised version makes more connections between facts. The connections are in bold for illustration. This factual synthesis is as important to an effective narrative as rule synthesis is to an effective discussion of the law in a legal analysis.

To achieve a style closer to the revised version than to the boring version, take some time to think about the story before you write. Who do you want the good guy to be? How would the good guy tell the story? What quotes and details can you include to help bring the story to life? How can you connect one fact to another to create a more fluid narrative?

9.4 | ORGANIZING THE FACTS

9.4.1 | Selecting Between a Chronological and a Topical Organization

I cannot offer any easy rules about how to organize a narrative. As a general rule, chronological order is best. However, chronological order does not always work. When your case cannot be broken down into series of events, then you may want to use a topical organization instead. A topical organization groups facts by category rather than sequence.

For example, a chronological order would work well for a car accident case. You could proceed through the events leading up to the crash, then relate the details of the crash, and then describe any subsequent developments. By contrast, a topical organization might work well for a case involving widespread employment discrimination by a particular company: one paragraph might describe limited opportunities for advancement by minorities; another might describe hiring discrimination; and another might describe retaliation against minorities who lodged discrimination complaints.

9.4.2 | Special Considerations When Using Chronological Order

Effective transitions. Chronological order does not require the exceptionally boring construction, "On February 2, 2009, ... Then, on March 21, ..." Dates are usually irrelevant and therefore should be omitted unless the timing of events is important to the issue you are analyzing. Instead of starting your paragraphs and sentences with dates, use topic sentences or, at least, transitional language. In the revised sample in section 9.3, the first paragraph does not start with a date. Instead, it states, "Curio had been a bus driver on the same line for 12 years. Then, one day, he picked up Spartacus Pullo." This sets the stage for the paragraph, which will provide the details about the encounter between Curio and

Pullo. Similarly, the second paragraph starts with a transition, "Earlier the same day," and then focuses on the events that preceded the encounter with Curio.

Logical paragraph breaks. Chronological order is also not an invitation to create a single paragraph for your entire narrative. You will need to figure out where to break your paragraphs. You should group paragraphs by the type of event or topic. In the revised sample in section 9.3, the first paragraph describes the attack on Curio and the second paragraph describes the events leading up to the attack. As another example, here are the first sentences of the paragraphs in the narrative from Appendix B, Sample A.

Sample Paragraph Breaks

Gator works for Fitness Functions, a company that sells fitness equipment...[Paragraph describes the company's use of paddleball as a recreational activity.]

Randolph saw Gator leaving from work one day as she was heading to play in the court...[Paragraph describes her invitation to play paddleball.]

Gator...had only recently been hired and was still on probationary status... [Paragraph describes his decision-making process regarding whether to accept the invitation.]

During his game with Randolph, Gator hit himself with his paddle...[Paragraph describes his injury and subsequent events.]

Facts that do not fit the chronology. Sometimes, certain facts do not fit in the chronology because they are not part of the sequence of events. You can put these nonchronological facts together either before or after the chronological narrative. For example, Appendix B, Sample A, describes the employer's facility and practices in a paragraph that precedes the sequence of events leading up to the employee's injury.

Sample Placement of Nonchronological Facts

Gator works for Fitness Functions, a company that sells fitness equipment. Fitness Functions has a paddleball court in its parking lot. It built the court to attract Gator's supervisor, Joyce Randolph, who was a famous racquetball player, to her current position as Director of Marketing and Sales. Randolph uses the court to play with employees and clients. She thinks paddleball is a good way to get to know her employees, boost morale, build team spirit, and keep employees in shape. The company provides paddles, balls, sneakers, and exercise clothes to "make[] it easy" for employees to play.

Randolph saw Gator leaving from work one day as she was heading to play in the court. She complimented Gator on bringing in a new client...and invited him to play

Cont.

with her later in the week. Gator responded that he would check his schedule and get back to her.

9.4.3 | Synthesis of Facts

A case file typically contains interview notes and deposition transcripts. Each set of notes or transcripts relates the testimony of a particular witness. Mirroring this organization, students are often tempted to organize their narrative by witness. For example, they might describe the plaintiff's testimony in one paragraph and then the plaintiff's mother's testimony in another paragraph. Bad idea. If you organize by witness, you will end up repeating the same facts over and over in different ways and, as a result, will drive your reader crazy. Just like you need to synthesize cases for your reader by organizing your rule explanation section by subrule rather than by case, you also need to synthesize the facts for your reader by organizing them in a logical fashion, as explained in section 9.4.1, rather than by witness.

9.5 | INCORPORATING PRINCIPLES OF GOOD PARAGRAPH STRUCTURE

A topical organization *requires* topic sentences, and even a chronological organization can sometimes benefit from topic sentences. Topic sentences in a narrative should not state conclusions, but should simply introduce the topic of the paragraph. Also, you want to avoid biased language in your topic sentences. For example, the sample narrative excerpt in section 9.3 starts one of its paragraphs by introducing Curio and then stating, "Then one day, he picked up Spartacus Pullo." This introduces the topic of the paragraph—the encounter between Curio and Pullo—without stating any conclusions or using biased language.

Another important consideration in organizing your narrative is to include transitional language at the start of each paragraph. The improved flow that results from transitional language helps the reader understand your organizational choices and helps the narrative read more like a story and less like an obituary. The first sentences from each paragraph of Appendix B, Sample A's factual background are provided below with the transitions bolded. Most of the transitions in this example help place the events in their proper timeframe without burdening the reader with unnecessary dates.

Sample Transitions

Gator works for Fitness Functions, a company that sells fitness equipment...[Paragraph describes the company's use of paddleball as a recreational activity.]

Cont.

Randolph saw Gator leaving from work **one day** as she was heading to play in the court...[Paragraph describes her invitation to play paddleball.]

Gator...had **only recently** been hired and was **still** on probationary status...[Paragraph describes his decision-making process regarding whether to accept the invitation.]

During his game with Randolph, Gator hit himself with his paddle...[Paragraph describes his injury and subsequent events.]

Section 12.2 provides more instruction on how to draft transitions.

9.6 | INCLUDING A PROCEDURAL HISTORY OF THE CASE

The narrative usually includes what lawyers refer to as the "procedural history" or "procedural posture." The procedural history is the story of the lawsuit or prosecution from the time it was commenced until the time of your memorandum or brief. In a civil case, the story of a lawsuit includes the complaint and the causes of action it alleges, the answer to the complaint, any motions and related court orders, the trial (if applicable), the verdict (if applicable), and any post-verdict orders or motions. In a criminal case, the story of the prosecution includes the indictment and the charges it asserts, the arraignment and plea, any motions and related court orders, the trial (if applicable), the verdict (if applicable), and any post-verdict orders or motions. Sometimes you may be preparing an analysis before a lawsuit has even been filed; you would not have a procedural history to include.

Usually, the procedural history fits best in the last paragraph of the narrative. The first paragraph is another option and works as long as the reader does not need to know the other facts to understand certain events in the procedural history. If, for example, the procedural history includes a motion to suppress evidence, you would probably want to save the procedural history for last because the reader would need to know about the evidence at issue before the reader could understand the significance of a motion to suppress it.

Sample Procedural History (at the end)

During his game with Randolph, Gator hit himself with his paddle. He filed for workers' compensation coverage for his resulting injuries. The company denied coverage. Gator is now considering filing an application for adjudication with the Workers' Compensation Appeals Board. (From Appendix B, Sample A.)

Sample Procedural History (at the beginning)

Our client, Hilary Lysander, lives and works as a licensed attorney in New York. Lysander is not licensed to practice law in California. The Attorney General of California has brought charges against her for violating California Business and Professions Code section 6125 by allegedly providing Derek Ptolemy with legal advice regarding California law without a license to practice in this state. (From Appendix B, Sample D.)

9.7 | AVOIDING STATEMENTS ABOUT THE LAW

The narrative should contain only factual assertions and not any statements about the law. A witness's testimony is a factual assertion. The provisions of a statute, however, are a legal matter and should be saved for your legal analysis.

ERROR Examples of Legal Assertions That Do Not Belong in the Factual Background

Workers' compensation permits coverage of injuries arising...

A local ordinance prohibited plaintiff's conduct.

The court denied the motion because case law provided that...

9.8 | AVOIDING CONCLUSIONS

The narrative should tell the story of the case without any conclusions about what the facts show or about the legal issues involved in the case. For example, if you are presenting the facts relevant to an analysis of an entrapment defense, you could not at any point in the narrative assert that the defendant *was* entrapped into committing a crime by the police. You could state that the defendant *claims* she was entrapped, however, since you would just be recounting the fact of what she claims rather than making the conclusion that she was entrapped. To further illustrate the difference between a legal conclusion and a factual statement that merely describes a party's contention, another example follows.

ERROR Example of Conclusory Language

Lysander violated California Business and Professions Code section 6125 by providing Derek Ptolemy with legal advice...

Revised Version

The Attorney General of California has brought charges against Lysander for violating California Business and Professions Code section 6125 by allegedly providing Derek Ptolemy with legal advice...

Factual Narrative Checklist

- ☐ Include an introductory sentence or paragraph that sets the stage by providing the who, what, when, and where.
- ☐ Include every fact and quotation you mention in your legal analysis. Double-check the narrative after you finish your legal analysis to ensure you have included everything.
- ☐ Tell a story. Use character development, perspective, plot development, and narrative detail.
- ☐ Think carefully about organization. Choose chronological or topical. For a topical organization, use topic sentences. For a chronological organization, avoid mundane dates and break paragraphs by type of event or topic.
- ☐ Do not organize by witness. Synthesize facts.
- ☐ Include a transition at the start of each new paragraph.

CHAPTER 9 SELF-TEST

1. What should the introductory paragraph of a factual background or statement of the facts do?
2. What should you do before beginning to draft a factual background or statement of the facts?
3. How can you achieve a more interesting narrative?
4. What does it mean to synthesize facts?
5. What is a procedural history?
6. Can you make statements about the law or state conclusions or opinions in a factual narrative?

See answers on page 339.

CHAPTER **10**

Issue Identification
Issue Statements and Questions Presented

Many types of legal documents also include a formal section that identifies the issue(s) that the document will analyze. This section is sometimes called the "issue statement," "question(s) presented," or "statement of the issue(s)." Although it is a small part of your document, the issue statement is important. It helps your reader understand the focus of your legal analysis. The issue statement provides the lens through which the reader will view your legal analysis. Drafting the issue statement is a challenging task. It often requires multiple rewrites.

10.1 | PUTTING THE ISSUE STATEMENT IN THE FORM OF A QUESTION

Many legal writers use the "whether" construction for an issue statement. However, you can avoid the grammatically incorrect "whether" construction by putting the issue statement in the form of a question.

ERROR **Example of "Whether" Construction**

Whether the sky is blue.

Sample Question Format

Is the sky blue?

10.2 | AIMING FOR SPECIFICITY

You are not analyzing a question for academic purposes. Your legal document is not a law review article. Rather, it is designed to solve a problem in your particular case. Therefore, it should be drafted in a manner that is specific to your case.

ERROR **Example of an Overly Generic Question**

Can a defendant establish entrapment where the government told her how to commit the crime and gave her all of the necessary materials?

Revised Version

Can **Nora Roberts** establish entrapment where the government **supplied all of the drugs she sold and told her how to contact the buyer and secure the deal?**

The bold portions of the revised version add the defendant's name and the specifics of the case.

10.3 | INCLUDING FACTUAL DETAIL

The issue statement should preview not just the nature of the question but also the key facts on which the answer to the question depends (in your judgment). This is the aspect of the issue statement with which students tend to struggle the most. Finish a draft of your legal analysis or, at least, develop a detailed outline for your analysis before you draft the issue statement. Think about the main reason(s) for your conclusion on the issue and identify the facts to which those reason(s) relate. Include those key facts in the issue statement.

You will likely struggle to choose which facts to include without making the issue statement too long and confusing. The idea is to preview the heart of your analysis of the issue. On what facts does the issue ultimately depend?

10.4 | IDENTIFYING THE CLAIM OR DEFENSE AT ISSUE

The issue statement should reference the claim or defense that is at issue. For example, "Can Nora Roberts establish entrapment..." tells the reader that the defense at issue is entrapment.

10.5 | IDENTIFYING THE KEY RULE LANGUAGE

The question should include the key element(s), test(s), or factor(s) on which your question turns. For example, in our entrapment example, we have to add the specific elements, tests, or factors on which entrapment depends. Including the key rule language gives the reader a better sense of where your analysis is going. The key rule language is bolded in the revised version below.

Sample Reference to Key Factors

To establish an entrapment defense, can Nora Roberts **prove significant governmental involvement in the drug sale for which she was charged and lack of any predis-position to commit the crime** where the government supplied all of the drugs she sold and told her how to contact the buyer and secure the deal, but she had engaged in similar transactions in the recent past without any prompting by the government?

Also keep in mind that the reader should not have to refer to a legal dictionary or some other part of your legal document to understand the question. In our entrapment example, no problem arises because "significant involvement" and "predisposition" are terms any reader can understand. The problem is more likely to arise where the key element, test, or factor is too esoteric or where the author includes a case reference in the question. For an example, see step 4 of the "Illustration of Perfecting an Issue Statement" in section 10.8.

10.6 | MATCHING THE FACTS TO THE RULE LANGUAGE

The key facts and the key element(s), test(s), or factor(s) that you include in your issue statement should match. The key rule language you include should indicate the relevance of the key facts you include.

ERROR Example of a Confusing Question

I o establish an entrapment defense, can Nora Roberts prove significant governmental involvement in the drug sale for which she was charged where she had engaged in similar transactions in the recent past?

This issue statement is confusing to the reader because there is no obvious connection between the fact of her past crimes and the factor of governmental involvement.

Revised Version (Good Matching)

To establish an entrapment defense, can Nora Roberts prove **significant governmental involvement** in the drug sale for which she was charged and lack of any predis-

Cont.

position to commit the crime where the **government supplied all of the drugs she sold and told her how to contact the buyer and secure the deal**, but she had engaged in similar transactions in the recent past without any prompting by the government?

In this revised version, the government's supply of the drugs and instructions on contacting the buyer relate to the factor of "governmental involvement," and her prior transactions relate to the factor of "predisposition."

10.7 | AVOIDING CONCLUSIONS

In drafting the issue statement, avoid assuming the answer to the question your legal analysis will address.

ERROR Example of Incorrectly Assuming the Answer

Can Nora Roberts establish entrapment where the government was significantly involved in the crime?

The clause "where the government was significantly involved" assumes an answer to a key question on which the analysis will turn—a major part of the analysis will focus on whether Roberts can establish significant involvement.

Revised Version

To establish an entrapment defense, can Nora Roberts prove significant_governmental involvement in the drug sale for which she was charged and lack of any predisposition to commit the crime where the government supplied all of the drugs she sold and told her how to contact the buyer and secure the deal, but she had engaged in similar transactions in the recent past without any prompting by the government?

The revised version correctly asks whether she can prove significant involvement under the facts of the case.

10.8 | PUTTING THE LESSONS TOGETHER

To illustrate the key lessons about issue statements, the following example will start with a terrible issue statement that violates all seven of the principles discussed in sections 10.1 to 10.7. It will then fix each problem.

Illustration of Perfecting an Issue Statement

Starting Point: A Terrible Issue Statement

Whether a person can be held liable for carelessly loaning a car to a drunk driver.

Step 1: Put It in Question Format

Can a person be held liable for carelessly loaning a car to a drunk driver?

Step 2: Change the Wording to Be Specific to the Case at Hand

Can Joe be held liable for carelessly loaning his car to Mary when she was drunk?

Step 3: Identify the Cause of Action at Issue

Can Joe be found **negligent** for carelessly loaning his car to Mary when she was drunk?

Step 4: Identify the Specific Element, Test, or Factor at Issue

Incorrect:

Can Joe be found negligent under the *Palsgraf* test for carelessly loaning his car to Mary when she was drunk?

Explanation of the Problem:

The reader has no idea what the *Palsgraf* test is. Instead of referencing a case, the author needs to use descriptive terminology for the test.

Correct:

Should Joe have foreseen, so as to be liable in negligence, that Mary, who was drunk, might be injured when he carelessly loaned his car to her?

Explanation of the Correction:

The reader is more likely to understand foreseeability than a reference to *Palsgraf*.

Step 5: Add the Facts That Will Determine the Answer to the Question

Should Joe have foreseen, so as to be liable in negligence, that Mary might be injured **when he carelessly loaned his car to her after she had consumed four beers and eight shots of vodka less than two hours before?**

Explanation of the Correction:

The key facts that follow the "when" help solidify the issue involved in this particular case.

Step 6: Check Whether the Key Rule and Key Facts Match

Look at the issue statement under step 5. Is it clear to you as the reader that Mary's consumption of alcohol is relevant to Joe's ability to foresee (i.e., predict) that she would get into an accident? Not unless he knew about it, right? So, to connect the test of fore-

Cont.

seeability to the facts of Mary's drinking, the writer needs to add that Joe knew about her drinking:

Should Joe have foreseen, so as to be liable in negligence, that Mary might be injured when he carelessly loaned his car to her **knowing** that she had consumed four beers and eight shots of vodka less than two hours before?

Step 7: Delete the Conclusory Language

The question as phrased in step 6 is biased because it includes the word "carelessly."

Should Joe have foreseen, so as to be liable in negligence, that Mary might be injured when he loaned his car to her knowing that she had consumed four beers and eight shots of vodka less than two hours before?

Ahhh, the perfect issue statement at last!

10.9 | USING FORMULAS FOR ISSUE STATEMENTS

When you sit down to write your first issue statement, you may be stunned by the seeming impossibility of creating a grammatically correct question that achieves all of the elements discussed in sections 10.1 to 10.7.

Here is an initial tip: keep the law on one side of the question and the facts on the other. In the following example, the underlined portion contains the rule language and the italicized portion contains the key facts from the case.

Example of Issue Statement Organization

<u>Should Joe have foreseen, so as to be liable in negligence, that Mary might be injured</u> *when he loaned his car to her knowing that she had consumed four beers and eight shots of vodka less than two hours before*?

In addition, the following two formulas may help you plug in the information you need without running into grammatical problems. These are not the only options, but they might help if you are struggling with including all of the necessary information while still creating a readable, grammatically correct question.

Option 1 Formula

To establish [insert cause of action or defense at issue], **can** [insert plaintiff's or defendant's name] [prove/establish/satisfy] [insert key element(s), test(s), factor(s)] **where** [insert key fact(s) on which your analysis will turn]?

Sample Using Option 1

To establish an entrapment defense, **can** Nora Roberts prove significant governmental involvement in the drug sale for which she was charged and lack of any predisposition to commit the crime **where** the government supplied all of the drugs she sold and told her how to contact the buyer and secure the deal, but she had engaged in similar transactions in the recent past without any government involvement?

Option 2 Formula

Given that [insert key facts], **can** [insert plaintiff's or defendant's name] [prove/establish/satisfy] [insert element(s), test(s) or factor(s) at issue] **so as to establish** [insert cause of action or claim at issue]?

Sample Use of Option 2

Given that the government supplied all of the drugs she sold and told her how to contact the buyer and secure the deal but she had engaged in similar transactions in the recent past without any government involvement, **can** Nora Roberts prove significant governmental involvement in the drug sale for which she was charged and lack of any predisposition to commit the crime **so as to establish** an entrapment defense?

In using these two formulas, choose appropriately between "prove," "establish," or "satisfy." A desired outcome or result is *proven* or *established*. A requirement or test is *satisfied*.

10.10 | ISSUE STATEMENTS FOR MULTIPLE ISSUES

Legal documents that address two or more separately analyzed, independent issues usually require a matching number of questions in the issue statement. When using two or more questions, enumerate them and use paragraph breaks. Issues are independent if the answer to one does not depend on or build on the answer to the other.

Sample Two-Question Issue Statement

1. Was the portfolio, resting on Schwartzberg's lap, sufficiently within his reach to enable the District Attorney to satisfy the immediate presence element of robbery?

Cont.

2. By forcefully entering the car, taking the keys, and ordering Schwartzberg to "Just stay put," did Fitzgerald reasonably cause sufficient fear to prevent Schwartzberg from attempting to retain or regain the portfolio and did these actions amount to a threat or display of force?

Another option is to use enumerated subparts within a single question. Subparts can be used for both independent and dependent sub-issues. They enable you to include more detail on the sub-issues without making the question unreadable. First draft an introductory clause that sets out the overarching issue (in the sample below, "To establish..."). The clause should end with a colon. Then break out the sub-issues into enumerated subparts. Each subpart should contain the rule language on one sub-issue and the related facts. For example, in the sample below, subpart (1) provides the rule language on subjective belief ("subjectively believed") and the relevant testimony that the employee felt he "needed" to play. Subpart (2) then provides the rule language on objective reasonableness ("belief was reasonable") and the relevant details regarding the nature of the invitation and evidence of pressure to participate.

Sample Two-Part Issue Statement

To establish workers' compensation coverage for injuries he sustained during an after-hours game of paddleball with his supervisor, can Gator show that:

1. His testimony that he felt he "needed" to play paddleball with his supervisor adequately proves that he subjectively believed his participation was an expectancy of his employment; and
2. His belief was reasonable because although no one ever suggested he needed to play, his supervisor invited him to play during a conversation about his job performance, a coworker had once told him that playing paddleball with the supervisor had helped her advance in the company, and the company supplied the equipment in the hope that the game would boost morale, foster team work, and keep employees fit?

When using the two-part format, draft an introductory clause that sets out the general issue and grammatically fits with the enumerated parts. The sample above uses "To establish [the element or defense at issue], can [party] prove that: (1)...; and (2)...." You can also use "to satisfy" instead of "to establish." For example: To satisfy the actual malice requirement, can Plaintiff prove with clear and convincing evidence that...

Question words can also be used for the introductory clause (did, could, etc.) along with a "where" or "given that":

Alternative Sample Two-Part Question

Did the Appellant meet her burden to prove actual malice by clear and convincing evidence where:

(1) She claims that the footage of her and her family was false because scenes were manipulated out of order; and

(2) She claims RBC acted recklessly when it juxtaposed scenes to make her parenting look worse than it actually was?

Of course, these are not the only possible phrasings, but are safe standbys.

Issue Statement Checklist

- ☐ Write the statement in the form of a question and include a question mark. Do not use "whether."
- ☐ Make the statement specific to your case and not generic.
- ☐ Include the key fact(s) that determine the answer to the question.
- ☐ Identify the claim or defense at issue.
- ☐ Identify the elements, tests, or factors on which your analysis of the issue relies.
- ☐ The facts you choose to include should match the elements, tests, or factors you choose to include.
- ☐ Do not state or suggest a conclusion. Do not phrase the question in a manner that assumes an answer. Do not use conclusory language.
- ☐ Consider using one of the formulas to prevent grammar trouble.

CHAPTER **10** SELF-TEST

1. What are the two most important components of a question presented or issue statement?
2. Do these two components have to match?

See answers on page 340.

SECTION **D**

THE DISCIPLINE OF WRITING

CHAPTER **11**

Plain Ole Good Writing

As a lawyer, you will not be writing novels or poetry. Nor will you be writing a philosophical piece designed to provoke thought and challenge your reader. Instead, you will write to inform and often to convince. To achieve these goals, simplicity and clarity are paramount. If you doubt this statement, imagine yourself as a judge reading hundreds of pages of court documents every day. Imagine your gratefulness for a brief that is easy to read and clear. Imagine your impatience with one that is full of so much fluff and flowery language that you can barely decipher the attorney's points. This chapter offers some techniques to achieve simplicity and clarity in your writing.

11.1 | ELIMINATING UNNECESSARY LANGUAGE

This lesson sounds simple enough. Cut out words that are not essential to the point of your sentence. However, achieving this goal requires a disciplined approach to self-editing. The process reminds me of removing the grime from the space between the tiles on a bathroom floor: the more energy you put into the process, the better the outcome, but oh boy, it is laborious! To achieve concise writing, read over your drafts word by word *hoping* to find words you can cut. You cannot achieve concise writing if you read over your drafts hoping to find perfection. If you find no errors, your writing will remain imperfect. Look forward to finding the flaws in your drafts as if they were flecks of gold.

Compare the following two examples.

Before Cutting Unnecessary Words

Next, Gator can show the objective reasonableness of his belief that participation in paddleball was required, by pointing to the job-related pressure. *Kidwell* establishes that specific job-related pressure can help establish the objective reasonableness of a belief, by looking at circumstances surrounding employment. *Kidwell v. Workers' Comp. Appeals Bd.*, 39 Cal. Rptr. 2d 540, 545 (Ct. App. 1995). Gator was on probationary status, and as such, was more susceptible to pressure when his superior, a former paddleball celebrity, invited him to play. Further, Gator had heard from a coworker that advancement in the company might depend on his participation, which also increased the pressure. The fact that he waited to call Randolph before accepting her invitation shows that he was cognizant of these elements and felt pressure to accept the invitation. Likewise, that Gator was not an avid paddleball player but ultimately decided to play, allows the inference that he felt job-related pressure to play.

After Trimming the Fat

Next, Gator reasonably believed participation in paddleball was required. Specific job-related pressure can help establish the objective reasonableness of a belief. *Kidwell v. Workers' Comp. Appeals Bd.*, 39 Cal. Rptr. 2d 540, 545 (Ct. App. 1995). Because Gator was on probationary status, he was more susceptible to pressure when his superior, a former paddleball celebrity, invited him to play. Further, Gator had heard from a coworker that advancement in the company might depend on his participation. Gator did not immediately accept. He was not an avid player. He accepted only due to the pressure he reasonably felt.

You may be wondering how you can convert your writing to something more like the concise example above. The short answer is that you have to look carefully at each sentence, identify the heart of the sentence, and question whether you need anything else. Here is the "before" example again with the unnecessary language underlined.

Example of Unnecessary Words

Next, Gator can show the objective reasonableness of his belief that participation in paddleball was required, by pointing to the job-related pressure. *Kidwell* establishes that specific job-related pressure can help establish the objective reasonableness of a belief, by looking at circumstances surrounding employment. *Kidwell v. Workers' Comp. Appeals Bd.*, 39 Cal. Rptr. 2d 540, 545 (Ct. App. 1995). Gator was on probationary status, and as such, was more susceptible to pressure when his superior, a former paddleball celebrity, invited him to play. Further, Gator had heard from a coworker that advancement in the company might depend on his participation, which also increased the pressure. The fact that he waited to call Randolph before accepting her invitation shows that

Cont.

he was cognizant of these elements and felt pressure to accept the invitation. Likewise, that Gator was not an avid paddleball player but ultimately decided to play, allows the inference that he felt job-related pressure to play.

Cutting unnecessary language requires discipline and a willingness to place your reader's needs first. Honestly assess how well your writing communicates your message and let go of language that interferes with this goal. One tip is to look for language like "show that," "belief that," "establishes that," "looking at," "the fact that," "the inference that," and "proves that." When you find this filler language, force yourself to rewrite the sentence without it.

11.2 | EDITING TOWARD A SIMPLE SUBJECT-VERB-OBJECT STRUCTURE

The core of a sentence is its subject, verb, and (sometimes) object.

Sentence Core

Laura likes apples.
↑ subject ↑ verb ↑ object

Embrace the sentence core as the model for your sentences, and you will make great strides toward simplicity and clarity.

11.2.1 | Eliminating Frivolous Additions to the Sentence Core

Someone might be tempted to throw in some adjectives and adverbs or even a verb clause to spice up the sentence core a bit.

Example of Frivolous Additions

Health-conscious Laura likes to eat apples slowly.

Does this make the sentence better or worse? These additional elements make the sentence more difficult to read. Are the additions necessary? What do they add? A separate sentence could have made the point that Laura is health-conscious. And we do not need "to eat" because eating is usually what we do with apples. Finally, "slowly" does not seem necessary either unless the pace of her eating is somehow central to the writer's point. The lesson here is that any additions you make to the reader's favorite sentence (subject-verb-object) should serve a purpose. Practice looking over your longer sentences to identify the sentence core and then question whether all of your additions are needed.

11.2.2 | Sticking to the Structure of the Sentence Core

As an experiment, let's mix up the order of our sentence core.

Example of Altering Sentence Core

Apples are liked by Laura.

The sentence is harder to read. The change might seem innocent in isolation, but consider the following example.

Example of Multiple Alterations

Apples are liked by Laura. Eating them constantly in class, Laura is always serving as a distraction in the classroom. The teacher, who simply hates distractions, glares at her constantly, but Laura is oblivious to her consternation and carries on as if she were the only person in the room. Her apple habit is not appreciated by the other students, who wish that she would wait until after class to eat.

When you add more sentences that depart from the subject-verb-object model, you create a paragraph that exercises your reader's mind in unpleasant ways. The situation would only get worse if you then moved from the simple topic of this paragraph to a complex discussion of the law.

Now look at the same paragraph with fewer departures from the subject-verb-object model (the subject, verb, and object are underlined).

Sample Revision to Keep the Structure of the Sentence Core

Laura likes apples. She eats them constantly in class. Every crunch is a distraction in the classroom. Our teacher hates distractions. She glares at Laura constantly, but Laura does not seem to care. Laura acts as though she were the only person in the room. The other students share the teacher's consternation, and we all wish that she would wait until after class to eat.

By keeping subject-verb-object order in each sentence, the revised paragraph achieves a simple, easy-to-read style. This frees the reader to focus on the writing's logic, not on its murky language.

11.2.3 | Appreciating the Beauty of the Sentence Core

The to-the-point rawness of the subject-verb-object model can take some getting used to. It may seem awkward at first—too simple, in fact. It may even pain you because removing syntactical distractions may expose gaps in your thinking. However, if you embrace the beauty of a simple sentence, you will discover that your words have more power than ever before.

Embracing the subject-verb-object model requires a careful review of your sentences. If you know you have a tendency to stray from the model, underline the subject, verbs, and objects in your sentences. This technique will identify sentences that need revision to make their subjects, verbs, and objects appear closer together and in the right order.

11.3 | AVOIDING SUPERSIZED SENTENCES

Periods are a necessary break for the reader, like a swimmer's breath at the end of a lap. Do not make your reader swim too long without a breath. A good rule of thumb is to comb through your draft for sentences two lines or longer. If you can cut your long sentences into shorter sentences, do it. Here is another tip: limit your sentences to the subject-verb-object core plus an introductory clause plus one additional piece of information.

Formula

Maximum Sentence = Intro + Core + One

Sample of the Formula Applied

Although he is dating Maria | Bill likes Laura | because she is more fun.

Intro | Core (subject-verb-object) | One additional piece of information

ERROR Example of a Violation

Although he is dating Maria, a very nice girl, Bill likes Laura because she is more fun, and, therefore, he is planning to break up with Maria tomorrow after the baseball game.

As demonstrated in the above example, each added element to the sentence makes it heavier. Aim for a nice light snack rather than a Big Mac meal.

One last tip for implementing the preceding lessons: watch out for words like "that," "which," "who," "whom," "in which," "such that," and "thereby." These words often signal sentence add-ons that make the sentence too heavy. Minimizing these add-ons also avoids the grammatical errors they often cause. Of course, you cannot completely eradicate the use of these words. However, if you search for them, you may find opportunities to simplify your sentences by breaking off the add-on and making it into its own sentence.

Example of Eliminating Add-Ons

Instead of: I keep trying to convince my brother that he does not need his old car, which would be perfect for me.

Write: I keep trying to convince my brother that he does not need his old car. It would be perfect for me.

Add-On Alerts

that, which, who, whom, in which, such that, thereby

11.4 | USING MORE BASIC, LESS FANCY WORDS

As a legal writer, you are writing either to convince or to inform. Either way, words that a reader might have to look up in the dictionary will only impede your purpose. Moreover, even if your reader knows the meaning of a word, simple is always easier to read than fancy.

For example, most people know all of the words in the following example, but it is still difficult to read and just plain strange.

ERROR **Example of Stilted Language**

As I left my domicile, I encountered a pedestrian walking his canine. He inquired whether I would sell my automobile because he was fastidiously searching for an alternative vehicle. He stated that he would provide substantial remuneration for my vehicle because he was astounded by its magnificence and surreptitious approach.

Most readers would much prefer the following more simple version.

Sample Revised Language

As I left my house, I saw someone walking his dog. He asked me whether I would sell my car. He said he had been looking for the right car for a while. He said my car is the first one he has been excited about because he likes the look and is amazed by its quietness. He said he would give me a good price.

This example may seem silly, but students often are tempted to use big words in their legal writing to sound smart. Ironically, these attempts to sound smart may have the opposite effect because stilted language in legal writing sounds no less silly to a seasoned lawyer or judge than the example above. Show your intelligence through the power of your logic, not through the size of your words.

Unfortunately, the legal sources you read will not always be models of simplicity. Although lawyers are moving away from legalese, even recent court opinions, statutes, and contracts may continue to use outdated language that is now foreign in common conversation. Legalese should be avoided in all contexts, but it is particularly counterproductive in communications to colleagues, clients, and courts.

Examples of Legalese to Avoid

aforementioned, heretofore, hereby, thereby, said document, wherefore

11.5 | ACTIVATING YOUR SENTENCES

Often a writer is still forming thoughts as she starts typing. If so, her sentences may not have the sharpest focus. Strong writers review their drafts to refocus sentences on the most important actor and action: the actor should be the subject of the sentence, and the action should be the verb. Two common errors tend to occur: nominalization and passive voice.

11.5.1 | Avoiding Nominalization

Nominalization disguises the action by using a noun form rather than a verb form. For example, "The court will make a determination whether to allow the suit to proceed." An effective writer reviews this sentence and asks, what is the most important action in this sentence? The sentence emphasizes the verb "make," but "make" is not an interesting action. Instead, the focus should be on the court's determination. Rearranging the sentence to use the verb "determine" rather than the noun "determination" helps focus the sentence: "The court will determine whether to allow the suit to proceed."

ERROR Nominalization Example 1

The awarding of damages is done by the jury.

Revision 1

The jury awards the damages.

ERROR Nominalization Example 2

The consideration of the plaintiff's position by the court will result in reversal.

Revision 2

When the court considers the plaintiff's position, it will reverse the judgment.

ERROR Nominalization Example 3

The sentence imposed by the jury was five years in prison.

Revision 3

The jury sentenced the defendant to five years in prison.

One hint in finding nominalizations is to look for *-ing* forms of verbs. If these verb forms are acting as nouns, as in "the awarding of damages," reword the sentence to avoid the *-ing* form. Another hint is to look for *-ion* endings. Often you can avoid using the *-ion* noun by replacing it with the verb form instead (e.g., changing "consideration" to "consider").

11.5.2 | Minimizing Passive Voice

A passive person is someone who waits for others to act. A passive sentence is one that fails to identify the actor or identifies the actor too late. A more active construction uses the actor as the subject of the sentence (in the subject-verb-object model).

ERROR Example of Passive Voice Problem

It was held that the plaintiff could not recover for liable.

This passive voice construction is unclear; "was held" does not identify who rendered the holding. Although the reader can figure out that the writer is referring to a court holding, why should the reader have to do the work when the writer could have been more clear?

Sample Active Voice Revision

The court held that the plaintiff could not recover for liable.

To catch passive voice problems in your writing, look for "it is/was/has been," "there is/was/has been," and the word "by." These are common signals of a passive sentence. When you find passive voice, revise to identify the subject (i.e., the actor) as in the following examples. The subject and verb are underlined in the revised sentences to illustrate the subject-verb structure that achieves active voice.

ERROR Passive Voice Example 1

The rule was changed by the court.

Active Voice Revision 1

The <u>court</u> <u>changed</u> the rule.

ERROR Passive Voice Example 2

There was a decision that I stay home.

Active Voice Revision 2

My mother decided that I should stay home.

ERROR Passive Voice Example 3

The wall was constructed by workmen.

Active Voice Revision 3

The workmen constructed the wall.

11.6 | SOME COMMON AND UGLY GRAMMAR GOOFS TO AVOID

Most of us have some weak spots in our mastery of grammar rules. Slaying our grammar ghouls, however, is important to our professional reputation as lawyers. Sloppy grammar significantly impedes your effectiveness as an advocate and even your job opportunities. Buy a grammar guide or style manual and keep it near as you write. Whenever you catch yourself wondering whether you need a comma, what verb tense to use, or any other grammatical question, consult your reference book. Internet searches are also helpful as long as the source is trustworthy (e.g., Purdue University's Online Writing Lab rather than someone posting a response while lounging on a floatie in her pool). The more you stop to look up grammar questions as they arise, the more automatic good grammar will become and the less often you will need to consult your grammar resources.

This text only briefly discusses some common errors; it does not replace a grammar guide or style manual. The following common errors are the type of glaring mistakes that tarnish the professional image you want your writing to convey. They are just plain ugly, and readers will notice them.

11.6.1 | Eliminating Parallelism Problems

List items should all follow the same grammatical form. You can choose to list all items as nouns, verbs, adjectives, or clauses, but do not switch back and forth. Ideally, you should also match the type of nouns, verbs, or other forms that you choose. Some illustrations of parallelism errors and revisions follow.

ERROR **Parallelism Error 1**

Courts need to ensure justice and equity and that everyone has access to the legal system.

↑ Noun ↑ Noun ↑ "that" clause

Revision 1

Courts need to ensure justice, equity, and equal access to the legal system.

↑ Noun ↑ Noun ↑ Noun

ERROR **Parallelism Error 2**

I want not only juice but also to eat berries.

↑ Noun ↑ Infinitive ("to" verb)

Revision 2

I want not only juice but also berries.

↑ Noun ↑ Noun

ERROR **Parallelism Error 3**

I am sure that you will be happy and are on a path to success.

↑ Future tense verb ↑ Present tense verb

Revision 3

I am sure that you will be happy and successful.

↑ Adjective ↑ Adjective

Alternative Revision 3

I am sure that you are on a path to happiness and success.

↑ Noun ↑ Noun

Sometimes you need a second conjunction to separate one list item from words to which it does not properly relate.

ERROR Missing Conjunction Example

I want to make sure that I am prepared for class, that my students learn, and be happy.

It is not clear whether "happy" relates to the teacher or her students.

Revision

I want to make sure that I am prepared for class and that my students are happy and learning.

Alternative Revision

I want to make sure that I am prepared for class and happy and that my students are learning.

Writing a new sentence often solves a parallelism problem, as in the following alternate revision.

Alternative Revision

I want to make sure that I am prepared for class and that my students are learning. However, I also want to be happy.

11.6.2 | Avoiding Dangling Modifiers

A modifier provides some special detail about another part of the same sentence (usually the subject). A modifier must be right next to the subject to which it relates. A dangling modifier is a grammatical error in which the modifier is divorced from its proper subject.

The erroneous sentence in this first example incorrectly suggests that the mother was crying rather than the baby. The revision solves the problem by removing the modifier and restructuring the sentence.

ERROR **Dangling Modifier Example 1**

Screaming loudly, the mother tried to console the baby.

Revision 1

The mother tried to console the baby, who was screaming loudly.

In this second example, the erroneous sentence has a modifier ("looking at the sky") that does not connect with the rest of the sentence ("we should pack up"). One of the sample revisions assumes that everyone was looking at the sky and the other assumes that only the speaker was looking at the sky.

ERROR **Dangling Modifier Example 2**

Looking at the sky, we should pack up.

Revision 2

Looking at the sky, we decided we should pack up.

Revision 2 Alternate

Looking at the sky, I decided we should pack up.

The third example shows a modifier ("hearing the arguments") that does not match the subject ("the motion"). Of course, a motion cannot hear an argument. The revision switches out the incorrect subject for the correct subject (the court hears the motion).

ERROR **Dangling Modifier Example 3**

Upon hearing the arguments, the motion was denied.

Revision 3

Upon hearing the arguments, the court denied the motion.

11.6.3 | Selecting Between "That," "Which," "Who," and "Whom"

These words introduce modifiers (see section 11.6.2). Modifiers are either restrictive or nonrestrictive. To select the right introductory word and punctuation, you need to correctly identify the type of modifier.

Restrictive modifiers use "that" or "who." Do not use a comma. A modifier is restrictive if it limits the group the sentence is about. In other words, removing the modifier would change the meaning of the sentence, or the sentence would not even make sense without the modifer.

Nonrestrictive modifiers use "which" or "who" and need commas. A modifier is nonrestrictive if the information it provides is extraneous. In other words, the information in the modifier could be placed in a separate sentence, and the remainder of the original sentence would make sense on its own.

The following example is incorrect because the author intends to limit the group the sentence is about. Not all dogs are annoying; only those that bark. If we take out the modifier, we are left with "A dog is annoying," which is not the meaning the author intended. The revision replaces "which" with the correct introductory word for restrictive modifiers, "that."

ERROR **Example of Incorrect Use of a Nonrestrictive Modifier**

A dog which barks is annoying.

Revision with a Restrictive Modifier

Dogs that bark are annoying. (Or, a dog that barks is annoying.)

In the next example, the erroneous sentence uses "that," the introductory phrase for a restrictive modifier, but the modifier should be nonrestrictive because the added information about the capabilities of the calculator is not necessary to the sentence. The capabilities could easily be explained in a separate sentence. The revision therefore uses the correct introductory word for nonrestrictive modifiers, "which," and inserts a comma.

ERROR **Example of Incorrect Use of a Restrictive Modifier**

My calculator that can add, subtract, divide, and multiply is pretty basic.

Revision with a Nonrestrictive Modifier

My calculator, which can add, subtract, divide, and multiply, is pretty basic.

Use "who" or "whom" for people. If the modified subject or object is a person, always use "who" or "whom." Use "who" when modifying a subject and "whom" when modifying an object. The same comma rules apply (use a comma for nonrestrictive modifiers only).

Sample Use of "Who" as a Restrictive Modifier

A person who is happy is a joy to be around.

Using "who" rather than "whom" is correct because in this first sample the additional information relates to the subject of the sentence ("a person"). No comma is used because the modifier is restrictive. We know it is restrictive because the author is referring to a certain category of people (those who are happy). Also, the sentence would not have the same meaning without the "who is happy" modifier. The author did not intend to say, "A person is a joy to be around."

Sample Use of "Who" as a Nonrestrictive Modifier

My father, who is away on business, is my best friend.

Using "who" rather than "whom" is correct because in this second sample the additional information relates to the subject of the sentence ("my father"). Commas are necessary because the modifier is nonrestrictive. We know that it is nonrestrictive because the additional information could have been in its own sentence as in, "My father is my best friend. He is away on business." This is a clue that the nonrestrictive modifier is correct.

Sample Use of "Whom"

The person to whom you are referring is not present.

Using "whom" is correct in this last example because the modifier refers to an object rather than to the subject ("the person"). No comma is used because the modifier is restrictive. We know it is restrictive because without the modifier, the sentence would not even make sense: "The person is not present."

11.7 | COMPARING APPLES TO APPLES

Sentences that compare two or more items must be complete comparisons and must compare like subjects. In legal writing, you might mistakenly violate this rule when comparing the facts of your client's case with the facts of a precedent case.

ERROR Example of an Incomplete Comparison

The *Jellyroll* case is even more compelling on this point.

The writing crafts an incomplete comparison. The reader wonders, "More compelling than what?"

Revised Version

The *Jellyroll* case is even more compelling on this point than the *Donut* case.

The revision inserts the other side of the comparison (the *Donut* case).

ERROR Example of a Faulty Comparison

Unlike *Elliot*, Keith's mother never relinquished custody

This example is incorrect because the sentence does not compare like subjects—the *Elliot* case is not a subject that is similar to Keith's mother.

Revised Version

Unlike the mother in *Elliot*, Keith's mother never relinquished custody

The revision inserts the comparable subject ("the mother in *Elliot*"). So now one mother is compared to another mother.

11.8 | BRUSHING UP ON POLITICAL CORRECTNESS

As lawyers, our words carry great weight. We constantly contribute to a discourse through which our society is governed. We therefore have a special responsibility to choose words that reflect the values of our society. Most students understand what politically correct language is and why it is important. Even so, using it correctly does not always come naturally to writers.

One area that creates problems for many writers is choosing gender-specific pronouns. When you refer to an abstract person rather than a specific individual, the best approach is to convert the sentence into the plural form. This avoids having to select either a male or female pronoun.

ERROR Not Politically Correct

A plaintiff must prove he was injured.

Using the male pronoun "he" in a generic statement may offend female readers.

Revised Version

Plaintiffs must prove they were injured.

11.9 | USING A STRUCTURED APPROACH TO IMPROVE YOUR GRAMMAR

This chapter covers only some of the most common style and grammar challenges. Develop a personalized checklist to catch the style and grammar issues you know you struggle with; add whatever comments your professor gives you to this checklist as well. Use your checklist in a focused and specific manner.

It is difficult to gain distance from your own writing, especially when you know *exactly* what ideas you are trying to convey. Often, the voice in your head makes you think you have created the perfect sentence when, in fact, you have not. A focused one-at-a-time approach to self-editing can combat the natural inclination to view your writing with a rose-colored lens. Go through your paper once looking for nominalizations. Then go through it a second time looking for passive voice. And so on. If you take this structured approach, you will improve. And all writers, no matter how strong, are always improving their writing.

Grammar and Style Checklist

- ☐ Review your sentences carefully to eliminate unnecessary filler language. For example, search for signal phrases like "show that," "belief that," "establishes that," "looking at," "the fact that," "proves that," and "the inference that."
- ☐ Mark the subject, verb, and object of your sentences and rephrase to bring your sentence closer to subject-verb-object structure.
- ☐ Do not exceed the maximum sentence formula: Intro + Core + One.
- ☐ Look for signals like "that," "which," "who," "whom," "in which," "such that," and "thereby." Break up sentences to avoid wordiness or eliminate these clauses if the additional information is not meaningful.
- ☐ Use basic words; do not get fancy.
- ☐ Search and destroy nominalizations.
- ☐ Search and destroy passive voice sentences.
- ☐ Check sentences that include "and" or "or" and check for parallelism.
- ☐ Search and destroy dangling modifiers.
- ☐ Check your use of "that," "which," "who," and "whom."
- ☐ Avoid using only the male (or female) pronoun for generic statements; revise using a plural pronoun.

GRAMMAR EXERCISES

To introduce you to a structured approach to self-editing, the following exercises cover common grammatical errors. You can apply one exercise at a time to the draft document on which you are working.

EXERCISE 1

Search for the word "by" and, whenever you find it, ask yourself the following:

Is it a passive sentence? (Clue: no subject)

Ex.: The rule was changed by the court.

If so, correct (identify and add the subject).

Ex.: The court changed the rule.

Have you used "by" to indicate a possessive relationship?

Ex.: The ruling by the court

If so, use a possessive instead.

Ex.: The court's ruling

EXERCISE 2

Now review your paper again, but this time look for words that end in:

-al	-ancy	-ence	-ent	-ity
-ance	-ant	-ency	-ion	-ment

Is the word a nominalization?

Ex.: The company's <u>success depended on</u> the physical fitness of its employees.

If so, change the noun phrase to an active verb.

Ex.: The company needed physically fit employees <u>to succeed</u>.

EXERCISE 3

Look at each sentence. Does a long clause separate the subject and verb?

Ex.: The <u>court</u>, after evaluating the evidence presented by the plaintiff regarding actual injury, <u>held</u> the statute of limitations barred the action.

If so, rephrase to bring the subject and verb closer together.

Ex.: After evaluating the evidence that the plaintiff presented regarding actual injury, the <u>court</u> <u>held</u> the statute of limitations barred the action.

EXERCISE 4

Look at each sentence. Does it start with "on," "by," "in," or an *-ing* verb?

(A) If so, do you have a comma before the subject of the sentence?
(B) And does the subject agree with the starting clause? (E.g., below, the contractor did the relying, so the sentence is okay.)

Ex.: Relying on the weather report, the contractor delivered the materials to the site.
Ex.: On March 20, I will go to the zoo.

EXERCISE 5

Search for the words "like," "similar to," "contrast," and "distinguish."

Check to make sure you are not comparing a noun to a case.

Ex.: Like *Williams*, the property was not on, attached to, or carried by the victim.

Change any offending sentences.

Ex.: Like the property in *Williams*, the property in this case was not on, attached to, or carried by the victim.

EXERCISE 6

Search for "it is/was/has been" and "there is/was/have been."

Unless the "it" refers to a specific noun, rephrase the sentence.

Ex.: It is provided that discovery triggers the limitations period.
Revise: The statute provides that discovery triggers the limitations period.
Ex.: The court held the statute of limitations barred the action. It was concerned, however, ...

No need to revise because "it" refers properly to the court.

EXERCISE 7

Search for the word "they."

Does the pronoun refer to a singular noun (e.g., the company or the court)?

If so, change to "it" or reword the sentence to avoid the problem.

Ex.: The company needed their employees to be physically fit.
Revise: The company needed its employees to be physically fit.

EXERCISE 8

Search for sentences three lines or longer.

Do they break the Max = Intro + Core + One rule?

Are the sentences clear?

Would it be clearer to break the sentences into separate sentences?

CHAPTER 12

Paragraph Structure

12.1 | PARAGRAPH COHESION

Earlier chapters have covered the first fundamental rule of effective paragraph structure: each paragraph starts with a topic sentence that states a thesis that the rest of the paragraph proves or edifies.

Paragraph Structure

Topic sentence + Proof

Chapter 4 covers paragraph structure by advising you to start rule explanation paragraphs with a topic sentence that states a subrule followed by case examples that prove the subrule. Similarly, Chapter 5 advises you to start each application paragraph with a topic sentence that states how a subrule plays out in your case and then follow with use of the four tools of effective application paragraphs to prove the topic sentence.

12.2 | TRANSITIONS

Since you have already learned the first rule of effective paragraph structure, you are ready to learn one more rule: start each paragraph with a transition to move the reader from the topic of the prior paragraph to the new paragraph's topic.

Using transitions changes your paper from a stormy sea that bounces your reader around to the point of sea-sickness to a gently flowing river that allows your reader to rest comfortably on her inner-tube while you navigate her through the logic of your argument. Transitions can be as simple as one word placed strategically within your topic sentence. However, often the best transitions are bridges that explicitly link the topic of the prior paragraph to the new topic.

12.2.1 | Adding Transitional Words

Sometimes a transition can be a word that indicates the relationship between the point of the new paragraph and the point of the previous one. Be sure to use a word that correctly characterizes the relationship.

If the topic of the new paragraph contradicts, qualifies, or limits the topic of the prior paragraph, use a transition of contrast:

- However, ...
- By contrast, ...

Sample Contrast Transition

Evidence that the employer sponsored or encouraged participation and benefited from the activity can establish reasonable expectancy... [followed by proof from case examples].

Sponsorship or encouragement, however, must be linked to the specific activity at issue... [followed by proof from case examples].

If the new paragraph adds another point related to the point of the prior paragraph, use a transition of addition:

- Moreover, ...
- In addition, ...
- Courts have also considered...

Sample Addition Transition

Implied pressure may be exacerbated when an employee is in a vulnerable position. [Followed by proof from case examples.]

In addition to evidence of pressure on an employee to participate in an activity, evidence that the employer sponsored or encouraged participation and benefited from the activity can establish reasonable expectancy. [Followed by proof from case examples.]

If the new paragraph presents a point that follows as a logical consequence from the point of the prior paragraph, use a transition of causal connection:

- Therefore, ...
- Consequently, ...
- As a result of...

Sample Causal Connection Transition

Entrapment is a disfavored defense because the police must have broad discretion in their investigatory tactics. [Followed by proof with case examples that show it is disfavored and that discuss the broad discretion point.]

Therefore, only an extreme level of police misconduct can create a colorable claim to the defense. [Followed by proof with case examples that show extreme misconduct is required.]

Another way of transitioning between paragraphs is to use transitional words of sequence:

- First, . . .
- Second, . . .
- Third, . . .

Sample Sequential Transition

Three factors are relevant to implied pressure: (1) the employment status of the plaintiff, (2) employer encouragement of and benefit from the activity, and (3) any connection between the activity and advancement in the workplace.

First, a vulnerable employment status can exacerbate implied pressure. [Followed by proof from case examples.]

Second, employer encouragement of and benefit from the activity can support a plaintiff's feeling of pressure. [Followed by proof from case examples.]

Third, a connection between the activity and advancement in the workplace is strong evidence of implied pressure. [Followed by proof from case examples.]

12.2.2 | Bridging the Topics

Words of transition are an easy out and are better than no transition. However, sometimes your reader needs more help to understand the connection between the topics of your paragraphs. You can use bridges to explicitly link the prior topic to the new topic. For example:

- Because of (topic A), (topic B)
- In light of (topic A), (topic B)
- Despite (topic A), (topic B)
- As a result of (topic A), (topic B)

In the following sample from *Rasul v. Bush*, 542 U.S. 466 (2004), bridging transitions and transitional words move the reader from one paragraph to the next. The transitions appear in boldface, and some citations have been edited.

EFFECTIVE PARAGRAPH STRUCTURE SAMPLE

RASUL EXCERPT	COMMENTS
Congress has granted federal district courts, "within their respective jurisdictions," the authority to hear applications for habeas corpus by any person who claims to be held "in custody in violation of the Constitution or laws or treaties of the United States." 28 U.S.C. §§ 2241(a), (c)(3). The statute traces its ancestry to the first grant of federal court jurisdiction: Section 14 of the Judiciary Act of 1789 authorized federal courts to issue the writ of habeas corpus to prisoners "in custody, under or by colour of the authority of the United States, or committed for trial before some court of the same." Act of Sept. 24, 1789, ch. 20, § 14, 1 Stat. 82. In 1867, Congress extended the protections of the writ to "all cases where any person may be restrained of his or her liberty in violation of the constitution, or of any treaty or law of the United States." Act of Feb. 5, 1867, ch. 28, 14 Stat. 385. *See* Felker v. Turpin, 518 U.S. 651, 659-660 (1996).	The first sentence introduces the topic of the Court's analysis (the statutory basis of habeas corpus). It is then expanded on with specifics. No transition is needed because this is the first paragraph of the Court's analysis.
Habeas corpus is, **however**, "a writ antecedent to statute, . . . throwing its root deep into the genius of our common law." Williams v. Kaiser, 323 U.S. 471, 484, n. 2 (1945) (internal quotation marks omitted). The writ appeared in English law several centuries ago, became "an integral part of our common-law heritage" by the time the Colonies achieved independence, Preiser v. Rodriguez, 411 U.S. 475, 485 (1973), and received explicit recognition in the Constitution, which forbids suspension of "the Privilege of the Writ of Habeas Corpus . . . unless when in Cases of Rebellion or Invasion the public Safety may require it," Art. I, § 9, cl. 2.	The transitional word "however" cues the reader that this paragraph's topic contradicts, qualifies, or limits the topic of the prior paragraph. The first sentence also introduces the topic of the paragraph (the common law origin of habeas corpus). The rest of the paragraph expands on the topic.
As it has evolved over the past two centuries, the habeas statute **clearly has expanded habeas corpus "beyond the limits that obtained during the 17th and 18th centuries."** Swain v. Pressley, 430 U.S. 372, 380, n. 13 (1977). But "at its historical core, the writ of habeas corpus has served as a means of reviewing the legality of Executive detention, and it is in that context that its protections have been strongest." INS v. St. Cyr, 533 U.S. 289, 301 (2001). See also Brown v. Allen, 344 U.S. 443, 533 (1953) (Jackson, J., concurring in result) ("The	The bolded language creates a bridging transition by referring to the topics of the prior two paragraphs (i.e., the evolution of habeas corpus). The underlined language introduces the topic of this

Cont.

RASUL EXCERPT	COMMENTS
historic purpose of the writ has been to relieve detention by executive authorities without judicial trial"). As Justice Jackson wrote in an opinion respecting the availability of habeas corpus to aliens held in U.S. custody: "Executive imprisonment has been considered oppressive and lawless since John, at Runnymede, pledged that no free man should be imprisoned, dispossessed, outlawed, or exiled save by the judgment of his peers or by the law of the land. The judges of England developed the writ of habeas corpus largely to preserve these immunities from executive restraint." Shaughnessy v. United States ex rel. Mezei, 345 U.S. 206, 218-219 (1953) (dissenting opinion).	paragraph: habeas corpus is historically a protection from executive imprisonment.
Consistent with the historic purpose of the writ, <u>this Court has recognized the federal courts' power to review applications for habeas relief in a wide variety of cases involving Executive detention, in wartime as well as in times of peace</u>. The Court has, for example, entertained the habeas petitions of an American citizen who plotted an attack on military installations during the Civil War, Ex parte Milligan, 71 U.S. 2 (1866), and of admitted enemy aliens convicted of war crimes during a declared war and held in the United States, Ex parte Quirin, 317 U.S. 1 (1942), and its insular possessions, In re Yamashita, 327 U.S. 1 (1946).	The bolded transitional clause refers back to the topic of the prior paragraph (the historical purpose of the writ). This is another example of a bridging transition. The underlined language introduces the topic of this paragraph (court review of habeas corpus in times of war).
The question now before us is whether the habeas statute confers a right to judicial review of the legality of Executive detention of aliens in a territory over which the United States exercises plenary and exclusive jurisdiction, but not "ultimate sovereignty."	This sentence transitions from the rule explanation to the rule application.

Next, compare the following erroneous paragraph to the revised version. The erroneous paragraph's topic sentence is too narrow to cover the entire paragraph because it covers only some students. By contrast, the revised version broadens the topic sentence to refer to both students who want to practice law and those who have other plans.

ERROR Example of Paragraph Cohesion Problem

Some students go to law school believing they want to practice law. They may have family members or friends who have convinced them the field is exciting and reward-

Cont.

ing. Or they may have enjoyed watching television shows about the legal field. But not all law students are like this. Some go to law school because they believe it will help them in other law-related fields such as politics.

Revised Version

Students have different reasons for going to law school. Some know they want to practice law. They may have family members or friends who have convinced them the field is exciting and rewarding. Or, they may have enjoyed watching television shows about the legal field. Others, however, go to law school because they believe it will help them in other law-related fields such as politics.

In the next example, the erroneous paragraph tries to cover two different topics (quick wit and professional demeanor). The revised version separates the two topics into their own paragraphs.

ERROR Example of Paragraph Cohesion Problem

Lawyers have to be quick on their feet. When examining a witness in front of a jury, a lawyer can be faced with unexpected testimony and must quickly change gears to address the new information. Similarly, when arguing in front of a judge, a lawyer often faces unexpected questions and must be able to divorce herself from her prepared comments to satisfy the concerns the judge expresses. Jurors expect lawyers to be courteous to witnesses and opposing counsel. Judges also expect lawyers to be respectful to everyone in the courtroom.

Revised Version

Lawyers have to be quick on their feet. When examining a witness in front of a jury, a lawyer can be faced with unexpected testimony and must quickly change gears to address the new information. Similarly, when arguing in front of a judge, a lawyer often faces unexpected questions and must be able to divorce herself from her prepared comments to satisfy the concerns the judge expresses.

Lawyers must complement quick wit with a professional demeanor. Jurors expect lawyers to be courteous to witnesses and opposing counsel. Judges also expect lawyers to be respectful to everyone in the courtroom.

Paragraph Structure Checklist

- ☐ For every paragraph in your analysis, check whether the entire paragraph relates to the topic sentence without veering off-topic. If you veer off-topic, either broaden the topic sentence or break the paragraph into two paragraphs by subtopic.
- ☐ For rule explanation paragraphs, check whether the topic sentence states a subrule that complies with the lessons of Chapter 4.
- ☐ For application paragraphs, check whether the topic sentence states a conclusion about your client's case using one of the subrules from your rule explanation.
- ☐ For every paragraph in your analysis except for the first paragraph, check that you have included a transition to link the new paragraph to the prior paragraph.

PART II

OBJECTIVE LEGAL WRITING

CHAPTER **13**

Overview of Objective Legal Writing
The Legal Research Memorandum

The next several chapters of this text focus on objective legal writing. Objective legal writing analyzes rather than persuades; it enables its reader, whether client or attorney, to make informed decisions about the case. To achieve this goal, it presents a balanced view of the law and the facts of the case.

This text focuses on the most formal genre of objective legal writing: the legal research memorandum. The legal research memorandum analyzes the law on a particular topic and then applies the law to a particular client's situation. It is an excellent tool for teaching objective legal writing because it covers all of the skills you will need. Keep in mind, however, that sometimes your professor, employer, or client will ask for only a portion of the full-sized memorandum—for example, a summary of the facts from a case file or an analysis of the law on a topic without an analysis of a client's case. You can take apart the pieces of the complete, formal memo to fulfill your specific needs.

13.1 | WHAT IS A LEGAL RESEARCH MEMORANDUM?

As soon as they hear you are entering law school, distant relatives and acquaintances are likely to call you with random legal questions. Hopefully, as a law student, you know to tell them that you have no sound legal advice to offer. Even as a lawyer, however, you will rarely be able to assess the merits of a case until you have conducted detailed legal research on the issues it raises. In many law offices, especially private law firms and government agencies, senior attorneys rely on junior attorneys to conduct legal research and evaluate the merits of a case. Usually, the senior attorney identifies very specific issues to evaluate and will ask for a memo detailing the research findings. Unlike the memos you are probably used to, a legal research memorandum is a formal and structured written product. Although senior attorneys may have their own stylistic and format preferences, there are identifiable standards for legal research memoranda that all attorneys will expect to be met. This text teaches you these universal standards and explains how to implement the TRAC organization in a legal research memorandum.

13.2 | GOALS

A legal research memorandum should achieve the following goals.

- Provide your informed opinion regarding the likely outcome of the case.
- Identify, explain, and exemplify the pertinent legal rules.
- Analyze how the rules apply to the case.
- Assess and identify risk for the client or senior attorney.

13.3 | TONE

A legal research memorandum is an objective, impartial assessment of the legal issues it addresses. It is designed to educate your senior attorney and, ultimately, the client. To serve this purpose:

- Provide your honest conclusion and not just what your senior attorney or client wants to hear.
- Provide all pertinent rules and not just the ones that seem to support your conclusion.
- Use impartial language.
- Identify and assess all possible arguments and not just those that support your conclusion.

13.4 | BASIC COMPONENTS

A legal research memorandum typically contains the following sections.

- Factual background (tells the story of your case) (covered in Chapter 9)
- Issue statement (identifies the questions your memorandum addresses) (covered in Chapter 10)
- Analysis (your TRAC analysis of the legal issue)
- Conclusion (briefly repeats your opinion and reasoning)

Different law offices may have different preferences. For example, some law offices may prefer to include a "brief answer" section, and others may call the various sections by slightly different names. Learn the preferences of your office and/or the particular person for whom you are writing the memo.

13.5 | OBJECTIVE FACTUAL NARRATIVES

Chapter 9 covers how to draft a well-written factual background. Writing a factual background in a legal research memorandum requires one additional technique: it needs to give equal attention to all relevant facts. After all, it is an objective piece of legal writing that calls for a balanced approach. Your factual background, therefore, must include facts that support both your conclusion and the counterarguments.

Because your memorandum is supposed to be objective and unbiased, avoid any wording that suggests you have a hidden agenda. Do not, for example, write that someone drank "heavily." Instead, tell the reader how much she drank. And do not characterize any of the parties or witnesses. For example, do not call the key witness against your client a "career criminal" or an "unreliable witness." To borrow a line from *Dragnet*, "Just the facts, ma'am."

13.6 | OBJECTIVE ISSUE IDENTIFICATION

Chapter 10 covers the issue statement. One special consideration in crafting an issue statement in a legal research memorandum is that it should ideally include key facts on both sides of the issue. Including only those facts that support your conclusion will not accurately reflect the balanced nature of the legal analysis in a legal research memorandum. Use a "but" to separate supportive from contradictory facts. Compare the following issues statements. (Key facts are bold.)

ERROR One-Sided Question

Can **Nora Roberts** establish entrapment where the government **supplied all of the drugs she sold and told her how to contact the buyer and secure the deal?**

Balanced Question

Can Nora Roberts establish entrapment where the government supplied all of the drugs she sold and told her how to contact the buyer and secure the deal, **but she had engaged in similar transactions in the recent past without any prompting by the government?**

The one-sided question mentions only the government's supply of the drugs and involvement in telling the defendant how to carry out the sale. These facts seem to lead the reader to think entrapment should be established. The more balanced version adds in some facts relevant to the counterargument.

Also, to further ensure the correct balanced presentation, the issue statement should not use conclusory or suggestive wording.

ERROR Example of Improperly Suggestive Wording

> Can Nora Roberts establish entrapment where the government overstepped its proper investigatory role?

Replace any conclusory language with the factual details that underlie the conclusion. The correct version of this issue statement above mentions the government's supply of the drugs and instructions on how to contact the buyer and secure the deal rather than saying that the government overstepped its role.

LEGAL RESEARCH MEMORANDUM "SHELL"

To: (Fill in the name of the assigning attorney)

From: (Fill in your name)

Date: (Fill in the date you turn in the memo)

Re: (Indicate the case name and the general subject matter of the memo)

FACTUAL BACKGROUND

Start with an introductory sentence that introduces the general nature of the case. Then, set forth all facts relevant to the questions you will be addressing in the memo. Any fact you mention in the analysis section should first be stated here in the factual background. Include all relevant facts, both good and bad. Write the facts objectively: no conclusions or loaded language. Write the facts using natural, prose-style language (no professorial or legal jargon).

ISSUE STATEMENT

Draft clear questions that adequately identify the issues the memo will analyze. You should have only one question per issue. The questions cannot be conclusory. They cannot assume any answers. They must include the key fact(s) pon which your analysis of the issue will depend. They should be worded in a manner specific to the case at hand. They should identify the element, test, or factor at issue in a manner that does not require advance knowledge of the reader.

ANALYSIS

This is the heart of your memo where you will discuss the law on the issue(s) and the cases you have read. You will also use the law to justify your conclusion on the issue and to explain and rebut counterarguments. Follow TRRRAAAC or one of the alternative organizations discussed in Chapter 6.

CONCLUSION

This section is usually an extremely brief wrap-up. Often, you will merely restate your thesis in the form of a conclusion. For example, "As analyzed above, Result X." However, if your analysis involves a balancing of factors, you may need to bring the factors together in the conclusion section as discussed in section 6.3 of this text.

CHAPTER **14**

The Brief Answer Section of a Legal Research Memorandum

The exact format of a legal research memorandum may vary by law office and even by attorney or client. If possible, determine whether the recipient of your memorandum wants you to include a "brief answer." If in doubt, include one.

A brief answer usually appears right after the issue statement. A brief answer must

(1) answer and match the issue statement and
(2) preview the reasons for your conclusion
(3) in a manner your reader can understand without reading the rest of the memorandum.

14.1 | ANSWERING THE ISSUE STATEMENT

The brief answer provides a yes-or-no response to the issue statement. The language and facts that appear in your issue statement should also appear in your brief answer. The following samples illustrate this technique: notice that the same rule language ("predisposition," "entrapment," "defense") and the same key facts ("recent petty thefts," "robbery") appear in the brief answer. Notice also that the "yes" answers the call of the question (whether he had a predisposition).

Sample Issue Statement

Did the Defendant have a predisposition to commit the robbery with which he is charged that would preclude him from asserting a defense of entrapment given that he had recently committed petty theft crimes?

Matching Brief Answer

Yes. Entrapment is not an available defense in this case. A defendant can escape conviction on a theory of entrapment only when he can prove he was not predisposed

Cont.

to commit the crime. Even if the government led the defendant to commit the crime, an entrapment defense will fail if there is any evidence that the defendant had committed similar acts in the recent past. In our case, Defendant's recent petty thefts establish predisposition to commit the robbery with which he is now charged and, therefore, make entrapment unavailable as a defense.

The purpose of the brief answer is to answer the question your memorandum will discuss. Although a legal memorandum is an objective piece of writing because its goal is to present the *right* answer and not necessarily the answer your supervisor or client wants to hear, you still need to be strategic about how you prepare the memorandum. Your supervisor and client are expecting an answer, and you want them to be confident in your conclusion. Therefore, state your conclusion confidently and firmly. Do not detract from your conclusion by including wishy-washy language like, "I think," or "maybe," or "could," or "should."

Occasionally, you may face a legal question that you cannot answer with certainty. In that case, you need to make an educated guess about what the court will do based on the rules and outcomes of the applicable precedent cases. Rather than using wishy-washy language that will only cause the reader to question your judgment, use words that convey some meaning about the probabilities. For example, "most likely" or "unlikely" convey more meaning to your reader than "maybe." If a weather reporter tells you it is "unlikely" to rain, you will probably go forward with your picnic. If he tells you it will "likely rain," you will probably opt for a movie instead. If, however, he tells you it "might" rain, you are left without any meaningful guidance and are probably wondering why you bothered tuning in. Do not let your reader wonder why she bothered tuning in. Give her some meaningful guidance.

14.2 | PREVIEWING YOUR REASONS

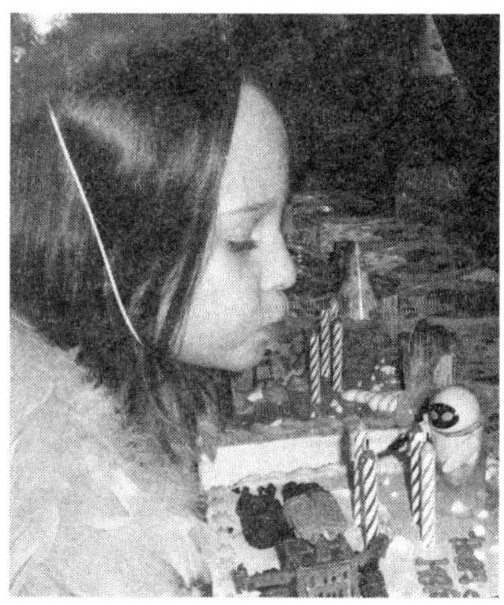

This is a four-year-old girl. Four-year-olds often do not like surprises, even if they are good surprises. Previewing your plans can help. For example, you might tell a four-year-old: "Tomorrow, we have to go grocery shopping in the morning. Then, we'll come home for a nap. Later, we can go for a swim in the pool." This puts her at ease. She knows what to expect. And, in the morning when you tell her it is time to go to the grocery store, she will be more cooperative than if you had never told her what to expect. You do not need to provide her with a list of all the things you are going to buy at the store. She just needs to know the general plan.

Treat your reader like a four-year-old. Lay out your general plans for the memorandum in a simple, clear manner. This means, of course, that you have formulated your plans. Finish a good outline before you start writing the brief answer. Also, return to the brief answer after you complete your analysis section to ensure that these two parts of your memorandum match. You may have ended up making slightly different points or articulating the points differently than you had anticipated when you first drafted the brief answer. Revise the brief answer so that it previews your analysis more accurately. And if you change the brief answer, you will have to change the issue statement to match.

14.3 | SETTING THE STAGE FOR YOUR REASONS

Now comes the tricky part. You are about to explain the law on your issue and the reasons for your conclusion. How are you supposed to craft a short paragraph that previews the reasons for your conclusion in a manner your reader can understand without reading the rest of the memorandum? The key is to stay big-picture at this point. Avoid terminology that requires explanation. State the main rule that governs your issue. You may also need to include a definitional rule or legal test to clarify the connection between your reasons and the main rule. Then state your reasons using the rule language you have introduced. The next example demonstrates how to provide the main rule and an overview of the reasons for your conclusion without assuming knowledge the reader may not yet have. In addition, you can find a sample brief answer in Appendix B, Sample B.

ERROR **Example of an Incomplete Brief Answer**

Entrapment is not an available defense in this case. The defendant in our case was predisposed to commit the crime.

This example uses a specific legal term, "predisposed," without explaining its meaning. The author has not provided a rule to set up the discussion of predisposition. In other words, she has not told us that predisposition is relevant to the entrapment defense. And the author does not provide an overview of the reasons for her conclusion that the defendant was predisposed to commit the crime.

Revised Version

Conclusion: no entrapment	Entrapment is not an available defense in this case.
Main rule: predisposition	A defendant can escape conviction on a theory of entrapment only when he can prove he was not predisposed to commit the crime.
Definition of predisposition: prior similar acts	Even if the government led the defendant to commit the crime, an entrapment defense will fail if there is any evidence that the defendant had committed similar acts in the recent past.
Reasons: his prior thefts show predisposition	In our case, the defendant's recent petty thefts establish predisposition to commit the robbery with which he is now charged and, therefore, make entrapment unavailable as a defense.

The revised version lays out the main rule: no entrapment when the defendant is predisposed to commit the crime. And the writer has previewed his reasons for concluding that the defendant was predisposed to the crime: his recent thefts. And he has provided the necessary definition of predisposition that connects his reason to the key legal rule:

Key Legal Rule ⟶	Definition to Link Reasons ⟶	Reasons
Predisposition	Recent similar crimes	His Prior Thefts

14.4 | ACHIEVING THE RIGHT AMOUNT OF DETAIL

In the brief answer, strike a balance between being too conclusory and too detailed. Omit details that are not necessary to preview the reasons for your conclusion. In the preceding example, it would have been too conclusory to write only, "In our case, entrapment is unavailable as a defense because the defendant was predisposed to commit the crime." Instead, including a reference to the defendant's "recent petty thefts" offers a fact that supports the conclusion. However, the author did not need to go into any detail about the dates or circumstances of the thefts. The reader does not need to know those details to understand how the author plans to support his conclusion.

Brief Answer Checklist

- ☐ Answer the issue statement with a yes, no, most likely, not likely, or other term that conveys probability.
- ☐ State the main rule (with a definitional rule or test if needed) and then an overview of the reasons that the main rule supports your conclusion.
- ☐ Include a definitional rule or test if necessary to link your reasons to the main rule.
- ☐ Use the same rule language and key facts you used in the issue statement.

CHAPTER **15**

The Analysis Section of a Legal Research Memorandum

The TRAC structure governs the organization of the analysis section in your legal research memorandum. Chapters 4 and 5 offer guidance on the construction of effective rule statement, rule explanation, and application paragraphs. This chapter explains where those lessons fit into the creation of a legal research memorandum and addresses the T and C components of TRAC in a memorandum.

To orient yourself, read the model analysis section that follows. The model uses the one-TRRRAAAC structure introduced in section 6.2. The model also labels the counterarguments and rebuttals within the application because these sections will be an important focus in this chapter. To emphasize the structure, the model provides only the topic sentences of each paragraph. You can refer to Appendix B, Sample A, for a full sample with similar annotations.

Model Analysis Section Structure

T
Thesis

The defendant's recent petty thefts establish predisposition to commit the robbery with which he is now charged and, therefore, make entrapment unavailable as a defense.

R
Rule statement

The defense of entrapment is available when the police lead defendants to commit crimes they would not otherwise have committed. To establish that the police led them to commit a crime, defendants must establish significant police involvement in designing or carrying out the crime. Moreover, defendants will not be able to prove they "would not otherwise have committed" a crime if they engaged in similar crimes in the recent past.

R
Rule explanation

The government becomes significantly involved in the commission of a crime where its agents not only supply the materials necessary to the crime but also direct the commission of the crime. *[In the rest of this paragraph, you would discuss at least one precedent case that proves and illustrates that supplying the materials and directing the crime establishes significant involvement.]*

Cont.

By contrast, merely supplying the materials necessary to the crime does not establish entrapment. *[In the rest of this paragraph, you would discuss at least one precedent case that proves and illustrates that merely supplying the materials is not sufficient.]* R Rule explanation

The final consideration is whether the defendant committed similar crimes in the recent past and, therefore, was predisposed to commit the crime. Courts have found that prior crimes are similar to the current crime where they involved the same underlying motivation. *[In the rest of this paragraph, you would discuss at least one precedent case that proves and illustrates that crimes involving the same underlying motivation establish predisposition.]* R Rule explanation

In this case, the defendant cannot establish the entrapment defense. The similarity between the defendant's recent prior crimes and the crime at issue will prove predisposition and, therefore, prevent the defense in this case. The prior crimes and the current crime involved the same underlying motivation. *[You would then prove this statement using comparisons to the cases that the rule explanation section used to explain predisposition.]* Transition sentence A Application (supportive)

The defendant could try to argue that his current crime involved physical aggression, an element missing from his prior crimes. *[Here, the author would use comparisons to cases discussed in the rule explanation section on predisposition to explain how the defendant could argue that physical aggression involves a different underlying motivation than theft crimes.]* A Application (counter-argument)

However, the physical aggression in this case was ultimately used to further the principal crime of theft and, therefore, does not erase the connection between his prior theft-related crimes and the crime at issue in this case. *[Here, the author would use either comparisons to cases or some underlying policy consideration discussed in the rule explanation section on predisposition to explain why the additional element of physical aggression would not refute predisposition.]* A Application (rebuttal)

Another possible argument in favor of the entrapment defense in this case is that the police not only supplied the materials necessary to the crime but also directed its commission. *[The author would then prove this statement using comparisons to the cases the rule explanation section used to explain significant involvement.]* However, courts have repeatedly stated that evidence of predisposition precludes the defense and therefore renders the degree of police involvement in the crime irrelevant. Because, as explained above, the defendant's prior crimes establish predisposition, the court will most likely decline to address the level of police involvement. A Application (counter-argument) A Application (rebuttal)

Conclusion[1]

The defendant will not be able to establish the defense of entrapment. Although he can prove significant police involvement in the crime, his prior similar crimes establish predisposition and, therefore, refute the defense. C Conclusion

1. In a one-TRRRAAAC structure, the C (conclusion) is contained in a separate "Conclusion" section of the memorandum rather than in the analysis section. In a TRRRAAAC by heading structure (section 6.3), each section will have a conclusion of the point it addresses, and then the "Conclusion" section will contain a global wrap-up of the entire memorandum.

The sample model structure shows you how the different parts of the analysis section fit together, but is not intended to suggest that you must have a certain number of REs, applications, counterarguments, or rebuttals. The illustration omits citations; do not forget that with the possible exception of topic sentences, every sentence in your rule statement and rule explanation paragraphs needs a citation. Citation is covered in Chapter 8.

Also, the one-TRRRAAAC organization is only one option for organizing an analysis section and may not always be the best organization. Consider other options, including TRRRAAAC by heading, TRARARAC, and the other structures discussed in Chapter 6. Full samples of legal research memoranda following TRRRAAAC (Samples A and B), TRRRAAAC by heading (Sample C), and TRARARAC (Sample D) are included in Appendix B.

15.1 | THE T IN TRAC: STATING YOUR THESIS

Before you proceed, stop for a minute and locate the thesis paragraph in Appendix B, Sample A. The first sentence in your analysis section usually states your thesis. You may be familiar with the term "thesis" from your prior writing experiences. Your thesis is the conclusion you are setting out to prove in the rest of the analysis section. The thesis in a legal research memorandum can be a single sentence or a short paragraph, but it must accomplish both of the following.

- It must convey a clear prediction about how the legal issue you were asked to address will play out in your case.
- It must be phrased specific to the legal issue you were asked to address.

15.1.1 | Stating a Clear Prediction

Although a legal research memorandum is an objective piece of writing because its goal is to present the *right* answer and not necessarily the answer your supervisor or client wants to hear, still be strategic about how you prepare the memorandum. Your supervisor and client are expecting an answer, and you want them to be confident in your conclusion. State your conclusion confidently and firmly. Do not detract from your conclusion by including wishy-washy language like, "I think," or "maybe," or "could," or "should."

Occasionally, you may face a legal question that you cannot answer with certainty. In that case, you need to make an educated guess about what the court will do based on the rules and outcomes of the applicable precedent cases. Rather than using wishy-washy language that will only cause the reader to question your judgment, use words that convey some meaning about the probabilities. For example, "most likely" or "unlikely," convey more meaning to your reader than "maybe." If a weather reporter tells you it is "unlikely" to rain, you will probably go forward with your picnic. If he tells you it will "likely rain," you will probably opt for a movie instead. If, however, he tells you it "might" rain, you are left without any meaningful guidance and are probably wondering why you bothered tuning in. Do not let your reader wonder why she bothered tuning in. Give her some meaningful guidance.

15.1.2 | Phrasing Your Thesis in Terms of the Issue at Hand

Rarely will anyone ask you to prepare a legal research memorandum on whether your client will win her case. The assignment would be too broad. Instead, associates are typically asked to research one or more specific issues about a case. Often, a case file will contain several legal research memoranda on various legal topics. Therefore, your thesis must clearly indicate the topic this legal research memorandum is addressing. Although you will also have a formal issue statement and perhaps even a brief answer preceding your analysis section, the thesis of your analysis section needs to be clear about the issue as well. Why? Legal readers do not always read a memorandum in a linear fashion like you would read a newspaper article. They skip around and read what they please. Each section should be clear on its own.

Suppose you are asked to analyze whether your client committed burglary when he used a stolen ATM card to withdraw money from an external ATM machine. The problematic element is a requirement that to prove burglary, the prosecution must show the perpetrator entered a building with the intent to steal. Your thesis should not be merely, "Our client will prevail," or even, "Our client did not commit burglary." Instead, the thesis should state your conclusion on the precise issue: "Our client did not commit burglary. The prosecution cannot establish that he entered a building to steal, an essential element of a burglary charge. The ATM machine was not a building."

15.2 | THE R AND A IN TRAC: RULE STATEMENT, RULE EXPLANATION, AND APPLICATION

After your thesis come your rule statement, rule explanation, and application. Stop here for a moment and locate these three components in Appendix B, Sample A.

Chapter 6 discusses various ways you can structure a legal analysis. This portion of the text presents some special considerations that arise when writing a legal research memorandum.

15.2.1 | Including Adverse Authority in Your Rule Statement and Rule Explanation

In a legal research memorandum, your goal is to enable the reader to reach her own conclusion about the issue you are analyzing so that she can make an intelligent decision about how to proceed in the case. Therefore, in addition to reaching a conclusion about the issue and developing arguments to support your conclusion, you must also present significant contrary arguments.

Your rule statement and rule explanation, therefore, should contain rules and cases that support not only your conclusion but also the rules and cases that support any significant counterarguments. In other words, your discussion of the law should include not only cases that reached the same result you are predicting in your case but also cases that reached the opposite result. For ease of reference, this text refers to the latter as "adverse cases." Adverse cases may be discussed as part of a rule explanation paragraph that focuses on supportive cases, but another option is to put some or all of the adverse cases in their own rule explanation paragraphs. Appendix B, Sample A, has examples of each approach, which are copied below. The first sample below uses the signal "compare," which is commonly used to synthesize supportive and adverse cases. When you use this signal, the parentheticals must support the point of your sentence (e.g., that subjective belief can be established unless the employee did not truly feel obligated to participate).

Excerpt from Annotated Sample: Combining Supportive and Adverse Cases

Combination of supportive cases: *Smith* and *Wilson* and adverse case: *City of Stockton*

Failing the subjective belief requirement seems to be a risk only when the employee did not truly feel obligated to participate. *Compare Smith v. Workers' Comp. Appeals Bd.*, 236 Cal. Rptr. 248, 254-55 (Ct. App. 1987) (holding that deceased teacher's wife's testimony that teacher went to a picnic because his department head asked him to, he felt he had a "responsibility" to go, and he believed he had to participate in a certain number of extracurricular activities satisfied the subjective element of the test to establish coverage for injuries sustained while he was windsurfing during the picnic), *and Wilson v. Workers' Comp. Appeals Bd.*, 239 Cal. Rptr. 719, 721 (Ct. App. 1987) (holding that police officer's testimony that he believed he had to keep in shape to stay on a special emergency unit satisfied the subjective element to establish coverage for an injury sustained while running off-duty), *with City of Stockton v. Workers' Comp. Appeals Bd.*, 38 Cal. Rptr. 3d 474, 483 (Ct. App. 2006) (denying coverage to officer injured while playing basketball when he admitted he could satisfy the job requirement of keeping in shape without playing basketball).

Excerpt from Annotated Sample: Separating Supportive and Adverse Cases

Supportive cases

In addition to evidence of pressure on an employee to participate in an activity, evidence that the employer sponsored or encouraged participation and benefitted from the activity can establish reasonable expectancy. Employer involvement and benefit can establish indirect encouragement by the employer that changes the voluntary nature of the activity and, therefore, requires coverage of resulting injuries. *Ezzy*, 194 Cal. Rptr. at 95. For example, in finding reasonable expectancy in *Ezzy*, the court pointed to evidence that the firm provided tee shirts and refreshments at the games and held a special banquet for participants. *Id.* The court also noted the benefit

Cont.

to the firm from increased morale. *Id.* Employer encouragement and benefit similarly played a large role in securing coverage in *Smith*, 236 Cal. Rptr. at 257-58 (relying on the school's role in planning the picnic at which the employee was injured including its collection of permission slips, advertisement of planning meetings, and payment for refreshments; the benefit of the picnic to the school through improved teacher-student relationships; and the school's general encouragement of teacher participation in extracurricular activities) and *Wilson*, 239 Cal. Rptr. at 722 (relying on the benefit to the police department from the ability of the employee's specially trained unit to handle situations too extreme for its standard force).

Sponsorship or encouragement, however, must be linked to the specific activity at issue. An employer's encouragement of general fitness, without any encouragement of the specific activity at issue, does not establish reasonable expectancy. For example, in *City of Stockton*, the employer required employees to remain fit, but employees did not undergo any specific fitness tests. *City of Stockton*, 38 Cal. Rptr. 3d at 483. The basketball game that caused the employee's injuries was off-premises, impromptu and not known to, much less encouraged by, the employer. *Id.* The court held that the employee could not reasonably believe his participation in such a game was expected. *Id.* at 483-84. The court explained that a general expectation of fitness does not lead to coverage for any activity the employee chooses to fulfill that expectation. *Id.* at 483. To allow such broad coverage would be contrary to the intent of the legislature to exclude coverage for injuries that are only remotely connected to employment. *Id.* at 479, 483; *see also Taylor v. Workers' Comp. Appeals Bd.*, 244 Cal. Rptr. 643, 645 (Ct. App. 1988) (finding no reasonable expectancy where employer informed employees that only approved fitness regimens would be entitled to coverage and employee's basketball game was not part of an approved regimen). Adverse cases

Whether you opt to combine supportive and adverse cases into one paragraph or address them in separate paragraphs, you must ensure you have synthesized the supportive and adverse cases. You must devote some time to reconciling the cases with one another. What is the dividing line that explains the divergent outcomes? Here are the two samples again. This time focus on the synthesizing topic sentences.

The rule explanation on subjective belief identifies a dividing line between supportive cases that found subjective belief and adverse cases that did not: failing the requirement is not a risk unless the employee did not truly feel obligated to participate. The cases did not say this explicitly. The author had to look at both supportive and adverse cases and reconcile the conflicting outcomes in a manner consistent with the reasoning in the cases.

Sample Synthesis: Subjective Belief

Failing the subjective belief requirement seems to be a risk only when the employee did not truly feel obligated to participate. *Compare Smith v. Workers' Comp. Appeals Bd.*, 236 Cal. Rptr. 248, 254-55 (Ct. App. 1987) (holding that deceased teacher's wife's testi-

Cont.

mony that teacher went to a picnic because his department head asked him to, he felt he had a "responsibility" to go, and he believed he had to participate in a certain number of extracurricular activities satisfied the subjective element of the test to establish coverage for injuries sustained while he was windsurfing during the picnic) *and Wilson v. Workers' Comp. Appeals Bd.*, 239 Cal. Rptr. 719, 721 (Ct. App. 1987) (holding that police officer's testimony that he believed he had to keep in shape to stay on a special emergency unit satisfied the subjective element to establish coverage for an injury sustained while running off-duty) *with City of Stockton v. Workers' Comp. Appeals Bd.*, 38 Cal. Rptr. 3d 474, 483 (Ct. App. 2006) (denying coverage to officer injured while playing basketball when he admitted he could satisfy the job requirement of keeping in shape without playing basketball).

Similarly, the rule explanation on the objective reasonableness of the employee's belief that participation is expected identifies a dividing line between the supportive and adverse cases on the implied pressure factor: encouragement establishes reasonable expectancy but only if the pressure is specific to the injury-causing activity. Notice how the case examples in the two paragraphs support this inferred dividing line.

Sample Synthesis: Objective Reasonableness

The topic sentences of these two paragraphs state a dividing line between the supportive and adverse cases on the implied pressure factor.

In addition to evidence of pressure on an employee to participate in an activity, evidence that the employer sponsored or encouraged participation and benefitted from the activity can establish reasonable expectancy. Employer involvement and benefit can establish indirect encouragement by the employer that changes the voluntary nature of the activity and, therefore, requires coverage of resulting injuries. *Ezzy*, 194 Cal. Rptr. at 95. For example, in finding reasonable expectancy in *Ezzy*, the court pointed to evidence that the firm provided tee shirts and refreshments at the games and held a special banquet for participants. *Id.* The court also noted the benefit to the firm from increased morale. *Id.* Employer encouragement and benefit similarly played a large role in securing coverage in *Smith*, 236 Cal. Rptr. at 257-58 (relying on the school's role in planning the picnic at which the employee was injured including its collection of permission slips, advertisement of planning meetings, and payment for refreshments; the benefit of the picnic to the school through improved teacher-student relationships; and the school's general encouragement of teacher participation in extracurricular activities) and *Wilson*, 239 Cal. Rptr. at 722 (relying on the benefit to the police department from the ability of the employee's specially trained unit to handle situations too extreme for its standard force).

Sponsorship or encouragement, however, must be linked to the specific activity at issue. An employer's encouragement of general fitness, without any encouragement of the specific activity at issue, does not establish reasonable expectancy. For example, in *City of Stockton*, the employer required employees to remain fit, but employees did not undergo any specific fitness tests. *City of Stockton*, 38 Cal. Rptr. 3d

Cont.

at 483. The basketball game that caused the employee's injuries was off-premises, impromptu and not known to, much less encouraged by, the employer. *Id.* The court held that the employee could not reasonably believe his participation in such a game was expected. *Id.* at 483-84. The court explained that a general expectation of fitness does not lead to coverage for any activity the employee chooses to fulfill that expectation. *Id.* at 483. To allow such broad coverage would be contrary to the intent of the legislature to exclude coverage for injuries that are only remotely connected to employment. *Id.* at 479, 483; *see also Taylor v. Workers' Comp. Appeals Bd.*, 244 Cal. Rptr. 643, 645 (Ct. App. 1988) (finding no reasonable expectancy where employer informed employees that only approved fitness regimens would be entitled to coverage and employee's basketball game was not part of an approved regimen).

Creating topic sentences that help synthesize supportive and adverse cases is not always easy. Understanding the reasoning behind the outcomes in the supportive and adverse cases (covered in Chapter 2) is the first step. Then you have to sit down with the cases and ponder how you can reconcile the cases to identify the dividing line(s) for your reader. The more inconsistent two case outcomes seem, the more you need to struggle to determine the dividing line. The struggle is the heart of good lawyering.

15.2.2 | Application in Legal Research Memoranda: Supportive Points, Counterarguments, and Rebuttals

Just as your rule explanation must include both supportive and adverse cases, your application must present both the points that support your conclusion and any significant counterarguments. You also need to rebut the counterarguments so that your reader can have confidence in your conclusion.

15.2.2.1 | Selecting Counterarguments

To fully inform your reader, your analysis must present all significant counterarguments. Because of the complexity and adaptability of the law, your prediction of the likely outcome of the case is unlikely to be foolproof. Most likely, a plausible argument for the opposite outcome exists. Find and present it. It takes effort to see the other side of an argument. Put aside all of the assumptions you have made — wipe the slate clean — and set out to prove the opposite conclusion. Students often make the mistake of trying to find a perfect counterargument. There is no such thing as a perfect counterargument. If you found a perfect counterargument, then you would have to change your conclusion. Counterarguments must be reasonable and must be supportable by the rules and case law. But they do not have to be immune from attack.

15.2.2.2 | Analyzing Counterarguments

Application paragraphs that present counterarguments should be as developed as any other application paragraph. These paragraphs should have topic sentences and should use the four tools for effective application paragraphs discussed in Chapter 5. In-depth counterargument paragraphs are particularly important because if you fail to explain the reasoning behind the counterargument, you will not be able to attack the reasoning in your rebuttal.

15.2.2.3 | Rebutting Counterarguments

A good rebuttal should explain why the counterarguments are faulty using the four tools for effective application paragraphs. Rebuttals should not merely repeat or refer to prior points. Instead, they should directly attack the counterarguments and expose their flaws. If you have adequately explained the reasoning behind the counterarguments, your rebuttal can attack the flaws in the reasoning. An alternative approach is to establish that the counterargument is not significant by weighing it against all of the other points you have made in support of your thesis *and explaining why it is less significant than the other points.* If using this alternative, you will need something from the case law to help you prove the counterargument is outweighed by your other points. Perhaps a case has actually stated that one factor should weigh more heavily than others. Or perhaps you can rely on an important policy consideration announced in a case to argue that the counterargument is outweighed by your other points. In any event, merely stating that a counterargument is outweighed will not be convincing.

Illustration of Rebuttal Techniques

Rule explanation

Mary likes fruits that have peels. For example, she loves apples. She explained to me once that peels are nutritious and that fruits with peels can be cleaned more thoroughly than those without peels. Mary will not eat fruits that do not have peels because she is afraid they may have harmful chemicals on them that cannot be completely washed away. She also told me that she loves fruits with peels because they tend to be juicier than other fruits.

Supportive application

Mary would like oranges. Like apple peels, orange peels protect the fruit from harmful chemicals.

Supportive application

In addition, oranges would satisfy Mary's desire for juicy fruits. Oranges are even juicier than apples, and, therefore, Mary is likely to enjoy oranges as much as apples.

Application counterargument

Arguably, Mary may not like oranges as much as apples because the peels are not edible and, therefore, will not provide nutrition.

Application rebuttal (weighing factors less effective)

However, because oranges are juicy and the peels protect the fruit from harmful chemicals, two of the three reasons why Mary likes fruit with peels are applicable to oranges.

Cont.

Moreover, oranges are not completely without nutrition. The inside of the fruit has Vitamin C. Therefore, despite their inedible peels, oranges are likely to be a good choice for Mary because they are juicy, protected from chemicals, and nutritious.

Application rebuttal (attacking counterargument's logic)

In this illustration, the weighing of the factors is not effective because we have nothing in the rule explanation that helps us establish that the presence of peels and the juiciness of oranges should outweigh the counterargument that the orange peels are not edible. The second rebuttal is more effective because it attacks the reasoning of the counterargument by establishing that oranges are nutritious even without their peels.

Now look at the following sample that involves legal analysis. Notice the use of the four tools for effective application paragraphs (case comparisons, court reasoning, factual detail, and commonsense inferences) in both the counterargument and the rebuttals.

Excerpt from Unannotated Sample Legal Research Memorandum: Counterarguments and Rebuttals

Savoranola may argue that *Valencia* is distinguishable because members of the public reasonably believed they *could* enter the kiosk without permission. The bank representative stated that he has occasionally permitted noncustomers to wait for the bus in the kiosk. The bank's failure to assert a possessory interest over the kiosk by asking loiterers to leave arguably removes any expectation of protection from intrusion the bank and its customers could otherwise reasonably expect. The absence of such an expectation is significant under *Davis*. *Davis* explained that the limits of the burglary statute should be based on the underlying rationale for the criminal sanction it imposes—the danger posed by the entry into an area reserved for only certain occupants. 958 P.2d at 1089. Because the kiosk was not reserved for customers, neither Savonarola nor the bank's representatives and customers would be likely to resort to violence in connection with his entry. Therefore, the underlying rationale for the high penalty associated with burglary arguably does not apply.

The counterargument includes a detailed analysis that uses the four tools for effective application paragraphs.

Savonarola's arguments are likely to fail. Although the bank's efforts to reserve the kiosk for customers were not consistent, the bank representative stated that he "usually" asks loiterers to leave. Therefore, the bank did assert its possessory interest in the kiosk. Moreover, no court has suggested that a building's owner forfeits his possessory interest merely by tolerating uninvited guests.

First rebuttal: bank's testimony rebuts failure to assert possession and no cases support the counter.

The court should also reject the argument that Savonarola's entry into the kiosk did not carry a risk of violence. *Davis* is distinguishable because the defendant did not enter any part of the building; he merely inserted a check in a window chute. Here, Savonarola walked into the kiosk. Unlike the check, Savonarola's entry into the kiosk implicates the rationale behind the criminal sanction for burglary. Once Savonarola passed through the kiosk door, he was in a confined space. Had someone guessed

Second rebuttal: Savonarola's presence in confined space of kiosk distinguishes the adverse case and establishes a risk of violence.

Cont.

that Savonarola was using a stolen card and confronted him, he might have resorted to violence to escape. The potential for violence was the same as if he entered the bank lobby and used the ATM card to withdraw money at the teller's window, an act that would clearly fall within the burglary statute. Therefore, the purpose behind the burglary penalties does not warrant a different result in this case.

15.2.2.4 | Organizing Counterarguments and Rebuttals in a Single TRRRAAAC Structure

Supportive points, counterarguments, and rebuttals are often structured like a debate: make your supportive point(s) first, then present the counterargument(s), then rebut the counterargument(s). In a single TRRRAAAC structure, all of the counterarguments and rebuttal, therefore, will appear at the end of your analysis section. This is the structure shown at the beginning of this chapter. Here is another example from Appendix B, Sample A. Just the topic sentences are shown here. You can review the complete document in Appendix B.

Counterarguments and Rebuttals in a One-TRRRAAAC Structure

Support **Application 1:** Gator can...establish his belief was reasonable. Evidence of implied pressure is strong.

Support **Application 2:** In addition, Fitness Functions sponsored and benefitted from the paddleball games.

Support **Application 3:** Fitness Functions' sponsorship of and benefit from paddleball distinguish this case from *City of Stockton* and *Taylor*...

Counterargument **Application 4:** Fitness Functions will need to argue that the pressure to play paddleball does not rise to the level of expectancy. The company can distinguish *Wilson* and *Kidwell* because in those cases, employees had to train to pass required fitness tests.... In this case, by contrast, Randolph merely invited Gator to play...

Rebuttal **Application 5:** The response to these arguments is that...Randolph's use of paddleball as an opportunity to discuss business with her employees transformed a recreational activity into a work-related activity...

15.2.2.5 | Organizing Counterarguments and Rebuttals in Alternative Structures

The organization of the analysis section in the alternative TRARARAC and TRATRATRAC structures described in Chapter 6 is similar. A sample legal research memorandum using the TRARARAC structure is included in Appendix B, Sample D. As the sample illustrates, the counterarguments and rebuttals in the alternative structures appear at the end of the analysis section just as in the TRRRAAAC structure modeled above. The main difference is that in the TRARARAC and TRATRATRAC structures, the discussion of the subrules and cases relevant to a particular counterargument or rebuttal appear right before the counterargument or rebuttal to which they relate.

Counterarguments and Rebuttals in a TRARARAC Structure

Rule explanation 1: The...definition of the practice of law is met when assistance goes beyond mere clerical functions and is tailored to the particularized needs of a client...	Supportive rule explanation
Application 1: In our case, Lysander's assistance with Ptolemy's lease was not merely clerical...	Supportive application
Rule explanation 2: Another relevant factor in determining when assistance becomes the practice of law is the context in which the assistance is provided. Acts are more likely to involve the practice of law if they are undertaken with an aura of legal expertise...	Rule explanation that sets up the counterargument
Application 2: Lysander could argue that she did not offer her advice with an "aura of expertise"...	Counterargument
Application 3: However, these arguments are not likely to prevail. First, Lysander's advice carried an "aura of expertise" just by virtue of her prior legal training in landlord tenant law...Second, while Lysander might have viewed her advice in a casual manner, Ptolemy clearly did not...	Rebuttal

15.2.2.6 | Organizing Counterarguments and Rebuttals in Analyses Divided by Headings

When you are using headings to separate multiple TRRRAAACs, TRARARACs, or TRATRATRACs, counterarguments may be presented and rebutted under the headings to which they are relevant. For example, if there is a significant counterargument to the specific conclusion you are reaching under heading A, present and rebut it at the end of section A and before the start of section B. You do not, however, have to include a counterargument under every heading. For an example of a counterargument and rebuttal tacked on at the end of a section, see section A in Appendix B, Sample C—the counterargument and rebuttal are labeled for you in the margin.

Alternatively, you may sometimes want to present a counterargument in its own section with its own heading. Take this approach only when the counterargument does not relate to any of your affirmative points but is based on separate subrules instead. The structure of a separate counterargument/rebuttal section in a TRRRAAAC by heading structure would look like the following illustration.

Illustration of an Independent Counterargument Section

Heading C identifies the sub-issue on which the counterargument is based.

T = thesis paragraph that previews the counterargument and your rebuttal.

Cont.

R = rule statement and rule explanation paragraph(s) that set(s) up the counterargument and the rebuttal
A = application paragraph(s) that explain(s) how the counterargument would be made and then rebut(s) the counterargument
C = conclusion reached through your rebuttal

Now look at the following sample. Section A supports the author's conclusion that the defendant practiced law without a California license. Section B presents and rebuts a counterargument. Because the counterargument in section B is not tied to the factor analyzed in section A, placing the counterargument and rebuttal in a separate section B is a logical choice. (For more information on the legal issue addressed in this analysis, refer to Appendix B, Sample D.)

Sample Separation of a Counterargument into Its Own Section

A. The Nature of Lysander's Advice

Section A is the supportive section of the analysis.

Lysander's assistance with Ptolemy's lease was the practice of law because it was tailored to his specific circumstances.

Assistance that goes beyond mere clerical functions and is tailored to the particularized needs of a client becomes the practice of law. *People v. Landlords Prof'l Servs.*, 264 Cal. Rptr. 548, 553 (Ct. App. 1989). In *Landlords*, an eviction services business, Landlords Professional Services (LPS), assisted clients in the preparation, filing, and resolution of unlawful detainer actions. *Id.* at 548-549. The court explained that a service like LPS would not be engaging in the practice of law if it merely "made forms available for the client's use, filled the forms in at the specific direction of the client, and filed and served those forms as directed by the client." *Id.* at 553. Similarly, the court concluded that providing a detailed manual on unlawful detainer actions would not be the practice of law. *Id.* On the other hand, any advice on a client's specific case would cross the line and become the practice of law. *Id.* Ultimately, the court held that LPS had engaged in the practice of law. *Id.* First, the court noted that the service had advertised that it "accomplished evictions" and invited prospective clients to "[c]all & talk" to its representatives about eviction procedures. *Id.* The court found that these advertisements "implie[d] its eviction services were not limited to clerical functions." *Id.* The court further noted that although an eviction may not appear to be a difficult procedure, it is still a "legal procedure carried out before a court with specific legal requirements for its accomplishment." *Id.* In addition, LPS addressed the "specific problems and concerns of its clients" during personal interviews. *Id.* For example, an employee advised a client that "it was unlawful to turn off the utilities to [the client's] rental" property. *Id.* Other cases have similarly clarified that while making forms available for clients may not constitute the practice of law, exercising judgment by selecting the right form to fulfill a client's specific needs does. *People v. Sipper*, 142 P.2d 960, 962 (Cal. App. Dep't Super. Ct. 1943) (holding that defendant had practiced law illegally when he advised a client to execute a trust

Cont.

deed to secure a loan), *overruled on other grounds by Murgia v. Municipal Court*, 540 P.2d 44, 54 (Cal. 1975); *In re Anderson*, 79 B.R. 482, 485 (Bankr. S.D. Cal. 1987) (holding that a bankruptcy typing service engaged in the unauthorized practice of law when it used information from client interviews to select and prepare bankruptcy schedules).

In our case, Lysander's assistance with Ptolemy's lease was not merely clerical. She did not merely make forms available to Ptolemy but rather selected the appropriate lease form for his particular needs. She searched for a *residential* lease specifically because he had told her he was leasing a residence. She also searched for a *California* lease because she knew his property was in California. Therefore, her provision of the lease alone involved the practice of law as did the selection of forms in *Sipper* and *Anderson*. However, her assistance did not end with the provision of the lease. She also reviewed the lease once it was completed. The review of the completed lease could have had only one purpose — to double check Ptolemy's adaptation of the form to his particular situation. Finally, Lysander's decision to advise Ptolemy that he could keep the tenant's deposit to cover the damage caused by her dog was even more clearly particularized to Ptolemy's circumstances. Ptolemy described the damage. Lysander even reviewed the lease again. Her advice, therefore, was informed by this specific information. She was not merely providing generalized instructions on landlord-tenant law. Under *Landlords*, advice so particularized to the specifics of a client's case involves the practice of law. 264 Cal. Rptr. at 553.

Section B presents a counterargument and rebuttal.

B. The Context of Lysander's Advice

Despite her attempted disclaimer of expertise and the casual tone of her communications with Ptolemy, Lysander's experience in landlord-tenant law led Ptolemy to rely on her advice to his detriment.

The thesis previews the counterargument (disclaimer & tone) and rebuttal (her legal experience).

Another relevant factor in determining when assistance becomes the practice of law is the context in which the assistance is provided. Acts are more likely to involve the practice of law if they are undertaken with an aura of legal expertise. In *Landlords*, the company argued that defining the practice of law to include all legal advice could lead to the absurd result of prohibiting advice between friends on legal matters. 264 Cal. Rptr. at 554. Without disagreeing that prohibiting advice between friends would be an absurd application of the statute, the court found that the hypothetical raised by LPS was too far from the facts of the case to be a concern. *Id.* The court again pointed to the advertisements published by LPS that suggested it could offer expertise on evictions. *Id.* at 553. In addition, one of its other employees handed out business cards that identified him as "Counselor." *Id.* The court found that because of the "aura of expertise" LPS had created, clients would be likely to view any advice offered by LPS as legal advice and would "undoubtedly" rely on the advice "perhaps to their serious detriment." *Id.* The court declined to limit the definition of the practice of law in a manner that would make the statute inapplicable "to situations in which the public requires protection." *Id.* at 554.

The rule explanation discusses the case on which the counterargument and rebuttal are based.

Lysander could argue that she did not offer her advice with an "aura of expertise." To the contrary, she specifically informed Ptolemy that she was not an expert on landlord tenant law and suggested she "might not be the right person" to offer

The first application paragraph sets forth the counterarguments.

Cont.

advice. She therefore attempted to dissuade Ptolemy from relying on her advice. Moreover, the contacts between Lysander and Ptolemy arguably raise the hypothetical dismissed as irrelevant in *Landlords*: advice on legal matters between friends. The court did not reject the contention that such an application of the statute would be absurd. The tenor of the communications between Lysander and Ptolemy suggest Lysander was offering her assistance merely as a friend. She disclaimed expertise. She joked about lunches as a perk of her advice. She used casual language that she would not use with a client. Imposing criminal penalties on Lysander for advising her former acquaintance in this context seems extreme.

The second appliction paragraph sets forth the rebuttals.

However, these arguments are not likely to prevail. First, Lysander's advice carried an "aura of expertise" just by virtue of her prior legal training in landlord tenant law. Her legal experience in this area was precisely the reason Ptolemy sought her advice. Although she attempted to disclaim expertise in her first communication with him, she presumably thought herself sufficiently qualified to offer the assistance; otherwise, she should have declined. Lysander should have realized that once she answered his legal questions, Ptolemy would be unlikely to seek out alternative legal counsel because he would assume she felt sufficiently qualified to answer. Second, while Lysander might have viewed her advice in a casual manner, Ptolemy clearly did not. He did not initially seek her out merely to renew their friendship. Rather, he contacted her for legal advice specifically. Therefore, even if *Landlords* can be read to have impliedly recognized that the statute was not designed to criminalize advice between friends, this is not such a case. Moreover, like *Landlords*, this case raises the need for public protection that underlies the statute. Ptolemy relied on her advice. As a result of his reliance, he faced an investigation by the authorities and suffered significant stress. The tenant was also a victim—an elderly woman unable, as a result of Ptolemy's retention of her security deposit, to afford the living assistance she urgently needed.

15.2.2.7 | Organizing Multiple Rebuttals

Rebut each counterargument you present. If you have only one counterargument, you only *need* one rebuttal. Of course, you *could* offer multiple rebuttals to the same counterargument. In any event, any rebuttals to a single counterargument should be placed right after the counterargument. If you offer multiple rebuttals to the counterargument, you could place the rebuttals in their own separate paragraphs or join them in a paragraph with a unifying topic sentence.

If you have more than one counterargument, you can either follow each counterargument with its rebuttal (counter 1, rebuttal 1, counter 2, rebuttal 2) or you can present all counterarguments and then follow with all of the rebuttals (counter 1, counter 2, rebuttal 1, rebuttal 2). The first approach benefits the reader by keeping related points closer to one another. An illustration follows. However, the second approach may sometimes be preferable if one point will rebut both counters at the same time or if the rebuttal points are closely related or dependent on one another.

Illustration of Multiple Rebuttals

In this case, the defendant cannot establish the entrapment defense. A transition sentence separates rule explanation and application.

The similarity between the defendant's recent prior crimes and the crime at issue will prove predisposition and, therefore, prevent the defense in this case. The prior crimes and the current crime involved the same underlying motivation. *[The author would then prove this statement using comparisons to the cases that the rule explanation section used to explain predisposition.]* Support

The defendant could try to argue that his current crime involved physical aggression, an element missing from his prior crimes. *[Here, the author would use comparisons to cases discussed in the rule explanation section on predisposition to explain how the defendant could argue that physical aggression involves a different underlying motivation than theft crimes.]* Counterargument 1

However, the physical aggression in this case was ultimately used to further the principal crime of theft and, therefore, does not erase the connection between his prior theft-related crimes and the crime at issue in this case. *[Here, the author would use either comparisons to cases or some underlying policy consideration discussed in the rule explanation section on predisposition to explain why the additional element of physical aggression would not refute predisposition.]* Rebuttal of counterargument 1

Another possible argument in favor of the entrapment defense in this case is that the police not only supplied the materials necessary to the crime but also directed its commission. *[The author would then prove this statement using comparisons to the cases the rule explanation section used to explain significant involvement.]* However, courts have repeatedly stated that evidence of predisposition precludes the defense and therefore renders the degree of police involvement in the crime irrelevant. Because, as explained above, the defendant's prior crimes establish predisposition, the court will most likely decline to address the level of police involvement. Counterargument 2 Rebuttal of counterargument 2

15.2.2.8 | Transitioning into Counterarguments and Rebuttals

You may have noticed from the samples in this chapter that the counterargument and rebuttal paragraphs use transitional language that clearly signals their purpose.

Sample Transitions

Fitness Functions will...argue Counter

The response to these arguments is... Rebuttal

Lysander could argue... Counter

However, these arguments are not likely to prevail... Rebuttal

This transitional language is essential. Standard transitional language like "will argue" or "can argue" signals to the reader that you are presenting a counterargument. Similarly, a transition like "The response is" or "This argument fails because" or even just "However" signals that you are now rebutting the counterargument. Without these transitions, your reader will be confused because your paragraphs will seem contradictory, and she may not understand how these points fit into your overall analysis.

15.2.2.9 | Distinguishing Between Counterarguments and Confounders

In the counterargument paragraphs of your analysis, present arguments that could support the opposite of the outcome your conclusion predicts.[2] An argument that, even if believed, would not support the opposite outcome is not a counterargument. You could think of such a partial argument as a confounder because it may confuse the analysis that supports your conclusion but it cannot defeat your conclusion. You should not ignore confounders, but you can address them in your supportive application paragraphs rather than saving them for the counterargument paragraphs. The counterargument paragraphs should present only arguments that would be dispositive if believed.

Sample Confounder Addressed in a Supportive Application Paragraph

Consistent with the case law discussed above, Savonarola should be found guilty of burglary. Under *Valencia*, the bank's outer boundary included the ATM kiosk because it was an enclosed area into which a reasonable person would believe that a member of the public could not pass without permission. Like a door or window, the kiosk affords protection from unauthorized intrusions. Indeed, the bank representative stated that the reason the bank built the kiosk was to protect customers from theft. **It does not matter that the external door of the kiosk does not lock.** As the court explained in *Valencia*, even an unlocked door provides expectation of protection because social norms preclude crossing such portals without permission. *Valencia*, 46 P.3d at 926. The bank representative confirmed that the bank did have this expectation. Specifically, he stated, "We figured that even without a lock, the doors are a deterrent." Because the bank reasonably expected the kiosk to offer protection from unauthorized intrusion, the "ultimate test" for entry is satisfied.

In the preceding sample from Appendix B, Sample B, the shaded sentence addresses a confounder. The point is not a counterargument because as the rest of the paragraph explains, the absence of a lock does not warrant an opposite outcome in the case. Someone might try to argue that the absence of a lock refutes the author's argument that the kiosk afforded protection from intrusion, so the point is worth addressing. However, because it is so easily rebutted under the case law, it is not worthy of a separate counterargument paragraph.

2. My colleague, Dov Waisman, inspired this section of the text by proposing a similar distinction.

Sample Counterargument in Its Own Paragraph

Fitness Functions will need to argue that the pressure to play paddleball does not rise to the level of expectancy. The company can distinguish *Wilson* and *Kidwell* because in those cases, employees had to train to pass required fitness tests. Fitness Functions employees did not need to play paddleball to satisfy an express job requirement. *Ezzy* can also be distinguished because in that case, a partner directly urged the law clerk to play by telling her "we'll see you" at the next game. *Ezzy*, 194 Cal. Rptr. at 92. In this case, by contrast, Randolph merely invited Gator to play. Moreover, no one with supervisory authority, including Randolph, ever suggested that employees should play paddleball. Although a coworker once advised Gator that he should play, she did not have supervisory authority and therefore cannot be considered to have been speaking as a representative of the company. Finally, Fitness Functions can argue that unlike participation in extracurricular activities in *Smith*, paddleball was not an overt aspect of employee evaluations. In sum, Fitness Functions can argue that expectancy should require more than a mere sense that participating in the activity will help get an "in" with the supervisor. Personal one-on-one time always helps advance a career. If the mere desire to become closer with a supervisor were sufficient, a supervisor could never invite an employee to play golf without worrying that a resulting injury would be subject to workers' compensation coverage.

This is a true counterargument because if all of the points in the paragraph are believed, a court would have to find that Gator's injury did not arise from a reasonable expectancy of employment. In other words, the author has fully explained how an opposite outcome could be reached.

The line between a confounder and a true counterargument may seem nebulous to you at first. So, take a disciplined approach. First, identify all of the points against you. Second, go through each point you have listed and think about whether the point would support an opposite conclusion if believed and whether it can reasonably be supported by the case law. If the point either does not support an opposite conclusion or is a "straw man" that can be easily rebutted, you might address the point as a confounder *if* it relates to one of your supportive application paragraphs, but it would not warrant its own counterargument paragraph.

Checklist for the Analysis Section

- ☐ Start with your thesis, phrased firmly and specifically to the issue you are analyzing.
- ☐ Next, include a rule statement paragraph that includes overarching rules.
- ☐ Then use rule explanation and application paragraphs to support your points and present and rebut any counterarguments.
- ☐ Address important counterarguments that could be dispositive of the case if believed.

Cont.

- ☐ Develop counterarguments with the same depth and using the same analytical process as in your supportive application paragraphs.
- ☐ Rebut every counterargument by exposing its logical flaws (and not merely repeating your earlier points).
- ☐ Use the four tools of effective application paragraphs in all application paragraphs, even counterarguments and rebuttals.
- ☐ Include transitional language for counterarguments and rebuttals.

CHAPTER 15 SELF-TEST

1. What should the first sentence of your analysis section do?
2. What does it mean to say that your discussion of the law (rule statement and rule explanation) are balanced?
3. What does it mean to say that your application is balanced?
4. Is there any difference between an application paragraph that supports your conclusion and one that presents a counterargument?
5. If a rebuttal cannot merely repeat the points that you made in favor of your conclusion, what should it do?
6. What is the difference between a confounder and a counterargument, and why does it matter?

See answers on page 340.

CHAPTER 16

The Conclusion Section of a Legal Research Memorandum

Now we have come to the end of the TRAC organization: the conclusion.

The final conclusion of your legal analysis in a legal research memorandum is separated from the analysis section with its own heading. Under that heading, briefly summarize your conclusion regarding the likely result in the case and your reasons for that conclusion. In most cases, this should be about one to three sentences. If you use headings in your analysis section, the conclusion section would be a broad wrap-up of all the points you have made. The conclusion might be longer if your analysis involved balancing factors because you would need to weigh any conflicting factors, as discussed in section 6.3.

Sample Conclusion

CONCLUSION

For the reasons explained above, Gator has a good claim for coverage and should therefore submit an application for adjudication with the Workers' Compensation Appeals Board.

PART III

PERSUASIVE WRITING

CHAPTER **17**

Overview of Persuasive Legal Writing
Briefs

The chapters that follow discuss legal briefs, a form of persuasive legal writing. Briefs are formal documents usually filed either in support of or in opposition to a motion. A motion is a party's formal request that the court in an ongoing case take a particular action (e.g., to dismiss the case, to order a disclosure of information, or to move the case to a different jurisdiction).

Briefs set forth, at a minimum, the relevant facts of the case in which the motion has been brought, a discussion of legal precedent relevant to the motion, and the party's arguments regarding how the legal precedent supports his or her position on the issue(s) raised in the motion.

As the chapters that follow explain, briefs apply all of the fundamental lessons of Part I but with a persuasive bent.

17.1 | GOALS

Your goal in writing a brief is to convince the court that your client should prevail on whatever motion is pending. Your brief should:

- Make your client's contentions clear and logical.
- Identify and explain the relevant legal rules in the most favorable light for your client but without misleading the reader.
- Anticipate and respond to your opponent's legal authority.
- Explain how the specific facts of your client's case support your client's contentions in light of the legal authority you have discussed while also anticipating and responding to your opponent's arguments.

Of course, you will not always persuade your reader, but you will have done your job if you accomplish these goals.

17.2 | TONE

The best-written briefs persuade through strategic choices that do not sacrifice integrity. To achieve the right balance, do the following.

- Always have your opponent's best facts, legal authority, and arguments in mind and address them head-on instead of avoiding them.
- Use every opportunity in the facts section, headings, and argument section to nudge the court in your client's direction by strategically selecting your focus, words, and organization.
- Gently slant your language to convey your client's point of view but avoid obviously biased language, overt emotional pleas, and self-righteous expressions. Do not make the judge roll her eyes.

17.3 | BASIC COMPONENTS

17.3.1 | List of Components

Brief components vary depending on the court in which the brief is filed and even sometimes the motion at issue. Chapters 22 and 23 present standard formats for appellate and trial-level briefs. At a minimum, most briefs have the following components.

- Caption or cover page
- Table of contents
- Table of authorities (as required)
- Question presented/statement of the issue
- Statement of facts/factual background
- Standard of review (appellate briefs only)
- Introduction or summary of the argument
- Argument
- Conclusion

17.3.2 | Description of Components

Each component is explained in detail in the chapters that follow. For now, here is a brief overview of what happens in each section.

Cover page (sections 22.1, 23.1)**:** All appellate briefs include cover pages. Trial-level briefs might use cover pages if they include tables. Cover pages have no pagination. They typically include the formal title of the case, case number, court, title of the brief, and attorney information.

Table of contents (Chapter 20)**:** The table of contents includes all of the sections and headings of the brief in order with the page number on which each begins. The table of contents is usually paginated with lowercase roman numerals.

Table of authorities *(Chapter 20)***:** The table of authorities contains a list of all cases, statutes, and other authority cited in the brief with the page number on which each is cited. The table of authorities' pagination continues from the table of contents' lowercase roman numerals.

Question presented *(appellate briefs and some trial briefs) (section 22.2)***:** This section contains a clearly drafted question or questions that adequately identify the issues that the brief will analyze. They include the key fact(s) on which your contentions depend and matching phrases from the relevant law, all geared toward predisposing the court to your client's position.

Standard of review *(appellate briefs only) (section 22.3)***:** This section states the relevant standard of review for the issue on appeal: de novo, abuse of discretion, or lack of substantial evidence. You must research the right standard for the issues raised in the appeal. Sometimes, the standard is simple. For example, all appeals from a summary judgment motion are reviewed de novo. Other times, the appeal might be governed by multiple standards that vary according to the issue, or the relevant standard for a particular issue might be subject to debate and, therefore, might require extensive analysis.

Introduction *(trial-level briefs) (section 23.2)* ***or summary of the argument*** *(appellate briefs) (section 22.4)***:** These sections aim to pack all of the brief's contentions into a condensed, highly persuasive synopsis. They typically include the action that you want the court to take, a powerful narrative that conveys your client's point of view, and either how existing law supports your contentions or why policy considerations support your contentions or both.

Argument *(Chapter 18 and section 23.4)***:** This is the bulk of the brief. This is where you will discuss the law on the issue(s) and the cases you have read. You do not want to detail your opponent's arguments, but you do need to anticipate and respond to them. Of course, you also need to present your favorable rules, cases, and facts. Follow TRRRAAAC by heading or one of the alternative organizations discussed in Chapter 6.

Conclusion: This section is usually an extremely brief wrap-up. Often, it restates that the court should take the action that you are requesting. For example, "For the foregoing reasons, this Court should affirm the judgment." However, if the preceding analysis involves a balancing of factors, the conclusion section may bring the factors together, as discussed in section 6.3.

CHAPTER **18**

Writing a Persuasive Factual Narrative

Both trial court and appellate court briefs contain a section that lays out the relevant facts of the case. This section might be referred to as statement of the case, factual background, or statement of facts. To decide which title to use, you should first consult the rules of the court to which you are submitting your brief. Some courts have rules that specify the components of briefs. Use the title that the rules use. If no court rules apply, then follow the convention of your law office. Finally, if you have neither court rules nor a law office convention that you need to follow, just choose the title you like best.

This chapter builds on Chapter 9, which discussed factual narratives generally. All of the considerations about which facts to include and how to organize the facts presented in Chapter 9 apply to briefs. Stop here and review Chapter 9 before proceeding.

This chapter supplements Chapter 9's lessons on storytelling by explaining how to incorporate strategy into your persuasive factual narrative. Your goal is to present the facts in the manner most beneficial to your client and in a narrative that builds sympathy toward your client. Your strategic choices should predispose the judge to accept your argument without losing credibility. The key to a successful factual narrative in a brief is to quietly, surreptitiously nudge the reader toward your position. But you need to walk a fine line. On the one hand, your brief should predispose the judge to your client's position. But, on the other hand, if it is too overtly biased, you will lose the judge's trust.

18.1 | FRAMING THE CASE STRATEGICALLY IN THE FIRST PARAGRAPH

The first paragraph of a factual narrative *needs* to identify the key players and general nature of the case so that the rest of the narrative makes sense to the reader. Review section 9.1 on the who, what, where, when facts that should be included in the first paragraph.

Ideally, the first paragraph should also frame the case in a manner that predisposes the reader to your client or your arguments. Framing mostly involves emphasis. Think about the arguments you plan to make and emphasize the factual details that will start nudging the reader in your direction. For example, compare the two paragraphs below. The first sample is from the Sample Appellee's Brief (Sample E) (the appellee is the party defending against the appeal). It frames the case in a manner that favors affirmance of the lower court's decision by emphasizing the reasons the lower court denied the defendant's motion to dismiss and the defendant's admission of her role in the bombing. By contrast, the second sample, which is from the Sample Appellant's Brief (Sample F), frames the case in a manner that favors reversal by emphasizing the reasons for the defendant's motion to dismiss and the lower court's failure to consider those reasons.

First Paragraph from Appellee's Brief

Defendant Reyna Forrest was found guilty of terrorism charges based on her role in the bombing of Lee King Autos that led to the death of the dealership's owner, Mr. King. (R. at 59.) Defendant does not dispute that she set and detonated the bomb that killed Mr. King but contends, in this appeal, that the trial court erroneously denied her pretrial motion to dismiss the indictment on outrageous conduct grounds. (R. at 63.) The trial court denied her motion because it concluded that the government's conduct in investigating Forrest's eco-terrorist group was not so "shocking to the universal sense of justice" that it required dismissal of her indictment. (R. at 59.)

First Paragraph from Appellant's Brief

The defendant, Reyna Forrest, has been convicted for the bombing of Lee King Autos. (R. at 59.) Before trial, she moved to dismiss her indictment on the basis of outrageous government conduct. (R. at 59.) In support of the motion, Ms. Forrest argued that she was coerced into participating in the bombing by a government informant named Sid Morlandia who manufactured the crime from start to finish, the government informant's sole motive was to obtain a conviction, and the FBI endangered the public. (R. at 51-52.) Despite these allegations, the trial court declined to dismiss the indictment. (R. at 52.) Ms. Forrest now appeals her conviction on the grounds of outrageous government conduct. (R. at 59.)

18.2 | CRAFTING THE PROCEDURAL HISTORY STRATEGICALLY

Procedural history is the history of the case to date from the filing of the complaint to the most recent procedural event (e.g., the filing of the motion you are now arguing or the filing of the appeal if you are preparing an appellate brief).

Procedural history usually fits best at the beginning of the facts section (as part of the introductory paragraph) or at the end of the facts section (as the last paragraph).

Slant the procedural history favorably toward your client, but do not *argue* in your facts section. Instead, *describe* the arguments stated in documents on file with the court. Here are the two samples from section 18.1 again. The bold language describes the arguments strategically.

First Paragraph from Appellee's Brief

Defendant Reyna Forrest was found guilty of terrorism charges based on her role in the bombing of Lee King Autos that led to the death of the dealership's owner, Mr. King. (R. at 59.) **Defendant does not dispute that she set and detonated the bomb that killed Mr. King** but contends, in this appeal, that the trial court erroneously denied her pretrial motion to dismiss the indictment on outrageous conduct grounds. (R. at 63.) **The trial court denied her motion because it concluded that the government's conduct in investigating Forrest's eco-terrorist group was not so "shocking to the universal sense of justice" that it required dismissal of her indictment.** (R. at 59.)

First Paragraph from Appellant's Brief

The defendant, Reyna Forrest, has been convicted for the bombing of Lee King Autos. (R. at 59.) Before trial, she moved to dismiss her indictment on the basis of outrageous government conduct. (R. at 59.) In support of the motion, **Ms. Forrest argued that she was coerced into participating in the bombing by a government informant named Sid Morlandia who manufactured the crime from start to finish, the government informant's sole motive was to obtain a conviction, and the FBI endangered the public.** (R. at 51-52.) **Despite these allegations,** the trial court declined to dismiss the indictment. (R. at 52.) Ms. Forrest now appeals her conviction on the grounds of outrageous government conduct. (R. at 59.)

Note that you should *not* argue in the procedural history. Instead, merely recite the arguments that were made in the documents that are part of the record on appeal. So, the sample paragraph from the appellee's brief states, "The trial court denied her motion because" and then states the exact reasons stated in the trial court's order. And the sample paragraph from the appellant's brief uses the language, "defense counsel argued that" and recounts the exact reasons stated in the motion that was filed with the trial court. Using language that clearly indicates that you are merely recounting what the documents say rather than stating the arguments yourself ensures that your reader will not think you are improperly arguing in the facts section.

In addition to describing your arguments in a favorable way, as in the examples above, you can also describe your opponent's arguments in an unfavorable way. For example, the sample paragraph from the appellant's brief states, "Despite these allegations, the trial court declined to dismiss the indictment." The beginning clause, "despite these allegations," naturally calls the trial court's decision into question by subtly suggesting the court overlooked important evidence.

18.3 | TELLING THE STORY FROM YOUR CLIENT'S POINT OF VIEW

After your introductory paragraph, which may also include procedural history, you can start to tell the story of the case. Before you start this step, pause and view the entire record with the right frame of mind. An objective factual narrative in a legal research memorandum takes an unbiased view of the facts. In persuasive writing, by contrast, you are with your client down in the trenches fighting to win your case. Think about how your client should tell the story to win over the sympathy of the judge. Choose your starting point strategically. Start with the best facts for your position.

To understand the importance of your starting point, compare the following two paragraphs. These are the second paragraphs from the appellee's brief and appellant's brief respectively. Notice that the appellee's brief focuses on the defendant's preexisting criminal activity and the destructiveness of her organization while the appellant's brief focuses on her devotion to legal environmental advocacy. Here the two different versions cancel each other out because each side has been strategic. However, if one of these briefs had failed to be strategic, the other brief would have struck a serious blow to the opponent. Do not be the one to submit the losing brief by failing to select a strategic starting point!

Second Paragraph from Appellee's Brief

Defendant participated in the bombing as a member of an eco-terrorist organization called EARTH. Although EARTH has one branch that engages solely in legal environmental advocacy, it has another branch, called the Crusaders, that engages in violence and sabotage to further its agenda. (R. at 14-15.) The Crusaders are suspecting of causing at least $30 million in damages and a number of deaths and accidents in Los Angeles alone. (R. at 15.) Defendant began as a member of the legal branch of EARTH but knowingly chose to join the Crusaders long before her role in the bombing for which she has been convicted. (R. at 40-41.) When Defendant joined the Crusaders, she knew it engaged in illegal acts of sabotage including spray-painting SUVs, sabotaging logging operations, and tree-spiking. (R. at 41, 45.) Defendant thereafter engaged in two illegal acts: spray-painting "Gas-Guzzler" on an SUV and puncturing the tires of construction vehicles. (R. at 41.) Prior to her role in the present bombing, Defendant also attended a meeting where she learned how to build an incendiary device, a task she claims she was "hopeless" at. (R. at 43-44.) Although she claims not to have known that the Crusaders resorted to violence, she was aware that EARTH was suspected of a recent bombing at Camp Pendleton that killed an officer and wounded others. (R. at 15, 45.)

Second Paragraph from Appellant's Brief

Prior to her encounters with the government informant, Ms. Forrest pursued her passion for environmental causes solely through nonviolent advocacy. (R. at 39-40.) At age 18, Ms. Forrest witnessed the destruction of her hometown of Valdez, Alaska, due to the 1989 Exxon oil spill. (R. at 39.) Deeply affected by this experience, she joined an environmental organization called EARTH and eventually became the leader of the EARTH chapter at her college. (R. at 40.) The chapter engaged only in legal environmental advocacy. (*R. at 40.*) After college, Ms. Forrest worked for a nonprofit organization devoted to advocating for environmental protection laws. (R. at 39.) Then, one day, a male member of EARTH asked to meet her for dinner. (R. at 39.) Expecting a date, Ms. Forrest was surprised to learn that the purpose of the meeting was to recruit her to join the eco-terrorist branch of EARTH called the Crusaders. (R. at 39-40.) Ms. Forrest decided to join the Crusaders only after several months of deliberation. (R. at 41.) At that time, she was aware that the Crusaders used sabotage to promote its agenda but was not aware that the group resorted to violence as well. (R. at 45.) True to her understanding that the group's "extralegal" methods were strictly nonviolent, her participation was limited to two nonviolent missions. On one occasion, she and other Crusaders sprayed the phrase "Gas Guzzler" on an SUV. (R. at 41.) On another occasion, they punctured the tires of construction vehicles at a new mall construction site. (R. at 41.) After puncturing the tires, Ms. Forrest and the other Crusaders draped a large banner over the entrance to the site. (R. at 41.) The purpose of the banner was to alert the construction workers not to use the vehicles so they would not be injured. (R. at 41.) No one was hurt in either situation. (R. at 41.) Indeed, in all of her years as a member of EARTH, she never met anyone she considered to be violent until she encountered Morlandia. (R. at 43.)

18.4 | SELECTING THE RIGHT FACTS

As you draft the rest of the factual narrative, you will need to select the right factual details to include. Here are some things to consider.

Include any fact you will use in your analysis (including any fact you will use in your rebuttals to the other side's arguments).

In addition, include key adverse facts even if you do not use them in your analysis. Notice, for example, that the sample paragraph from the appellant's brief discloses the appellant's prior crimes. She could not have omitted this information because the government would obviously rely on her prior crimes to argue that she was not coerced into committing the crime.

Finally, you may want to include some less relevant facts if they help build sympathy for your client even if you do not plan to mention them in your argument section. For example, the sample paragraph from the appellant's brief includes details about her legal environmental advocacy efforts. These are not important facts to the issue addressed in the brief, but they help build sympathy for the defendant.

In sum, ask yourself:

- Am I going to refer to this fact in my argument section? If yes, include it in the factual narrative.
- Is the other side going to refer to this fact in its argument section? If yes, include it unless you are convinced it is irrelevant.
- Does it help build sympathy for my client or my arguments? If yes, include it in your facts section even if it is not directly relevant. But use this technique sparingly; do not include too many irrelevant facts.

18.5 | INCORPORATING GENTLY SLANTED DESCRIPTIVE LANGUAGE

As you put your client's side of the story on paper, strategy should be your guiding principle. One technique is to use descriptive language to slant the narrative favorably toward your client and your arguments. But avoid overly biased terms.

ERROR Examples of Overly Loaded Terms

The Defendant is a villain, who has repeatedly committed sabotage to further her political agenda.

The Defendant was a criminal long before she crossed paths with Agent Morlandia.

Both "villain" and "criminal" are too accusatory and inflammatory to use to describe one of the parties in your case. Instead of using these labels, rely on facts instead, as in the following example.

Revised Version

The Defendant committed two serious acts of sabotage before ever meeting Agent Morlandia. On one occasion, she slashed the tires of construction vehicles. On another occasion, she defaced someone's SUV with a spray-painted political message.

This sentence achieves the same result as the language above, but it appears more objective because it states facts. The use of the adjective "serious" is appropriate because it is a fair characterization of the facts and is not inflammatory to the same degree as calling the defendant a "villain" or "criminal."

Example of Appropriately Descriptive Language

In a surprising turn of events, Adhemar appeared at the rendezvous site where Defendant was to pick up Morlandia. (R. at 28-29.)

In this example, the descriptive language, "surprising turn of events," is a fair characterization of the facts in the *Forrest* case (see Sample E) because the testimony established that no one expected Adhemar's appearance. Try to incorporate some descriptive language in your factual narrative to help tell the story of the case from your client's perspective and to help call the reader's attention to significant facts.

18.6 | SELECTING YOUR WORDS STRATEGICALLY

Sometimes creating the right impression of an event is as simple as selecting the right adjective, verb, or noun. Pay attention to your word choice as you draft your facts section, especially when addressing important facts. Effective word choice takes discipline. Stop yourself and sift through your vocabulary to find the right word with the right connotation. In the examples below, notice how the underlined words give a completely different impression of the events without misrepresenting the facts or using inflammatory language.

Example of Strategic Word Choice

Plaintiff's word choice: Defendant sped through the red light and crashed into Plaintiff's car without even touching his breaks.

Defendant's word choice: Defendant missed the red light and Plaintiff's car was coming on so fast that he had no time to react. The cars collided.

Example of Strategic Word Choice

Prosecution's word choice: Defendant fired his gun haphazardly without pausing to think about where the bullets might end up.

Defendant's word choice: Caught up in the excitement of the moment, Defendant fired a celebratory shot straight up into the air not anticipating that anyone would be hurt.

18.7 | VARYING THE AMOUNT OF DETAIL FOR STRATEGIC EFFECT

Another technique to help the facts look better for your client is to add detail to emphasize favorable facts and omit detail to downplay unfavorable facts. Compare the following two examples. The first sentence illustrates how a defendant in a car collision case might downplay his alcohol consumption. The second sentence illustrates how the plaintiff might add detail to emphasize the defendant's drinking.

Example of Minimal Detail to Downplay a Bad Fact

Defendant had consumed some alcohol over the course of the evening.

Example of More Detail to Emphasize a Favorable Fact

Defendant had been drinking glass after glass of straight vodka all night and decided he needed one more shot just as he was leaving to drive home.

Quotations from testimony create even more emphasis:

Example of Testimony Quotation to Emphasize a Favorable Fact

Defendant's glass was "never empty" because "the vodka just kept coming." As he was leaving to drive home, the defendant asked for one last shot "for the road."

When you are writing your factual narrative, comb through the witnesses' testimony to find helpful quotes that can help create the view of the facts that best supports your client's position. For the bad facts that you must disclose, think carefully about your phrasing to neutralize their effect on the reader.

18.8 | DEALING WITH BAD FACTS

18.8.1 | Placement of Bad Facts

To the extent possible, hide each bad fact in the middle of an otherwise favorable paragraph (though, of course, the placement has to make sense). A reader's attention is naturally drawn to the beginning and end of each paragraph. Therefore, placing a fact in the middle of the paragraph helps to deemphasize it. Sometimes this may mean coming up with some last point about the facts of the case to avoid ending the paragraph on an unfavorable note.

Example of Strategic Placement

As part of its undercover operation, the FBI used informants to obtain information about EARTH's leadership and terrorist activities. (R. at 16.) Defendant's motion to dismiss was based entirely on the actions of one of these informants—Sid Morlandia. (R. at 59.) Morlandia was the FBI's most successful informant; he was the closest the FBI had ever come to penetrating EARTH's mid-level leadership in the nine years of its operation. (R. at 16, 18-19.) Morlandia's success in gaining the trust of EARTH's leadership was so crucial to the FBI's goals that **the FBI continued to use him even after it began to suspect that he might be misleading the FBI and that he might have participated in arson in Sylmar.** (R. at 18-19.) The FBI believed it could still get useful information from Morlandia while watching him more closely to ensure his allegiance. (R. at 19.)

In the preceding excerpt from the appellee's brief, the government deals with the damaging fact that the FBI was using a known terrorist to infiltrate EARTH. The fact is disclosed in the middle of the paragraph (in bold). Rather than end the paragraph with the unfavorable fact, the government adds an additional sentence that helps detract from the significance of the unfavorable fact.

18.8.2 | Strategic Juxtaposition

You should also try to find a favorable related fact that can help detract from a bad fact's significance. You can think of the favorable fact as a "neutralizing fact." The neutralizing fact can be in its own sentence after you have disclosed the unfavorable fact. Or the neutralizing fact can be contained in the same sentence as the unfavorable fact with an "although" or similar clause. When using this technique, you always want to put the neutralizing fact *after* the unfavorable fact.

Example of a Juxtaposing Sentence

Despite her cheery disposition, Rachel is dogmatic and stubborn.

The preceding sample deemphasizes Rachel's cheery disposition by following it with the statement that she is dogmatic and stubborn. Compare the following example that has the opposite effect.

Example of a Juxtaposing Sentence

Although Rachel is dogmatic and stubborn, she has a cheery disposition.

For additional examples of "although" clauses that downplay adverse facts, refer to Annotations 4, 7, and 15 of the Sample Appellee's Brief (Sample E).

18.8.3 | Strategic Use of Passive Voice

Another technique for deemphasizing bad facts is to use passive voice to dissociate your client from a bad act. Compare the following two sentences. The first uses the active voice to emphasize the defendant's role in causing the plaintiff's injury whereas the second uses passive voice to take the defendant out of the image created by the sentence.

Plaintiff's Version: Active Voice

Defendant's product injured Plaintiff when it spontaneously burst into flames.

Defendant's Version: Passive Voice

Plaintiff was injured when the toaster caught on fire.

18.9 | USING CLEAR NAME REFERENCES

When referring to the parties in an appellate brief, avoid using "Appellant" and "Appellee" because the reader may have trouble remembering who is who. It is much easier for the reader if you use "Plaintiff" and "Defendant" or, even better, the actual names of the parties. For individuals, you can use their last names. For entities, you can use a shortened version of the name (e.g., George's instead of George's Repair Shop).

18.10 | CITING TO THE RECORD

If you have not yet noticed from the samples, every statement in the facts section of a brief must be supported by a citation to the page in the record that proves it. In appeals, the parties prepare a paginated Record on Appeal and use "R. at ___" to cite to the right page. The "R." stands for "Record on Appeal." The *Bluebook* permits but does not require parentheses around the citations. Whichever format you select, be consistent.

Example of Citation to the Record in an Appellate Brief

The sky is blue. (R. at 15.) There are no clouds. (R. at 16.)

Lawyers preparing a brief for a trial court do not have a paginated record to which to cite. Instead, they submit supporting declarations that include key documents or transcripts that provide the proof of any factual assertions they want to make in their briefs. A trial court brief cites to these declarations and exhibits.

Example of Citation to Declaration Exhibits in a Trial Court Brief

The sky is blue. (Turner Decl., ¶ 4, exh. A, p. 4.)

Facts Section Checklist

- ☐ Review the checklist at the end of Chapter 9.
- ☐ Include all relevant facts, even unfavorable facts.
- ☐ Draft your first introductory paragraph strategically. Make sure it has the right emphasis for your client's position.
- ☐ Tell the story from your client's point of view. Think about your starting point strategically.
- ☐ Make your discussion of any procedural history into another opportunity to get the court to view the case from your client's point of view.
- ☐ Use the following techniques to make your facts section surreptitiously persuasive:
  - Gently slanted descriptive language
  - Strategic word selection
  - Variation of the amount of detail depending on whether you want to emphasize or downplay a fact
  - Careful placement of bad facts (hide bad facts in the middle of a paragraph if possible but make sure the placement makes logical sense too)
  - Strategic juxtaposition (follow bad facts with good facts that detract from their significance)
  - Strategic use of passive voice
- ☐ In appellate briefs, do not refer to parties as Appellant and Appellee.
- ☐ Include record cites for each sentence.

CHAPTER **19**

The Argument Section of a Brief

The lessons covered in Chapters 3 through 12 apply to briefs as well as legal research memoranda. The main difference between a brief and a memorandum is that a brief must be strategic. This chapter covers strategic considerations that are particular to brief writing.

19.1 | SELECTING AN ORGANIZATIONAL STRUCTURE

Most briefs involve more than one issue or sub-issue. Therefore, the multiple TRAC structure covered in section 6.3 is most likely the best fit for a brief, but with the possible modifications covered in sections 6.4 through 6.7. In particular, the use of narratives discussed in section 6.5 can be extremely beneficial in drafting a brief because narratives can ground your legal arguments in a factual context that will help persuade the court to side with your client. Select your structure strategically. Which structure best emphasizes your favorable arguments and permits you to respond to the other side's arguments in a way that does not emphasize them?

19.2 | THE T IN TRAC: STRUCTURING YOUR ARGUMENTS

Briefs nearly always involve a complex analysis that requires a multiple-TRAC organization. You will therefore use all three forms of T discussed in Chapter 6: a single thesis sentence in an undivided subsection (6.1); a main umbrella paragraph that introduces your first tier of subheadings (A., B., C., etc.); and mini-umbrella paragraphs for any subsection that is further divided into sub-subheadings (1., 2., 3., etc.). The content is no different in briefs than in legal research memoranda except that briefs require more overt persuasive techniques, including persuasive roadmaps and core theory statements. These new techniques are explained in more detail in sections 19.2.1 and 19.2.2. For now, here is a sample that shows you the components of an umbrella paragraph in a brief. Some of these components can be moved around. However, the thesis sentence, which states the broad conclusion, usually precedes the rule statement, and the rule statement usually precedes the roadmap.

Sample Umbrella

This Court should reverse the judgment because Plaintiff has demonstrated triable Issues on newsworthiness.

Thesis sentence

Core theory

The District Court's grant of summary judgment in favor of Defendant was erroneous. Defendant's decision to reveal Plaintiff's identity in its article and thereby expose her previously private battle with depression was unjustified and unduly intrusive.

Rule statement

To preserve the quality of life that legal protection of our private lives engenders, reasonable limitations on the public's right to information are necessary. *Virgil v. Time, Inc.*, 527 F.2d 1122, 1128 (9th Cir. 1975). The media does not have the unrestricted right to "pry into [] unnewsworthy private affairs." *Id.*

Under California law, three factors determine when the media has gone too far: "the social value of the facts published, the depth of the article's intrusion into ostensibly private affairs, and the extent to which the party voluntarily acceded to a position of public notoriety." *Kapellas v. Kofman*, 459 P.2d 912, 922 (Cal. 1969); *accord Shulman v. Grp. W Prods., Inc.*, 955 P.2d 469, 482 (Cal. 1998). The social value and depth of intrusion factors both require the application of community mores, a function entrusted to the jury. *See Virgil*, 527 F.2d at 1130 n.13 (concluding that the determination of whether published facts are of legitimate public interest involves the application of community mores and, therefore, should be "largely" left to the jury). The role of the court is limited to determining whether a jury question is presented. *Id.* at 1130. Summary judgment is appropriate only when there is no room for "differing views" on either the state of community mores or on how they apply to the facts of the case. *Id.*

Transition to roadmap

Plaintiff does not challenge the general newsworthiness of Defendant's article on work-life balance among female attorneys in law firms. However, "while the general subject matter of a publication may be newsworthy, it does not necessarily follow that all information given in the account is newsworthy." *Times-Mirror Co. v. Superior Court*, 244 Cal. Rptr. 556, 562 (Ct. App. 1988). Defendant's decision to identify Plaintiff by name in the article is not entitled to protection under the three factors identified in *Kapellas*. First, she did nothing to invite public notoriety. Second, Defendant's disclosure of her identity carried no social value because it did nothing to further the article's message. Third, any slight relevance her identity might have had would be insufficient to counterbalance the severity of Defendant's intrusion into her personal life.

Roadmap

A. Plaintiff was an average citizen who did not engage in any conduct that would attract public attention.

19.2.1 | Thesis Sentences and Core Theory

The first sentence of an argument section is usually a thesis sentence that states the result you are seeking or the trial court error you are asserting and a broad statement of your conclusion on the issue.

Sample Thesis Sentences

This Court should affirm the judgment because recovery for defamation in this case would violate Defendant's First Amendment rights.

This Court should reverse the judgment because the government's conduct in this case exceeded due process limits.

The trial court's decision to grant summary judgment was erroneous because Defendant's due process rights were not violated.

The trial court correctly granted summary judgment because Plaintiff failed to establish that Defendant published a provably false factual assertion.

The thesis sentence and core theory work together. The core theory is a more specific statement of the central theme for the brief. The core theory sentence in your umbrella should be a powerful statement that encompasses all of the points you will make in your brief. You may want to include some narrative details with the core theory sentence to make it more vivid.

The core theory can be placed right after the thesis sentence at the beginning of the umbrella (as in the sample umbrella at the start of section 19.2) or can be saved for near the end of the umbrella as a lead-in to your roadmap (as in the Sample Appellant's Brief (Sample F) and Sample Appellee's Brief (Sample E)).

Compare the core theories from the sample briefs below.

Core Theory and Narrative Details from Sample Appellant's Brief

The dangers of overzealous law that underlie the outrageous conduct theory are evident in this case. Ms. Forrest was a nonviolent environmental activist who had only participated in two minor acts of vandalism prior to becoming caught up in the criminal plan devised by the government's informant. The informant first coerced her into committing the crime by threatening her life and then directed every aspect of the plan.

Core Theory Sentence from Sample Appellee's Brief

This is not one of the rare cases that require overturning an otherwise justified conviction.

Ideally, the core theory is not confined to the umbrella but is a theme to which subsequent headings, thesis sentences, and wrap-ups connect. For example, consider how the following excerpts from the Sample Appellee's Brief (Sample E) pick up on and carry forward the two-part theme from the core theory sentence: the rareness of the defense and the justification behind the conviction.

Later Excerpts from Sample Appellee's Brief

> **A. The government's conduct satisfies a five-factor test developed by this Court to limit outrageous government conduct claims.**
>
> **B. The government's conduct was not outrageous because it was designed to intercept active terrorists...**
>
> **In the thesis paragraph of B:** "Defendant was drawn into the planned bombing by her own terrorist organization."
> **In the wrap-up at the end of B:** "She was not 'lawfully and peacefully minding [her] own business.'"
> **In the wrap-up at the end of D:** "This Court cannot reverse the conviction on such attenuated grounds without risking significant interference with the success of necessary undercover operations."
> **In the wrap-up at the end of E:** "[N]one of the conduct on which Defendant relies is sufficiently outrageous to support the drastic remedy of dismissing the indictment...."

To ensure that you spot opportunities to tie your points back to your core theory, you could print out your core theory sentence and keep the printout on your desk as you write or create a temporary header with the core theory to constantly remind yourself of the theme.

To construct a strong core theory, think about both the legal rules on the issue and human nature. Judges are humans. Moreover, they are *socially conscious* humans who want their work to have a positive impact on society. Picture yourself in that role. How can you frame the case (with the applicable legal rules in mind) in a way that will appeal to the judge's desire to do the right thing? Sometimes this may mean focusing the brief on an emotional element of the case. For example, the Sample Appellant's Brief (Sample F) focuses on the "overzealous law enforcement" language from one of the cases and then ties it to the inherent unfairness of the government informant's coercive tactics to get the defendant to commit her first-ever act of violence. Other times, the emotion may not be on your side and you need to focus on some greater policy concern instead. For example, the Sample Appellee's Brief (Sample E) focuses on the limited nature of the defense and the justifications the government offered for its sting operation.

Here are some common themes you might consider depending on the legal issues you are addressing and the facts of your client's case:

- Fairness to the parties
- Stare decisis (i.e., the need for consistency)
- Separation of powers (e.g., courts do not want to usurp the role of the legislature by creating new law)
- States' rights (to self-govern without undue restriction)
- Public safety
- Limited court information (e.g., appellate courts hesitate to overturn other adjudicative bodies that have directly observed witnesses or have more experience with the issues involved)

- Efficiency of the court system
- Efficiency of government administration
- Costs/harm to individuals or society in general

19.2.2 | Persuasive Roadmaps

Sections 6.3.2 and 6.3.3 on multiple-TRAC organization introduced the need to preview the conclusions you will reach under each heading and subheading. This is a roadmap. Each new tier of headings needs its own roadmap, as discussed in section 6.3.3.

Enumeration of the points in the roadmap is fairly typical in briefs, as the following sample shows.

Sample Roadmap with Enumeration

Defendant's decision to identify Plaintiff by name in the article is not entitled to protection under the three factors identified in *Kapellas*. First, she did nothing to invite public notoriety. Second, Defendant's disclosure of her identity carried no social value because it did nothing to further the article's message. Third, any slight relevance her identity might have had would be insufficient to counterbalance the severity of Defendant's intrusion into her personal life.

However, give yourself some flexibility to discard enumeration if you think your roadmap will flow better without it. Here is an example of a roadmap that does not use enumeration.

Sample Roadmap Without Enumeration

This case...presents both of the main factual circumstances that have warranted dismissals of indictments on due process grounds: over-involvement in criminal activity and coercive tactics. Moreover, the government's conduct was improper even under the five-factor test on which the government relies to justify its tactics.

With or without enumeration, the roadmap should list the points that you make in the headings that follow. The first roadmap (in your first umbrella paragraph) previews the first subtier of headings. The sample roadmap without enumeration above, for example, lists three points: over-involvement, coercion, and improper conduct under the five-factor test. Take a moment to look at the Sample Appellant's Brief (Sample F) and notice that these three points correspond to headings A. (The government informant's role in...the bombing...), B. (The government informant's use of coercion...), and C. (The government informant's conduct...fails the five-factor test...).

The first umbrella does not need to roadmap more specific points you make in smaller subdivisions of the brief (e.g., A.1., A.2.); save those roadmaps for the mini-umbrellas. For example, the Sample Appellant's Brief (Sample F) makes three points in its section A regarding the government informant's role in the bombing. Those three points are carved out in subsections 1., 2., and 3. They are roadmapped not in the initial umbrella but in a separate mini-umbrella paragraph that appears under heading A. and before the first subheading 1.

Sample Mini-Umbrella

A. The government informant's role in planning and executing the bombing shocks the universal sense of justice.

Thesis

Rule to set up roadmap

Roadmap

The government's conduct requires reversal of the conviction on due process grounds because the government's involvement in the bombing was excessive. This Court has held that an indictment must be dismissed when the government manufactured the crime to secure a conviction rather than to protect the public from ongoing criminal activity. *Bogart*, 783 F.2d at 1436, 1438. Ms. Forrest's conviction must be reversed under this standard for the following three reasons. First, Morlandia completely manufactured the bombing from start to finish. Second, at the time Morlandia approached Ms. Forrest, she was not engaging in or planning any illegal activity. Third, Morlandia was motivated by pressure to obtain a conviction.

1. The government and its informant manufactured the crime from start to finish.

19.2.3 | Thesis Paragraphs Without Roadmaps

Sections that are not subdivided do not need roadmaps since they are making only one point. Begin these sections with a thesis sentence or paragraph. You may want to include one or more rules if necessary to lead in to your first rule explanation paragraph's topic sentence. These rules can be integrated into the thesis paragraph or separated into a rule statement paragraph. When integrated, rules usually fit best between a broad thesis and a more specific thesis that is linked to the rule, as in the sample below.

Sample Thesis with Rule Included

Defendant committed the unauthorized practice of law on several occasions. The practice of law includes legal advice and legal document preparation even when not connected to a court proceeding. *Birbrower, Montalbano, Condon & Frank, P.C. v. Superior Court*, 949 P.2d 1, 5 (Cal. 1998). Defendant's provision of and review of her acquaintance's lease and subsequent advice that he could retain his tenant's deposit to cover damage caused by her pet squarely fits this definition.

Thesis sentences may seem repetitive of the headings especially when you have a section that only needs one thesis sentence. (Chapter 20 discusses the need to draft persuasive headings.) However, legal readers do not always read briefs in a linear fashion. They may read the headings separately from the text. You can avoid monotony by changing the wording a bit from the heading, as in the samples below.

Sample Thesis Sentence

1. The government and its informant manufactured the crime from start to finish.

The degree of control the informant exercised over the bombing exceeds constitutional limits on government involvement in criminal activity.

Sample Thesis Sentence

2. The government's over-involvement in the bombing led Ms. Forrest to commit a crime she would not otherwise have committed.

The conviction should be reversed because the Defendant was not planning to bomb a car dealership or commit any similar act until the government's informant approached her with the plan.

19.3 | THE R IN TRAC: PERSUASION IN THE DISCUSSION OF THE LAW

19.3.1 | A Refresher: Where Is the R?

Sections 6.3.2 and 6.3.3 explain that in a multiple-TRAC organization, the rule statement must be moved around to fit the structure of the analysis. You will undoubtedly need some rule statement in your first umbrella paragraph to set up your first subtier of headings. You may also need additional rule statements in your mini-umbrellas and thesis paragraphs. Rule explanation should start in the first undivided subdivision. The following sample contains an initial rule statement in the main umbrella paragraph before heading A. and a second rule statement in the mini-umbrella paragraph under heading A. It then starts the first rule explanation under heading 1.

Sample Rules in Multiple-TRAC Organization

Main umbrella starts under first heading

The Court should reverse the conviction because the government's investigative tactics exceeded Due Process Limits.

Broad conclusion *(part of main umbrella)*

The trial court's denial of Ms. Forrest's motion to dismiss the indictment was erroneous because the government's conduct in this case exceeded due process limits.

First rule statement *(part of main umbrella)*

The United States Supreme Court has recognized that the Due Process Clause of the Constitution imposes limits on the methods law enforcement may use to obtain convictions and, accordingly, convictions obtained through improper means are barred. *United States v. Russell*, 411 U.S. 423, 431 (1973) ("we may some day be presented with a situation in which the conduct of law enforcement agents is so outrageous that due process principles would absolutely bar the government from invoking judicial processes to obtain a conviction"). Unlike the defense of entrapment, a claim of outrageous government conduct may be successful even when the defendant was predisposed to commit the crime. *Hampton v. United States*, 425 U.S. 484, 495 (1976)....

The availability of a dismissal based on outrageous government conduct is necessary to guard against "'the dangers of overzealous law enforcement.'" *United States v. Twigg*, 588 F.2d 373, 380 (3d Cir. 1978)....

Core theory and roadmap *(part of main umbrella)*

The dangers of overzealous law enforcement that underlie the outrageous conduct theory are evident in this case.... This case thus presents both of the main factual circumstances that have warranted dismissals of indictments on due process grounds: over-involvement in criminal activity and coercive tactics. Moreover, the government's conduct was improper even under the five-factor test on which the government relies to justify its tactics.

A. The government informant's role in planning and executing the bombing shocks the universal sense of justice.

Mini-umbrella

Thesis *(part of mini-umbrella)*

Rule statement *(part of mini-umbrella)*

Roadmap *(part of mini-umbrella)*

The government's conduct requires reversal of the conviction on due process grounds because the government's involvement in the bombing was excessive. This Court has held that an indictment must be dismissed when the government manufactured the crime to secure a conviction rather than to protect the public from ongoing criminal activity. *Bogart*, 783 F.2d at 1436, 1438. Ms. Forrest's conviction must be reversed under this standard for the following three reasons. First, Morlandia completely manufactured the bombing from start to finish. Second, at the time Morlandia approached Ms. Forrest, she was not engaging in or planning any illegal activity. Third, Morlandia was motivated by pressure to obtain a conviction.

1. The government and its informant manufactured the crime from start to finish.

Thesis

The degree of control the informant exercised over the bombing exceeds constitutional limits on government involvement in criminal activity.

Cont.

The Due Process Clause limits the extent to which the government can involve itself in criminal activity. In *Greene*, for example, the court dismissed an indictment on bootlegging charges largely because of the government agent's role in setting up, supplying and continuing the bootlegging operation. *Greene*, 454 F.2d at 786-87. Specifically, the agent had offered to find a still site, still equipment and an operator. *Id.* at 786....

First rule explanation

19.3.2 | Persuasive Rule Statements

When drafting a rule statement in a brief, be strategic in your selection of rules, articulation of those rules, choice of connectors, and synthesis of the rules. Compare the rule statement portion of the appellee's brief with the rule statement portion of the appellant's brief. Notice the different pictures they paint.

Appellant's Rule Statement

The United States Supreme Court has recognized that the Due Process Clause of the Constitution imposes limits on the methods law enforcement may use to obtain convictions and, accordingly, convictions obtained through improper means are barred. *United States v. Russell*, 411 U.S. 423, 431 (1973) ("we may some day be presented with a situation in which the conduct of law enforcement agents is so outrageous that due process principles would absolutely bar the government from invoking judicial processes to obtain a conviction"). Unlike the defense of entrapment, a claim of outrageous government conduct may be successful even when the defendant was predisposed to commit the crime. *Hampton v. United States*, 425 U.S. 484, 495 (1976) (Powell, J., concurring), 497 (Brennan, J., dissenting); *see also United States v. Bogart*, 783 F.2d 1428, 1432 (9th Cir. 1986) (explaining that the concurring and dissenting Justices in *Hampton* comprised a majority to support the availability of an outrageous government conduct claim regardless of the defendant's criminal predisposition).

The availability of a dismissal based on outrageous government conduct is necessary to guard against "'the dangers of overzealous law enforcement.'" *United States v. Twigg*, 588 F.2d 373, 380 (3d Cir. 1978) (quoting *Sherman v. United States*, 356 U.S. 369, 381 (1958) (Frankfurter, J., concurring)). This overzealousness is not merely theoretical but has warranted dismissals of indictments in several federal cases. *Twigg*, 588 F.2d 373; *United States v. West*, 511 F.2d 1083 (3d Cir. 1975); *Greene v. United States*, 454 F.2d 783 (9th Cir. 1971); *United States v. Gardner*, 658 F. Supp. 1573 (W.D. Pa. 1987); *United States v. Batres-Santolino*, 521 F. Supp. 744 (N.D. Cal. 1981); *see also United States v. Luttrell*, 889 F.2d 806, 813-14 (9th Cir. 1989) (finding that indictment should be dismissed if government did not have reason to investigate defendants prior to presenting them with an opportunity to engage in criminal conduct and remanding for a factual determination of whether such a reason existed); *United States v. Archer*, 486 F.2d 670, 677 (2d Cir. 1973) (dismissing indictment on other grounds but stating it might have

Cont.

found government's authorization of crimes by government agents to be sufficiently outrageous to warrant dismissal on due process grounds).

Appellee's Rule Statement

The possibility that the Supreme Court might "some day" bar a conviction when the government's conduct is far outside the bounds of decency, *United States v. Russell*, 411 U.S. 423, 431 (1973), has not yet been realized. In the thirty-nine years since *Greene v. United States*, 454 F.2d 783 (9th Cir. 1971) first dismissed an indictment on the ground that the government's excessive involvement in criminal activity violated the Due Process Clause, no Supreme Court decisions and only five federal court decisions have ever dismissed an indictment or overturned a conviction on this ground. *United States v. Twigg*, 588 F.2d 373 (3d Cir. 1978); *United States v. West*, 511 F.2d 1083 (3d Cir. 1975); *United States v. Gardner*, 658 F. Supp. 1573 (W.D. Pa. 1987); *United States v. Valdovinos-Valdovinos*, 588 F. Supp. 551 (N.D. Cal. 1984), *rev'd*, 743 F.2d 1439 (9th Cir. 1985); *United States v. Batres-Santolino*, 521 F. Supp. 744 (N.D. Cal. 1981); *see also United States v. Luttrell*, 889 F.2d 806 (9th Cir. 1989) (remanding for further fact-finding); *United States v. Bogart*, 783 F.2d 1428 (9th Cir. 1986) (also remanding for further fact-finding). Dismissal of an indictment remains an extraordinary remedy reserved for only the most egregious conduct. *See Hampton v. United States*, 425 U.S. 484, 495 (1976) (Powell, J., concurring) (recognizing that government participation in crime "ordinarily will be fully justified in society's 'war with the criminal classes'" (quoting *Sorrells v. United States*, 287 U.S. 435, 453 (1932) (Roberts, J., concurring))). Indeed, the cases of outrageous conduct are so rare that the Supreme Court has yet to approve or require a dismissal.

To craft a rule statement strategically:

1. Include only necessary rules and favorable rules.

   If the reader cannot understand the law on the issue without the rule, then the rule is necessary.

   For example, both the appellant and the appellee had to identify the door that *Russell* left open for the outrageous conduct defense.

   A rule is favorable if it helps your client's position.

   For example, appellee includes the rule, "Dismissal of an indictment remains an extraordinary remedy reserved for only the most egregious conduct." The rule helps appellee argue that the court was correct not to dismiss the indictment. Appellant, of course, does not include this rule because it is neither necessary nor favorable.

2. For the rules you choose to include, select strategically among different articulations of the rules. Three different court opinions may state the same rule differently. Choose the articulation that favors your position.

   For example, the appellant's brief selects the phrasing "improper means" while the appellee's brief selects "far outside the bounds of decency."

"Improper means" sounds like a lower standard than "far outside the bounds of decency." Although the the rule is the same, the more strategic phrasing can help predispose the judge to the author's position.

3. Order the rules logically but strategically to emphasize your strongest points.

   For example, the appellee's brief quickly discloses the dicta in *Russell* that opened the door to the outrageous conduct defense. But it immediately follows that disclosure with a true statement that the Supreme Court has never applied the dicta.

19.3.3 | Rule Explanations

Section 4.3 explains how to draft effective rule explanations. Like in any legal analysis, each rule explanation paragraph in a brief should start with a transition and a topic sentence that states a subrule (express or inferred from the cases). A few special considerations apply to rule explanations in briefs, however.

19.3.3.1 | Discarding Objectivity

In briefs, every subrule stated in a rule explanation paragraph's topic sentence must favor your client. The paradox, however, is that briefs must disclose adverse authority. Section 19.5 explains how to include adverse authority in your rule explanation in a manner that still favors your client.

19.3.3.2 | Increasing Your Use of Inferred Subrules

Inferred subrules are critical to a strategic discussion of the law in a brief. Because briefs should be more strategic in how they explain the law, quoting express rules from the cases often falls flat. They should synthesize or contextualize the law in a way that favors your position. Of course, your inferred subrules must be well supported by the relevant body of case law. Ideally, inferred subrules should be proven with more than one case example. And they cannot be inconsistent with any binding authority in your jurisdiction except perhaps for an errant, older case. If your inferred rule is well supported despite an errant case, you can disclose the errant case with a "*but see*" parenthetical as in the sample below.

Sample Rule Explanation with an Inferred Rule and a *"But See"* Parenthetical at the End

Undercover agents often must engage in "unsavory conduct," including the use of threatening language, to maintain their cover. *See Luttrell*, 889 F.2d at 812 (stating, "Undercover agents are actors. The success of their performance requires the delivery

Cont.

of lines appropriate to their characters. The agents' mere delivery of language alone... may be necessary to the investigation of established criminal activity."). Accordingly, courts have repeatedly rejected threatening language by an undercover agent as a ground to dismiss an indictment. *See, e.g., United States v. Emmert*, 829 F.2d 805, 812 (9th Cir. 1987). In *Emmert*, two government agents negotiated a drug deal with the defendant and some other accomplices. *Id.* at 807. When the deal failed to go through, one of the accomplices asked the undercover agents for some money up front and expressed concern that one of the agents was a policeman. *Id.* In response, one of the agents said, "Maybe we'll do the deal in an airplane and if something goes wrong, we'd have one parachute and guess who'd come down without one." *Id.* And the other agent said she had three words for the defendant's accomplice, "R.I.P." *Id.* A few months later, the defendant was able to put the deal together and was arrested at the scene. *Id.* In rejecting these threats as a reason to dismiss the indictment, the court stated that "[e]xpress or implied threats may be warranted under certain circumstances" and "may not always constitute outrageous conduct." *Id.* at 811. The court concluded that the threats aimed at Emmert were "scarely more than bluster" and were "ordinary bargaining tactics in drug deals." *Id.* at 812. It further explained that "government agents may need to engage in such unsavory conduct to maintain their cover." *Id.* The court concluded that the threats were necessary to allay suspicions about the undercover agents. *Id.*; *see also United States v. McQuin*, 612 F.2d 1193, 1195-96 (9th Cir. 1980) (holding that agent's threat to kill defendant for failing to complete planned robbery did not violate due process when viewed in light of the "vulgarity and 'puffing' engaged in by all participants in the criminal venture"); *accord United States v. Reynoso-Ulloa*, 548 F.2d 1329 (9th Cir. 1977). *But see Greene v. United States*, 454 F.2d 783, 786 (9th Cir. 1971) (noting veiled threat by agent to pressure defendants into production of bootleg alcohol as one fact supporting dismissal of the indictment).

19.3.3.3 | Trimming Out Some Details

The goal of briefs is to persuade rather than to educate the reader. Therefore, choose carefully the details you include in a brief's rule explanation. Exclude information that is not critical to proving your topic sentence as long as the exclusion does not mislead or confuse the reader.

Guidelines for Case Examples in Briefs

1. Use a full case example only when the case is critically important to your position or its details are needed to prove your points in application. Section 4.3.3.4 discusses how to determine when you need a full case example.
2. Omit nearly all background information in a full case example. Go right to the facts, holding, and reasoning that prove your topic sentence.
3. Take extra time to go back to your full case examples and delete unnecessary details that do not aid your points.
4. To maximize the persuasiveness of your rule explanation, be even more alert to the need for bridges between a full case example and additional parenthetical examples. Section 4.3.3.3 discusses the use of bridges.

19.4 | THE A IN TRAC: APPLICATION

Chapter 5 covers the basic tools of effective application paragraphs, all of which are critical to an effective brief. Chapter 6 discusses many options for the placement of application paragraphs within each subdivision of an analysis. These lessons are no different in brief writing.

19.5 | ANTICIPATORY REBUTTAL IN RULE EXPLANATIONS AND APPLICATION

If your legal writing course covered objective legal writing before persuasive legal writing, you most likely learned to include a detailed analysis of any significant counterpoints to your thesis. A persuasive brief, however, does not give the opponent any free air time. No client wants to pay a lawyer to do the opponent's job. Therefore, briefs do not explain the opponent's arguments.

On the other hand, a brief must respond to the opponent's strongest authority and points. This is the art of anticipatory rebuttal, which is absolutely crucial to the effectiveness of a brief.

Anticipatory rebuttal requires first that you understand all of the significant arguments your opponent might make. Although the brief will be slanted in your favor, your research should be objective. As you gather and read cases, think both about what aspects of the case law will help you and about what aspects of the case law will help your opponent. Read and understand adverse cases. Think critically about your supportive cases to identify the reasoning or facts that your opponent might highlight to distinguish them. Do not make the mistake of narrowly focusing on your client's view of the case. The same is true of your review of the facts of your case. Think about which facts your opponent is likely to exploit and how.

Once you identify the key cases and arguments your opponent will likely use, you can start thinking about how to respond to them. Anticipatory rebuttal does not happen in any one place in your brief. It is scattered throughout in a strategic manner. The sections that follow discuss several methods of anticipatory rebuttal. You will likely want to use a combination of these methods.

19.5.1 | Rule Explanation Topic Sentences That Limit Adverse Authority

This technique looks at a batch of adverse cases and identifies a shared, relevant fact pattern that distinguishes them from your case. It works best when your characterization can fairly cover *all* or *nearly all* of the directly on-point adverse cases on a particular topic.

Example of a Limiting Rule Explanation Sentence

The cases in which courts have reversed convictions on due process grounds involve not sting operations that target criminal organizations but the targeting of a specific individual without reason to suspect the individual is currently engaged in criminal activity. *See Twigg*, 588 F.2d at 381 (holding that the government violated due process when it asked an informant to reestablish contact with an acquaintance who was not engaged in any illicit drug activity and an agent thereafter "implanted the criminal design" in the defendant's mind and enabled him to carry it out); *West*, 511 F.2d at 1086 (reversing drug-related convictions where the defendant had not previously engaged in drug deals); *Greene*, 454 F.2d at 786 (reversing conviction where a government agent initiated contact with the defendant without any reason to suspect the defendant was then engaged in illegal activity); *Gardner*, 658 F. Supp. at 1576-77 (concluding that an agent violated due process when he "persisted over a period of time in inducing and persuading the Defendant to commit the crime in question with sole motive and intention of overcoming the obvious reluctance of the Defendant to commit the alleged crime in question"); *Valdovinos-Valdovinos*, 588 F. Supp. at 556 (finding that INS engaged in outrageous conduct when in the hope of catching and convicting transporters of illegal aliens, its agents told ineligible Mexican citizens that they could lawfully cross the border); *Batres-Santolino*, 521 F. Supp. at 751 (finding that due process was violated when rather than infiltrating an existing drug ring, a government agent "persuaded defendants to create one").

In this sample, the cases are all adverse to the appellee's position. The topic sentence, however, limits their applicability to cases that do not involve sting operations. Later, in application (below), the appellee will argue that the government conduct in the instant case did involve a sting operation and, therefore, all of these adverse cases are distinguishable. You might notice that the application also compares supportive cases that held that sting operations were lawful (*Morgan*, *Mitchell*, and *Shaw*).

Example of Corresponding Application Paragraph

Here, Forrest's conviction is squarely within due process grounds for at least two reasons. First, she was caught as the result of a general undercover investigation that did not target her specifically but, instead, was aimed more widely at her known terrorist organization. Morlandia did not target Forrest and convince her to commit a crime for the purpose of obtaining her conviction. Rather, her conviction resulted from a general undercover operation designed to protect the public by thwarting the terrorist activities of her organization. The FBI set up the operation as a wide web to catch whatever criminal conduct came its way much like the sting operations in *Morgan*, *Mitchell* and *Shaw*. Because it targeted a known criminal operation, the FBI's undercover operation has a "settled place in law enforcement." *Id.* Forrest became caught in the web because of her prior involvement in EARTH's terrorist activities. EARTH's leadership wanted

Cont.

Forrest to assist in the bombing to evaluate her worth to the organization. (R. at 31.) Thus, Forrest was targeted by her own criminal organization and not by the FBI. Morlandia's role in initiating and planning the bombing was designed to earn the trust of EARTH's leadership by demonstrating he could "motivate" (R. at 30); Forrest's conviction was not the goal (R. at 20). Therefore, this is not a case where the government got lucky and obtained a conviction in an otherwise arbitrary effort to induce innocent citizens to commit crimes.

If the pattern stated in your rule explanation topic sentence covers most but not all cases, you will need to disclose contrary authority to avoid misrepresentation to the court. You should use a "*but see*" parenthetical at the end of the paragraph for this purpose. Section 19.3.3.2 provides a sample of a "*but see*" parenthetical.

Usually, brief writers prefer to use parentheticals rather than full case examples for adverse cases. Full case examples might place undue emphasis on adverse cases. Occasionally, however, you might need the details from the adverse case in order to distinguish it. When you need to discuss an adverse case in full, you can use a limiting rule explanation topic sentence to downplay its significance and set up the point on which you plan to distinguish it.

In the example below, the appellee deals with the adverse case, *Hampton*, by emphasizing the narrow scope of the defense the court introduced and pulls quotes from the case that emphasize the need to give the police wide latitude. Later, in application, the appellee argues that the narrow defense does not apply to the case at hand because the agent's tactics were necessary.

Example of Limiting Rule Explanation Topic Sentence with Full Discussion of Adverse Case

The door left open by Justice Powell's concurring opinion in *Hampton* for an outrageous conduct claim was very narrow. While agreeing with the plurality opinion that the government does not commit outrageous conduct merely by supplying drugs to catch drug traffickers, the concurring opinion left open the possibility that government *over*-involvement in crime might constitute a due process violation. 425 U.S. at 495 (Powell, J., concurring). However, Justice Powell emphasized that government conduct would have to "reach a demonstrable level of outrageousness before it could bar conviction." *Id.* at 495, n.7. He noted the difficulty law enforcement faces in battling the trafficking of narcotics and the necessity for undercover operations to detect drug offenses and acknowledged that government participation in crime "ordinarily will be fully justified in society's 'war with the criminal classes.'" *Id.* (quoting *Sorrells*, 287 U.S. at 453 (Roberts, J., concurring)). The only hints dropped in the concurring opinion regarding when government involvement in crime would violate due process were a citation to *Greene*, 454 F.2d 783 and quotations from *United States v. Archer*, 486 F.2d 670, 676-

Cont.

77 (2d Cir. 1973). *Hampton*, 425 U.S. at 493, nn.3 & 4 ("'[i]t would be unthinkable, for example, to permit government agents to instigate robberies and beatings merely to gather evidence to convict other members of a gang of hoodlums'"; the courts should be "'extremely reluctant to sanction" "participation in activities that result in injury to the rights of [] citizens") (quoting *Archer*, 486 F.2d at 676-77)).

19.5.2 | "Sneaky Jab" Rule Explanation Topic Sentences

This technique subtly refutes an argument you expect your opponent to make by using case law to establish that the argument is not relevant. An inferred rule or a favorable synthesis of the adverse and supportive cases works well. I like to call this a sneaky jab.

Sample Sneaky Jab

In applying factor two, the courts have not solely focused on the government's facilitation of the particular criminal act at issue. To the contrary, courts have declined to find outrageous conduct when the defendant was capable of committing similar crimes without the government's involvement even if the government facilitated the particular crime for which the defendant was charged. In *Williams*, for example,... (From Sample Appellee's Brief (Sample E), Annotation 40.)

The sneaky jab does not look like a rebuttal. It looks like a natural part of the author's analysis. However, its purpose is to rebut the other side's likely argument—in the above example, that the government's conduct was outrageous because its informant facilitated the bombing by providing explosives and devising a plan. The second sentence "To the contrary..." is supported by a case example, *Williams*, in which the court denied the defense even though the government had facilitated the crime.

19.5.3 | Juxtaposition in Rule Explanation Topic Sentences

Another technique to deal with adverse cases is to juxtapose the adverse point of law with a related point of law that supports your position. The favorable point must logically detract from the significance of the unfavorable point. This technique is similar to a sneaky jab, but a bit less sneaky since the adverse point is actually identified.

The juxtaposition can be created using either an "although" clause or two sentences.

19.5.3.1 | "Although" Clause Juxtaposition

When using the "although" construction, start the sentence with "although" followed by the adverse point. Then insert a comma at the end of the clause. Then state the supportive point:

"Although [Bad Thing], [Good Thing]."

Sample "Although" RE Topic Sentence

Although "unwarranted physical, or perhaps mental, coercion" may shock the conscience, *Bogart*, 783 F.2d at 1438, the courts have recognized that undercover agents often must engage in "unsavory conduct," including the use of threatening language, to maintain their cover, *Luttrell*, 889 F.2d at 812 (stating, "Undercover agents are actors. The success of their performance requires the delivery of lines appropriate to their characters. The agents' mere delivery of language alone...may be necessary to the investigation of established criminal activity."). Accordingly, courts have repeatedly rejected threatening language by an undercover agent as a ground to dismiss an indictment. *See, e.g., United States v. Emmert*, 829 F.2d 805, 812 (9th Cir. 1987). In *Emmert*,...(From the Sample Appellee's Brief (Sample E), Annotation 52.)

Notice that your attention is drawn away from the point that coercion may be grounds for outrageous government conduct and to the point the author wants you to focus on—the need for agents to use threatening language to maintain their cover.

"Although" rule explanation topic sentences require a citation for both the unfavorable point and the favorable point. You may either imbed the citations in the sentence or use "*compare...with...*".

Sample Imbedded Citation

Although "unwarranted physical, or perhaps mental, coercion" may shock the conscience, *Bogart*, 783 F.2d at 1438, the courts have recognized that undercover agents often must engage in "unsavory conduct," including the use of threatening language, to maintain their cover, *Luttrell*, 889 F.2d at 812 (stating, "Undercover agents are actors. The success of their performance requires the delivery of lines appropriate to their characters. The agents' mere delivery of language alone...may be necessary to the investigation of established criminal activity.").

Sample *"Compare...With"* Citation

Although unwarranted government coercion may shock the conscience, the courts have recognized that undercover agents often must use language that could be con-

Cont.

strued as threatening in order to maintain their cover. *Compare Bogart*, 783 F.2d at 1438 (recognizing that "unwarranted physical, or perhaps mental, coercion" may shock the conscience), *with Luttrell*, 889 F.2d at 812 (stating, "Undercover agents are actors. The success of their performance requires the delivery of lines appropriate to their characters. The agents' mere delivery of language alone...may be necessary to the investigation of established criminal activity.").

Select between these options based on the heft of your citations. The imbedded option works well when you are citing only one case for each part of the sentence. When you want to include multiple parentheticals, use "*compare... with*" or the two-sentence option discussed in the next section.

19.5.3.2 | Two-Sentence Juxtaposition

In lieu of the "although" sentence, you can use two sentences. The first sentence states the adverse point, and the second sentence starts with a word of contrast like "however" or "but" and uses the favorable point to detract from the significance of the adverse point.

Sample Two-Sentence Juxtaposition

"Unwarranted physical, or perhaps mental, coercion" may shock the conscience. *Bogart*, 783 F.2d at 1438. However, the courts have recognized that undercover agents often must engage in "unsavory conduct," including the use of threatening language, to maintain their cover. *Luttrell*, 889 F.2d at 812 (stating, "Undercover agents are actors. The success of their performance requires the delivery of lines appropriate to their characters. The agents' mere delivery of language alone... may be necessary to the investigation of established criminal activity").

This method can accommodate multiple parentheticals better than the "although" clause because it physically separates the adverse citations from the supportive citations. You can even insert a paragraph break between the two parts to avoid an overly long rule explanation paragraph. For example, if the author wanted to cite more than just the *Bogart* case for the adverse point in the sample above, it could be helpful to insert a paragraph break after the adverse citations and before the "However" sentence. See 15.2.1 for an example.

19.5.3.3 | Considerations When Juxtaposing Rules

When crafting a juxtaposing rule explanation topic sentence, always place the adverse point before the positive point. The positive point rebuts the adverse point:

Although [bad thing], [good thing].

Also, keep in mind that the adverse point and the positive point should be logically related to one another. The positive point should limit or otherwise detract from the significance of the adverse point.

ERROR Example of Unclear "Although" Clause

Although Jane is shy, she likes math

This sentence makes no sense because Jane's math skills have no obvious relationship to her shyness. The sentence has to be tweaked to clarify the relationship.

Corrected Version

Although Jane is shy, she lights up during math exercises.

Now the reader understands the connection between the fact the author wants to deemphasize (her shyness) and the positive point (her ability to overcome her shyness due to her enthusiasm for math).

19.5.4 | Deciding Which Adverse Cases to Rebut

The number one rule is that you *must* disclose adverse authority that directly counters any statement you make in your paper. And, to be safe, include authority that might possibly be construed as directly countering any statement you make in your paper. Do not mislead the court. The court relies on lawyers to make honest statements about the law. Nothing will harm you or your client more than hiding the truth from the court. If in doubt, disclose.

If a disclosure is not required to avoid dishonesty, be strategic. How likely is it that the opponent will cite the case or make the argument the case stands for? And how strong is your rebuttal? The more likely the point will come up and the stronger your rebuttal, the more the balance tips in favor of including an anticipatory rebuttal.

19.5.5 | Anticipatory Rebuttal in Applications

You can use the same anticipatory rebuttal techniques in applications to rebut bad facts. When juxtaposing, remember to put the bad stuff first: Although [bad fact], [good fact]. And the good fact should be logically connected to the bad fact so that it detracts from its significance.

Sample "Although" Clause in Application

Although Forrest claimed she was "hopeless" at constructing bombs and had never obtained explosives for a prior EARTH operation (R. at 43-44), she was a member of an organization that the FBI believed had stockpiled large amounts of explosives (R. at 19), had carried out a bombing of army barracks (R. at 15), and had trained its members in the construction of explosives (R. at 24, 43). (From Sample Appellee's Brief (Sample E), Annotation 42.)

You do not need to use the magic word "although." The idea is simply to address adverse facts in a manner that does not call attention to them but, instead, calls attention to why they are not important. The "sneaky jab" technique discussed in section 19.5.2 for rule explanations can also be used in applications.

Sample Sneaky Jab Without "Although"

In *Williams*, the court found that a difference in degree does not detract from the similar nature of crimes. 547 F.3d at 1201. Similarly, here, the increased danger posed by the bombing does not make it dissimilar from her prior acts of terrorism. (From Sample Appellee's Brief (Sample E), Annotation 35.)

This "sneaky jab" anticipates and rebuts the argument that the bombing was not similar to the defendant's prior crimes because it was more dangerous than her prior acts of vandalism.

Argument Section Checklist

- ☐ Review checklists from Chapters 4, 5, and 6.
- ☐ Select an organizational structure (Chapter 6).
- ☐ Include an initial umbrella under your main heading that includes
  - a thesis (e.g., affirm/reverse),
  - a core theory,
  - a rule statement, and
  - a roadmap of headings A., B., C., etc.
- ☐ Make your rule statement persuasive.
  - Include only necessary rules and favorable rules.
  - Select the articulation of each rule that best supports your client's position.
  - Order the rules logically but strategically to emphaze your client's position.
- ☐ Include mini-umbrellas for any section A., B., C., etc., that is further subdivided into sections 1., 2., 3., etc. These should include at least a thesis and roadmap and possibly a rule statement paragraph if needed to link your first rule explanation paragraph in the section to the stopping point of your initial rule statement paragraph.

Cont.

- ☐ In all other sections, include at least a thesis sentence.
- ☐ Ensure your rule explanation paragraphs are strategic.
  - Use "although" clauses, inferred rules, or two-sentence "however" constructions to limit or downplay the adverse cases.
  - Except in rare situations, do not devote full case examples to adverse cases—use parentheticals instead.
- ☐ Ensure your application paragraphs are strategic.
  - Do not explain counterarguments; use anticipatory rebuttal instead.
  - Use "although" clauses to deal with bad facts.

CHAPTER **19** SELF-TEST

1. What are the components of an umbrella paragraph of a brief?
2. How do you make your rule statement persuasive?
3. What are some differences between objective rule explanation and persuasive rule explanation?
4. How do you deal with adverse authority in a manner that still emphasizes your client's position?
5. What comes first in an "although" statement—the good stuff you want to emphasize or the bad stuff you want to deemphasize?
6. You also need to think about anticipatory rebuttal of bad facts. How do you handle that?

See answers on page 340.

CHAPTER 20

Point Headings

Point headings state arguments in complete grammatical sentences. They divide a brief's argument section into smaller, more digestible pieces. Point headings serve two important goals: (1) to make your organization clear and logical to the reader; and (2) to provide a complete and persuasive outline of your brief.

For ease of reference, this textbook uses the following terminology for different levels of point headings. This chapter follows the structure for tiered headings discussed in section 6.3.3. Keep in mind that conventions may vary by law office or court.

Main heading or overall heading. This is the heading that covers your entire analysis of an issue. Sometimes, your brief may have two or more entirely separate and unrelated issues. Then you should use a main heading for each separate issue. If you have only one main heading, you do not need to enumerate it. If you use more than one main heading, a typical convention is to use roman numerals (I., II., etc.) to enumerate main headings.

Subheadings. These are the headings numbered by capital letters A., B., C., etc.

Sub-subheadings. These are the headings numbered by ordinals 1., 2., 3., etc.

20.1 | MAIN HEADINGS

A main heading states your overall conclusion on an issue.

Each main heading should state a result and a reason. The result is the procedural action you want the court to take. In an appeal, for example, you would ask the court to affirm or reverse the judgment. The reason is the general, overall justification for the result you seek.

ERROR **Example of Heading That Fails to State a Reason**

The Court should affirm the judgment.

ERROR **Example of Heading That Fails to State a Result**

The government's efforts to infiltrate Defendant's terrorist organization did not violate fundamental fairness.

Sample Heading

The Court should affirm the judgment because the government's efforts to infiltrate Defendant's terrorist organization did not violate fundamental fairness.

The reason stated in the main heading must be broad enough to encompass all of the arguments stated in subheadings A., B., C., etc. It is better to word the heading broadly than to list each point. A list is usually too cumbersome for a heading.

For example, the sample main heading above, which is from the Sample Appellee's Brief (Sample E), states that the court should affirm because the government's conduct did not violate fundamental fairness. This is sufficiently broad to encompass every point made in the brief. Imagine the long wordy heading that would have resulted if the main heading had tried to list all of the points stated in headings A. through E.

20.2 | SUBHEADINGS AND SUB-SUBHEADINGS

After your main heading, you can subdivide initially into sections A., B., C., etc., and then you may want to further subdivide some sections into subsections 1., 2., 3., etc. Section 6.3.4 discusses how to decide when to subdivide.

Subheadings and sub-subheadings do not need to state results like "the Court should affirm the judgment." They state only reasons that support the conclusion stated in the heading under which they fall. In the sample below, notice that headings A. through C. each state a reason why the "government's tactics exceeded due process limits," and headings 1. through 3. under heading A. each state a reason why the informant's role "shocks the universal sense of justice." Each lower-tier heading provides a more specific point that supports the higher-tier heading under which it falls.

Sample Tiered Headings

The Court should reverse the conviction because the government's investigative tactics exceeded due process limits.

A. The government informant's role in planning and executing the bombing shocks the universal sense of Justice.

1. The government and its informant manufactured the crime from start to finish.

2. The government's over-involvement in the bombing led Ms. Forrest to commit a crime she would not otherwise have committed.

3. The informant's eagerness to procure Ms. Forrest's involvement in the bombing resulted from the FBI's threat that it would arrest him for terrorism.

B. The government's informant's use of coercion to convince Ms. Forrest to help him execute the bombing was fundamentally unfair.

C. The government's conduct in this case fails the five-factor test some courts have used to uphold convictions against claims of outrageous government conduct.

Persuasive subheadings and sub-subheadings are specific. A subheading can be general *only if* it is followed by sub-subheadings that provide the specifics. In the sample headings above, subheading A. is more general ("informant's role in planning and executing") because sub-subheadings 1., 2., and 3. provide more specifics about the aspects of the informant's role that were offensive. By contrast, subheadings B. ("use of coercion") and C. ("five-factor test") are more specific because they are not followed by sub-subheadings.

20.3 | HEADING STYLE TIPS

Do not phrase any headings in a manner that assumes knowledge or requires cross-reference to other parts of the brief. Each heading should be self-contained.

ERROR **Example of Heading that Assumes Knowledge**

Defendant is unlikely to reoffend because of his family situation.

This example assumes the reader knows enough about the defendant's family situation to understand what aspect of his family life supports the author's point.

Is it because his mother keeps him locked in a closet? By contrast, the revision below more clearly refers to the defendant's strong family ties as the relevant consideration.

Sample Heading

Defendant has strong family ties that will help keep him away from crime.

Keep your headings very simple: no long, unnecessarily wordy sentences. As a rule of thumb, aim for two lines and try to not go over three.

Do not put citations or case references in the headings.

20.4 | FORMATTING HEADINGS

Heading format varies from office to office and even from attorney to attorney within an office. This chapter presents one common formatting convention for headings. You should refer to one of the sample briefs as you read this section.

20.4.1 | Formatting Rules for All Headings

- All headings are single-spaced.
- All headings are complete sentences.
- All headings end with a period.
- All headings are in bold.
- All headings are in normal sentence format with the first word and proper nouns capitalized.

20.4.2 | Formatting Rules for Main Heading

- The main heading is not numbered unless you have more than one (then you enumerate I., II., etc.).
- Start the heading at the left margin; do not indent.

Sample Main Heading

This Court should affirm the judgment because the government's efforts to infiltrate Defendant's terrorist organization did not violate fundamental fairness.

20.4.3 | Formatting Rules for Subheadings

- Subheadings are numbered by capital letter (A., B., C., etc.).
- Start the capital letter one-half inch from the left margin; then start the text after another one-half inch and justify on the left.

Sample Subheading

A. Under a five-factor test established by this Court to limit outrageous government conduct claims, the government's conduct in this case did not require dismissal of the indictment.

20.4.4 | Formatting Rules for Sub-subheadings

- Sub-subheadings are numbered by ordinals (1., 2., 3., etc.).
- Start the number one inch from the left margin; then start the text a half-inch from the number and justify on the left.

Sample Sub-subheading

1. At the time of her first contact with the government's informant, Defendant was an active member of a terrorist organization, and she had previously committed terrorist acts.

Point Heading Checklist

☐ All headings
- Do not assume any knowledge on the part of the reader.
- No long, unnecessarily wordy sentences (2-3 lines).
- No citations or case references.

☐ Main heading(s)
- Start at the left margin.
- Use roman numerals (I., II., III., etc.) if more than one; if only one, do not number.
- Bold.
- End with a period.
- State both a result (affirm/reverse) and a reason (because…).

☐ Subheadings
- Use capital letters A., B., C., etc.
- Indent the letter one-half inch and the text another half-inch and left-justify.
- State more specific points that support the main heading.

Cont.

- Must be sufficiently specific to persuade the reader unless the section is further subdivided into sub-subheadings.
- Bold.
- End with a period.

☐ Sub-subheadings
- Use ordinals 1., 2., 3., etc.
- Indent ordinal one inch from left margin and indent text another half-inch and left-justify.
- State more specific points that support the subheading.
- Must be sufficiently specific to persuade the reader.
- Bold.
- End with a period.

CHAPTER 21

Tables

Typically, briefs that are ten pages or more should contain a table of contents and table of authorities. Even if the court does not require these tables, include them as a convenience for your reader.

A table of contents always includes the section dividers and headings in the brief and the page numbers at which they begin. A table of authorities always includes an alphabetized list of cases, statutes, and other sources cited in the brief with their page numbers. The table of contents precedes the table of authorities. The tables are ordinarily paginated separately from the rest of the brief using lowercase roman numerals (i., ii., iii., etc.).

Apart from these basic requirements, formatting and other specifics may vary. This chapter provides some common conventions that apply to tables.

21.1 | TABLE OF CONTENTS

Label your table of contents with its own "Table of Contents" heading. Select a typeface convention such as all caps, bold, and underlined.

Under the "Table of Contents" heading, list the major divisions of your brief at the left margin: e.g., Table of Authorities, Question Presented, Statement of the Case, Standard of Review, Summary of the Argument, Argument, Conclusion. Choose a typeface convention for these divisions such as all caps.

List the main heading(s) in your brief at the margin.

Indent one-half inch under each main heading and list any subheadings that appear.

Indent another one-half inch under each subheading and list any sub-sub-headings that appear.

The text of each heading should be indented by one-half inch from its lettering or enumeration and left-justified.

Check to make sure you have a period after every heading.

Insert the starting page of each heading.

Use a series of periods to separate the heading from the page number with a space between each period.

TABLE OF CONTENTS ❶

1. For the title at the top of the page, use all caps, bold, and underline.
2. When listing each portion of the document (e.g., Table of Authorities, Question Presented), use all caps but do not bold or underline. These section names will be in bold and underlined in the text but not in the Table of Contents.
3. Each heading after the main heading is indented one-half inch before the enumeration or lettering and another half-inch before the text. Remove bolding but keep capitalization the same as in the text. Left-justify. Double-check that each heading ends with a period.

Your word processing program may generate the table of contents and table of authorities for you. However, you still need to code your brief correctly and carefully edit the tables to ensure they are accurate, complete, and neat. In other words, you should still learn about the components and conventions of tables.

21.2 | TABLE OF AUTHORITIES

The table of authorities lists every source you cite in your brief. It includes headings (in all caps) that divide the citations by type: cases, constitutional provisions, statutes, and miscellaneous. Some writers also prefer to separate federal cases from state cases and federal statutes from state statutes. The "miscellaneous" category includes treatises, law review articles, Restatements of the Law, or any source that does not fall under one of your other categories. Omit any categories that are not applicable to your paper. For example, if you do not cite a constitutional provision, delete that section from your table of authorities.

Order the sources alphabetically within each category. Include the full citation form. Retain italics or underlining. When copying and pasting the citations from the text of your brief into the table, be sure to delete the pinpoint cite/jump page. Forgetting to delete the pinpoint cite is the most common mistake in the table of authorities.

Include each page on which the source appears. If the source is cited on more than five pages, you may use "passim" to indicate the source is cited frequently throughout the brief.

When listing multiple sections of a statutory code or secondary source, arrange the section numbers in numerical order from lowest to highest. Numbers come before letters, so a code that starts with a volume number will precede a code that starts with a title.

<u>TABLE OF AUTHORITIES</u> (1)

CASES (2)

Affiliated Capital Corp. v. City of Houston, 735 F.2d 1555 (5th Cir. 1984) 44 (3)

Armendariz v. Penman, 31 F.3d 860 (9th Cir. 1994) 20

Bartell v. Lohiser, 215 F.3d 550 (6th Cir. 2000) 24

Behrens v. Pelletier, 516 U.S. 229 (1996) 12 (4)

Bibeau v. Pac. N.W. Research Fund, Inc., 188 F.3d 1105 (9th Cir. 1999) 23

Bigelow v. Virginia, 421 U.S. 809 (1975) 39

Fischer Sand & Aggregate Co. v. City of Lakeville, 874 F. Supp. 957 (D. Minn. 1994). 36 (5)

Nadel v. Regents of the Univ. of Cal., 34 Cal. Rptr. 2d 188 (Ct. App. 1994) 36

Richardson v. McKnight, 521 U.S. 399 (1997). 21, 22, 23, 24

Wyatt v. Cole, 504 U.S. 158 (1992) . . . . passim (6)

CONSTITUTIONAL PROVISIONS

U.S. Const. amend. I 3

STATUTES

28 U.S.C. § 1291 (West 1993) 4 (7)

28 U.S.C. § 1331 (West 1993) 5 (8)

42 U.S.C. § 3604(c) (West 1994). 15

Cal. Gov't Code § 12955(g) (West 2003) 11, 16

MISCELLANEOUS

Restatement (Second) of Torts § 90 cmt. a (1965) 23

Restatement (Second) of Torts § 90 cmt. c (1965) 24

Paul Rich, *American Voluntarism, Social Capital, and Political Culture*, 565 Annals Am. Acad.
    Pol. & Soc. Sci. 15 (1999 . . . . 42 (9)

1. For the title at the top of the page, use all caps, bold, and underline.
2. Cases is all caps, no bold, no underline.
3. Put cases in alphabetical order.
4. Delete pinpoint cites/jump pages.
5. Keep italics and abbreviations.
6. Use passim if cited on more than five pages.
7. Numbers come before letters.
8. Arrange sections of same code in numerical order.
9. Indent second line.

CHAPTER **22**

Appellate Brief Conventions

Most components of a great appellate brief are the same as for any other brief. The lessons in Chapters 18 through 21 regarding the statement of facts, argument, point headings, and tables apply to all briefs.

This chapter addresses a few components that are specific to appellate briefs. First, all appellate briefs contain a caption and a "question(s) presented" or "statement of the issue(s)" section. Additional requirements vary by jurisdiction. Federal appellate courts, for example, require a "jurisdictional statement," a "statement of the case," and a "summary of the argument." They also set a mandatory order for these components. Other appellate courts may require a "standard of review." When preparing briefs as an attorney, consult the rules of the court to which you are submitting your brief to determine which components are required. Ask for some sample briefs from your colleagues to determine whether your law office has a standard format.

22.1 | THE CAPTION OF AN APPELLATE BRIEF

Trial court briefs typically use a pleading format with the party information and a caption box at the left margin. Appellate briefs, however, have a separate caption page. The court may require that the caption page be a particular color depending on the type of brief you are submitting. Always consult your court's local rules regarding the formatting of briefs and obtain from your law office a sample of the same type of brief you are drafting.

Typically, an appellate brief caption includes the name of the court, the case number, the name of the case, the title of your brief, your name, and the party that you are representing. Font size, bolding, or lines typically set apart the information and create an aesthetic appeal.

SAMPLE CAPTION

IN THE

UNITED STATES COURT OF APPEALS

FOR THE NINTH CIRCUIT

CASE NO. 09-55923

UNITED STATES

v.

REYNA FORREST

BRIEF FOR THE APPELLEE

John Doe
Attorneys for the Appellee

22.2 | QUESTION(S) PRESENTED/STATEMENT OF THE ISSUE(S)

Whereas trial court briefs are directed toward achieving a particular order from the court (e.g., summary judgment, judgment notwithstanding the verdict, an order compelling discovery), appeals are directed toward the review of trial court decisions. They must raise a particular legal question that the appellate court can properly answer. Hence, a "question(s) presented" section is a necessary component of an appellate brief. You might also hear the question presented referred to as a "statement of the issue(s)." Check your court's rules to determine whether they require that the question presented or statement of the issue be put in a particular location in the brief. If no rules specify the location, you might decide to place this section either before or after the statement of the facts.

Chapter 10 discusses the general attributes of effective issue identification. All of the same lessons apply to a question presented or statement of the issue section of an appellate brief. Review Chapter 10 now before continuing.

To adapt the Chapter 10 lessons to brief writing, you merely need to be strategic. You should not include the opposing viewpoint in your question, and you should phrase the question so that there seems to be only one reasonable answer (the answer you want the court to reach). Be sure that you leave no doubt as to which side you are on. On the other hand, you want to *appear* impartial. Instead of using conclusory or biased language, your goal is to *surreptitiously* persuade your reader. To obtain a persuasive bent, locate the most favorable rule language for your position, include the facts that match the favorable rule language, and play a little with your word choice. Consider the differences in the samples below between the objective question and the two competing persuasive questions.

Sample Objective v. Persuasive Questions Presented

Objective Issue Statement Appropriate for a Legal Research Memo

Did Savonarola "enter" the bank so as to be guilty of burglary when he walked into the ATM kiosk adjacent to the bank and used a stolen ATM card to withdraw money from the ATM machine given that the kiosk was completely enclosed and shared a wall with the bank but had no lock on the external door and did not share a roof with the bank?

Persuasive Question Presented in Favor of Savonarola

Did Savonarola interfere with the possessory interest of the occupants of the bank and thereby raise a significant risk of violence to warrant the stiffer penalties that burglary carries when he did not enter the bank but merely used an ATM machine in an unlocked kiosk that was not reserved exclusively for bank customers?

Persuasive Question Presented in Favor of the Prosecution

Was the ATM kiosk from which Savonarola stole money using someone else's ATM card part of the outer boundary of the bank so that his entry into the kiosk satisfies the entry requirement of the burglary statute where the kiosk shared a wall and a door with the bank and the bank owners built the kiosk to provide protection to their customers?

Go through the same steps when drafting your question presented:

1. Look at the rule language from the favorable cases that you use in your rule explanation and incorporate it into the question.
2. Add facts that connect well to the rule language you have chosen.
3. Tweak your word choices to have a subtle impact on the court's view of you or your opponent.

In the boxes below, the question presented from the Sample Appellant's Brief (Sample F) is deconstructed to illustrate how the question presented matches the language from supportive rule explanation and application paragraphs.

Sample Question Presented

Are the dangers of overzealous police tactics that underlie the outrageous police conduct defense sufficiently implicated to warrant dismissal of the indictment against Ms. Forrest for her limited role in a car dealership bombing on due process grounds where an FBI informant used a veiled threat to recruit Ms. Forrest to participate in the bombing on which her charges are based, Ms. Forrest had no prior intention of participating in a violent crime and no history of violent criminal activity, and the informant planned the bombing, obtained the explosives from the FBI, trained Ms. Forrest, provided explicit directions under which she was acting at every stage of the operation, accompanied her to the crime scene, and waited to drive her away while she planted the explosives pursuant to his instructions?

Corresponding Excerpts from the Argument Section

Rule language pulled from the main rule statement paragraph: The availability of a dismissal based on outrageous government conduct is necessary to guard against "'the dangers of overzealous law enforcement.'"

Rule language pulled from the first rule explanation: The Due Process Clause limits the extent to which the government can involve itself in criminal activity. In *Greene*, for example, the court dismissed an indictment...because of the government agent's role in setting up, supplying, and continuing the [] operation.

Rule language pulled from the third rule explanation: Government's involvement in initiating and directing criminal activity is particularly offensive when the "government generate[s] new crimes" by a defendant who was not otherwise engaged in or planning criminal activity.

Rule language pulled from another rule explanation: Unwarranted physical or mental coercion by the government independently requires dismissal....

Facts pulled from the first application: Morlandia provided all of the materials, investigated the location of the crime, determined where and how to strike, and obtained explosives. He also trained her and instructed her at every stage.

Facts pulled from the second application: Forrest was not planning any criminal activity and was reluctant to participate. She had never engaged in violence before.

Fact pulled from a later application: Morlandia threatened her life.

22.3 | STANDARD OF REVIEW

You always need to discuss the standard of review in an appellate brief. Check your court's rules to determine whether a separate section is required and where it should be placed. When a standard of review section is included, it must come after the question presented/issue statement. If your brief does not include a separate standard of review section, you still must state the standard somewhere. If the standard is simple and nondebatable, you could put it in the main umbrella section of your argument (e.g., Sample F puts the standard in the first sentence of the argument section). If it is more complex or debatable, you may need to devote your first subheading in the argument to establishing the right standard.

Appellate courts are a higher authority than trial courts, but they actually have less power than trial courts in some important ways. Appellate courts are not free to simply review the case and determine the right outcome for the parties. They may do only the following:

1. Review questions of law de novo
2. Review questions of fact to determine whether they were supported by substantial evidence
3. Review discretionary decisions of the trial courts to determine whether they were abuses of discretion

The standard of review can have a significant impact on the scope of the appellate court's power and, therefore, is a critical issue to address and state correctly.

The "substantial evidence" standard is the most difficult for the appellant. As long as some valid evidence supports the outcome in the trial court, the appellate court must affirm, even if contradictory evidence was also introduced. The substantial evidence standard is typically applied to resolutions of factual disputes. Appellate courts are hesitant to become involved in factual disputes because unlike trial courts and juries, they do not get to hear and see witness testimony in person.

The appellant does not fare much better under an "abuse of discretion" standard. Under this standard, the appellant must show that the trial court's decision was arbitrary or relied on an incorrect application of the law. Many trial court decisions, including most discovery and evidentiary orders, are reviewed for an abuse of discretion.

"De novo" review is the most favorable for the appellant. Questions of law and decisions on some dispositive motions (e.g., summary judgment) are reviewed de novo. Unlike abuse of discretion and substantial evidence review, de novo does not require any deference to the trial court's decision. The appellate court reviews the issue with its own independent analysis.

You may find the applicable standard of review stated in the cases you read while researching your issue. If not, you will need to separately research the standard of review. A standard of review may be specific to the type of action you want the court to undo. For example, appellate courts review the trial courts' decisions on dispositive motions de novo. They review discovery and evidentiary orders for an abuse of discretion. Or the standard of review may depend on the type of legal issue you are addressing and whether it is a question of law or a question of fact.

You may sometimes be faced with conflicting results. Sometimes, for example, an order reviewable for an abuse of discretion raises a question of law subject to de novo review. And some legal issues raise a mixed question of law and fact. In these more complex situations, your discussion of the standard of review may be quite involved and will require careful research and synthesis of the case law that governs the conflicting standards.

Sample Simple Standard of Review

STANDARD OF REVIEW

Summary judgment is reviewed de novo and, accordingly, should be affirmed if correct even if the trial court's reasons for granting summary judgment were erroneous or incomplete. *Buss v. Superior Court*, 65 Cal. Rptr. 2d 366, 383 (Ct. App. 1997).

22.4 | SUMMARY OF THE ARGUMENT

Many appellate courts require the parties to include a "summary of the argument" section in their briefs. The summary of the argument is typically placed between the statement of facts and the argument. The summary of the argument is the equivalent of an introduction in a trial court brief. As a first step, it should track the organization of your brief including all tiers of headings. However, the summary of the argument must do much more than list the points you will address in your headings.

The summary of the argument is the court's first peek at your contentions. If it is not well written, it may also be the last peek the court bothers to give your brief. You must grab the court's attention.

This section of the brief is the most fun to write. You need to refer to the legal principles you will present and apply in your argument section. However, you do not and should not bog your summary down with citations. Instead, this is your chance to zoom out for the court and present a big-picture snapshot for the court. Hit your theme hard and be sure to indicate the compelling policy or fairness considerations that support your position. Persuade, persuade, persuade!

The ideal organization for a summary of the argument is to start broad and end broad with a roadmap of your headings in the middle.

First paragraph. Paint a vivid picture for your client's position. Grab the reader's attention and encourage an emotional connection to your client's point of view. Invoke sympathy, outrage, frustration, or worry as appropriate to your client's arguments. Include compelling narrative details and tie them to policy considerations. Indicate the result you want the court to reach (e.g., affirm/reverse).

Middle paragraph(s). Introduce the legal issue. Roadmap your headings and subheadings. Provide some factual detail to make each point persuasive. Strike a balance between providing enough detail to be persuasive but not so much detail that the summary becomes too long and repeats your argument section. Use rule language in these paragraphs, but do not detail the applicable rules.

Last paragraph. Zoom out. Bring the reader back to the big picture. Connect the points you have roadmapped in the middle paragraphs to the policy considerations you introduced in the first paragraph. Make a last appeal to your reader's sense of right and wrong. End with the result you are seeking.

Sample Summary of the Argument, Appellant

The first paragraph should grab the reader's attention and encourage an emotional connection to your position. In this example, the author invokes sympathy for the defendant and outrage over the government's conduct. It contains both factual details and a reference to the legal standard (shocks the universal sense of justice). The factual details should be relevant to the legal issue(s) your brief will address. In this sample, the included facts regarding her lack of prior violence and the government's involvement in the bombing are later emphasized in the subsequent argument section of the brief.

The Appellant, Ms. Forrest, was a nonviolent environmental activist whose worst transgressions were minor acts of vandalism that posed no risk of physical harm. However, on a day that would forever change her life, she detonated explosives at an auto dealership. At the heart of her progression from a nonviolent activist to an accomplice in a bombing is the government's reckless empowerment of a known terrorist who ultimately coerced, directed, and enabled Ms. Forrest to commit the crime. The government's involvement in the bombing, including its decision to supply the explosives, shocks the universal sense of justice and warrants reversal of the conviction.

The next paragraph introduces the general legal principle at issue in the case (egregious government conduct as a defense) and begins roadmapping the headings. *Russell* was the lead case on the outrageous conduct defense.

In *United States v. Russell*, 411 U.S. 423, 431 (1973), the Court recognized that a civilized society must place some outer limits on the investigative tactics of law enforcement. When these limits are crossed, the potential harm to our criminal justice system is sufficiently egregious to justify barring the government from obtaining a conviction. Here, the government's degree of involvement in the bombing crossed the line in at least three respects.

Cont.

The paragraph below previews section A.1. of the brief. The point is stated using the rule language (start to finish). Then factual details flush out the point. In providing factual detail, strike a balance between including enough detail to be persuasive but not so much detail that the paragraph becomes long and repeats your argument section.

First, the government encouraged its informant, a known terrorist, to direct the bombing from start to finish and supplied the necessary explosives. The informant recruited Ms. Forrest to participate in the bombing, located and surveyed the target, planned all logistics, obtained and stored explosives provided by the government, trained Ms. Forrest on how to detonate the explosives, and directed all of Ms. Forrest's actions. Testimony established that Ms. Forrest did not have the necessary skills or contacts to have completed such a mission on her own. The government enabled a crime that would not otherwise have occurred.

The following paragraph covers section A.2.

Second, Ms. Forrest was not engaged in or planning any criminal activity prior to her first contact with the government's informant. She was, in fact, highly reluctant to participate in the bombing when the informant first attempted to recruit her and gave in only when she believed the informant was threatening her life.

The next paragraph covers section A.3.

Third, the government encouraged its informant's excessively zealous tactics by threatening to arrest him if he failed to facilitate some convictions and tolerated the tactics out of desperation to justify a failing eight-year project. Its desperation is perhaps best illustrated by its willingness to not only supply explosives to the informant but to also permit him to store the explosives in a public facility.

The next paragraph covers section B, which is not further subdivided.

Heading C is not previewed because it is an anticipatory rebuttal section (i.e., the entire section is devoted to rebutting opposing arguments). Sometimes, you will want to include rebuttals in your summary but other times, the rebuttal may not make sense out of context. Here, for example, it would have been cumbersome to explain the five-factor test that the rebuttal in section C responds to.

In addition to the government's over-involvement in the initiation, planning, and execution of the bombing, the coercion of Ms. Forrest's involvement in the crime warrants reversal of the conviction. After Ms. Forrest initially refused to participate in the bombing because she could not "do something like that," the informant menacingly commented that he "hope[d] [she would] make the right decision" and that "we cannot take chances with defectors." Fearing for her life, she then acquiesced and promised to "do what was required."

The final paragraph should bring the reader back to the big picture. In this example, the reader is brought back to the starting point of the summary in the first paragraph—the unfairness to the defendant and the egregiousness of the government's conduct.

Admittedly, Ms. Forrest was not completely innocent. Although she professed a belief that she had joined a nonviolent organization, she likely knew that at least some of its members endorsed violence. She also had embraced illegal, though nonviolent, tactics in the past. However, she would never have been at that dealership setting the explosives if not for the coercive and directive conduct of the government's informant.

Cont.

Lee King would be alive, and Ms. Forrest would not be facing a life in prison. This is a quintessential case of the government manufacturing a crime that would not otherwise have occurred. Reversal of the conviction is necessary to preserve the integrity of our justice system. The government must adhere to some basic principles of fairness or be barred from invoking judicial process to sanction its misguided suspension of morality.

Sample Summary of the Argument, Appellee

The first paragraph builds sympathy for the government's position by dispelling the image of the defendant as a peaceful, innocent bystander.

Defendant is seeking to invoke the rarely successful defense of outrageous government conduct to excuse her role in the bombing of a car dealership that led to the death of its owner. Although Defendant claims to be an innocent victim of government entrapment, she in fact was a member of a dangerous eco-terrorist organization. She had participated in prior acts of terrorism and had even attended a bomb-making training session.

The second paragraph introduces the legal standard on the issue (shocking to the universal sense of justice) and includes factual details that build sympathy for the government's position.

Government conduct will bar a conviction only if it violates fundamental fairness and is shocking to the universal sense of justice required by the Due Process Clause. Far from shocking the universal sense of justice, the government's efforts in this case were devoted to protecting the public from a dangerous and destructive terrorist organization. The government had been trying to infiltrate the leadership of this organization for eight years without any success. It suspected the group had stockpiled a large amount of explosives and was planning another large-scale attack. Faced with a virtually impenetrable leadership, the government resorted to the use of an inside informant. The informant was to carry out the planning of the bombing but keep the government updated so that it could intercept the perpetrators prior to the detonation of the explosives. The plan developed with the informant was the government's best hope to date in the investigation. However, a last-minute unforeseen turn of events prevented the government from stopping the bombing.

The next paragraph previews sections A.1.–A.3. Notice that although a list format is used, each item in the list includes not just a conclusion (e.g., that she was not innocent) but also a reason (she was an active member of a terrorist organization). This is as short on detail as you would want to get.

Federal courts have created a five-factor test to limit the availability of the outrageous conduct defense and thereby protect law enforcement's ability to employ a broad range of investigative tactics. Defendant cannot pass the five-factor test because (1) Defendant was not an otherwise innocent citizen ensnared by government trickery but, instead, was an active member of a terrorist organization; (2) the organization had proven itself capable of carrying out bombings without government involvement and therefore the government's role did not enable the crime; and (3) the government's plan to use the bombing to ingratiate its informant with the leadership of the organi-

Cont.

zation was an appropriate investigative tactic given its intent to intercede before the bombing could be carried out.

The paragraph below previews sections B–E. Again, both conclusions and reasons are provided for each point.

Moreover, this case does not resemble other cases in which the defense has succeeded. First, Defendant was not an innocent citizen unfairly targeted by the government but, to the contrary, was caught up in the bombing as a result of her preexisting membership in a terrorist organization. Second, the government did not plan to participate in any crimes. In the past, the defense has been successful when the government participated in *real* crimes. Here, the government planned to intercept the conspirators prior to the completion of the bombing. Third, although the informant admittedly pressured the Defendant to participate in the bombing, the lines he delivered were necessary to his role as an informant. Fourth, the government's use of a known terrorist as an informant does not shock the universal sense of justice. Given the secrecy of the organization, the government had little choice. No other efforts had been successful.

The last paragraph brings the reader back to the big picture and connects the points to an important policy consideration: the need to provide latitude to law enforcement.

Stripped to its core, this case involves a sting operation gone awry. The headline was surely a bad one, but the government envisioned a much different result. If the government had intercepted the bombing as planned, the informant might finally have achieved the seemingly impossible task of infiltrating the leadership of Defendant's terrorist organization. Given some time, the government's plan might well have thwarted future dangerous crimes. The lead FBI agent, Agent Tu, might have been hailed as a hero. The plan's ultimate failure cannot be the basis of a claim of outrageous conduct. If sting operations were deemed outrageous upon their failure, law enforcement would be severely impeded. Defendant was a victim of her own poor decisions and is not entitled to evade conviction or her role in the death of Lee King.

22.5 | FEDERAL APPELLATE COURT BRIEFS

The federal appellate courts require several special sections and require that advocates follow an exact order. Under Federal Rule of Appellate Procedure 28, all briefs by an appellant must include the following and in this order:

(1) a corporate disclosure statement (when applicable)
(2) a table of contents, with page references;
(3) a table of authorities—cases (alphabetically arranged), statutes, and other authorities—with references to the pages of the brief where they are cited;
(4) a jurisdictional statement, including:
  (A) the basis for the district court's or agency's subject matter jurisdiction, with citations to applicable statutory provisions and stating relevant facts establishing jurisdiction;

(B) the basis for the court of appeals' jurisdiction, with citations to applicable statutory provisions and stating relevant facts establishing jurisdiction;
(C) the filing dates establishing the timeliness of the appeal or petition for review; and
(D) an assertion that the appeal is from a final order or judgment that disposes of all parties' claims, or information establishing the court of appeals' jurisdiction on some other basis;

(5) a statement of the issues presented for review;
(6) a concise statement of the case setting out the facts relevant to the issues submitted for review, describing the relevant procedural history, and identifying the rulings presented for review, with appropriate references to the record (see Rule 28(e));
(7) a summary of the argument, which must contain a succinct, clear, and accurate statement of the arguments made in the body of the brief, and which must not merely repeat the argument headings;
(8) the argument, which must contain:
(A) appellant's contentions and the reasons for them, with citations to the authorities and parts of the record on which the appellant relies; and
(B) for each issue, a concise statement of the applicable standard of review (which may appear in the discussion of the issue or under a separate heading placed before the discussion of the issues);

(9) a short conclusion stating the precise relief sought; and
(10) the certificate of compliance, if required by Rule 32(a)(7).

Some of these components are formulaic and are not addressed in this textbook. However, this section describes the jurisdictional statement and the statement of the case. The issue statement, statement of facts, tables, summary of the argument, and argument sections are discussed in earlier sections.

22.5.1 | Jurisdictional Statement

To complete a jurisdictional statement, you need to understand the basis of federal jurisdiction. Most frequently, the basis is either federal question jurisdiction (i.e., the case involves the application of the United States Constitution, a federal statute or regulation, or a treaty) (28 U.S.C. § 1331) or diversity jurisdiction (i.e., the parties are diverse in citizenship and the amount in controversy exceeds $75,000) (28 U.S.C. § 1332).

Then, to comply with section 4B of Rule 28, you need to understand the basis of appellate jurisdiction. 28 U.S.C. § 1291 provides jurisdiction over all appeals from "final decisions" of the district courts unless the party can seek direct review by the Supreme Court (a narrow exception). The "final decision" in a case is usually the formal judgment entered in favor of one of the parties after a verdict or dispositive motion. However, the meaning of "final decision" encompasses a complex body of law. If you have any question whether your case has had a "final decision" rendered, research the issue. In limited circumstances, a federal appellate court may review nonfinal decisions ("interlocutory orders"). Again, this is a complex area of law and would need to be fully researched.

If your appeal fits the standard scenario: federal question or diversity jurisdiction and appeal from a final judgment, your jurisdictional statement is likely to be very basic. In addition to the statutory basis for jurisdiction, you would simply need the date of the final judgment and the date of the appeal. In more complex cases in which jurisdiction is questionable, you may end up having a mini-brief in the jurisdictional statement.

From Sample F

JURISDICTIONAL STATEMENT

The Central District of California had jurisdiction over this case because the Defendant was charged with two federal crimes. 28 U.S.C. § 1331 (2006). A judgment and commitment order was entered on December 11, 2009. Defendant filed this appeal on December 21, 2009. This Court has jurisdiction over the appeal from the final judgment pursuant to section 1291. *Id.* § 1291.

22.5.2 | Statement of the Case

Federal Rule of Appellate Procedure 28 refers to a statement of facts as a "statement of the case." It includes, however, the same content and requires the same techniques discussed in Chapter 18. The procedural history paragraph in the statement of the case must "briefly indicat[e] the nature of the case, the course of proceedings, and the disposition below." As an example, the procedural history paragraph from the Sample Appellant's Brief (Sample F) follows.

From Sample F

STATEMENT OF THE CASE

The defendant, Reyna Forrest, has been convicted for the bombing of Lee King Autos. (R. at 59.) Before trial, she moved to dismiss her indictment on the basis of outrageous government conduct. (R. at 59.) In support of the motion, Ms. Forrest argued that she was coerced into participating in the bombing by a government informant named Sid Morlandia who manufactured the crime from start to finish, the government informant's sole motive was to obtain a conviction, and the FBI endangered the public. (R. at 51-52.) Despite these allegations, the trial court declined to dismiss the indictment. (R. at 52.) Ms. Forrest now appeals her conviction on the grounds of outrageous government conduct. (R. at 59.)

Sample F shows how the rest of the statement of the case (i.e., the facts section) would follow this procedural history paragraph. As Chapter 18 explains, procedural history can also be put at the end of the facts section.

CHAPTER **23**

A Memorandum of Points and Authorities

A brief submitted in support of or in opposition to a motion in a trial court is usually entitled a "memorandum of points and authorities." Motions can challenge the right of a party to offer a particular type of evidence or to seek certain information from the other parties. They can seek to dispose of the case early before trial. They can even be brought after trial to convince the court that the jury got its verdict wrong or that an error occurred during the trial that requires a new trial.

A memorandum of points and authorities is like any other brief, and the lessons in Chapters 18 through 21 regarding the statement of facts, argument, point headings, and tables apply to it. This chapter addresses some nuances that are specific to memoranda of points and authorities. Practicing lawyers always need to consult and follow the rules of the particular trial court in which they are filing their briefs because the court may have special requirements. Students, by analogy, should follow their professor's instructions as the equivalent of the court's rules.

23.1 | CAPTION OF A MEMORANDUM OF POINTS AND AUTHORITIES

Memoranda of points and authorities typically use a pleading format with the party information and a caption box at the left margin. Many courts require that they be prepared with line numbers as in Appendix B, Sample G. The information required in the caption and first page of the brief is particular to the court to which you are submitting the brief but typically includes case identifying information, judge's name, courtroom number, hearing date and time, and the title of the brief. The title of the brief should indicate the type of motion and which side you are on: e.g., "Memorandum of Points and Authorities in Support of the Defendant's Motion for Summary Judgment" or "Memorandum of Points and Authorities in Opposition to the Defendant's Motion for Summary Judgment." A short memorandum can begin its text right under the caption on the same page, but memoranda ten pages or longer will need a table of contents and table of authorities. The tables should start on separate pages as discussed in Chapter 21 and illustrated in Sample G.

23.2 | INTRODUCTION

After the caption and the tables, the first section of a memorandum of points and authorities is usually the introduction. If you read section 22.4 on the summary of the argument, you will find this discussion of an introduction in a memorandum of points and authorities to be very similar. However, a key difference is that the introduction must be must shorter than a summary of the argument—no more than three paragraphs (and if using three, at least one of the paragraphs should be very short as in the samples that follow).

The key lesson remains the same, however. The main role of the introduction in a memorandum of points and authorities, like the summary in an appellate brief, is to grab the court's attention. The introduction is the court's first peek at your contentions. If it is not well written, it may also be the last peek the court bothers to give your brief. Ideally, it should include (1) some persuasive facts that help build sympathy for your client's position; (2) a connection between those facts and the legal issue addressed in the motion; and (3) an appeal to policy considerations or, at least, the judge's sense of justice. In the course of achieving these goals, the introduction also needs to clearly state the type of motion addressed and the issue it raises.

Persuasive facts. Paint a vivid picture for your client's position. Grab the reader's attention and encourage an emotional connection to your client's point of view. Invoke sympathy, outrage, frustration, or worry as appropriate to your client's arguments. Include compelling narrative details and tie them to policy considerations.

Introduction to the legal issue. Connect the factual details you included to the legal issue addressed in the motion. Explain why the facts do or do not warrant the relief requested in the motion. You can also roadmap the main points of your brief here as long as you keep the roadmap short and simple—e.g., roadmap your headings A., B., C., etc., but not subsidiary points within each section (A.1., A.2., A.3., etc.).

Policy considerations. Zoom out. Bring the reader back to the big picture. Connect the points you have roadmapped to the policy considerations you will highlight in your brief. Make a last appeal to your reader's sense of right and wrong. End with the result you are seeking.

Sample Introduction, Moving Party

This sample first identifies the basic issue and type of motion.

The Appellant, Ms. Forrest, seeks to dismiss her indictment on the ground that it was obtained in violation of her Due Process rights through outrageous government conduct.

Cont.

Then it proceeds to grab the reader's attention and encourage an emotional connection to the client's position by revealing key sympathetic facts. The author invokes sympathy for the defendant and outrage over the government's conduct. The factual details in the introduction should relate to the legal issue(s) your brief will address. In this sample, the included facts regarding her lack of prior violence and the government's involvement in the bombing are later emphasized in the application paragraphs.

The paragraph then roadmaps some of the points that will be made in the brief: (1) the informant's large role in the crime; (2) the use of threats; (3) the enablement of the crime by the government via explosives and training.

Ms. Forrest was a nonviolent environmental activist whose worst transgressions were minor acts of vandalism that posed no risk of physical harm. However, on a day that would forever change her life, she detonated explosives at an auto dealership. At the heart of her progression from a nonviolent activist to an accomplice in a bombing is the government's reckless empowerment of its informant, a known terrorist who ultimately coerced, directed, and enabled Ms. Forrest to commit the crime. With the government's knowledge, its informant used threats to overcome Ms. Forrest's reluctance to participate in the bombing, located and surveyed the target, planned all logistics, obtained and stored explosives *provided by the government*, trained Ms. Forrest on how to detonate the explosives, and directed all of Ms. Forrest's actions.

The last paragraph connects the facts and roadmap to the legal standard (shocks the universal sense of justice) and one of the key considerations in its application (manufacturing a crime). It also brings in a policy consideration (fairness and the danger of an abusive government).

The government's involvement in the bombing shocks the universal sense of justice and warrants dismissal of the indictment on Due Process grounds. This is a quintessential case of the government manufacturing a crime that would not otherwise have occurred. Dismissal of the indictment is necessary to preserve the integrity of our justice system. The government must adhere to some basic principles of fairness or be barred from invoking judicial process to sanction its misguided suspension of morality.

Sample Introduction, Opposition to Motion

The first paragraph introduces the basic issue and builds sympathy for the government's position by dispelling the image of the Defendant as a peaceful, innocent bystander.

In her Motion to Dismiss the Indictment, Defendant is seeking to invoke the rarely successful defense of outrageous government conduct to excuse her role in the bombing of a car dealership that led to the death of its owner. Although Defendant claims to be an innocent victim of government entrapment, she in fact was a member of a dangerous eco-terrorist organization. She had participated in prior acts of terrorism and had even attended a bomb-making training session.

The second paragraph introduces the legal standard on the issue (shocking to the universal sense of justice) and connects pro-government facts to that standard. It also brings in an important policy consideration: the need to provide latitude to law enforcement.

Government conduct will bar a conviction only if it violates fundamental fairness and is shocking to the universal sense of justice required by the Due Process Clause. Far from shocking the universal sense of justice, the government's efforts in this case were

Cont.

devoted to protecting the public from a dangerous and destructive terrorist organization. The government had been trying to infiltrate the leadership of this organization for eight years without any success. It suspected the group had stockpiled a large amount of explosives and was planning another large-scale attack. Faced with a virtually impenetrable leadership, the government resorted to the use of an inside informant to set up a sting operation. If the government had intercepted the bombing as planned, future dangerous crimes would have been avoided. The plan's ultimate failure cannot be the basis of a claim of outrageous conduct. If sting operations were deemed outrageous upon their failure, law enforcement would be severely impeded.

It ends by stating the action the prosecution wants the court to take.

Defendant was a victim of her own poor decisions and is not entitled to evade conviction for her role in the death of Lee King. The motion to dismiss should be denied.

23.3 | QUESTION PRESENTED/ISSUE STATEMENT AND STATEMENT OF FACTS

After the introduction, you might need to include a question presented/issue statement if required by the court. Questions presented/issue statements are covered in section 22.2.

Next comes the statement of facts, which is covered in Chapter 18. In a memorandum of points and authorities, the last procedural event to include is the motion itself.

23.4 | ARGUMENT

All of the lessons from Chapter 19 on the argument section apply equally to appellate briefs and memoranda of points and authorities. Point headings, covered in Chapter 20, must also be used.

Strategic considerations in drafting your arguments and headings may be slightly different in memoranda of points and authorities than in appellate briefs. First, whereas appellate briefs must focus on the applicable standard of review (see section 22.3), memoranda of points and authorities must focus on the procedural standard for the motion at issue. For example, in most jurisdictions, a motion for summary judgment must be denied if there are any triable issues of fact, and any factual dispute must be resolved in favor of the party opposing the motion. Different standards apply to discovery motions, post-trial motions, motions to dismiss (or demurrers), motions to exclude evidence from trial, and so on. Research the most favorable articulation of the standard governing the motion you are bringing or opposing. Although there is no special section of the memorandum in which to place the standard, it is typically set forth in the umbrella paragraph and referred to throughout the brief, particularly in the wrap-up conclusions for each subdivision (A., B., C., etc.) of the argument.

In Sample G, the motion to dismiss does not have a procedural standard because it presents an issue of law for the court to decide. If you faced a motion for summary judgment, you could include the summary judgment standard in about the same place that the sample mentions that the motion to dismiss the indictment is a question of law (indicated in the excerpt from Sample G below).

Sample Umbrella with Procedural Standard Excerpt from Sample G

ARGUMENT

The Court should dismiss the indictment because the government's investigative tactics exceeded due process limits.

This Court should dismiss the indictment because the government's conduct in this case exceeded due process limits.

The United States Supreme Court has recognized that the Due Process Clause of the Constitution imposes limits on the methods law enforcement may use to obtain convictions and, accordingly, convictions obtained through improper means are barred. *United States v. Russell*, 411 U.S. 423, 431 (1973) ("we may some day be presented with a situation in which the conduct of law enforcement agents is so outrageous that due process principles would absolutely bar the government from invoking judicial processes to obtain a conviction"). Unlike the defense of entrapment, a claim of outrageous government conduct may be successful even when the defendant was predisposed to commit the crime. *Hampton v. United States*, 425 U.S. 484, 495 (1976) (Powell, J., concurring); *id.* at 497 (Brennan, J., dissenting); *see also United States v. Bogart*, 783 F.2d 1428, 1432 (9th Cir. 1986) (explaining that the concurring and dissenting justices in *Hampton* comprised a majority to support the availability of an outrageous government conduct claim regardless of a defendant's criminal predisposition). The motion to dismiss the indictment raises a question of law for the court to decide rather than the jury. *United States v. Gardner*, 658 F. Supp. 1573, 1577 (W.D. Pa. 1987). Procedural standard

Some experts may comment that, as compared to appellate briefs, trial-level briefs should focus more on application of precedent cases and less on loftier policy arguments. In truth, however, while appellate courts may have more power to create new law than trial courts, they are no more eager to do so. Therefore, both appellate briefs and trial-level briefs really need to use the same strategy: focus primarily on the application of precedent and use policy considerations as an additional persuasive tool. Policy considerations will take on a larger role and fill more of the pages of a brief when the motion or appeal asks a court to tread new territory in the law—that is, when existing precedent cannot answer the legal question. It may be true that a motion in a trial court that relies primarily on policy considerations (because it lacks controlling precedent) is likely to fail while the appeal may have a slightly better chance of success, but this truth does not change the strategy in your briefs. Essentially, then, the only real difference between an argument section in an appellate brief and one in a memorandum of points and authorities is the need to focus the former on the standard of review applicable to the appeal and the latter on the procedural standard that governs the motion.

23.5 | CONCLUSION AND SIGNATURE BLOCK

After the argument, include a one- or two-sentence conclusion section and signature block, as shown in Appendix B, Sample G. The conclusion should ask for the action you want the court to take (i.e., grant or deny the motion).

APPENDIX **A**

SELF-TEST ANSWERS

ANSWERS TO CHAPTER 1 SELF-TEST

1. Interact with the material through highlighting, writing questions to follow up with your professor about, and tagging helpful samples.
2. Use the material as you write.
3. Follow professor feedback closely; use a check-off system to make sure you have addressed every comment.
4. Develop a personalized self-editing checklist that focuses on the areas in which you need improvement.

ANSWERS TO COURT HIERARCHY SELF-TEST

1. The viability of the lawsuit is an open issue. Your court will have to make up its own mind. If you had to argue about the issue in court, you would need to discuss both court opinions and argue in favor of the one that supports your client's position.
2. They can sue. No reason to even mention the disagreement between the lower-level appellate courts.
3. They can sue, but because the supreme court has not weighed in on the issue, it is not a slam dunk. The neighbors might be able to convince a new court of appeal to disagree with its sibling court. The new court is unlikely to disagree with its sibling court, but it could.
4. They cannot sue. The state's opinion trumps the federal court's opinion because the issue is one of state law.

ANSWERS TO READING A COURT OPINION SELF-TEST

1. Case analysis sheets and rule charts are important prewriting steps.
2. Court reasoning includes the logical connections the court makes to bridge the gap between the legal rules and the case facts.

ANSWERS TO CHAPTER 4 SELF-TEST

1. The purpose of rule statement is to introduce the more detailed discussion of the law to come in the rule explanation paragraphs by providing an overview of the rules pertinent to the legal issue.
2. Broad rules come before more narrow rules.
3. Stop RS and start RE when you start to feel like the reader will want to see an example to explain or prove the rule.
4. "Connectors" refers to language that connects the rules to one another and clarifies the relationship between the rules.
5. REs consist of the following components: topic sentence, transition, and case examples.
6. The topic sentence should state a subrule that you have pulled or inferred from the cases that the paragraph will describe. (In a question of first impression, it would make a statement about the law in other jurisdictions or make a point in favor of or against a particular interpretation.)
7. It should state a clear rule like, "If it rains, I will not go to the beach," rather than wishy-washy language like, "Whether I go to the beach will depend on the weather." In general, avoid "consider," "whether," or "a factor" except as transitional language into a more explicit topic sentence.

8. A full case example includes the facts, holding, and reasoning of the case, in that order.
9. Underline the reasoning in the opinion, track the same steps in your case example, and use some key quoted language.
10. A parenthetical is a note about a case placed in parentheses. It is less than one full sentence long. It must include the holding and key facts that relate to the subrule stated in your topic sentence; it may also include some key court reasoning.
11. A parenthetical follows the full case example at the end of the paragraph. Do not place a parenthetical in the middle of a full case example.
12. A bridge is a sentence to join the end of a full case example and a parenthetical. You need a bridge if the last sentence of the full case example does not state a generalizable point that can be supported by the parenthetical. For example, if your case example ends with a fact from the first case, it will not flow into the parenthetical cite to another case without a bridge.

ANSWERS TO CHAPTER 5 SELF-TEST

1. An application paragraph applies the information about the law that you included in your rule explanation (and rule statement) to assess or argue the outcome of your case.
2. An application paragraph should match one of your rule explanation paragraphs, including use of the same rule language from the topic sentence and use of some of the language in the court's reasoning that you included in the rule explanation.
3. The topic sentence of an application paragraph should make a statement about your case that matches one of your rule explanation topic sentences. For example, if your rule explanation paragraph's topic sentence states that it is fun to visit national parks, then your matching application paragraph's topic sentence would state that it would be fun to visit Yosemite because it is a national park.
4. The comparison sentence in this question is not grammatically parallel and is nonspecific. Compare: Like the employee in *Smith*, who left his duties as a cashier to do jumping jacks in the parking lot, our client left her duties as a waitress... (now client is compared to the like subject, the employee in *Smith*, and details are added).
5. Use some of the language from the court's reasoning that you include in your rule explanation as you are proving your points in application. Follow the same steps of logic that the court went through to prove its conclusion.
6. Go back through the fact file for your case and highlight good details, even quotations, that support the points that you are exploring in your memo or brief.

ANSWERS TO CHAPTER 6 SELF-TEST

1. In the TRRRAAAC structure, all of your rule statement and rule explanations come before any of your application paragraphs.
2. This is a bit of a trick question. Any section that is not further subdivided will have its own TRRRAAAC. However, if a section A. is divided into subsections 1. and 2., you will have an umbrella under heading A., and then subsections 1. and 2. will each have their own TRRRAAAC.
3. An umbrella includes a thesis, rule statement, and preview of the conclusions you reach in the headings that come under the umbrella. A main umbrella (the umbrella before your first subdivision) will always include rule statement—i.e., the rules needed to set up the subdivisions. Smaller subdivisions, however, may or may not need a rule statement depending on whether you need any rules to set up the subdivisions.

4. It depends. If you have only one tier of headings, you will have one umbrella. If you have multiple tiers of headings, you will also have an umbrella before each new tier.
5. An umbrella always comes right before the subdivisions that it sets up.
6. TRARARAC is best for a factor-balancing analysis.
7. TRARARAC has separate paragraphs for rule explanation and application; TRATRATRAC has a thesis, rule explanation, and application in each paragraph.
8. TRATRATRAC works best when each point can fit neatly within a reasonably sized paragraph. If the paragraphs are too long, switch to TRARARAC.
9. Narratives are tied to the T. Wherever a T occurs in the various structures discussed in this chapter, you can fit a narrative as part of the thesis.
10. You do not need to use the exact same structure in each subdivision of your brief. Each new heading gives you freedom to adopt the structure that is best for that section of your paper.

ANSWERS TO CHAPTER **8** SELF-TEST

1. Consult the rules of your citation manual because which reporter to cite to varies.
2. A jump page or pinpoint cite is the exact page of the source that supports your sentence.
3. You do not need a signal if you are quoting the source or paraphrasing it. If any inferential reasoning is needed to see how the source supports your sentence, you need to use *see*.
4. Yes, signals are italicized or underlined.
5. You must indicate whether a case has been overruled or a statute has been abrogated.
6. String cites usually use semicolons between sources.
7. Use *id.* to refer to the same source that you most recently cited when that cite appears alone.
8. Include a jump page or pinpoint cite with *id.* when the new sentence is supported by a different page of the source than the previous cite to the source.
9. No. Instead of using the full cite again, you can use the short form: *Smith*, 12 Cal. Rptr. at 211.
10. Capitalize court, defendant, and plaintiff when referring to the court deciding your case and the defendant and plaintiff in your case. Do not capitalize them when referring to another court or a defendant or plaintiff in another case.

ANSWERS TO CHAPTER **9** SELF-TEST

1. The introductory paragraph of a factual narrative generally includes: who, what, when (maybe), and where (maybe).
2. When getting ready to write a factual narrative, review the fact file and highlight important details including quotations and specifics.
3. Do not simply string details together; take your time in telling the story. Develop the characters by providing some detail and work on making connections between facts.
4. Do not organize your narrative by witness or document but by chronology and/or topic.
5. The procedural history should include the significant events in the court case to date—e.g., motion that was filed, jury's decision, date of appeal.
6. No. The factual narrative should include only facts.

ANSWERS TO CHAPTER 10 SELF-TEST

1. The two main componets of issue identification are factual details and key rule language.
2. You should choose the factual details that are relevant to the rule language that you chose so that the reader understands the potential relevance of the factual details.

ANSWERS TO CHAPTER 15 SELF-TEST

1. The first sentence in the analysis section should state your thesis, i.e., how you think the case will turn out on the legal issue that your memo will address.
2. Give equal space to rules and cases that support and question your conclusion.
3. Fully analyze significant counterarguments to your conclusion.
4. There is no difference between a supportive application and counterargument except for the addition of transitional language like, "Plaintiff may argue..."
5. A rebuttal should find flaws in the logic of the counterargument or explain why your other points outweigh the counterargument.
6. A confounder is a fact or point that confuses your analysis but that, even if believed, would be insufficient to warrant a contrary result to your conclusion. The difference matters because confounders can be analyzed within your supportive paragraphs whereas counterarguments must be separately analyzed and rebutted.

ANSWERS TO CHAPTER 19 SELF-TEST

1. The umbrella includes the thesis, core theory, rule statement, roadmap.
2. In persuasive writing, pick articulations of the rule that are favorable for your position, select rules strategically, use connectors, and synthesize the rules in a favorable manner to emphasize the good stuff for your client's position.
3. Persuasive rule explanation requires that every topic sentence makes a statement that is good for your client's position (no neutral or unfavorable statements). You may need to use more inferred subrules than express subrules to achieve this result. In briefs, it is also more important to be concise and trim out unnecessary details.
4. The magic is in the topic sentences. You want your rule explanation topic sentences to limit the bad cases in a manner that will make it easy to distinguish your case and/or juxtapose unfavorable subrules with favorable ones that detract from their significance.
5. In an "although" type of juxtaposition, the bad stuff always comes first. Emphasis is placed on the good stuff that follows.
6. Your application paragraphs can use strategic juxtaposition and "although" clauses to explain away the bad facts.

APPENDIX **B**

SAMPLES

SAMPLE A. ONE-TRRRAAAC LEGAL RESEARCH MEMORANDUM

To: Supervising Attorney ❶

From: Junior Associate

Date: October 20, 2006

Re: Gator v. Fitness Functions; Coverage of Recreational Activities ❷

---
❸

FACTUAL BACKGROUND ❹

Mark Gator is seeking workers' compensation coverage of an injury he sustained while playing paddleball with his supervisor after work on a court in his employer's parking lot. ❺

Gator works for Fitness Functions, a company that sells fitness equipment to health clubs, hotels, and spas. Fitness Functions has a paddleball court in its parking lot. It built the court to attract Gator's supervisor, Joyce Randolph, who was a famous racquetball player, to her current position as Director of Marketing and Sales. Randolph uses the court to play with employees and clients. She thinks paddleball is a good way to get to know her employees, boost morale, build team spirit, and keep employees in shape. The company provides paddles, balls, sneakers, and exercise clothes to "make[] it easy" for employees to play. ❻

Randolph saw Gator leaving from work one day as she was heading to play in the court. She complimented Gator on bringing in a new client, expressed her desire to see continued successes from him, and invited him to play with her later in the week. Gator responded that he would check his schedule and get back to her. ❼

1. The caption should be double-spaced and in the same font as the rest of the memo.
2. The "Re" line should provide the case name plus the research topic.
3. The solid line between the caption and text is a common format, but your office or your professor may use another format.
4. Memos typically have at least four sections: factual background, issue statement, analysis, and conclusion. The name of the sections and how they are formatted (bolding, underlining, etc.) can vary.

   In the factual background, you will recount the facts of your client's case that are relevant to the issue you are analyzing in the memo. The story should be presented impartially and should include both favorable and unfavorable facts.
5. Include an introductory paragraph to state the general nature of the case and focus on your client's point of view. This writer's client is Gator; therefore, she frames the case in terms of what he wants. By contrast, the employer's lawyer might have started with a sentence like, "Fitness Functions is defending a claim for workers' compensation brought by ..."

   The purpose of the introductory paragraph is to give the reader a context for the facts that follow. Note that you still have to go into all of the pertinent details again in the body of your factual background.
6. There is no easy rule on how to organize a factual background. Usually, a chronological organization is easiest for a reader. However, often some facts will not fit in the chronology. This memo solves the problem by having an initial paragraph after the introductory paragraph that presents the background information.
7. The chronology of events starts here. When you are presenting a narrative in chronological order, you should not use a drab presentation like, "On July 2, x happened. On July 4, y happened." Dates should be used only when they are important to the legal issues the memo will address and should be integrated more naturally and less rigidly into the narrative. Here, for example, the author uses "one day" instead of bombarding the reader with an irrelevant date.

* The sample memoranda are single-spaced with an extra space between paragraphs. If you need to double-space your memorandum, then you should not include an extra space between paragraphs.

8 Gator, a sales employee working under Randolph, had only recently been hired and was still on probationary status at the time. Despite reservations about playing with Randolph because she was "very good and extremely competitive," Gator agreed to play because he "wanted to be on her good side" and felt he "needed to play." In making this decision, he considered what a coworker had once told him: she felt playing with Randolph had helped her advance in the company by giving her an "in," and Randolph often discussed business while playing with her.

9 During his game with Randolph, Gator hit himself with his paddle. He filed for workers' compensation coverage for his resulting injuries. The company denied coverage. Gator is now considering filing an application for adjudication with the Workers' Compensation Appeals Board.

ISSUE STATEMENT

10 Was Gator's after-hours game with his supervisor on his employer's paddleball court a reasonable expectancy of employment and, therefore, subject to workers' compensation coverage when no supervisor ever suggested he needed to play but he felt he needed to play to advance in the company, a coworker had once told him playing had helped her advance, and his employer supplied the equipment in the hope that the game would boost morale, foster team work, and keep employees fit?

ANALYSIS

11 Gator is entitled to coverage because paddleball was a reasonable expectancy of his employment with Fitness Functions. T

8. You will need to decide where to start new paragraphs. Break paragraphs by event or topic. The prior paragraph, for example, covered the invitation to play paddleball. This paragraph covers Gator's decision to accept the invitation. And the next paragraph covers the game and its results (injuries and litigation).

   The fact file for this sample memo consisted of witness statements, police reports, interview notes, and similar documents. Notice that the facts are presented as a narrative and not as "Gator stated x, y, and z. Randolph stated a, b, and c." You want to tell a story for the reader rather than flatly recounting who attested to what. Like in this example, you want to synthesize the witness statements into a narrative for the reader. You should use the narrative approach even when the exact words of the witness are important. You can work in the exact words by putting quotation marks around them—like "very good and extremely competitive" in this example. Using quotation marks allows you to signify these are exact words without stepping out of the narrative with a "he said."
9. End the factual background with an indication of what, if anything, has happened in the case to date.
10. Generally, issue statements have two key components: (1) the legal question, and (2) the key facts on which your answer to the question relies.

    In this example, the key legal question is whether playing paddleball was a reasonable expectancy of employment (this is what workers' compensation coverage would depend on). The author, therefore, includes "reasonable expectancy" in the issue statement.

    Notice the inclusion of key facts like that the game was after-hours. Also, because the memo is objective, it is best to include both the facts that support your conclusion and those that relate to any counterarguments you will present. Here, "no one ... ever suggested" is a fact that goes against the author's conclusion that the game was a reasonable expectancy of employment. The conjunction "but" is used to separate this "bad" fact from the facts that support the author's conclusion. Look at your application paragraphs to identify the facts that played a key role in your analysis.
11. **T** = Thesis
    The analysis section should begin with your thesis, phrased firmly and in a manner that is specific to the issue you are analyzing.

    The thesis in this sample, for example, does not merely state that he is entitled to coverage but states the conclusion on the issue—i.e., reasonable expectancy.

    The thesis can be a sentence or a short paragraph.

RS Labor Code section 3600, subdivision (a)(9), excludes from workers' compensation (12) coverage injuries arising from "voluntary participation in any off-duty recreational, social, or athletic activity not constituting part of the employee's work-related duties, except where these activities are a reasonable expectancy of, or are expressly or impliedly required by, the employment." Cal. Labor Code § 3600(a)(9) (West 2003). The exception for activities that (13) are a reasonable expectancy of employment applies when (1) the employee subjectively believes participation in the activity is expected; and (2) the employee's belief is objectively reasonable. *Ezzy v. Workers' Comp. Appeals Bd.*, 194 Cal. Rptr. 90, 93 (Ct. App. 1983).

RE1 The first part of the test, subjective belief, is satisfied by an employee's professed belief (14) that participation was required. Indeed, a belief that one *should* participate is sufficient. In *Ezzy*, for example, a law clerk was injured while playing on her firm's softball team. *Id.* at 91. She testified that because the team did not have enough female players to satisfy the league's rules, she felt she "should" play when a partner handed her a tee shirt and game schedule and said, "At the next one, we'll see you there." *Id.* at 92. Her statement under oath was sufficient to satisfy the subjective belief requirement. *Id.* at 96.

RE2 Failing the subjective belief requirement seems to be a risk only when the employee (15) did not truly feel obligated to participate. *Compare Smith v. Workers' Comp. Appeals Bd.*, 236 Cal. Rptr. 248, 254-55 (Ct. App. 1987) (holding that deceased teacher's wife's testimony (16) that teacher went to a picnic because his department head asked him to, he felt he had a "responsibility" to go, and he believed he had to participate in a certain number of extracurricular activities satisfied the subjective element of the test to establish coverage for injuries sustained while he was windsurfing during the picnic), *and Wilson v. Workers' Comp. Appeals Bd.*, 239 Cal. Rptr. 719, 721 (Ct. App. 1987) (holding that police officer's testimony that he believed he had to keep in shape to stay on a special emergency unit

12. **RS** = Rule Statement
After the thesis comes the rule statement paragraph. As explained in section 4.2, this paragraph should start with the rule that requires the element or establishes the defense at issue. Here, the element is the reasonable expectancy requirement.
13. Next, the rule statement paragraph should provide the basic rule(s) that govern your issue. In this case, the author identifies the two-prong test that applies to the reasonable expectancy requirement. Section 4.2 discusses the use of connectors to link the rules in the rule statement paragraph. Here, the author uses the "mobile" approach to connectors. The two-prong test stated in the second sentence is linked to the starting-point rule stated in the first sentence through repetition of the key phrase in the starting-point rule—i.e., "reasonable expectancy."
14. **RE** = Rule Explanation
After the rule statement paragraph, you should have several paragraphs that explain and exemplify the meaning of the key rule(s). This is your rule explanation (RE).
The RE is organized into separate paragraphs, each of which presents and exemplifies a subrule (i.e., pattern, definition, policy consideration) that helps define the key rule(s) you state in your rule statement paragraph. The subrule is stated in the topic sentence of the paragraph. The topic sentence does not have to be the first sentence. Sometimes, as in this example, you may want to start with a transitional sentence or one that leads up to the specific subrule on which your paragraph will focus. Here, the discussion of *Ezzy* is focused on the specific point that "should" is enough.
15. A new topic sentence for a new RE paragraph.
16. This RE contains examples of parentheticals. Parentheticals are an effective method of providing additional examples to edify the subrule stated in the topic sentence without boring the reader with a bunch of "In case X, ..." sentences. A parenthetical should focus on the key fact(s), holding, and reasoning that relate to the subrule stated in the topic sentence of the paragraph. Here, for example, the topic sentence states that subjective belief is satisfied unless the employee did not feel obligated to participate. The parentheticals therefore focus on the key facts and holding regarding whether the employee truly felt obligated to participate. Parentheticals usually start with an *-ing* verb a court can perform, like "holding," "stating," "finding," etc. Do not start a new sentence within a parenthetical.

satisfied the subjective element to establish coverage for an injury sustained while running off-duty), *with City of Stockton v. Workers' Comp. Appeals Bd.*, 38 Cal. Rptr. 3d 474, 483 (Ct. App. 2006) (denying coverage to officer injured while playing basketball when he admitted he could satisfy the job requirement of keeping in shape without playing basketball).

17 Because the subjective element is easily met, most cases turn on the reasonableness of the employee's belief. Even as to this second element, however, courts have been liberal in RE3
18 their interpretation of "expectancy" and have found it satisfied based merely on "implied pressure" on an employee to participate in the activity at issue. *Smith*, 236 Cal. Rptr. at 254 ("[E]vidence demonstrating and proving express or implied pressure upon the employee serves to establish the objective reasonableness of that employee's belief that he or she
19 was required to participate."). The need to participate in the activity to remain or advance
20 in employment can establish implied pressure. *See Wilson*, 239 Cal. Rptr. at 722. In *Wilson*, a
21 police officer claimed coverage for injuries sustained while running on his own time off work premises. *Id.* at 719. Police officers in the plaintiff's special emergency unit were tested four times per year, and those in his age group had to run two miles in seventeen minutes. *Id.*
22 at 722. The court found that the plaintiff reasonably believed he had to keep in shape to
23 remain in the unit and was therefore entitled to coverage. *Id.* It reasoned that it would be "unrealistic" to think that such a requirement could be met without off-duty exercise. *Id.* The court similarly found implied pressure satisfied in *Kidwell v. Workers' Comp. Appeals Bd.*, 39 Cal. Rptr. 2d 540, 545-46 (Ct. App. 1995), where a police officer was injured while practicing long jumps at home, because testimony established that promotion and benefits were contingent on passing a long jump test and that passing the test required practice.

24 Implied pressure may be exacerbated when an employee is in a vulnerable position. RE4
See Smith, 236 Cal. Rptr. at 257 (noting that the employee was more vulnerable to pressure because as a temporary instructor, he needed to participate in extracurricular activities to

17. The first sentence of this RE transitions from the topic of the prior RE paragraph.
18. The second sentence then states an introductory rule that implied pressure satisfies the expectancy requirement.
19. The true topic sentence is actually the third sentence that defines implied pressure more specifically. The rest of the paragraph will prove this definition, i.e., that a need to participate to remain or advance in employment can establish implied pressure.
20. Here, the author is using a full case example to explain the implied pressure subrule. Notice that she starts with the basic nature of the case—here, the plaintiff's injury and what he is seeking (in this case, workers' compensation coverage).
21. Next, she relates the key facts relating to the topic of this particular paragraph—implied pressure.
22. Next, she states the holding on the issue at hand—reasonable expectancy was established.
23. And lastly, she states the reasoning. In this example, the reasoning was pretty sparse. Often, it will take a few sentences to get out all of the court's reasons for its holding on the point the paragraph is addressing.
24. The topic sentence for this RE is about vulnerability of position as a factor in reasonable expectancy. Notice that the author here uses a case, *Ezzy*, that she also used earlier in the memo on a different topic. Because you should be organizing your RE by subrule and not by case, you may end up using the same case in different paragraphs as in this sample memo. When reusing a case, avoid repetition. For example, this author's earlier reference to *Ezzy* is in a paragraph devoted to the subjective belief test (refer to the paragraph that goes with Annotation 14). In that earlier paragraph, the author related the basic nature of the case (law clerk injured while playing on softball team), the holding on subjective belief, and the court's reasoning (the clerk's statement under oath that she felt she should play in the game). Here, in the second reference to *Ezzy*, the author does not repeat that the clerk was injured in the game. She assumes this knowledge because it was related earlier. Here, she focuses on the holding (reasonable belief), facts (the client's position as a law clerk) and reasoning (law clerk would naturally feel pressure from partner) relevant to the topic of this paragraph (vulnerable position as a factor in reasonable belief).

better his chances of being rehired); *Ezzy*, 194 Cal. Rptr. at 95 (finding that a law clerk's belief that her participation in a softball game was expected was reasonable based in part on the pressure a law clerk would naturally feel when urged to participate in a softball game by a partner at the firm).

RE5 In addition to evidence of pressure on an employee to participate in an activity, evidence that the employer sponsored or encouraged participation and benefited from the activity can establish reasonable expectancy. Employer involvement and benefit can establish indirect encouragement by the employer that changes the voluntary nature of the activity and, therefore, requires coverage of resulting injuries. *Ezzy*, 194 Cal. Rptr. at 95. For example, in finding reasonable expectancy in *Ezzy,* the court pointed to evidence that the firm provided tee shirts and refreshments at the games and held a special banquet for participants. *Id.* The court also noted the benefit to the firm from increased morale. *Id.* Employer encouragement and benefit similarly played a large role in securing coverage in *Smith*, 236 Cal. Rptr. at 257-58 (relying on the school's role in planning the picnic at which the employee was injured including its collection of permission slips, advertisement of planning meetings, and payment for refreshments; the benefit of the picnic to the school through improved teacher-student relationships; and the school's general encouragement of teacher participation in extracurricular activities), and *Wilson*, 239 Cal. Rptr. at 722 (relying on the benefit to the police department from the ability of the employee's specially trained unit to handle situations too extreme for its standard force). 25

RE6 Sponsorship or encouragement, however, must be linked to the specific activity at issue. An employer's encouragement of general fitness, without any encouragement of the specific activity at issue, does not establish reasonable expectancy. For example, in *City of Stockton*, the employer required employees to remain fit, but employees did not undergo any specific fitness tests. *City of Stockton*, 38 Cal. Rptr. 3d at 483. The basketball game that caused the employee's injuries was off-premises, impromptu, and not known to, much less encouraged by, the employer. *Id.* The court held that the employee could not reasonably believe his participation in such a game was expected. *Id.* at 483-84. The court explained that a general expectation of fitness does not lead to coverage for any activity the employee chooses to fulfill that expectation. *Id.* at 483. To allow such broad coverage would be contrary to the intent of the legislature to exclude coverage for injuries that are only remotely connected to employment. *Id.* at 479, 483; *see also Taylor v. Workers' Comp. Appeals Bd.*, 244 Cal. Rptr. 643, 645 (Ct. App. 1988) (finding no reasonable expectancy where employer informed employees that only approved fitness regimens would be entitled to coverage and employee's basketball game was not part of an approved regimen). 26 27

25. This RE starts with a transitional sentence to connect to the prior RE. The topic sentence follows: "Employer involvement . . . can establish . . ."

26. The preceding paragraphs focus on what can establish reasonable expectancy. This paragraph focuses on when reasonable expectancy is lacking. The separation of positives (what can satisfy the element) and negatives (what is insufficient) often works well as a way of organizing RE paragraphs. However, it is not the only option. Do not feel that you must separate positives and negatives or that you must do positives before negatives.

27. This discussion of *City of Stockton* is a well-developed case example. Notice that the facts come first followed by the holding (no reasonable belief) and the reasoning. The author takes two sentences to explain the reasoning. She not only explains that an employer's general encouragement of exercise does not lead to coverage but also provides the broader policy reason behind this finding (it would be contrary to legislative intent to cover remotely connected injuries). The broader policy will later be helpful to his conclusion (refer to Annotation 37).

(28) Moreover, merely condoning an activity does not create a sufficient connection to employment to warrant liability. *See Tensfeldt v. Workers' Comp. Appeals Bd.*, 77 Cal. Rptr. 2d 691, 698 (Ct. App. 1998) (denying coverage for city employee's basketball injury when employees were allowed but not encouraged to play basketball at a city gym); *Todd v. Workers' Comp. Appeals Bd.*, 243 Cal. Rptr. 925, 927 (Ct. App. 1988) (denying coverage for employee's basketball injury when employer did nothing to encourage the game other than allow employees to install a hoop on the premises using some of the employer's material). RE7

(29) Based on the case law explained above, a court would be likely to find coverage in this (30) case. Gator's subjective belief that he was expected to play paddleball can be established by his testimony that he thought he needed to play to advance in the company. His use of (31) the word "needed" even more clearly demonstrates a belief in expectancy than did Ezzy's use of the word "should." *Ezzy*, 194 Cal. Rptr. at 92. Moreover, unlike the employee in *City of Stockton*, Gator never admitted that paddleball was optional. Therefore, Gator should be able to establish the requisite subjective belief. A1

(32) Gator can also establish that his belief was reasonable. Evidence of implied pressure is strong. Like the vulnerable positions of the employees in *Smith* and *Ezzy*, Gator's proba- (33) tionary status made him particularly susceptible to pressure. Moreover, playing paddleball with Randolph was necessary to advance in the job. Randolph invited Gator to play while complimenting his job performance and expressing a desire to see continued successes. The coupling of a discussion of job performance with an invitation to play paddleball justifies Gator's impression that paddleball and advancement in the company were related. Indeed, Randolph admitted that she uses paddleball games as an opportunity to discuss business with employees. Therefore, by turning down paddleball, an employee would necessarily be turning down an opportunity to discuss business with the Director. No ambitious employee A2

28. The author does not provide a full case example in this paragraph. Sometimes, when you are merely establishing a point of law (here, that an employer's tolerance of a certain activity does not make the employer liable for injuries that result from the activity) and the point is one that does not require factual detail to illustrate, parentheticals will suffice. See section 4.3.3.4.
29. **A** = Application
    This is the transition sentence from RE to application of the rules to the case at hand.
30. After the transition sentence, you should state your first point. Here, the author's first point is that Gator subjectively believed his participation was expected.
31. Notice that the author does not merely say that "needed" is similar to "should." An analogy must explain the importance of the similarity to the rules. Here, the author explains that "needed" conveys a belief that participation is expected.
32. The author will present two points on the objective reasonableness test. In this paragraph, she argues that Gator faced implied pressure to participate in the game. In the next paragraph, she establishes that the employer sponsored the activity. Notice that each paragraph has a topic sentence that states the point it will make. Notice also that the points the author is making in application correspond to the subrules she identified in RE. It should be clear in each paragraph of application which subrule you are applying. Repeating the same key terminology in application that you use in RE helps accomplish this consistency. Here, the author uses "implied pressure" just as she uses "implied pressure" in RE3. And in the next paragraph, she uses "sponsorship" just as she uses "sponsorship" in her RE5.
33. The two points the author makes in this paragraph correspond to the two subrules she earlier establishes on "implied pressure"—vulnerability of position and testimony that participation was necessary to remain or advance in the job. The first point about position is relatively straightforward. The author merely has to tie Gator's probationary status to the pressure factor. However, the second point about advancement is more complex. Notice the depth of the author's analysis of this second point. She takes facts from the case file and explains how they demonstrate that paddleball was tied to advancement in the job. Rather than just stating which facts are similar to the precedent cases, the author explains the relevance of the similarities to the subrule she is applying in this paragraph (advancement).

would refuse such an invitation. Just like it would have been unrealistic to think that the police officers in *Wilson* and *Kidwell* could have passed their employers' fitness tests without training, it would be unrealistic to think that Gator would have the same opportunity to advance if he turned down one-on-one time with Randolph on the paddleball court. The possible adverse effect of a refusal on Gator's advancement justifies his feeling of pressure.

A3 In addition, Fitness Functions sponsored and benefited from the paddleball games. 34
Fitness Functions went beyond the *Ezzy* employer's provision of shirts and refreshments at softball games. Fitness Functions built a court on the premises and provided all necessary supplies — even sneakers and exercise clothes. This sponsorship of paddleball supports Gator's belief that his participation was expected. In addition, like the *Ezzy* employer, Fitness Functions benefited from employee participation in the recreational activity. Randolph believed that paddleball increased morale. It also enabled Randolph to foster her relationships with her employees much like the picnic improved teacher-student relationships in *Smith*. Fitness Functions' sponsorship of and benefit from paddleball distinguish this case from *City of Stockton* and *Taylor*, where the employers encouraged physical fitness in general but not the specific injury-causing activities, and from *Tensfeldt* and *Todd*, where the employers merely condoned the injury-causing activities.

A4 Fitness Functions will need to argue that the pressure to play paddleball does not rise to 35
the level of expectancy. The company can distinguish *Wilson* and *Kidwell* because in those
COUNTERARGUMENT cases, employees had to train to pass required fitness tests. Fitness Functions employees 36
did not need to play paddleball to satisfy an express job requirement. *Ezzy* can also be distinguished because in that case, a partner directly urged the law clerk to play by telling her "we'll see you" at the next game. *Ezzy*, 194 Cal. Rptr. at 92. In this case, by contrast, Randolph merely invited Gator to play. Moreover, no one with supervisory authority, including Randolph, ever suggested that employees should play paddleball. Although a coworker once advised Gator that he should play, she did not have supervisory authority and therefore cannot be considered to have been speaking as a representative of the company. Finally, Fitness Functions can argue that unlike participation in extracurriculars in *Smith*, paddleball was not an overt aspect of employee evaluations. In sum, Fitness Functions can argue that expectancy should require more than a mere sense that participating in the activity will help get an "in" with the supervisor. Personal one-on-one time always helps advance a career. If the mere desire to become closer with a supervisor

34. This application paragraph is devoted to the sponsorship/encouragement and benefit factors. In RE, the author devotes three paragraphs to these factors—the first covers what can prove sponsorship/encouragement and benefit, the second establishes that merely condoning is not encouragement, and the third establishes that the encouragement must be tied to the specific activity. Here, in application, the author addresses each subrule and in the same order. Sometimes, you may not be able to address subrules in the exact order you use in RE. For example, one factor may relate only to your counterargument. However, when possible, apply subrules in the same order you present them in RE. The consistency helps the reader follow your organization.

35. Here, the author turns to counterarguments. The first sentence clearly transitions from the support for her conclusion to counterarguments by starting with "Fitness Functions will need to argue ..." You always need a transition sentence before your counterarguments. Signaling whose arguments you are presenting can be an effective transition, as in this example.

36. If the author stopped here, she would have identified but not explained the counterarguments. In a legal research memo, counterarguments deserve as much attention as the support for your conclusion because your analysis is supposed to be balanced to enable the reader to make an intelligent decision about how to proceed in the case. Here, for example, the rest of the paragraph explains how the listed differences from *Wilson*, *Kidwell*, and *Ezzy* support denial of coverage.

were sufficient, a supervisor could never invite an employee to play golf without worrying that a resulting injury would be subject to workers' compensation coverage.

(37) The response to these arguments is that more is present in this case than a mere desire to get an "in" with the supervisor. Randolph's use of paddleball as an opportunity to discuss business with her employees transformed a recreational activity into a work-related activity. Paddleball was a necessary step toward advancing in the company and, therefore, a reasonable expectancy of the job. If Gator had any doubt that paddleball and advancement are connected at Fitness Functions, that doubt would have been erased by Randolph's comments about his job performance, which were uttered in the same breath as her invitation to play paddleball. Moreover, as discussed above, Fitness Functions encouraged employees to play paddleball by building a court on its property and providing equipment and clothes. These facts demonstrate a substantial connection between participation in paddleball and employment at Fitness Functions and, therefore, should be enough to entitle Gator to coverage. A5 REBUTTAL

CONCLUSION (38)

For the reasons explained above, Gator has a good claim for coverage and should therefore submit an application for adjudication with the Workers' Compensation Appeals Board. C

37. Now, the author turns to rebuttal of the counterarguments. Notice again the use of a transition. Like counterarguments, rebuttals require a transition because you are changing gears. The transition here is "The response to these arguments is . . ."

A rebuttal should do more than merely repeat prior points. Instead, it should point out the weaknesses in the counterargument (e.g., "more is present in this case than a mere desire to get an 'in' with the supervisor") and explain why the counterargument is not persuasive (here, all of the facts recited by the author in this paragraph "demonstrate a substantial connection between participation in paddleball and employment at Fitness Functions"). Broad policies and rules can often be helpful in making rebuttals because they bring the reader back to the most fundamental and important principles. Here, for example, the reader points to "substantial connection" to distinguish the case from the type of remote connection the court in *City of Stockton* said the legislature did not intend to cover. (Refer to Annotation 27.)

38. The conclusion should usually be very brief. Think of it as a period at the end of a sentence. Its purpose is mostly to let the reader know you are finished.

SAMPLE B. ONE-TRRRAAAC LEGAL RESEARCH MEMORANDUM WITH BRIEF ANSWER (NO ANNOTATIONS)

To: Sylvia Artoon, Senior Deputy District Attorney

From: Junior Associate

Date: November 22, 2010

Re: Geraldo Savonarola Case

FACTUAL BACKGROUND

This office has charged Geraldo Savonarola with burglary for his use of a stolen ATM card to obtain cash from an ATM kiosk adjacent to the victim's bank.

The ATM card that Savonarola stole belonged to Eloise Abelard. Savonarola had been dating Abelard for several months and was living with her at the time of the incident. Abelard saw Savonarola steal her card and called her bank to deactivate the card. She was, however, too late, and Savonarola had already used the card to withdraw $300 from Abelard's account.

Savonarola made the withdrawal from an ATM kiosk at Abelard's bank. The kiosk and the bank are adjacent but share only one wall. The kiosk's other three walls and its ceiling jut out from the shared wall. The kiosk has two doors: one unlocked door opens to the outside and another locked door opens into the bank through the shared wall. The bank manager told our investigators that the purpose of the kiosk was to provide some protection for customers using the ATM. He stated, "We figured that even without a lock, the doors are a deterrent [to theft]." Although the bank manager usually asks loiterers to leave the kiosk, he has occasionally permitted noncustomers to wait for the bus in the kiosk during off-hours.

Abelard reported the theft shortly after it occurred. The police arrested Savonarola the same day at his place of employment. The bank's security video shows Savonarola entering the kiosk and using an ATM card to obtain cash on the day in question. The bank's log also confirms the withdrawal from Abelard's account.

ISSUE STATEMENT

Did Savonarola "enter" the bank so as to be guilty of burglary when he walked into the ATM kiosk adjacent to the bank to use a stolen ATM card to withdraw money from the ATM machine given that the kiosk was completely enclosed and shared a wall with the bank but had no lock on the external door and did not share a roof with the bank?

BRIEF ANSWER

Yes. Although Penal Code section 459 requires an "ent[ry]" into a "building" to support a burglary charge, we can establish that Savonarola entered the bank when he entered the ATM kiosk. The relevant case law establishes two key principles. First, a structure's outer boundary includes any element that encloses an area into which a reasonable person would believe he could not enter without permission. Second, the potential for violence that can occur when a person interferes with another's possessory interest in a building warrants the higher penalties that a burglary charge carries. Both principles support a burglary charge in this case. A reasonable person would understand that permission was needed to enter the ATM kiosk, and Savonarola's act carried a potential for violence because he might have resorted to violence to escape the kiosk if detected or customers might have resorted to violence to stop him from escaping.

ANALYSIS

We can establish that Savonarola entered a building and therefore committed burglary when he entered the bank kiosk and used the victim's ATM card to withdraw money from her bank account.

To establish burglary under California law, the prosecution must establish that the defendant "enter[ed]" a "building" "with the intent to commit . . . larceny or felony." Cal. Penal Code § 459 (West 2004). The entry requirement distinguishes burglary from other theft crimes by emphasizing interference with the possessory interest of a building's occupants. *People v. Davis*, 958 P.2d 1083, 1089 (Cal. 1998). As explained by the California Supreme Court, the higher penalties burglary charges carry "are based primarily upon a recognition of the . . . danger that the intruder will harm the occupants in attempting to perpetrate the intended crime or to escape and the danger that occupants will in anger or panic react violently to the invasion." *Id.* Because burglary is based on the dangers inherent in an intrusion, "'[t]he ultimate test of whether a burglarious entry has occurred must focus on the protection the owners or inhabitants of a structure reasonably expect.'" *People v. Valencia*, 46 P.3d 920, 924 (Cal. 2002) (quoting *People v. Nible*, 247 Cal. Rptr. 396, 399 (Ct. App. 1988)).

Even the "slightest partial entry" of the outer boundary of a building constitutes an entry. *Id.* at 925. Consistent with the "ultimate test" that the California Supreme Court adopted in *Valencia*, a building's outer boundary includes any element that encloses an area into which a reasonable person would believe that a member of the general public could not pass without authorization. *Id.* at 926. In *Valencia*, the court found that the defendant had entered a house when he removed a window screen with a screwdriver even though he did not successfully open the window. *Id.* at 927. The court reasoned that a screen window announces that intrusion is unauthorized. *Id.* The court also noted that an element of a structure need not offer physical protection to be considered part of the building's outer boundary. *Id.* at 926. "[W]hat matters is not whether a reasonable person would believe that a given element of a building provides some physical protection against unauthorized intrusion, but simply whether a reasonable person would believe that a member of the general public needed authorization to pass beyond it." *Id.* at 926-27. The court noted with approval a prior holding that "'even an open door . . . affords some expectation of protection from unauthorized intrusion because reasonable persons understand the social convention that portals may not be crossed without permission.'" *Id.* at 926 (quoting *Nible*, 247 Cal. Rptr. at 399).

The outer boundary of a building also includes any integral part of the structure of the building. *People v. Franco*, 250 P. 698, 699 (Cal. Ct. App. 1926). In *Franco*, the defendant stole shoes from showcases that were located on the external walls of a shoe store along a stairway that led from the sidewalk down to the store. *Id.* at 698. The court stated that with respect to the types of structures it covers, the burglary statute "has the very broadest significance and meaning and is very comprehensive." *Id.* at 699. The court noted that the roof of the building covered the showcases and therefore concluded that the showcases were "part of the store proper." *Id.*

On the other hand, if the defendant's act does not invade the possessory interest of a building's occupants, then the stiffer penalties under the burglary statute are not justified. *Davis*, 958 P.2d at 1089. In *Davis*, the defendant submitted a forged check to a drive-up check-cashing facility by inserting it into a chute in the window of the facility. *Id.* at 1084. Although previous cases had found entry based upon the slightest intrusion into the air space of a building, the court stated that courts must "establish reasonable limits as to what constitutes an entry . . . for the purposes of the burglary statute" to avoid expanding the statute to "absurd proportions." *Id.* at 1087. In determining the appropriate limits, the court considered the interest sought to be protected by the burglary statute. *Id.* at 1088. The statute was originally intended to protect the sanctity of a person's home. *Id.* Although it has since been expanded by the legislature to cover other buildings, it is still "based primarily upon a recognition of . . . the danger the intruder will harm the occupants in attempting to perpetrate the intended crime or to escape and the danger that the occupants will in anger or panic react violently to the invasion." *Id.* at 1089. These dangers exist only when the defendant has invaded the possessory interest of a building's occupants. *Id.* The court analogized the insertion of the forged check into the window chute to mailing a forged check to a bank, inserting a stolen ATM card into an ATM, and returning library books through a chute and concluded that none of these acts violate an occupant's possessory interest. *Id.* at 1089-90. Therefore, they do not constitute entry under the burglary statute. *Id.* at 1090. By contrast, in *Valencia*, the court concluded that removing the window screen did carry the potential for violence because a homeowner would be just as likely to react violently to removal of the screen as to penetration of the window itself. *Valencia*, 46 P.3d at 927.

Consistent with the case law discussed above, Savonarola should be found guilty of burglary. Under *Valencia*, the bank's outer boundary included the ATM kiosk because it was an enclosed area into which a reasonable person would believe that a member of the public could not pass without permission. Like a door or window, the kiosk affords protection from unauthorized intrusions. Indeed, the bank representative stated that the reason the bank built the kiosk was to protect customers from theft. It does not matter that the external door of the kiosk does not lock. As the court explained in *Valencia*, even an unlocked door creates an expectation of protection because social norms preclude crossing such portals without permission. *Valencia*, 46 P.3d at 926. The bank representative confirmed that the bank did have this expectation. Specifically, he stated, "We figured that even without a lock, the doors are a deterrent." Because the bank reasonably expected the kiosk to offer protection from unauthorized intrusion, the "ultimate test" for entry is satisfied.

Moreover, the kiosk was an integral part of the structure of the bank. Just as the casements in *Franco* were part of the store proper, the kiosk was part of the bank proper. Like the casements, the kiosk was attached to one of the exterior walls of the building. Giving the statute its broadest interpretation, as directed by the court in *Franco*, the court should conclude that when Savonarola entered the kiosk, he entered the bank.

Savoranola may argue that *Valencia* is distinguishable because members of the public reasonably believed they *could* enter the kiosk without permission. The bank representative stated that he has occasionally permitted noncustomers to wait for the bus in the kiosk. The bank's failure to assert a possessory interest over the kiosk by asking loiterers to leave arguably removes any expectation of protection from intrusion the bank and its customers could otherwise reasonably expect. The absence of such an expectation is significant under *Davis*. *Davis* explained that the limits of the burglary statute should be based on the underlying rationale for the criminal sanction it imposes — the danger posed by the entry into an area reserved for only certain occupants. 958 P.2d at 1089. Because the kiosk was not reserved for customers, neither Savonarola nor the bank's representatives and customers would be likely to resort to violence in connection with his entry. Therefore, the underlying rationale for the high penalty associated with burglary arguably does not apply.

Savonarola may also argue that the kiosk was not an integral part of the bank's structure because unlike the casements in *Franco*, the kiosk did not share a roof with the bank.

Savonarola's arguments are likely to fail. Although the bank's efforts to reserve the kiosk for customers were not consistent, the bank representative stated that he "usually" asks loiterers to leave. Therefore, the bank did assert its possessory interest in the kiosk. Moreover, no court has suggested that a building's owner forfeits his possessory interest merely by tolerating uninvited guests.

The court should also reject the argument that Savonarola's entry into the kiosk did not carry a risk of violence. *Davis* is distinguishable because the defendant did not enter any part of the building; he merely inserted a check in a window chute. Here, Savonarola walked into the kiosk. Unlike the check, Savonarola's entry into the kiosk implicates the rationale behind the criminal sanction for burglary. Once Savonarola passed through the kiosk door, he was in a confined space. Had someone guessed that Savonarola was using a stolen card and confronted him, he might have resorted to violence to escape. The potential for violence was the same as if he entered the bank lobby and used the ATM card to withdraw money at the teller's window, an act that would clearly fall within the burglary statute. Therefore, the purpose behind the burglary penalties does not warrant a different result in this case.

Finally, the attempt to distinguish *Franco* should also fail. Although the casements happened to share a roof with the shoe store in that case, the court's focus was on the physical and functional connection between the casements and the store. Here, the kiosk shared a wall with the bank; it was no less integral to the bank than were the casements to the shoe store in *Franco*.

CONCLUSION

For the reasons explained above, we have a good chance of successfully prosecuting Savonarola for burglary.

SAMPLE C. TRRRAAAC BY HEADING LEGAL RESEARCH MEMORANDUM

To: Supervising Attorney

From: Junior Associate

Date: October 20, 2006

Re: Gator v. Fitness Functions; Coverage of Recreational Activities

---

FACTUAL BACKGROUND

Mark Gator is seeking workers' compensation coverage of an injury he sustained while playing paddleball with his supervisor after work on a court in his employer's parking lot.

Gator works for Fitness Functions, a company that sells fitness equipment to health clubs, hotels, and spas. Fitness Functions has a paddleball court in its parking lot. It built the court to attract Gator's supervisor, Joyce Randolph, who was a famous racquetball player, to her current position as Director of Marketing and Sales. Randolph uses the court to play with employees and clients. She thinks paddleball is a good way to get to know her e mployees, boost morale, build team spirit, and keep employees in shape. The company provides paddles, balls, sneakers, and exercise clothes to "make[] it easy" for employees to play.

Randolph saw Gator leaving from work one day as she was heading to play in the court. She complimented Gator on bringing in a new client, expressed her desire to see continued successes from him, and invited him to play with her later in the week. Gator responded that he would check his schedule and get back to her.

Gator, a sales employee working under Randolph, had only recently been hired and was still on probationary status at the time. Despite reservations about playing with Randolph because she was "very good and extremely competitive," Gator agreed to play because he "wanted to be on her good side" and felt he "needed to play." In making this decision, he considered what a coworker had once told him: she felt playing with Randolph had helped her advance in the company by giving her an "in," and Randolph often discussed business while playing with her.

During his game with Randolph, Gator hit himself with his paddle. He filed for workers' compensation coverage for his resulting injuries. The company denied coverage. Gator is now considering filing an application for adjudication with the Workers' Compensation Appeals Board.

ISSUE STATEMENT

To establish workers' compensation coverage for injuries he sustained during an after-hours game of paddleball with his supervisor, can Gator show that:

1. His testimony that he felt he "needed" to play paddleball with his supervisor adequately proves that he subjectively believed his participation was an expectancy of his employment; and

2. His belief was reasonable because although no one ever suggested he needed to play, his supervisor invited him to play during a conversation about his job performance, a coworker had once told him that playing paddleball with the supervisor had helped her advance in the company, and the company supplied the equipment in the hope that the game would boost morale, foster team work, and keep employees fit?

ANALYSIS

1 Gator is entitled to coverage because paddleball was a reasonable expectancy of his employment with Fitness Functions. Labor Code section 3600, subdivision (a)(9), excludes from workers' compensation coverage injuries arising from "voluntary participation in any off-duty recreational, social, or athletic activity not constituting part of the employee's work-related duties, except where these activities are a reasonable expectancy of, or are expressly or impliedly required by, the employment." Cal. Labor Code § 3600(a)(9) (West 2003). The exception for activities that are a reasonable expectancy of employment applies when (1) the employee subjectively believes participation in the activity is expected; and (2) the employee's belief is objectively reasonable. *Ezzy v. Workers' Comp. Appeals Bd.*, 194 Cal. Rptr. 90, 93 (Ct. App. 1983). Gator's paddleball game with his supervisor meets this standard for two reasons. First, Gator believed that participation was expected by his boss. Second, his belief was reasonable because Fitness Functions created implied pressure for its employees to play paddleball and encouraged and benefited from its employees' participation. UMBRELLA

A. Subjective Belief

Gator's testimony that he felt he needed to play paddleball with Randolph satisfies the subjective belief requirement. T

Subjective belief is satisfied by an employee's professed belief that participation was required. Indeed, a belief that one *should* participate is sufficient. In *Ezzy*, for example, a law clerk was injured while playing on her firm's softball team. 194 Cal. Rptr. at 91. She testified that because the team did not have enough female players to satisfy the league's rules, she felt she "should" play when a partner handed her a tee shirt and game schedule and said, "At the next one, we'll see you there." *Id.* at 92. The court found her statement under oath was sufficient to establish her subjective belief of expectancy. *Id.* at 96. RE1

Failing the subjective belief requirement seems to be a risk only when the employee did not truly feel obligated to participate. *Compare Smith v. Workers' Comp. Appeals Bd.*, 236 Cal. Rptr. 248, 254-55 (Ct. App. 1987) (holding that deceased teacher's wife's testimony that teacher went to a picnic because his department head asked him to, he felt he had a "responsibility" to go, and he believed he had to participate in a certain number of extracurricular activities satisfied the subjective element of the test to establish coverage for injuries sustained while he was windsurfing during the picnic), *and Wilson v. Workers' Comp. Appeals Bd.*, 239 Cal. Rptr. 719, 721 (Ct. App. 1987) (holding that police officer's testimony that he believed he had to keep in shape to stay on a special emergency unit satisfied the RE2

1. The umbrella should include general rules that are relevant to all sections of the analysis. The umbrella should stay broad and, therefore, will have only a rule statement and no rule explanation. Notice that this umbrella paragraph sets up the headings by identifying the two tests that then become the two major divisions of the analysis (subjective belief and reasonableness).

subjective element to establish coverage for an injury sustained while running off-duty), *with City of Stockton v. Workers' Comp. Appeals Bd.*, 38 Cal. Rptr. 3d 474, 483 (Ct. App. 2006) (denying coverage to officer injured while playing basketball when he admitted he could satisfy the job requirement of keeping in shape without playing basketball).

[A] [C] Based on the case law explained above, Gator's subjective belief that he was expected to play paddleball can be established by his testimony that he thought he needed to play to advance in the company. His use of the word "needed" even more clearly demonstrates a belief in expectancy than did Ezzy's use of the word "should." Moreover, unlike the employee in *City of Stockton*, Gator never admitted that paddleball was optional. Therefore, Gator should be able to establish the requisite subjective belief.

B. Reasonableness of the Belief

[UMBRELLA] Gator can also establish that his belief that his participation was expected was reasonable. [2] Courts have been liberal in their interpretation of "expectancy" and have found it satisfied based merely on "implied pressure" on an employee to participate in the activity at issue. *Smith*, 236 Cal. Rptr. at 254 ("[E]vidence demonstrating and proving express or implied pressure upon the employee serves to establish the objective reasonableness of that employee's belief that he or she was required to participate."). In addition, an employer's indirect encouragement of the activity may change the voluntary nature of the activity and therefore may warrant coverage of the resulting injuries. *Ezzy*, 194 Cal. Rptr. at 95. In this case, Gator has evidence to support both implied pressure and indirect encouragement and, therefore, can satisfy the reasonableness requirement.

1. Implied Pressure to Participate

[T] Gator can establish implied pressure to play paddleball based on his vulnerable status as a probationary employee and the strong connection between paddleball and job advancement at Fitness Functions.

[RE1] A need to participate in the activity to remain or advance in employment may establish implied pressure. *See Wilson*, 239 Cal. Rptr. at 722. In *Wilson*, a police officer claimed coverage for injuries sustained while running on his own time off work premises. *Id.* at 719. Police officers in the plaintiff's special emergency unit were tested four times per year, and those in his age group had to run two miles in seventeen minutes. *Id.* at 722. The court found he reasonably believed he had to keep in shape to remain in the unit and was therefore entitled to coverage. *Id.* It reasoned that it would be "unrealistic" to think that such a requirement could be met without off-duty exercise. *Id.* The court similarly found implied pressure satisfied in *Kidwell v. Workers' Comp. Appeals Bd.*, 39 Cal. Rptr. 2d 540, 545-46 (Ct. App. 1995), where a police officer was injured while practicing a long jump at home, because testimony established that promotion and benefits were contingent on passing a long jump test and that passing the test required practice.

[RE2] Implied pressure may be exacerbated when an employee is in a vulnerable position. *See Smith*, 236 Cal. Rptr. at 257 (noting that the employee was more vulnerable to pressure

2. Another umbrella ("mini-umbrella") is needed for Section B to introduce the rules that set up the two subdivisions 1. (implied pressure) and 2. (indirect encouragement). Like the umbrella for the entire memo, this umbrella includes only a rule statement and no rule explanation.

because as a temporary instructor, he needed to participate in extracurricular activities to better his chances of being rehired); *Ezzy*, 194 Cal. Rptr. at 95 (finding that a law clerk's belief that her participation at the softball game was expected was reasonable based in part on the pressure a law clerk would naturally feel when urged to participate in a softball game by a partner).

[A1] Evidence of implied pressure is strong in Gator's case. Like the vulnerable positions of the employees in *Smith* and *Ezzy*, Gator's probationary status made him particularly susceptible to pressure. Moreover, playing paddleball with Randolph was necessary to advance in the job. Randolph invited Gator to play while complimenting his job performance and expressing a desire to see continued successes. The coupling of a discussion of job performance with an invitation to play paddleball justifies Gator's impression that paddleball and advancement in the company were related. Indeed, Randolph admitted that she uses paddleball games as an opportunity to discuss business with employees. Therefore, by turning down paddleball, an employee would necessarily be turning down an opportunity to discuss business with the Director. No ambitious employee would refuse such an invitation. Just like it would have been unrealistic to think that the police officers in *Wilson* and *Kidwell* could have passed their employers' fitness tests without training, it would be unrealistic to think that Gator would have the same opportunity to advance in the company if he turned down the opportunity for one-on-one time with Randolph on the paddleball court. The possible adverse effect of a refusal on Gator's advancement justifies his sense of pressure.

[A2 COUNTERARGUMENT] Fitness Functions will need to argue that the pressure to play paddleball does not rise to the level of expectancy. The company can distinguish *Wilson* and *Kidwell* because in those cases, employees had to train to pass required fitness tests. Fitness Functions employees did not need to play paddleball to satisfy an express job requirement. *Ezzy* can also be distinguished because in that case, a partner directly urged the law clerk to play by telling her "we'll see you" at the next game. In this case, by contrast, Randolph merely invited Gator to play. Moreover, no one with supervisory authority, including Randolph, ever suggested that employees should play paddleball. Although a coworker once advised Gator he should play, she did not have supervisory authority and therefore cannot be considered to have been speaking as a representative of the company. Finally, Fitness Functions can argue that unlike participation in extracurriculars in *Smith*, paddleball was not an overt aspect of employee evaluations. In sum, Fitness Functions can argue that expectancy should require more than a mere sense that participating in the activity will help get an "in" with the supervisor. Personal one-on-one time always helps advance a career. If the mere desire to become closer with a supervisor were sufficient, a supervisor could never invite an employee to play golf without worrying that a resulting injury would be subject to workers' compensation coverage.

[A3 REBUTTAL] The response to these arguments is that more is present in this case than a mere desire to get an "in" with the supervisor. Randolph's use of paddleball as an opportunity to discuss business with her employees transformed a recreational activity into a work-related activity. Paddleball was a necessary step towards advancing in the company and, therefore, a reasonable expectancy of the job. If Gator had any doubt that paddleball and advancement are connected at Fitness Functions, that doubt would have been erased by the coupling of Randolph's invitation with comments about his job performance. These

C facts demonstrate a substantial connection between participation in paddleball and employment at Fitness Functions and, therefore, should entitle Gator to coverage.

2. Indirect Encouragement of the Activity

T Gator can also establish indirect encouragement of paddleball by Fitness Functions in light of the company's involvement in and benefit from the activity.

RE1 Employer involvement and benefit can establish indirect encouragement by the employer that changes the voluntary nature of the activity and, therefore, requires coverage of resulting injuries. *Ezzy*, 194 Cal. Rptr. at 95. For example, in finding reasonable expectancy in *Ezzy*, the court pointed to evidence that the firm provided tee shirts and refreshments at the games and held a special banquet for participants. *Id.* Employer encouragement and benefit similarly played a large role in securing coverage in *Smith*, 236 Cal. Rptr. at 257-58 (relying on the school's role in planning the picnic at which the employee was injured including its collection of permission slips, advertisement of planning meetings, and payment for refreshments; the benefit of the picnic to the school through improved teacher-student relationships; and the school's general encouragement of teacher participation in extracurricular activities) and *Wilson*, 239 Cal. Rptr. at 722 (relying on the benefit to the police department from the ability of the employee's specially trained unit to handle situations too extreme for its standard force).

RE2 Sponsorship or encouragement, however, must be linked to the specific activity at issue. An employer's encouragement of general fitness, without any encouragement of the specific activity at issue, does not establish reasonable expectancy. For example, in *City of Stockton*, the employer required employees to remain fit but did not undergo any specific fitness tests. *City of Stockton*, 38 Cal. Rptr. 3d at 483. The basketball game that caused the employee's injuries was off-premises, impromptu, and not known to, much less encouraged by, the employer. *Id.* The court held that the employee could not reasonably believe his participation in such a game was expected. *Id.* at 483-84. The court explained that a general expectation of fitness does not lead to coverage for any activity the employee chooses to fulfill that expectation. *Id.* at 483. To allow such broad coverage would be contrary to the intent of the legislature to exclude coverage for injuries that are only remotely connected to employment. *Id.* at 479, 483; *see also Taylor v. Workers' Comp. Appeals Bd.*, 244 Cal. Rptr. 643, 645 (Ct. App. 1988) (finding no reasonable expectancy where employer informed employees that only approved fitness regimens would be entitled to coverage and employee's basketball game was not part of an approved regimen).

RE3 Moreover, merely condoning an activity does not create a sufficient connection to employment to warrant liability. *See Tensfeldt v. Workers' Comp. Appeals Bd.*, 77 Cal. Rptr. 2d 691, 698 (Ct. App. 1998) (denying coverage for city employee's basketball injury when employees were allowed but not encouraged to play basketball at a city gym); *Todd v. Workers' Comp. Appeals Bd.*, 243 Cal. Rptr. 925, 927 (Ct. App. 1988) (denying coverage for employee's basketball injury when employer did nothing to encourage the game other than allow employees to install a hoop on the premises using some of the employer's material).

A The evidence in this case demonstrates company sponsorship of and benefit from the paddleball games. Fitness Functions went well beyond the *Ezzy* employer's provision of tee shirts and refreshments at softball games. Fitness Functions built a court on the premises and provided all necessary supplies — even sneakers and exercise clothes. Also, like the *Ezzy* employer, Fitness Functions benefited from employee participation in paddleball through increased morale. Moreover, paddleball enabled Randolph to foster her relationships with her employees. This benefit to work relationships is similar to the improved teacher-student relationships the court pointed to in *Smith* and, therefore, helps justify coverage of Gator's injury. Notably, unlike the employers' mere encouragement of general physical fitness in *City of Stockton* or *Taylor*, Fitness Functions encouraged and benefitted from paddleball specifically. Moreover, the great degree of encouragement discussed above distinguishes this case from *Tensfeldt* and *Todd*, where the employers merely condoned the activity at issue. Based on Fitness Functions' involvement in and benefit from the paddleball games on its property, Gator's injuries from the paddleball game fall within the scope of workers' compensation coverage. C

CONCLUSION

For the reasons explained above, Gator has a good claim for coverage and should therefore submit an application for adjudication with the Workers' Compensation Appeals Board.

SAMPLE D. TRRRAAAC LEGAL RESEARCH MEMORANDUM

To: Patrick O'Malley

From: Junior Associate

Date: November 16, 2011

Re: Hilary Lysander; Unauthorized Practice of Law in California

---

FACTUAL BACKGROUND

Our client, Hilary Lysander, lives and works as a licensed attorney in New York. Lysander is not licensed to practice law in California. The Attorney General of California has brought charges against her for violating California Business and Professions Code section 6125 by allegedly providing Derek Ptolemy with legal advice regarding California law without a license to practice in this state.

Ptolemy, an acquaintance of Lysander's from college, solicited advice from her regarding the lease of property he owns in California because he knew Lysander had done some landlord-tenant work in law school. Their contact regarding the lease consisted of several e-mails exchanged between Lysander in her New York office and Ptolemy in California. Because she used her work account, Lysander's e-mails all contained her job title, "Associate," in the signature block. In addition to the e-mails, Lysander and Ptolemy discussed the lease over lunch in California on two occasions.

In his first e-mail to Lysander, Ptolemy explained that he had run into an old friend in New York who had reminded him of Lysander and provided her contact information. He then explained that he was in the process of leasing his property in California and asked Lysander whether she had "a form residential lease" that she could send him. Lysander was pleased to hear from her law school friend and decided to help him. She spent approximately ten minutes searching for a standard lease agreement for Ptolemy and then sent one to him via e-mail. In her e-mail, Lysander told Ptolemy that the form she was attaching "should serve your purposes." She also remarked, "My law firm would charge you $60 for that. But we won't tell them. Just buy me lunch, and we'll call it even."

After Ptolemy and his tenant filled out the lease form, he e-mailed the completed lease back to Lysander. Ptolemy asked Lysander to review the lease for "any big problems." Subsequently, via e-mail, Lysander replied, "It looks okay to me." She wrote, "At this point, I think I've put in enough work on this to warrant upscaling our lunch. How about that fancy French place across the street from my firm's office? They have the best wine list in town!"

Shortly thereafter, Lysander's law firm sent her to work in its California office for a few days. While she was in California, Ptolemy and Lysander met for lunch. During lunch, Ptolemy informed Lysander that he had collected a security deposit from his tenant, but he had not cashed the check yet. Lysander failed to advise Ptolemy that, under a local ordinance, he needed to deposit the check in an interest-bearing account.

Over the next five months, Ptolemy and Lysander had little contact apart from some "chit chat" by e-mail. Then, an issue arose between Ptolemy and his tenant. The tenant was moving out, and Ptolemy discovered that her dog had damaged the property. Ptolemy e-mailed Lysander to explain the dispute and to ask her whether he could retain his tenant's deposit to cover the damage. Lysander replied via e-mail, "Keeping the deposit seems reasonable." Lysander also explained that she would be in California in a few days and suggested Ptolemy buy her lunch again. She offered to review the lease over lunch to see what it said about the deposit.

Ptolemy and Lysander did indeed meet for lunch. Lysander reviewed the lease and did not alter her original advice regarding the deposit. Thereafter, Ptolemy cashed the deposit check and refused to turn the money over to the tenant. Because Ptolemy retained the deposit, his tenant, an elderly woman, was not able to secure the assisted living arrangement that she urgently needed. She complained to the authorities, and Ptolemy was investigated. He suffered great stress in the course of the investigation.

ISSUE STATEMENT

Did Lysander engage in the unauthorized practice of law when she (1) provided a form lease to Ptolemy for his California property; (2) reviewed and approved his completion of the form; and (3) advised him that he could keep his tenant's security deposit to cover damages caused by the tenant's dog?

ANALYSIS

Lysander's actions did constitute the unauthorized practice of law in California and thus violated section 6125 of the California Business and Professions Code. Her assistance was sufficiently particularized to Ptolemy's needs and specialized in nature to be considered the practice of law. Moreover, Ptolemy relied on her advice to his detriment. T

Section 6125 of the California Business and Professions Code states: "No person shall practice law in California unless the person is an active member of the State Bar." Cal. Bus. & Prof. Code § 6125 (West 2003). The prohibition against the unauthorized practice of law was designed to safeguard the public by ensuring that legal services are provided only by qualified individuals. *Birbrower, Montalbano, Condon & Frank v. Superior Court*, 949 P.2d 1, 5 (Cal. 1998), *superseded by statute on other grounds*, Cal. Civ. Proc. Code § 1282.4 (West 2007 & Supp. 2011); *People v. Landlords Prof'l Servs.*, 264 Cal. Rptr. 548, 551 (Ct. App. 1989). The practice of law includes not only courtroom appearances but also "'"legal advice and counsel" and "the preparation of legal instruments and contracts by which legal rights are secured."'" *Baron v. City of Los Angeles*, 469 P.2d 353, 357 (Cal. 1970) (quoting *People v. Merchants' Protective Corp.*, 209 P. 363, 365 (Cal. 1922), *superseded by statute on other grounds*, Cal. Bus. & Prof. Code § 6160 (West 2003)). RS

The above definition of the practice of law is met when assistance goes beyond mere clerical functions and is tailored to the particularized needs of a client. *Landlords Prof'l Servs.*, 264 Cal. Rptr. at 553. In *Landlords*, an eviction services business, Landlords Professional Services (LPS), assisted clients in the preparation, filing, and resolution of unlawful detainer RE1 actions. *Id.* at 548-49. The court explained that a service like LPS would not be engaging in the practice of law if it merely "made forms available for the client's use, filled the forms in at the specific direction of the client, and filed and served those forms as directed by the client." *Id.* at 553. Similarly, the court concluded that providing a detailed manual on unlawful detainer actions would not be the practice of law. *Id.* On the other hand, any advice on a client's specific case would cross the line and become the practice of law. *Id.* Ultimately, the court held that LPS had engaged in the practice of law. *Id.* First, the court noted that the service had advertised that it "accomplished evictions" and invited prospective clients to "[c]all & talk" to its representatives about eviction procedures. *Id.* The court found that these advertisements "implie[d] its eviction services were not limited to clerical functions." *Id.* The court further noted that although an eviction may not appear to be a difficult procedure, it is still a "legal procedure carried out before a court with specific legal requirements for its accomplishment." *Id.* In addition, LPS addressed the "specific problems and concerns of its clients" during personal interviews. *Id.* For example, an employee advised a client that "it was unlawful to turn off the utilities to [the client's] rental" property. *Id.* Other cases have similarly clarified that while making forms available for clients may not constitute the practice of law, exercising judgment by selecting the right form to fulfill a client's specific needs does. *In re Anderson*, 79 B.R. 482, 485 (Bankr. S.D. Cal. 1987) (holding that a bankruptcy typing service engaged in the unauthorized practice of law when it used information from client interviews to select and prepare bankruptcy schedules); *People v. Sipper*, 142 P.2d 960, 962 (Cal. App. Dep't Super. Ct. 1943) (holding that defendant had practiced law illegally when he advised a client to execute a trust deed to secure a loan), *overruled on other grounds by Murgia v. Municipal Court*, 540 P.2d 44, 54 (Cal. 1975).

A1 In our case, Lysander's assistance with Ptolemy's lease was not merely clerical. She did not merely make forms available to Ptolemy but rather selected the appropriate lease form for his particular needs. She searched for a *residential* lease specifically because he had told her he was leasing a residence. She also searched for a *California* lease because she knew his property was in California. Therefore, her provision of the lease alone involved the practice of law as did the selection of forms in *Sipper* and *Anderson*. However, her assistance did not end with the provision of the lease. She also reviewed the lease once it was completed. The review of the completed lease could have had only one purpose — to double-check Ptolemy's adaptation of the form to his particular situation. Finally, Lysander's decision to advise Ptolemy that he could keep the tenant's deposit to cover the damage caused by her dog was even more clearly particularized to Ptolemy's circumstances. Ptolemy described the damage. Lysander even reviewed the lease again. Her advice, therefore, was informed by this specific information. She was not merely providing generalized instructions on landlord-tenant law. Under *Landlords*, advice so particularized to the specifics of a client's case involves the practice of law. 264 Cal. Rptr. at 553.

RE2 Another relevant factor in determining when assistance becomes the practice of law is the context in which the assistance is provided. Acts are more likely to involve the practice of law if they are undertaken with an aura of legal expertise. In *Landlords*, the company argued that defining the practice of law to include all legal advice could lead to the absurd result of prohibiting advice between friends on legal matters. 264 Cal. Rptr. at 554. Without disagreeing that prohibiting advice between friends would be an absurd application of the statute, the court found that the hypothetical raised by LPS was too far from the facts of the case to be a concern. *Id.* The court again pointed to the advertisements published by LPS that suggested it could offer expertise on evictions. *Id.* at 553. In addition, one of its other employees handed out business cards that identified him as "Counselor." *Id.* The court found that because of the "aura of expertise" LPS had created, clients would be likely to view any advice offered by LPS as legal advice and would "undoubtedly" rely on the advice "perhaps to their serious detriment." *Id.* The court declined to limit the definition of the practice of law in a manner that would make the statute inapplicable "to situations in which the public requires protection." *Id.* at 554.

A2 COUNTERARGUMENT

Lysander could argue that she did not offer her advice with an "aura of expertise." To the contrary, she specifically informed Ptolemy that she was not an expert on landlord-tenant law and suggested she "might not be the right person" to offer advice. She therefore attempted to dissuade Ptolemy from relying on her advice. Moreover, the contacts between Lysander and Ptolemy arguably raise the hypothetical dismissed as irrelevant in *Landords*: advice on legal matters between friends. The court did not reject the contention that such an application of the statute would be absurd. The tenor of the communications between Lysander and Ptolemy suggest Lysander was offering her assistance merely as a friend. She disclaimed expertise. She joked about lunches as a perk of her advice. She used casual language that she would not use with a client. Imposing criminal penalties on Lysander for advising her former acquaintance in this context seems extreme.

A3 REBUTTAL

However, these arguments are not likely to prevail. First, Lysander's advice carried an "aura of expertise" just by virtue of her prior legal training in landlord tenant law. Her legal experience in this area was precisely the reason Ptolemy sought her advice. Although she attempted to disclaim expertise in her first communication with him, she presumably thought herself sufficiently qualified to offer the assistance; otherwise, she should have declined. Lysander should have realized that once she answered his legal questions, Ptolemy would be unlikely to seek out alternative legal counsel because he would assume [1] she felt sufficiently qualified to answer. Second, while Lysander might have viewed her advice in a casual manner, Ptolemy clearly did not. He did not initially seek her out merely to renew their friendship. Rather, he contacted her for legal advice specifically. Therefore, even if *Landords* can be read to have impliedly recognized that the statute was not designed to criminalize advice between friends, this is not such a case. Moreover, like *Landlords*, this case raises the need for public protection that underlies the statute. Ptolemy relied on her advice. As a result of his reliance, he faced an investigation by the authorities and suffered significant stress. The tenant was also a victim — an elderly woman unable, as a result of Ptolemy's retention of her security deposit, to afford the living assistance she urgently needed.

1. Note that the author bases the counterargument and the rebuttal on the same RE paragraph. Sometimes you will need separate REs for the counterargument and rebuttal. In the TRARARAC and TRATRATRAC structures, each RE would be placed right before its corresponding application—so, the RE that sets up the counterargument would come right before the counterargument, and the RE that sets up the rebuttal would come right after the counterargument and right before the rebuttal: supportive R, supportive A, counter R, counter A, rebuttal R, rebuttal A.

CONCLUSION

As analyzed above, Lysander engaged in the unauthorized practice of law in California under section 6125 of the Business and Professions Code when she advised Ptolemy on the specifics of his California residential lease.

SAMPLE E. APPELLEE'S BRIEF

IN THE

UNITED STATES COURT OF APPEALS

FOR THE NINTH CIRCUIT

CASE NO. 09-55923

UNITED STATES

v.

REYNA FORREST

BRIEF FOR THE APPELLEE

John Doe
Attorneys for the Appellee

Note: The table of contents and table of authorities have been omitted from this sample. See Sample F, Sample Appellant's Brief, for sample tables.

QUESTION PRESENTED

Did the investigation of Defendant, a member of the eco-terrorist organization EARTH, constitute outrageous government conduct so grossly shocking to the universal sense of justice to warrant dismissal of the indictment against her for bombing a car dealership, when the FBI, hoping to locate a suspected stockpile of explosives and ultimately disable the terrorist organization, authorized its informant to feign cooperation in the bombing to gain the trust of EARTH's leadership? 1

STATEMENT OF FACTS

Defendant Reyna Forrest was found guilty of terrorism charges based on her role in the bombing of Lee King Autos that led to the death of the dealership's owner, Mr. King. (R. at 59.) Defendant does not dispute that she set and detonated the bomb that killed Mr. King but contends, in this appeal, that the trial court erroneously denied her pretrial motion to dismiss the indictment on outrageous conduct grounds. (R. at 63.) The trial court denied her motion because it concluded that the government's conduct in investigating Forrest's eco-terrorist group was not so "shocking to the universal sense of justice" that it required dismissal of her indictment. (R. at 59.) 2

Defendant participated in the bombing as a member of an eco-terrorist organization 3
called EARTH. Although EARTH has one branch that engages solely in legal environmental 4
advocacy, it has another branch, called the Crusaders, that engages in violence and sabotage to further its agenda. (R. at 14-15.) The Crusaders are suspected of causing at least $30 million in damages and a number of deaths and accidents in Los Angeles alone. (R. at

1. In briefs, the QP should select rule language and key facts strategically. Here, for example, the author emphasizes the high burden the defendant must meet ("so grossly shocking..."). By contrast, the Sample Appellant's Brief (Sample F) emphasizes the overzealousness of police conduct.

   In addition, this QP emphasizes favorable facts and describes them in a way that predisposes the reader to find that the FBI acted appropriately (e.g., "hoping to locate a suspected stockpile..." and "disable the terrorist organization"). By contrast, the QP in the appellant's brief emphasizes the informant's role in the bombing and the lack of any prior violence by the defendant.
2. The first paragraph of the facts section needs to introduce the basic nature of the case (here, that Forrest was convicted of terrorism but claims outrageous government conduct bars her indictment). In addition, the first paragraph is often a good place for the procedural history, as in this example. Be sure to include the main procedural events in the action (here, the motion to dismiss, the court's denial of the motion, her conviction, and the appeal). Do not forget to include the appeal in the procedural history. Also, try to portray the procedural history in a light that is favorable for your position. Here, for example, the respondent emphasizes the reasons that the court denied the defendant's motion and defendant's admission of her role in the bombing. This helps predispose the court to reject the appeal. Take a moment to compare this to the first paragraph of the appellant's brief, which emphasizes the reasons for her motion and the court's disregard of those reasons.
3. Notice that this facts section starts by emphasizing the defendant's preexisting criminal activity in EARTH and the destructiveness of the group. This again helps predispose the court to reject her appeal. Take a moment to compare this to the second paragraph of the appellant's brief, which starts with her passion for environmental causes and legal advocacy.
4. This "although" clause is a subtle strategic choice. It downplays the legal efforts of the group by immediately emphasizing its violent activities.

5 15.) Defendant began as a member of the legal branch of EARTH but knowingly chose to join the Crusaders long before her role in the bombing for which she has been convicted. (R. at 40-41.) When Defendant joined the Crusaders, she knew it engaged in illegal acts of
6 sabotage including spray-painting SUVs, sabotaging logging operations, and tree-spiking. (R. at 41, 45.) Defendant thereafter engaged in two illegal acts: spray-painting "Gas-Guzzler" on an SUV and puncturing the tires of construction vehicles. (R. at 41.) Prior to her role in the present bombing, Defendant also attended a meeting where she learned how to build
7 an incendiary device, a task she claims she was "hopeless" at. (R. at 43-44, 46.) Although she claims not to have known that the Crusaders resorted to violence, she was aware that EARTH was suspected of a recent bombing at Camp Pendleton that killed an officer and wounded others. (R. at 15, 45.)

8 Eco-terrorist groups like Defendant's organization are the number one domestic threat in the United States. (R. at 14-15.) When the FBI first became aware of EARTH in 1994, it tried conventional methods of detecting EARTH's illegal activities. (R. at 15.) However, information about EARTH's planned terrorist acts was "tightly controlled and segmented," and continued to evade the FBI's detection. (R. at 15.) And as EARTH's organization grew, its structure became even more "complex and secretive." (R. at 15.) The FBI was unable to penetrate EARTH's leadership and had obtained arrests of only low-level EARTH members. (R. at 15.) Indeed, even the low-level perpetrators were difficult to catch. (R. at 15.) In hopes of disabling EARTH, the FBI initiated an undercover operation in 2001. (R. at 16.) The goal of the undercover operation was to penetrate EARTH's leadership and thwart EARTH's terrorist activities. (R. at 16.)

As part of its undercover operation, the FBI used informants to obtain information about EARTH's leadership and terrorist activities. (R. at 16.) Defendant's motion to dismiss was based entirely on the actions of one of these informants — Sid Morlandia. (R. at 59.) Morlandia was the FBI's most successful informant; he was the closest the FBI had ever come to penetrating EARTH's mid-level leadership in the nine years of its operation. (R. at 16, 18-19.) Morlandia's success in gaining the trust of EARTH's leadership was so crucial to the FBI's goals that the FBI continued to use him even after it began to suspect he might be

5. The same strategy is used here to downplay her prior legal activity and instead emphasize her role in the terrorist wing. Notice the use of the word "knowingly"— a strategic adverb to help paint a negative picture of the defendant.
6. The word choice here is strategic. Using "Defendant" instead of her name depersonalizes the defendant to the advantage of the prosecution. Do not use "Appellee" or "Appellant," however. Because the appellee and appellant vary (e.g., the defendant is not always the appellant), the appellate party designations can confuse the reader. If you want to use a party designation, use "Defendant" or "Plaintiff" or "the Prosecution" (in a criminal case). By contrast, the appellant's brief personalizes the defendant by using her name.
7. Another strategic "although" clause. Here, the author downplays Forrest's testimony that she did not know about the violence by juxtaposing it with other testimony that detracts from her credibility.
8. Topic sentences help the flow of your paragraphs and, in persuasive writing, have the added benefit of focusing your reader on the point you hope he or she will take away from the paragraph. Topic sentences in persuasive writing should favor your client's view of the case. Topic sentences in the facts section cannot state conclusions; they must state facts. However, they can paint a picture. The record pages cited here establish that eco-terrorism is the number one threat in the U.S. The insertion of the language "like Defendant's organization" helps subtly slant the facts in favor of the government. The rest of the paragraph should relate back to the topic sentence— here, the threat posed by EARTH.

misleading the FBI and that he might have participated in an arson in Sylmar. (R. at 18-19.) The FBI believed it could still get useful information from Morlandia while watching him [9] more closely to ensure his allegiance. (R. at 19.)

The FBI seemed to come closer to its goal of bringing down EARTH when, in May 2009, [10] high-level Crusaders selected Morlandia for possible promotion within the organization. (R. at 18.) However, to ensure his promotion, Morlandia had to successfully complete a [11] high-risk operation for EARTH. (R. at 30.) A high-ranking Crusader named Bishop Adhemar [12] ("Adhemar") instructed Morlandia to plan and execute a bombing of a car dealership. (R. at 30.) Adhemar also told Morlandia that he was to recruit Forrest to join the mission. (R. at 30.) Adhemar told Morlandia that both he and Forrest were being tested. (R. at 30.) The Crusaders planned to assess Morlandia based on his ability to motivate Forrest and plan the action. (R. at 30.) They also planned to use the mission to "see" what Forrest was capable of. (R. at 31.)

When Morlandia reported the conversation to the FBI, the FBI encouraged Morlandia to [13] carry out the assignment because it was a prime opportunity to earn the trust of the EARTH leadership and gather useful intelligence. (R. at 20, 31.) Moreover, the FBI had recently received information that EARTH was "planning something big" and had allegedly smuggled large amounts of explosives into Los Angeles. (R. at 19.) Learning the location or planned [14] purpose of these stockpiled explosives became the FBI's top priority and Morlandia was its "best shot." (R. at 19.) The FBI planned to intercept the bombing before it was executed and pretend to permit Morlandia's escape so that he could return to his undercover role in EARTH. (R. at 19.)

9. This paragraph contains an unfavorable fact about the FBI's continued use of Morlandia but manages to end on a favorable note that detracts from the significance of the bad fact. You want to try not to begin or end paragraphs with unfavorable facts. Of course, you must maintain a logical flow; you cannot place a random fact in the middle of a paragraph if it does not fit there. The key is figuring out what in the record could help detract from the bad fact.
10. Topic sentences help guard against the monotony of a strict chronology and enable strategic characterizations of the facts. Here, the topic sentence introduces the topic of the paragraph (the initiation of the bombing plan) and focuses the reader's attention on the connection between the bombing and the FBI's legitimate goals.
11. This paragraph now starts the chronology of pertinent events that continues to the end of the facts section. Paragraph breaks are inserted when moving on to a new event or topic. This paragraph covers EARTH's tapping of Morlandia for the mission that led to the Defendant's arrest.
12. This sentence is a subtle characterization of the facts to favor the government. The record states merely that Morlandia was told he was being considered for promotion and would be assessed during this mission. This sentence makes a logical connection that is not explicitly stated in the facts—that his promotion was tied to his success in planning the bombing.
13. This sentence is another example of characterizing the facts. The record just states that the FBI encouraged him to carry out the assignment and, separately, that the FBI hoped he would earn the trust of EARTH's leadership. This sentence connects those facts in a logical manner that supports the client. Juxtaposing facts in a logical and favorable manner is a key skill in drafting a subtly persuasive facts section.
14. Notice the selective use of quotes from the record in this and other paragraphs. Including quotations that make your client look good or the opponent look bad is a key method of painting a vivid picture that can help predispose the reader to your client's position. Choose favorable quotes that carry relevance to the issue(s) your brief will address.

To carry through with the plan, Morlandia contacted Defendant as instructed by Adhemar. (R. at 42.) Adhemar had told Morlandia that he would be monitoring his conversation with Defendant and assessing his efforts to recruit her. (R. at 42.) To demonstrate a commitment to the task, Morlandia attempted to motivate Defendant to participate through
(15) discussing the threats of global warming. (R. at 30.) Although Defendant hesitated at first, Morlandia's appeal to Defendant's fervor for environmental causes led her to "think that he was right" about the bombing. (R. at 42.) However, she declined to give an affirmative answer. (R. at 42.) Morlandia stopped the conversation at that point and called her back
(16) many hours later. (R. at 42.) Defendant expressed some lingering doubt. (R. at 42.) Knowing that Adhemar was monitoring their conversation, Morlandia said, "You do understand we cannot take chances with defectors." (R. at 42-43.) Defendant subsequently agreed to participate. (R. at 43.)

As instructed by Adhemar, Morlandia took the lead in planning the bombing. (R. at 30.) Morlandia attempted to get Adhemar to reveal the location of the suspected stockpile of explosives but failed. (R. at 43.) When Morlandia tried to get Adhemar to tell him where he could find explosives, Adhemar told him that he needed to obtain the necessary explosives on his own as part of EARTH's assessment of his ability to lead. (R. at 43.) Because the FBI wanted Morlandia to rise in the ranks in the hope of obtaining meaningful intelligence, it provided the necessary explosives to Morlandia. (R. at 43.) The FBI instructed Morlandia to keep the agency up to date so that it could ultimately intercept the bombing before the
(17) explosives were used. (R. at 44.) The FBI did not put any tracking device on Morlandia or the explosives, however, because it feared sacrificing his cover. (R. at 30.)

Defendant met Morlandia in advance of the bombing to train for the mission. (R. at 44.) She learned how to set and detonate the explosives. (R. at 44.) She also learned about the details of the plan. (R. at 44.) Then, on the night of the bombing, she drove to the storage facility where Morlandia had stored the explosives. (R. at 44.) She drove to the facility by herself, loaded the explosives into her car, and then drove to meet Morlandia. (R. at 44.) Morlandia knew the FBI planned to intercept the bombing; Defendant did not. (R. at 43.)

(18) In a surprising turn of events, Adhemar appeared at the rendezvous site where Defendant was to pick up Morlandia. (R. at 28-29.) At trial, Morlandia hypothesized that Adhemar appeared because he may have suspected that Morlandia was serving as an informant. (R. at 29.) In any event, Adhemar was carrying a gun and ordered Morlandia to change the target to another dealership. (R. at 29.) Morlandia feared he would be shot if he failed to comply or if he tried to escape to contact the FBI. (R. at 29.) So, he remained in the

15. Another strategic "although" clause. Here, the author downplays the bad fact that Morlandia overcame Forrest's hesitation by juxtaposing it with the more favorable fact that she was easily persuaded.
16. The phrase "many hours later" is strategic. By contrast, the appellant's brief uses the phrase "the same night." Both phrases are accurate, but they create different emphases that support the respective parties' positions.
17. The author includes an adverse fact about the FBI's failure to track the explosives but focuses the reader's attention on the FBI's legitimate reason for not using a tracking device.
18. Here is an example of using descriptive language to subtly slant the story in favor of the writer's client. Characterizing the change in target as a "surprising turn of events" is a fair characterization of the facts (which provide that the government was planning to intercept the bombing at the original planned location) and helps build sympathy for the brief's later arguments that the government did not act inappropriately.

car with Adhemar and Defendant as they drove to the new target. (R. at 29.) Upon arrival, Morlandia and Adhemar remained in the car as Defendant set the explosives. (R. at 43.) Defendant enthusiastically exclaimed, "This is for my daughter," before she planted the explosives. (R. at 44.) Once they drove away a safe distance, Defendant detonated the explosives. (R. at 44.)

Because of the last-minute change in the target, the FBI was unable to intercept the bombing. (R. at 20.) The agency apprehended Defendant only after the bombing killed the owner of the car dealership that Adhemar had chosen as the new target. (R. at 20, 44.)

STANDARD OF REVIEW

A trial court's decision to dismiss for outrageous government conduct is subject to de novo review. *United States v. Bogart*, 783 F.2d 1428, 1431 (9th Cir. 1986). 19

ARGUMENT

This Court should affirm the judgment because the government's efforts to infiltrate Defendant's terrorist organization did not violate fundamental fairness. 20

The trial court correctly denied Defendant's motion to dismiss the indictment because the government's conduct did not violate Due Process. 21

The possibility that the Supreme Court might "some day" bar a conviction when the government's conduct is far outside the bounds of decency, *United States v. Russell*, 411 U.S. 423, 431 (1973), has not yet been realized. In the thirty-nine years since *Greene v. United States*, 454 F.2d 783 (9th Cir. 1971), first dismissed an indictment on the ground that the government's excessive involvement in criminal activity violated the Due Process Clause, 22

19. The standard of review is not a rule relating to the issue but, instead, a procedural rule relating to the appellate court's proper role. Selecting the right standard of review can be a very big deal—critical to the outcome of the appeal. Attorneys must research it carefully and potentially spend some number of pages proving the standard that favors the client. Other times, the standard is clear and not debatable and can be established in a single sentence as in this example.
20. Your argument section should begin with an overall heading that states, in broad terms, the reason that your client should prevail. You might have two or more of these headings depending on how many issues you are addressing. However, this sample addresses only one issue (the outrageous conduct defense) and therefore has only one overall heading. The conclusion should be phrased in terms of the action by the appellate court you are seeking (affirmance or reversal) or perhaps as an assertion regarding the propriety of the trial court's actions (the trial court erred or the trial court correctly held). The reason should be broad enough to encompass all of your subheadings to follow.
21. The first sentence of the main umbrella (i.e., the thesis sentence) should state the result you are seeking (here, a holding that the trial court was correct) and the overarching reason (the government's conduct did not violate due process). The reason stated here must be broad enough to encompass all of your arguments.
22. This is the rule statement paragraph. In briefs, the RS paragraphs should be strategic. Carefully select the rules and quotations that are favorable to your position. Here, the appellee starts by emphasizing the absence of a Supreme Court decision applying the defense whereas the appellant's RS paragraph in Sample F opens by emphasizing the reasons for the defense (to prevent convictions based on improper police conduct).

23 no Supreme Court decisions and only five federal court decisions have ever dismissed an indictment or overturned a conviction on this ground. *United States v. Twigg*, 588 F.2d 373, 380 (3d Cir. 1978); *United States v. West*, 511 F.2d 1083, 1086 (3d Cir. 1975); *United States v. Gardner*, 658 F. Supp. 1573, 1579 (W.D. Pa. 1987); *United States v. Valdovinos-Valdovinos*, 588 F. Supp. 551, 558 (N.D. Cal. 1984), *rev'd*, 743 F.2d 1439 (9th Cir. 1985); *United States v. Batres-Santolino*, 521 F. Supp. 744, 753 (N.D. Cal. 1981); *see also United States v. Luttrell*, 889 F.2d 806, 813-14 (9th Cir. 1989) (remanding for further fact-finding relevant to the defendant's claim); *United States v. Bogart*, 783 F.2d 1428, 1438 (9th Cir. 1986) (also
24 remanding for further fact-finding). Dismissal of an indictment remains an extraordinary remedy reserved for only the most egregious conduct. *See Hampton v. United States*, 425 U.S. 484, 495 (1976) (Powell, J., concurring) (recognizing that government participation in crime "ordinarily will be fully justified in society's 'war with the criminal classes'" (quoting *Sorrells v. United States*, 287 U.S. 435, 453 (1932) (Roberts, J., concurring)). Indeed, the cases of
25 outrageous conduct are so rare that the Supreme Court has yet to approve or require a dismissal.

26 This is not one of the rare cases that require overturning an otherwise justified conviction. To the contrary, the government's efforts to infiltrate Defendant's terrorist organization meet the criteria of a five-factor test this Court has developed to protect the government from unfounded outrageous conduct claims. *United States v. Bonanno*, 852 F.2d 434, 437-38 (9th Cir. 1988). Moreover, none of the conduct on which Defendant relies warrants reversal. First, the government did not target Defendant for prosecution but, rather, properly set up an undercover operation designed to ferret out existing terrorists. Second, the government did not authorize or participate in any crimes. Third, the statements by the informant that Defendant claims led her to participate in the bombing were central to his assumed role as a member of Defendant's terrorist organization and, therefore, were not misconduct. Finally, the informant's unrelated and unauthorized crimes cannot be attributed to the government.

23. When lower courts have come to conflicting conclusions about the legal issue you are addressing, appellate courts appreciate an overview of what the lower courts have held with respect to the issue. Notice the strategic emphasis in this paragraph on the absence of a Supreme Court case and the small number ("only five") of cases that have applied the defense. By contrast, the appellant's brief focuses on the importance of the defense and the "several" cases that have applied it. Strategic word choice like "only five" v. "several" can have a significant impact on how the reader views your position.
24. The inclusion of the extraordinary remedy rule is strategic. The appellant's brief omits this statement and instead emphasizes that the defense is not merely theoretical but has actually been applied to reverse convictions.
25. This sentence has no citation because it is pointing out the absence of a case on point. Before making such a statement, you must be 100% confident that your research is exhaustive and has revealed no such case.
26. The main umbrella includes a "core theory" and a "roadmap." Ideally, the core theory provides a powerful statement that encompasses all of the points you will make in your brief. Here, the core theory (stated in the first sentence of this paragraph) is that the defense is rarely applied and that the conviction in this case was fully justified. It is also helpful if the core theory builds off of (i.e., transitions well from) your RS paragraph. Here, the core theory carries over the focus in the RS paragraph on how rarely the defense is applied.

    The core theory is followed by a "roadmap." The roadmap should correspond to your subheadings A., B., C., etc. (but do not include previews of your sub-subheadings 1., 2., 3., etc.—these are saved for the roadmaps in your mini-umbrellas under headings A., B., C., etc.). Notice how closely the language in the list matches the headings below. This consistency helps the reader understand the structure of your brief. Enumeration (first, second, etc.) also helps.

A. **The government's conduct satisfies a five-factor test developed by this Court to limit outrageous government conduct claims.** 27

The government's conduct in this case was permissible under a five-factor test developed by this Court to limit claims of outrageous government conduct.

A claim of outrageous government conduct is technically not a defense. *United States v. Williams*, 547 F.3d 1187, 1199 (9th Cir. 2008). Instead, the claim seeks to invoke the Due Process Clause of the United States Constitution to dismiss an otherwise justified conviction. *Id.* Accordingly, defendants asserting a claim of outrageous government conduct must meet a "high standard" of proof by demonstrating that the "government's conduct violates fundamental fairness and is 'shocking to the universal sense of justice mandated by the Due Process Clause.'" *Id.* (quoting *United States v. Gurolla*, 333 F.3d 944, 950 (9th Cir. 2003)). To keep claims of outrageous government conduct properly limited to "shocking" conduct, this Court has established five factors that help define "fundamental fairness." When these five factors are satisfied, the claim will fail: (1) the defendant was already involved in a continuing series of similar crimes, or the charged criminal enterprise was already in process at the time the government agent became involved; (2) the agent's participation was not necessary to enable the defendant to continue the criminal activity; (3) the agent used artifice and stratagem to ferret out criminal activity; (4) the agent infiltrated a criminal organization; and (5) the agent approached persons already contemplating or engaged in criminal activity. *Bonanno*, 852 F.2d at 437-38; *accord Williams*, 547 F.3d at 1199. 28

Under this test, Defendant's claim fails because (1) Defendant was already engaging in terrorist activity; (2) Defendant had the resources to complete the bombing without the government; and (3) the government's use of artifice and stratagem was necessary to take down Defendant's terrorist organization. 29

1. **At the time of her first contact with the government's informant, Defendant was an active member of a terrorist organization, and she had previously committed terrorist acts.**

Factors one, four, and five of the *Bonanno* test are satisfied in this case because at the time of her first contact with Morlandia, Defendant was an active member of EARTH, a criminal organization, and she had engaged in prior terrorist acts. 30

27. Headings A., B., C., etc. state specific reasons for the general conclusion stated in your overall heading. Here, the specific reason is that the conduct fails the five-factor test.
28. When a section A., B., C., etc. is going to be subdivided into subheadings as in this section, the heading A., B., C., etc. should be followed by an RS, thesis, and roadmap similar to the structure of the initial paragraph(s) under your main heading. Here, for example, the paragraph provides some broad rules relating to the topic of heading A. (the five-factor test that limits the defense). Then it ends with a thesis and roadmap (see next annotation).
29. This is the thesis and roadmap of points 1., 2., and 3. Notice how closely the language here tracks the headings below.
30. Sections that are not further subdivided, like this section 1., should start with a thesis. The thesis is usually just one sentence that states the point of the section. The sentence will look a lot like the heading under which it falls. However, you should try to change the wording a bit, as in this example, to avoid monotony.

(31) *Bonanno* does not require that the defendant was already planning the particular crime
(32) at issue prior to the government's involvement. As long as the defendant committed similar crimes in the past and was still engaged in an ongoing criminal enterprise at the time of her first contact with the government agent, factors one, four, and five are satisfied. *Williams*, 547 F.3d at 1201. In *Williams*, the court affirmed a conviction for a robbery that was initiated
(33) by government agents. *Id.* at 1192-93. The defendant had developed detailed plans to rob a bank with an "experienced crew" that he had used in prior robberies. *Id.* at 1191-93. The agents diverted the defendant from his plans to rob the bank by proposing a robbery of a fictitious drug stash house instead. *Id.* at 1192-93. The agents arrested the defendant when he showed up at the location where the stash house robbery was supposed to take place. *Id.* The court found that the initiation of the stash house robbery by the agents did not warrant reversal of the conviction in light of the defendant's past robberies and his existing plan to rob a bank with his "crew." *Id.* at 1200-01. The court rejected the defendant's argument that the defense should apply because the robbery of illicit drugs from the stash house was more serious than his planned bank robbery. *Id.* at 1201. The court found that this difference between the two otherwise similar plans was irrelevant to the defense. *Id.*
(34) Other cases have similarly rejected claims of outrageous conduct where the defendant had engaged in past crimes and continued to participate in a criminal organization. *See, e.g., United States v. Mayer*, 490 F.3d 1129, 1141 (9th Cir. 2007) (holding that the government's role in arranging defendant's travel was not outrageous conduct that would bar defendant's conviction for travel with intent to engage in illicit sexual conduct with minors where the FBI agent had met defendant at a conference of an organization that fostered sexual molestation of children and defendant had told an FBI agent that he had traveled to Thailand for sex in the past).

Like Williams, Forrest was engaged in a continuing series of crimes. Prior to meeting Morlandia, Forrest had spray-painted an SUV and punctured the tires of construction vehicles at a new mall construction site. (R. at 41.) Like the bombing of the Hummer dealer-
(35) ship, these prior incidents were acts of terrorism designed to intimidate the public to further the goals of EARTH. In *Williams*, the court found that a difference in degree does not detract

31. This is the first RE paragraph in the brief. All of your topic sentences should clearly favor your client's position. This topic sentence emphasizes that the defense should be denied when the defendant has committed similar crimes in the past and is still engaged in an ongoing criminal enterprise.
32. This is an inferred rule. *Williams* does not make this exact statement but does, as the case example demonstrates, fairly prove the truth of the inferred rule. Inferred rules are even more common in briefs than in research memos because it is more important in briefs to describe the law in a manner that supports your points.
33. Case examples should focus on the information about the case that supports your topic sentence. This paragraph is very long for a brief. This length is warranted here only because the *Williams* case was a crucial case on the issue. Later REs in this sample use only parentheticals.
34. This is an example of a bridging sentence to link the end of a full case example to additional parentheticals.
35. Prove your points in application paragraphs with a combination of the four tools discussed in Chapter 5 (comparison sentences, court reasoning, specific facts, and common sense). Here, the commonsense reasoning is that her prior acts were designed to intimidate the public. And the paragraph uses the *Williams* court's reasoning to explain away the difference in degree between her prior acts and the bombing. These points are tied to the first factor (a continuing series of crimes).

from the similar nature of crimes. *Williams*, 547 F.3d at 1201. Similarly, here, the increased [36] danger posed by the bombing does not make it dissimilar from her prior acts of terrorism. The first *Bonanno* factor is, therefore, met.

Moreover, Forrest was a member of a criminal organization that was planning criminal activity. She remained an active member of the terrorist branch of EARTH and had even attended a training session on how to construct a bomb. (R. at 43-44, 46.) Her ongoing [37] membership in EARTH was no different than Williams's ongoing relationship with his "experienced crew" or Mayer's continuing membership in a sex crimes group. Morlandia did [38] not approach an innocent citizen but, rather, merely infiltrated a terrorist organization and connected with Forrest as a member of that organization. There is no reason to believe that were it not for this mission, Forrest would have suddenly become a law-abiding citizen. To the contrary, her continued participation in EARTH's terrorist activities suggests she would have continued her criminal activity. Accordingly, the fourth and fifth *Bonanno* factors are [39] also met.

2. With the resources available to her through her terrorist organization, Defendant could have carried out the bombing without the involvement of the government.

Factor two of the *Bonanno* test is satisfied in this case because Forrest was capable of carrying out the bombing without the government's involvement.

In applying factor two, the courts have not solely focused on the government's [40] facilitation of the particular criminal act at issue. To the contrary, courts have declined to find outrageous conduct when the defendant was capable of committing similar crimes without the government's involvement even if the government facilitated the particular crime for which the defendant was tried. In *Williams*, for example, the stash house robbery [41] was fabricated by the government and, therefore, the exact criminal acts for which he was arrested would not have occurred but for the government's involvement. *Williams*, 547 F.3d at 1193-93. Nonetheless, the court concluded that the second *Bonanno* factor was satisfied because Williams was already planning a similar bank robbery with his "experienced crew." *Id.* at 1200.

36. The point here about a "difference in degree" is an example of an anticipatory rebuttal, a.k.a. "sneaky jab." The appellant's brief argues that the government led her to commit a violent act completely different in nature from her prior minor criminal acts. The appellee does not discuss this counterargument at all. Instead, in anticipation of the appellant's argument, this sentence goes right to the rebuttal.
37. Remember to check your comparison sentences for parallelism. Here, "relationship" matches "membership."
38. Here, the comparison is tied back to the legal rules. Remember to establish the relevance of the comparison by tying it to the conclusion you are trying to prove.
39. Each section should have its own wrap-up sentence.
40. Here is another sneaky jab. This sentence anticipates and rebuts the appellant's argument that the government facilitated the bombing by providing explosives Forrest could not have obtained on her own.
41. If you want to use a case in two different RE paragraphs, you do not need to repeat details you included in your first discussion of the case. Just add the details that are necessary to prove your topic sentence (here, that facilitation of the crime does not always result in dismissal).

42 Here, as a member of EARTH, Forrest had the ability to carry out bombings without the government's assistance. Although Forrest claimed she was "hopeless" at constructing bombs and had never obtained explosives for a prior EARTH operation (R. at 43-44), she was a member of an organization that the FBI believed had stockpiled large amounts of explosives (R. at 19), had carried out a bombing of army barracks (R. at 15), and had trained its members in the construction of explosives (R. at 24, 43.) Morlandia happened to be the person EARTH chose to plan the operation, but EARTH could have chosen someone else to carry out the mission with Forrest. The evidence regarding EARTH's activities suggests that Forrest's membership in EARTH would have enabled her to obtain explosives and carry out the bombing without Morlandia's assistance. Just as the government's initiation of and role in planning the stash house robbery did not bar Williams's conviction, Morlandia's role in planning the bombing should not bar Forrest's conviction. Rather, the second factor of the *Bonanno* test is satisfied based on Forrest's ability to carry out a bombing as a member of EARTH.

3. The government needed to use artifice and stratagem to thwart a suspected major attack by Defendant's terrorist organization.

Factor three of the *Bonanno* test is satisfied in this case because the government's conduct was devoted to infiltrating an existing terrorist organization and thwarting its planned criminal activity.

43 Certain crimes can be effectively thwarted only through the government's use of artifice and stratagem to infiltrate an organization and gain the trust of its members. *See Russell*, 411 U.S. at 432 (recognizing the necessity of infiltration of drug rings); *Bogart*, 783 F.2d at 1438 (finding that the use of artifice and stratagem to infiltrate a criminal organization is not outrageous conduct). Artifice and stratagem may legitimately include participation in the activities of the criminal organization and even provision of supplies. *See Russell*, 411 U.S. at 432 (stating that agents may offer valuable items that a drug ring requires in order to earn the trust of its members); *United States v. Winslow*, 962 F.2d 845, 849 (9th Cir. 1992) (holding that defendant's conviction for planning to bomb a gay bar was not barred by due process where, in an effort to infiltrate defendant's violent anti-homosexual organization, an undercover agent bought the defendant a gun, paid for the defendant's trip to the city of the planned attack, and paid for gunpowder the defendant used to construct the bomb); *United States v. Allen*, 955 F.2d 630, 631 (9th Cir. 1992) (rejecting outrageous conduct claim where government allowed dealer to sell illegal drugs and keep the proceeds in exchange for information on his customers and the manufacturing process); *United States v. Ahluwalia*, 807 F. Supp. 1490, 1497 (N.D. Cal. 1992) (finding that government did not violate due process when, in an effort to ferret out corruption, it provided real work permits in exchange for bribes).

42. Another sneaky jab. "Although" clauses are a great way to disclose an adverse point but immediately rebut it. The adverse point is in the "although" clause and then the rebuttal follows the comma.

43. Here is an example of an RE paragraph comprised solely of parentheticals. Use this approach for straightforward points that you do not expect will be debated and that are sufficiently simple and specific.

Here, all of Morlandia's interactions with Forrest were devoted to infiltrating EARTH and, more specifically, to gaining information regarding a suspected impending large-scale attack. The government hoped that through his role in planning the bombing of the car dealership, Morlandia would earn the trust of the leadership and eventually obtain intelligence regarding the location of EARTH's recent stockpile of explosives and planned attacks. (R. at 20.) The government planned to intercept the bombing before its fruition and secretly enable Morlandia's escape so that he could continue to earn the trust of the leadership. (R. at 20, 32.) Because the FBI authorized his role in planning the bombing to serve important investigative objectives, the third *Bonanno* factor is satisfied. Notably, his provision of the explosives is substantially similar to the undercover agent's provision of bomb materials that the court in *Winslow* concluded was not outrageous conduct. Moreover, since the FBI did not condone any actual criminal activity, its use of Morlandia was much less objectionable than the government's continued use of an illegal drug supplier in *Allen*.

Because all five *Bonanno* factors are satisfied in this case, the Court should affirm the judgment and uphold the conviction.

B. The government's conduct was not outrageous because it was designed to intercept active terrorists rather than to target Defendant for prosecution.

The government did not single out Defendant and pursue her conviction at all costs. (44) To the contrary, Defendant was drawn into the planned bombing by her own terrorist (45) organization.

Although courts have suggested that outrageous conduct may be established where (46) the government manufactured the crime from start to finish, *e.g., Bogart*, 783 F.2d at 1436, (47) courts have declined to bar convictions even when the criminal plan was entirely initiated and controlled by the government but was part of a general sting operation to which the defendant was drawn on his own accord. In *Morgan v. Robinson*, 156 F. Supp. 2d 1133, 1148 (C.D. Cal. 2001), for example, the court upheld a conviction even though the government initiated the crime and managed it from start to finish and even though the defendant had not engaged in similar crimes before. The defendant was convicted of soliciting lewd and lascivious conduct with an underage child after responding to an ad placed by the police department that offered "schoolgirl escorts." *Id.* at 1147. Defendant's conduct was limited to showing up at the time and place specified by the police. *Id.* Despite the evidence that the defendant had not previously planned to solicit an underage escort and the lack of any participation by the defendant in the planning of the crime, the court found that the police department's conduct was not outrageous. *Id.* at 1148. In reaching this conclusion, the court cited previous cases that had found the police could legitimately set up fictitious illegal

44. This is a nice example of a thesis that states the same point as the heading but uses different language to avoid monotony.
45. Because unlike section A., section B. is not subdivided, section B. does not need an RS or a roadmap.
46. Another sneaky jab "although" clause. Notice how the citation is handled. Chapter 19 discusses various options for handling the citations in these sneaky jab RE topic sentences.
47. The second part of this topic sentence introduces an inferred rule that detracts from the significance of the adverse rule contained in the "although" clause.

operations and place ads to catch those predisposed to the criminal activity at issue. *Id.* (citing *United States v. Mitchell*, 915 F.2d 521 (9th Cir. 1990), and *United States v. Johnson*, 855 F.2d 299, 304-05 (6th Cir. 1988)).

48 Sting operations aimed at a preexisting criminal organization do not offend the universal sense of justice. Indeed, they further justice because they are designed to protect the public by catching those predisposed to commit crime. *See Williams*, 547 F.3d at 1201 (stating that the fake robbery set up through the government's sting operation should be commended rather than condemned because it avoided harm to the public from the real robbery defendants would have otherwise committed). Accordingly, courts are less likely to reverse a conviction where the defendant's conduct reveals she was predisposed to the crime. In *Mitchell*, the government had created a sting operation to catch pedophiles. *Mitchell*, 915 F.2d at 524. As part of the sting operation, the government mailed unsolicited offers to suspected pedophiles for the purchase of child pornography and arranged purchases to obtain convictions. *Id.* The defendant was arrested when, in response to the government's solicitations, he paid for the purchase of pornography from the fictitious illegal operation. *Id.* at 523-24. In rejecting the due process claim, the court recognized that engineering criminal activity from start to finish may violate due process but found that even though the government had orchestrated the criminal enterprise, due process was not violated because the defendant willingly purchased the pornography without any pressure from the government. *Id.* at 526. The court distinguished *Greene* on the ground that in *Greene*, the police applied coercion to induce the defendant to commit the crime at issue. *Id.; see also Shaw v. Winters*, 796 F.2d 1124, 1125-26 (9th Cir. 1986) (rejecting outrageous conduct claim where government agent "took the lead" in offering to sell the defendant stolen food stamps and arranging the sales and where the defendant had not previously purchased stolen food stamps but was a willing purchaser once they were offered).

49 By contrast, the cases in which courts have reversed convictions on due process grounds involve not sting operations that target criminal organizations but the targeting of a specific individual without reason to suspect the individual is currently engaged in similar criminal activity. *See Twigg*, 588 F.2d at 381 (holding that government violated due process when it asked an informant to reestablish contact with an acquaintance who was not engaged in any illicit drug activity and agent thereafter "implanted the criminal design" in the defendant's mind and enabled him to carry it out); *West*, 511 F.2d at 1086 (reversing drug-related convictions where the defendant had not previously engaged in drug deals);

48. The three sentences at the start of this RE are an example of rule synthesis. In persuasive writing, be sure the synthesis is favorable to your position. Here, the connection between the importance of sting operations (stated in the first two sentences) and the predisposition factor (stated in the third sentence) was not stated explicitly in the cases. Instead, the author fit these concepts together in a logical manner that supports the appellee's arguments that the government's involvement in the bombing in this case was part of a sting operation and, therefore, not outrageous conduct.

49. This paragraph addresses the adverse authority by characterizing it in a way that helps distinguish this case. Taking down adverse authority in this way can be very effective in convincing the court to find in your client's favor. It only works, however, if you can take down all of your opponent's cases. There is no point in doing this if it leaves a confounding case that you cannot distinguish on some other basis.

Greene, 454 F.2d at 786 (reversing conviction where a government agent initiated contact with the defendant without any reason to suspect the defendant was then engaged in illegal activity); *Gardner*, 658 F. Supp. at 1576-77 (concluding that an agent violated due process when he "persisted over a period of time in inducing and persuading the Defendant to commit the crime in question with sole motive and intention of overcoming the obvious reluctance of the Defendant to commit the alleged crime in question"); *Valdovinos-Valdovinos*, 588 F. Supp. at 556 (finding that INS engaged in outrageous conduct when in the hope of catching and convicting transporters of illegal aliens, its agents told ineligible Mexican citizens they could lawfully cross the border in the hope of catching and convicting their transporters); *Batres-Santolino*, 521 F. Supp. at 751 (finding that due process was violated when rather than infiltrating an existing drug ring, government agent "persuaded defendants to create one"). When the government targets a specific defendant without reason to suspect he is engaged in criminal activity, the motive appears to be to secure a conviction rather than to protect the public from criminal activity. *Twigg*, 588 F.2d at 381 (stating that agent's conduct was offensive because it "generated new crimes by the defendant merely for the sake of pressing criminal charges against him when . . . he was lawfully and peacefully minding his own business"); *see also Bogart*, 783 F.2d at 1438 (finding that police conduct shocks the conscience in the "hopefully few cases where the crime is fabricated entirely by the police to secure the defendant's conviction rather than to protect the public from the defendant's continuing criminal behavior").

The Ninth Circuit explored the difference between a legitimate sting operation and the illegitimate targeting of an apparently innocent defendant in *Luttrell*. In *Luttrell*, the defendants were convicted of possession and trafficking of counterfeit credit card drafts in a scheme initiated by and planned primarily by an informant who was acting under government instructions. 689 F.2d at 807. There was no evidence that the defendants had engaged in any criminal activity in the past. *Id.* at 808 n.3. The court rejected the government's role in initiating and planning the scheme as a basis for reversing the conviction and remanded the case only for the court to consider whether the government had any basis to suspect that one of the defendants was involved in illegal activity prior to the informant's initiation of the crime. *Id.* at 811, 814. The court explained, "[w]e think that police officers violate constitutional norms when, without reasoned grounds, they approach apparently innocent individuals and provide them with a specific opportunity to engage in criminal conduct." *Id.* at 813. The court further distinguished between "[u]ndercover investigations aimed at known or suspected criminal operations," which have a "settled place in law enforcement," and "[o]perations directed at targets whom the police have no reason to suspect" which may "occasionally uncover evidence of a crime" but are inefficient and arbitrary. *Id.*

Here, Forrest's conviction is squarely within due process grounds for at least two reasons. First, she was caught as the result of a general undercover investigation that did not target her specifically but, instead, was aimed more widely at her known terror- 50

50. Additional roadmaps like this one can be great organizational tools for application paragraphs when you plan to make more than one point within the paragraph.

ist organization. Morlandia did not target Forrest and convince her to commit a crime for the purpose of obtaining her conviction. Rather, her conviction resulted from a general undercover operation designed to protect the public by thwarting the terrorist activities of her organization. The FBI set up the operation as a wide web to catch whatever criminal conduct came its way much like the sting operations in *Morgan*, *Mitchell*, and *Shaw*. Because it targeted a known criminal operation, the FBI's undercover operation has a "settled place in law enforcement." 689 F.2d at 813. Forrest became caught in the web because of her prior involvement in EARTH's terrorist activities. EARTH's leadership wanted Forrest to assist in the bombing to evaluate her worth to the organization. (R. at 31.) Thus, Forrest was targeted by her own criminal organization and not by the FBI. Morlandia's role in initiating and planning the bombing was designed to earn the trust of EARTH's leadership by demonstrating he could "motivate" (R. at 30); Forrest's conviction was not the goal (R. at 20). Therefore, this is not a case where the government got lucky and obtained a conviction in an otherwise arbitrary effort to induce innocent citizens to commit crimes.

Second, even if the facts had been different and Morlandia had selected Forrest himself, Forrest's active participation in a known terrorist organization made her an entirely appropriate target of the undercover operation. She was not "lawfully and peacefully minding [her] own business." *Twigg*, 588 F.2d at 381. Accordingly, Morlandia's role in approaching Forrest about the bombing and planning it does not warrant reversal of the judgment.

C. The government's conduct was not outrageous because the government did not plan to participate in any crimes.

The outrageous conduct claim should be rejected in this case because the government did not support or otherwise involve itself in any criminal activity.

51 The door left open by Justice Powell's concurring opinion in *Hampton* for an outrageous conduct claim was very narrow. While agreeing with the plurality opinion that the government does not commit outrageous conduct merely by supplying drugs to catch drug traffickers, the concurring opinion left open the possibility that government *over*-involvement in crime might constitute a due process violation. 425 U.S. at 495 (Powell, J., concurring). However, Justice Powell emphasized that government conduct would have to "reach a demonstrable level of outrageousness before it could bar conviction." *Id.* at 495 n.7. He noted the difficulty law enforcement faces in battling the trafficking of narcotics and the necessity for undercover operations to detect drug offenses and acknowledged that government participation in crime "ordinarily will be fully justified in society's 'war with the criminal classes.'" *Id.* (quoting *Sorrells*, 287 U.S. at 453 (Roberts, J., concurring)). The only hints dropped in the concurring opinion regarding when government involvement in crime would violate due process were a citation to *Greene*, 454 F.2d 783, and quotations from *United States v. Archer*, 486 F.2d 670, 676-77 (2d Cir. 1973). *Hampton*, 425 U.S. at 493 nn.3 & 4 ("'[i]t would be unthinkable, for example, to permit government agents to instigate

51. Section C. is another example of how to address adverse authority by characterizing it in a way that you can easily distinguish from your case. The REs will work together to establish that the defense should not apply where the government has merely staged false crimes rather than participated in real crimes.

robberies and beatings merely to gather evidence to convict other members of a gang of hoodlums'"; the courts should be "'extremely reluctant to sanction'" "participation in activities that result in injury to the rights of [] citizens") (quoting *Archer*, 486 F.2d at 676-77)).

Both *Archer* and *Greene* involved government participation in real crimes rather than government-staged crimes. In *Archer*, the defendant faced corruption charges after he fell into a trap set by law enforcement officials. *Archer*, 486 F.2d at 672-74. Officials had arrested an agent on phony charges in the hope that the agent would become a customer for corruption and thereby "some evidence of corruption would surface" in the New York criminal justice system. *Id.* at 672. In the course of staging the phony arrest, the government encouraged its agents to commit several crimes including falsification of records and perjury. *Id.* at 672-74. When the defendant took the bait, he was arrested on bribery-related charges. *Id.* at 672. The court ultimately dismissed the indictment on other grounds, but suggested that it otherwise might have found the government's conduct was sufficiently outrageous to dismiss the indictment. *Id.* at 677. The court pointed out that while the typical narcotics sting operation involves no criminal intent on the part of the government, in this case, the government involved itself in actual crimes. *Id.* at 675. By authorizing crimes that victimized the court, members of law enforcement, and the grand jury, the government had engaged in conduct more offensive than the mere inducement of the sale of narcotics to catch drug traffickers. *Id.* Similarly, in *Greene*, the government and its agent aided the defendant's unlawful bootlegging operation for over two-and-one-half years before finally arresting him. *Greene*, 454 F.2d at 786. One of the court's main reasons for dismissing the indictment on due process grounds was the government's "direct[] and continuous[]" involvement "over such a long period of time in the creation and maintenance of criminal operations." *Id.* at 787. *But see Williams*, 547 F.3d at 1201 n.11 (noting that the government agent's phony plan to rob a fictitious stash house did not "instigate a robbery or beating 'merely to gather evidence to convict'" the defendant but, instead, was designed to catch a dangerous group of robbers in a controlled sting operation).

Here, the government did not sanction any actual crimes. The government used Morlandia solely to gather intelligence necessary to thwart EARTH's activities. Although the government authorized Morlandia to plan the bombing of a car dealership, it planned to intercept the collaborators before they could plant the explosives. (R. at 20, 32.) Therefore, unlike the government officials in *Greene* and *Archer*, the FBI agents in this case did not participate in any criminal activity. Like the sting operation in *Williams*, the government's plan to intercept the bombing and arrest the conspirators was legitimately aimed at preventing rather than sanctioning criminal activity. The last-minute decision of EARTH's leadership to change the target and Morlandia's decision to carry out the bombing of the new target was not sanctioned by the government and, therefore, cannot support an outrageous conduct claim.

D. The government informant's responses to Defendant's initial hesitation were part of his assumed role as an active terrorist and, therefore, do not establish a due process violation.

Morlandia's conversations with Defendant regarding the bombing must be viewed in the context of his assumed role as an active terrorist. When viewed in this context, his statements did not require dismissal of the indictment.

52 Although "unwarranted physical, or perhaps mental, coercion" may shock the conscience, *Bogart*, 783 F.2d at 1438, the courts have recognized that undercover agents often must engage in "unsavory conduct," including the use of threatening language, to maintain their cover, *see Luttrell*, 889 F.2d at 812 (stating, "Undercover agents are actors. The success of their performance requires the delivery of lines appropriate to their characters. The agents' mere delivery of language alone . . . may be necessary to the investigation of established criminal activity."). Accordingly, courts have repeatedly rejected threatening language by an undercover agent as a ground to dismiss an indictment. *See, e.g., United States v. Emmert*, 829 F.2d 805, 812 (9th Cir. 1987). In *Emmert*, two government agents negotiated a drug deal with the defendant and some other accomplices. *Id.* at 807. When the deal failed to go through, one of the accomplices asked the undercover agents for some money up front and expressed concern that one of the agents was a policeman. *Id.* In response, one of the agents said, "Maybe we'll do the deal in an airplane and if something goes wrong, we'd have one parachute and guess who'd come down without one." *Id.* And, the other agent said she had three words for the defendant's accomplice, "R.I.P." *Id.* A few months later, the defendant was able to put the deal together and was arrested at the scene. *Id.* In rejecting these threats as a reason to dismiss the indictment, the court stated that "[e]xpress or implied threats may be warranted under certain circumstances" and "may not always constitute outrageous conduct." *Id.* at 811. The court concluded that the threats aimed at Emmert were "scarely more than bluster" and were "ordinary bargaining tactics in drug deals." *Id.* at 812. It further explained that "government agents may need to engage in such unsavory conduct to maintain their cover." *Id.* The court concluded that the threats were necessary to allay suspicions about the undercover agents. *Id.*; *see also United States v. McQuin*, 612 F.2d 1193, 1195-96 (9th Cir. 1980) (holding that agent's threat to kill defendant for failing to complete planned robbery did not violate due process when viewed in light of the "vulgarity and 'puffing' engaged in by all participants in the criminal venture"); *accord*
53 *United States v. Reynoso-Ulloa*, 548 F.2d 1329 (9th Cir. 1977). *But see Greene*, 454 F.2d at 786 (noting veiled threat by agent to pressure defendants into production of bootleg alcohol as one fact supporting dismissal of the indictment).

Morlandia's statement that EARTH would not "take chances with defectors" (R. at 42-43) was, like the threats in *Emmert*, "scarcely more than bluster." *Emmert*, 829 F.2d at 812. Indeed, the statement is much weaker than the fairly direct death threats uttered by the agents in *Emmert*, *Reynoso-Ulloa*, and *McQuin*. Moreover, just like an undercover narcotics agent, Morlandia needed to take on a certain persona to be believable as a mid-level member of a terrorist organization. Morlandia could have reasonably concluded that Forrest would become suspicious if he let her refuse the mission without any threat of retribution. He was merely delivering lines appropriate to his assumed role. This Court

52. Another sneaky jab. And another example of rule synthesis that reconciles case law in a way that favors the author's position.
53. Try to avoid the "but see" approach to handling adverse cases. It is not very effective. However, sometimes one confounding case seems to go against an inferred rule that is otherwise supported by the weight of case law. If you have no way of synthesizing that case but need to disclose it to avoid misrepresentation, the "but see" is your last resort.

cannot reverse the conviction on such attenuated grounds without risking significant interference with the success of necessary undercover operations.

E. The informant's unrelated crimes cannot establish outrageous government conduct because the government did not authorize them.

The government's decision to continue to use Morlandia as an informant despite its suspicion that he had participated in the Sylmar arson and may have been acting as a double agent did not constitute outrageous conduct. Use of criminals to catch worse criminals is a common, accepted investigative tactic.

Infiltration of a criminal organization often requires the use of criminals as informants. In *United States v. Simpson*, 813 F.2d 1462, 1469 (9th Cir. 1987), the government used a known heroin addict and prostitute as an informant to facilitate its investigation of a heroin dealer. When the defendant argued that the government's continued use of the informant despite her numerous arrests was outrageous conduct, the court responded, "We find no authority supporting the defendants' claim that the continued use of an informant known to be committing unrelated crimes without the government's urging or approval raises due process concerns." *Id.* at 1470. The court explained that it is "unrealistic" to expect law enforcement officers to "ferret out criminals without the help of unsavory characters." *Id.* Because the informant's illegal acts were "neither encouraged nor condoned" by the government, they did not constitute excessive government involvement in crime. *Id.* at n.9.

Accordingly, Morlandia's unrelated arson and other suspected terrorist activities cannot be the basis of an outrageous government conduct claim. To deprive law enforcement officials of the ability to use suspected terrorists as informants would cripple their efforts to combat terrorism. The lead FBI agent testified to the extreme difficulty faced by the FBI in its efforts to ferret out the leaders of this secretive, effective eco-terrorist group. (R. at 15-16.) It would be completely unrealistic to expect them to have any success in thwarting the group's activities without resorting to using its active members as informants.

Because the five *Bonanno* factors are satisfied in this case and none of the conduct on which Defendant relies is sufficiently outrageous to support the drastic remedy of dismissing the indictment, the judgment should be affirmed.

CONCLUSION

For the reasons explained above, all *Bonanno* factors are satisfied and the Court should affirm the judgment.

Dated: March 14, 2010

Respectfully submitted,

____

John Doe
Attorney for the Appellee

SAMPLE F. APPELLANT'S BRIEF FRAP 28 FORMAT

IN THE

UNITED STATES COURT OF APPEALS

FOR THE NINTH CIRCUIT

CASE NO. 09-55923

UNITED STATES

v.

REYNA FORREST

BRIEF FOR THE APPELLANT

John Doe
Attorneys for the Appellant

TABLE OF CONTENTS

Page

TABLE OF AUTHORITIES

CASES

JURISDICTIONAL STATEMENT

The Central District of California had jurisdiction over this case because the Defendant was charged with two federal crimes. 28 U.S.C. § 1331 (2006). A judgment and commitment order was entered on December 11, 2009. Defendant filed this appeal on December 21, 2009. This Court has jurisdiction over the appeal from the judgment pursuant to section 1291. 28 U.S.C. § 1291 (2006).

ISSUE STATEMENT

Are the dangers of overzealous police tactics that underlie the outrageous police conduct defense sufficiently implicated to warrant dismissal of the indictment against Ms. Forrest for her limited role in a car dealership bombing on due process grounds where an FBI informant used a veiled threat to recruit Ms. Forrest to participate in the bombing on which her charges are based, Ms. Forrest had no prior intention of participating in a violent crime and no history of violent criminal activity, and the informant planned the bombing, obtained the explosives from the FBI, trained Ms. Forrest, provided explicit directions under which she was acting at every stage of the operation, accompanied her to the crime scene, and waited to drive her away while she planted the explosives pursuant to his instructions?

STATEMENT OF THE CASE

The defendant, Reyna Forrest, has been convicted for the bombing of Lee King Autos. (R. at 59.) Before trial, she moved to dismiss her indictment on the basis of outrageous government conduct. (R. at 59.) In support of the motion, Ms. Forrest argued that she was coerced into participating in the bombing by a government informant named Sid Morlandia who manufactured the crime from start to finish, the government informant's sole motive was to obtain a conviction, and the FBI endangered the public. (R. at 51-52.) Without disagreeing that the government engaged in questionable conduct, the trial court declined to dismiss the indictment. (R. at 52.) Ms. Forrest now appeals her conviction on the grounds of outrageous government conduct. (R. at 59.)

Prior to her encounters with the government informant, Ms. Forrest pursued her passion for environmental causes solely through nonviolent advocacy. (R. at 39-40.) At age 18, Ms. Forrest witnessed the destruction of her hometown of Valdez, Alaska, due to the 1989 Exxon oil spill. (R. at 39.) Deeply affected by this experience, she joined an environmental organization called EARTH and eventually became the leader of the EARTH chapter at her college. (R. at 40.) The chapter engaged only in legal environmental advocacy. (R. at 40.) After college, Ms. Forrest worked for a nonprofit organization devoted to advocating for environmental protection laws. (R. at 39.) Then, one day, a male member of EARTH asked to meet her for dinner. (R. at 39.) Expecting a date, Ms. Forrest was surprised to learn that the purpose of the meeting was to recruit her to join the eco-terrorist branch of EARTH called the Crusaders. (R. at 39-40.) Ms. Forrest decided to join the Crusaders only after several months of deliberation. (R. at 41.) At that time, she was aware that the Crusaders used sabotage to promote its agenda but was not aware that the group resorted to violence as well. (R. at 45.) True to her understanding that the group's "extralegal" methods were strictly nonviolent, her participation was limited to two nonviolent missions. On one occasion, she and other Crusaders sprayed the phrase "Gas Guzzler" on an SUV. (R. at 41.) On another occasion, they punctured the tires of construction vehicles at a new mall construction site. (R. at 41.) After puncturing the tires, Ms. Forrest and the other Crusaders draped a large banner over the entrance to the site. (R. at 41.) The purpose of the banner was to alert the construction workers not to use the vehicles so they would not be injured. (R. at 41.) No one was hurt in either situation. (R. at 41.) Indeed, in all of her years as a member of EARTH, she never met anyone she considered to be violent until she encountered Morlandia. (R. at 43.)

Morlandia's role as a government informant began after the FBI caught and arrested him for his involvement in a tree-spiking incident. (R. at 16.) Morlandia identified himself as a Crusader, and the FBI agreed to release him in exchange for his service as an informant against the Crusaders. (R. at 17.) The FBI hoped he would gain the Crusaders' trust and work his way up the ranks of the organization so that the FBI could eventually take down the group. (R. at 18.) The FBI continued to trust Morlandia in this role even after they suspected him of participating in an arson at a housing development while he was an informant and without informing the FBI. (R. at 19.)

Morlandia and Ms. Forrest first crossed paths after a high-level Crusader assigned Morlandia to plan the bombing at issue in this case. (R. at 31.) The high-level Crusader specifically instructed Morlandia to recruit Ms. Forrest. (R. at 31.) Morlandia understood that Ms. Forrest was a "very green" "rookie." (R. at 31.) When Morlandia reported his assignment to the FBI, the FBI encouraged him to proceed with the plans for the bombing to earn the trust of the Crusaders' leadership. (R. at 19-20.)

Morlandia subsequently set out to obtain Ms. Forrest's participation. (R. at 31.) When Morlandia first communicated the plan to her, Ms. Forrest responded that she "didn't think [she] could do something like that." (R. at 42.) She "had never done anything dangerous to others before" and "had no intent to do so." (R. at 42.) Prior to her first conversation with Morlandia, she had attended a meeting where she was instructed on how to make incendiary devices, but she was "quite hopeless at it" and never intended to use the training. (R. at 46.)

In response to Ms. Forrest's refusal to participate in the bombing, Morlandia launched into a lengthy speech about the dangers of oil dependency and the role of SUV companies in perpetuating it and even commented that Ms. Forrest's three-year-old daughter faced an "uncertain future." (R. at 42.) Distressed by Morlandia's speech, Ms. Forrest stated that she needed to think about his proposal. (R. at 42.) Morlandia, however, did not give her much time. (R. at 42.) He called her back the same night. (R. at 42.) In this second conversation, he questioned her loyalty and stated, "I hope you'll make the right decision." (R. at 42.) He then warned her, "you do understand we cannot take chances with defectors." (R. at 42-43.) At that point, Ms. Forrest feared for her safety if she refused. (R. at 43.) As a result of her fear, she told Morlandia she would "do what was required." (R. at 43.)

After Morlandia secured Ms. Forrest's involvement, he proceeded to plan the bombing, scope out the target, determine the appropriate time to strike, and procure the difficult-to-obtain explosives from the FBI. (R. at 31-32.) It is unclear whether the Crusaders would have otherwise been able to obtain such powerful explosives. (R. at 32.) Morlandia also secured a location to store them and trained Ms. Forrest. (R. at 43-44.) On the morning of the incident, Ms. Forrest obtained the explosives from the storage facility in which Morlandia had stored them, picked up Morlandia, and drove to the dealership. (R. at 43.) Morlandia waited at the crime scene while Ms. Forrest planted and detonated the explosives (R. at 43), and he drove the getaway car (R. at 12). At all times during the preparation and execution of the bombing, Ms. Forrest was acting under Morlandia's explicit instructions. (R. at 42-43.) Ms. Forrest never wanted or expected to participate in this or any violent criminal activity and has stated that she will "regret it until the day [she] dies[s]." (R. at 41.)

SUMMARY OF THE ARGUMENT

The Appellant, Ms. Forrest, was a nonviolent environmental activist whose worst transgressions were minor acts of vandalism that posed no risk of physical harm. However, on a day that would forever change her life, she detonated explosives at an auto dealership. At the heart of her progression from a nonviolent activist to an accomplice in a bombing is the government's reckless empowerment of a known terrorist who ultimately coerced, directed, and enabled Ms. Forrest to commit the crime. The government's involvement in the bombing, including its decision to supply the explosives, shocks the universal sense of justice and warrants reversal of the conviction.

In *United States v. Russell*, 411 U.S. 423, 431 (1973), the Court recognized that a civilized society must place some outer limits on the investigative tactics of law enforcement. When these limits are crossed, the potential harm to our criminal justice system is sufficiently egregious to justify barring the government from obtaining a conviction. The government's degree of involvement in the bombing crossed the line in at least three respects.

First, the government encouraged its informant, a known terrorist, to direct the bombing from start to finish and supplied the necessary explosives. The informant recruited Ms. Forrest to participate in the bombing, located and surveyed the target, planned all logistics, obtained and stored explosives provided by the government, trained Ms. Forrest on how to detonate the explosives, and directed all of Ms. Forrest's actions. Testimony established that Ms. Forrest did not have the necessary skills or contacts to have completed such a mission on her own. The government enabled a crime that would not otherwise have occurred.

Second, Ms. Forrest was not engaged in or planning any criminal activity prior to her first contact with the government's informant. She was, in fact, highly reluctant to participate in the bombing when the informant first attempted to recruit her and gave in only when she believed the informant was threatening her life.

Third, the government encouraged its informant's excessively zealous tactics by threatening to arrest him if he failed to facilitate some convictions and tolerated the tactics out of desperation to justify a failing eight-year project. Its desperation is perhaps best illustrated by its willingness to not only supply explosives to the informant but to also permit him to store the explosives in a public facility.

In addition to the government's over-involvement in the initiation, planning, and execution of the bombing, the coercion of Ms. Forrest's involvement in the crime warrants reversal of the conviction. After Ms. Forrest initially refused to participate in the bombing because she could not "do something like that," the informant menacingly commented that he "hope[d] [she would] make the right decision" and that "we cannot take chances with defectors." Fearing for her life, she then acquiesced and promised to "do what was required."

Admittedly, Ms. Forrest was not completely innocent. Although she professed a belief that she had joined a nonviolent organization, she likely knew that at least some of its members endorsed violence. She also had embraced illegal, though nonviolent, tactics in the past. However, she would never have been at that dealership setting the explosives if not for the coercive and directive conduct of the government's informant. Lee King would be alive, and Ms. Forrest would not be facing a life in prison. This is a quintessential case of the government manufacturing a crime that would not otherwise have occurred. Reversal of the conviction is necessary to preserve the integrity of our justice system. The government must adhere to some basic principles of fairness or be barred from invoking judicial process to sanction its misguided suspension of morality.

ARGUMENT

The Court should reverse the conviction because the government's investigative tactics exceeded due process limits.

A trial court's decision to dismiss for outrageous government conduct is subject to de novo review. *United States v. Luttrell*, 889 F.2d 806, 812 (9th Cir. 1989). The trial court's denial of Ms. Forrest's motion to dismiss the indictment was erroneous because the government's conduct in this case exceeded due process limits.

The United States Supreme Court has recognized that the Due Process Clause of the Constitution imposes limits on the methods law enforcement may use to obtain convictions, and, accordingly, convictions obtained through improper means are barred. *United States v.*

Russell, 411 U.S. 423, 431 (1973) ("we may some day be presented with a situation in which the conduct of law enforcement agents is so outrageous that due process principles would absolutely bar the government from invoking judicial processes to obtain a conviction"). Unlike the defense of entrapment, a claim of outrageous government conduct may be successful even when the defendant was predisposed to commit the crime. *Hampton v. United States*, 425 U.S. 484, 495 (1976) (Powell, J., concurring); *id.* at 497 (Brennan, J., dissenting); *see also United States v. Bogart*, 783 F.2d 1428, 1432 (9th Cir. 1986) (explaining that the concurring and dissenting justices in *Hampton* comprised a majority to support the availability of an outrageous government conduct claim regardless of the defendant's criminal predisposition).

The availability of a dismissal based on outrageous government conduct is necessary to guard against "'the dangers of overzealous law enforcement.'" *United States v. Twigg*, 588 F.2d 373, 380 (3d Cir. 1978) (quoting *Sherman v. United States*, 356 U.S. 369, 381 (1958) (Frankfurter, J., concurring)). This overzealousness is not merely theoretical but has warranted dismissals of indictments in several federal cases. *Twigg*, 588 F.2d 373, 380; *United States v. West*, 511 F.2d 1083, 1086 (3d Cir. 1975); *Greene v. United States*, 454 F.2d 783, 786-87 (9th Cir. 1971); *United States v. Gardner*, 658 F. Supp. 1573, 1579 (W.D. Pa. 1987); *United States v. Batres-Santolino*, 521 F. Supp. 744, 753 (N.D. Cal. 1981); *see also United States v. Luttrell*, 889 F.2d 806, 813-14 (9th Cir. 1989) (finding that indictment should be dismissed if government did not have reason to investigate defendants prior to presenting them with an opportunity to engage in criminal conduct and remanding for a factual determination of whether such a reason existed); *United States v. Archer*, 486 F.2d 670, 677 (2d Cir. 1973) (dismissing indictment on other grounds but stating it might have found government's authorization of crimes by government agents to be sufficiently outrageous to warrant dismissal on due process grounds).

The dangers of overzealous law enforcement that underlie the outrageous conduct theory are evident in this case. Ms. Forrest was a nonviolent environmental activist who had participated in only two minor acts of vandalism prior to becoming caught up in the criminal plan devised by the government's informant. The informant first coerced her into committing the crime by threatening her life and then directed every aspect of the plan. This case thus presents both of the main factual circumstances that have warranted dismissals of indictments on due process grounds: over-involvement in criminal activity and coercive tactics. Moreover, the government's conduct was improper even under the five-factor test on which the government relies to justify its tactics.

A. The government informant's role in planning and executing the bombing shocks the universal sense of justice.

The government's conduct requires reversal of the conviction on due process grounds because the government's involvement in the bombing was excessive. This Court has held that an indictment must be dismissed when the government manufactured the crime to secure a conviction rather than to protect the public from ongoing criminal activity. *Bogart*, 783 F.2d at 1436, 1438. Ms. Forrest's conviction must be reversed under this standard for the following three reasons. First, Morlandia completely manufactured the bombing from start to finish. Second, at the time Morlandia approached Ms. Forrest, she was not engaging in or planning any illegal activity. Third, Morlandia was motivated by pressure to obtain a conviction.

1. The government and its informant manufactured the crime from start to finish.

The degree of control the informant exercised over the bombing exceeds constitutional limits on government involvement in criminal activity.

The Due Process Clause limits the extent to which the government can involve itself in criminal activity. In *Greene*, for example, the court dismissed an indictment on bootlegging charges largely because of the government agent's role in setting up, supplying, and continuing the bootlegging operation. *Greene*, 454 F.2d at 786-87. Specifically, the agent had offered to find a still site, still equipment, and an operator. *Id.* at 786. In addition, the agent had actually provided two thousand pounds of sugar to ensure the continued operation of the still. *Id.* And the government agent was the only customer of the operation he had helped to create. *Id.* at 787. The court concluded that this conduct rose to a level of "creative activity" "substantially more intense and aggressive than the level of such activity charged against the government in prior entrapment cases." *Id.* It found that "when the government permits itself to become enmeshed in criminal activity, from beginning to end, to the extent which appears here, the same underlying objections which render entrapment repugnant to American criminal justice are operative." *Id.; see also Twigg*, 588 F.2d at 380 (basing dismissal of indictment in part on government's role in providing a location, supplies, and necessary expertise to enable the defendants' production of narcotics and on the court's conclusion that although defendants raised capital for the operation, the agent was "completely in charge" of the drug laboratory).

Extensive government involvement in criminal activity is particularly offensive when it enables crimes that would otherwise not have occurred. *Gardner*, 658 F. Supp. at 1567 (applying a four-factor test that includes consideration of whether the crime "would not have occurred but for the government's assistance"); *see also Bogart*, 783 F.2d at 1435 n.7 (recognizing the four-factor test without explicitly adopting it). Accordingly, the inability of the defendant to successfully commit the crime absent government involvement may support dismissal of the indictment. In *Twigg*, for example, due process prevented the government from obtaining a conviction for the manufacture of narcotics when the defendants lacked the expertise and may have lacked the ability to obtain a key ingredient to commit the crime absent the government's involvement. *Twigg*, 588 F.2d at 380. The court further found that the assistance provided by the defendants was "minimal and then at the specific direction of" the agent. *Id.* at 381. Similarly, the court in *Batres-Santolino*, 521 F. Supp. at 751, based its dismissal of a drug indictment partly on its conclusion that it was "inconceivable that [the defendants] could have entered the secretive world of international drug smuggling on their own" when they had never imported cocaine before and had no foreign source of supply of their own. Therefore, the court concluded that "government agents 'manufactured' a crime that . . . could not and would not have been committed if [the informant] had not inveigled defendants into it and offered to provide them with an otherwise unavailable source of supply of the illegal drug they were to import." *Id.*

Based on the case law explained above, the conviction should be reversed because Morlandia manufactured the crime from start to finish. Like the agent in *Twigg*, Morlandia was "completely in charge" of the criminal enterprise. *Twigg*, 588 F.2d at 380. Not only did he plan the entire mission, but he also provided all the materials necessary to carry out the mission. Without any assistance from Ms. Forrest, Morlandia investigated the location of the crime, determined where and how to strike, and obtained the explosives from the FBI. (R. at 31-32.) In fact, Ms. Forrest's participation in the crime was even more minor than that of the defendants in either *Greene* or *Twigg*. Whereas the defendants in *Greene* manufactured bootleg alcohol, and the defendants in *Twigg* raised capital for the operation and arranged for distribution of the product, Ms. Forrest's participation in the crime was limited to following Morlandia's specific instructions. (R. at 43-44.) In fact, Morlandia had to train Ms. Forrest in advance on how to set up the explosives. (R. at 43-44.) Moreover, the bombing in this case could not have been committed without the government's involvement. Like the defendants in *Batres-Santolino*, who were novices incapable of engaging in drug smuggling without the government's assistance, Ms. Forrest similarly lacked the expertise to execute the bombing on her own. Although Ms. Forrest had been trained on how to make incendiary devices, Ms. Forrest testified that she was "hopeless at that kind of stuff." (R. at 43-44.) Therefore, it is unlikely she could have made the explosives necessary to carry out the bombing. Moreover, she did not have a source from which to obtain explosives. (R. at 42.) The government's provision of the explosives was critical to Ms. Forrest's ability to commit the crime. As in *Batres-Santolino*, *Twigg*, and *Greene*, the government's enablement of a crime that would otherwise not have occurred exceeds due process limits on government involvement in criminal activity and should have resulted in a dismissal of the indictment.

2. The government's over-involvement in the bombing led Ms. Forrest to commit a crime she would not otherwise have committed.

The conviction should be reversed because the Defendant was not planning to bomb a car dealership or commit any similar act until the government's informant approached her with the plan.

Courts have found that the government's involvement in initiating and directing criminal activity is particularly offensive when the "government generate[s] new crimes" by a defendant who was not otherwise engaged in or planning criminal activity. *Twigg*, 588 F.2d at 381. In *Twigg*, defendants Neville and Twigg challenged their convictions on charges of illegal drug manufacture. *Id.* at 374. The speed laboratory for which they were arrested had been originally proposed by an informant. *Id.* at 380. Although the informant had operated a speed laboratory with Neville more than three years earlier, neither Neville nor Twigg was engaged in any illegal activity at the time the informant contacted Neville to propose setting up a new laboratory. *Id.* at 375 n.2. Neville was immediately receptive to the idea and never expressed any hesitation. *Id.* at 376. Despite Neville's willing participation in the scheme, the court found that the government's role in originating the criminal plan and supplying the indispensable expertise needed to run the laboratory violated due process and required reversal of both defendants' convictions. *Id.* at 381. The court explained that "fundamental fairness does not permit [the courts] to countenance" the "generat[ion] of new crimes by the defendant . . . when, as far as the record shows, he was lawfully and peacefully minding his own affairs." *Id.*; *see also Bogart*, 783 F.2d at 1435 n.7 (recognizing ongoing criminal activity as a factor some courts have considered); *West*, 511 F.2d at 1086 (suggesting that whereas the government's provision of materials to make illegal drugs would not be outrageous where the government suspected the defendant was engaged in illegal drug activity, the result should be different where the defendant had not previously been engaged in drug transactions); *Gardner*, 658 F. Supp. at 1576 (considering absence of any ongoing criminal activity by defendant prior to his contact with government agent as one factor supporting dismissal of indictment).

The prior innocence of the defendant, however, does not appear to be a necessary element of establishing an outrageous conduct claim. In *Batres-Santolino*, for example, the court dismissed the indictment, 521 F. Supp. at 753, because even though at least one of the defendants had dealt cocaine on a small scale before, *id.* at 749, none of the defendants had ever imported cocaine prior to the encouragement of government agents, *id.* at 751.

Moreover, a vague, unrealized intent to engage in the type of crime at issue does not preclude an outrageous government conduct claim when the government's encouragement of the crime was central to its commission. In *Greene*, for example, the government reinitiated contact with the defendants at a time when they were released on bail after arrests that resulted from a successful sting operation that "terminated" their bootlegging operation. 454 F.2d at 784, 787. In response to the government agent's telephone call, which was intended merely to confirm that his cover had not been compromised, the defendants revealed that they were planning to get back into bootlegging. *Id.* at 785. They did not, however, have a still at the time and encountered various difficulties in getting their operation up and running again. *Id.* The government agent's subsequent involvement in the "creation and maintenance" of their bootlegging operation, including the supply of two thousand pounds of sugar, led the court to dismiss the indictment on due process grounds. *Id.* at 786-87.

In this case, as in *Twigg*, the defendant was not engaged in or planning any criminal activity. In fact, whereas defendant Neville was an enthusiastic participant in the crime conceived by the informant, Ms. Forrest was extremely reluctant to assist Morlandia in the bombing. She told Morlandia that she "didn't think [she] could do something like that" and acquiesced only after he warned her that EARTH could not "take chances with defectors." (R. at 42-43.) Therefore, Morlandia's role in creating new crime by Ms. Forrest was even more pronounced than the government's role in *Twigg*.

Although Ms. Forrest was a member of the Crusaders and had committed two minor acts of vandalism prior to her contact with Morlandia (R. at 41), neither her prior crimes nor her mere membership in a terrorist organization justifies Morlandia's solicitation and direction of her involvement in the bombing. Just as the minor drug transactions previously engaged in by one of the defendant's in *Batres-Santolino* did not indicate he would have engaged in the large-scale importation of drugs for which he was arrested, Ms. Forrest's minor acts of vandalism do not suggest she would have engaged in a bombing of a car dealership absent Morlandia's initiation and planning of the crime. Moreover, while her membership in EARTH might suggest a vague intent to someday engage in some type of sabotage in furtherance of EARTH's goals, she was neither engaged in nor planning any criminal act. Since the *Greene* defendants' hope of reestablishing a bootleg operation did not affect the availability of the outrageous conduct defense where the government's involvement was instrumental in their ability to realize that hope, Ms. Forrest's membership in EARTH should not bar her from asserting the defense. Morlandia's substantial role in creating and carrying out the plan for the bombing was even more egregious than the government's role in encouraging and supporting the bootleg operation in *Greene*. In this case, the government not only offered encouragement and supplies, but also decided all of the details of the plan for the bombing and directed Ms. Forrest's involvement. Accordingly, reversal of the conviction is even more warranted here than it was in *Greene*.

3. The informant's eagerness to procure Ms. Forrest's involvement in the bombing resulted from the FBI's threat that it would arrest him for terrorism.

The informant's conduct in this case was outrageous because he was motivated solely by a desire to secure a conviction to avoid his own imprisonment.

It is unclear whether courts must address the motive of the government in inducing the crime. *See Bogart*, 783 F.2d at 1436, 1438 (stating initially that "criminal sanction is not justified when the state manufactures crimes that would otherwise not occur" but later adding "to secure the defendant's conviction rather than to protect the public from the defendant's continuing criminal behavior"). In any event, none of the decisions reversing convictions on the ground of outrageous government conduct have discussed specific evidence of the government's motives. Instead, those courts that have considered motive a factor have found the factor satisfied by the lack of any criminal activity by the defendant at the time of the investigation. *See Twigg*, 588 F.2d at 381 (finding the government "generated new crimes by the defendant merely for the sake of pressing criminal charges" based on the lack of evidence that the defendants were engaged in criminal activity prior to the informant's proposal to create a speed laboratory); *United States v. Valdovinos-Valdovinos*, 588 F. Supp. 551, 556 (N.D. Cal. 1984) (holding that an undercover operation that circulated its telephone number in an unregulated manner and then advised callers from Mexico that it was acceptable to enter the United States without proper immigration papers constituted "the generation by police of new crimes merely for the sake of pressing criminal charges"), *rev'd on other grounds*, 793 F.2d 1436 (9th Cir. 1985); *Batres-Santolino*, 521 F. Supp. at 752 (concluding, based on the lack of any evidence that defendants were engaged in ongoing illegal activity when the government prompted them to import drugs, that the government "implant[ed] in the mind of an innocent person the disposition to commit the alleged offense and induce[d] its commission in order that they may prosecute") (quoting *Sherman*, 356 U.S. at 372).

Moreover, the motive of the government in inducing crime by someone who is not currently engaged in or contemplating criminal activity is suspect even when the government is not specifically targeting the particular defendant. In *Valdovinos-Valdovinos*, the undercover operation aimed to apprehend transporters of illegal aliens. 588 F. Supp. at 553. The government used its undercover telephone number to encourage Mexican citizens to cross the border illegally so that it could catch the aliens' transporters. *Id.* The defendant was arrested for transporting one of the Mexican citizens the government had encouraged to cross the border illegally. *Id.* at 554. Despite the legitimate goal of catching transporters, the court found that the generation of crimes by falsely telling Mexican citizens they could cross the border legally was a violation of due process. *Id.* at 556. Similarly, in *Twigg*, the court held that the agent's "specific direction" of defendant Twigg's actions in furtherance of the crime required reversal of his conviction even though Twigg was brought into the conspiracy by an acquaintance and not by the agent. 588 F.2d at 382.

As discussed above in Subsection 2, Ms. Forrest was not engaged in or planning criminal activity before Morlandia recruited her for the bombing. Therefore, as in *Twigg*, *Batres-Santolino*, and *Valdovinos-Valdovinos*, the Court should infer that the government's role in the bombing was designed to secure a conviction rather than to protect the public from any ongoing criminal activity by Ms. Forrest. Moreover, such an inference has much greater support in this case because the trial testimony provides specific evidence that

Morlandia was motivated by a desire to secure a conviction. After an eight-year-long investigation of EARTH that produced relatively few leads or convictions, the FBI in this case exerted pressure on its agents to obtain convictions or face reassignment. (R. at 22.) In particular, Agent Tu threatened Morlandia that he might be arrested if his role as informant did not lead to some arrests. (R. at 34.) The FBI was so desperate to substantiate its operation that it encouraged overzealous law enforcement. This encouragement prompted Morlandia to lead Ms. Forrest, a relatively harmless environmental advocate, into a serious crime that claimed the life of an innocent man.

Although the FBI's undercover EARTH operation was designed to uncover important intelligence and thwart terrorist activities, *Valdovinos-Valdovinos* established that the broader purpose of a sting operation does not justify the generation of new crimes. 588 F. Supp. at 556. Just as it was wrong to induce aliens to cross the border illegally so that the government could catch their transporters in *Valdovinos-Valdovinos*, it was wrong to induce Ms. Forrest to commit arson in the attenuated hope that Morlandia's role in the mission might eventually enable him to gather some useful intelligence on EARTH's operations. In fact, the government's conduct in this case is even more outrageous than in *Valdovinos-Valdovinos* given the high likelihood of harm to the public that was inherent in the government's plan to intercept the bombing at the last minute. Moreover, as in *Twigg*, the government's specific direction of Ms. Forrest's actions in furtherance of the bombing is no less offensive merely because EARTH, rather than Morlandia, chose to bring her into the plan.

Because the government in this case involved itself in the generation of new crimes by Ms. Forrest in the absence of any evidence that she had been engaging in or planning criminal activity, the conviction should be reversed.

B. The government's informant's use of coercion to convince Ms. Forrest to help him execute the bombing was fundamentally unfair.

The government informant coerced Ms. Forrest into participating in the bombing by threatening her life. The Due Process Clause forbids the government from inducing crime through coercion and therefore requires reversal of the conviction.

In addition to the generation of new crimes by the government, unwarranted physical or mental coercion by the government independently requires dismissal of an indictment on due process grounds. *Bogart*, 783 F.2d at 1438. In *Rochin v. California*, 342 U.S. 165, 174 (1952), the Supreme Court reversed a conviction because it had been obtained through excessive physical coercion. Upon entering the defendant's home, the police saw some capsules. *Id.* at 166. The defendant then swallowed the capsules. *Id.* The police "jumped" on the defendant and tried unsuccessfully to extract the capsules. *Id.* They then brought him to the hospital and directed a doctor to forcibly pump his stomach. *Id.* The court found that the police conduct in obtaining the evidence of the defendant's drug possession offended principles of fair play and decency and, therefore, required reversal of his conviction on due process grounds. *Id.* at 173.

Although no court has yet relied exclusively on mental coercion to dismiss an indictment on due process grounds, the court in *Greene* did justify dismissal in part on mental coercion. *Greene*, 454 F.2d at 787. The court's finding of coercion rested on the following facts. When the defendants told the government agent they were having difficulty reestablishing their bootlegging operation, the agent, who was posing as a member of a drug ring, told them that "the boss [was] on [his] back." *Id.* at 785. Several months later, the defendants delivered alcohol from the new operation. *Id.* At trial, the defendants claimed that their discussions about the bootlegging operation were designed merely to impress the agent and that "they were reluctant to act and might never have produced any bootleg alcohol without the prodding of [the agent]." *Id.* at 786. The court found that the agent's statement "could only be construed as a veiled threat" and this threat was one of the reasons the court dismissed the indictment. *Id.* at 787. Mental coercion has similarly been recognized as a potential factor favoring dismissal in *Bogart*, 783 F.2d at 1435 n.7 (recognizing that one factor that courts have used to support dismissal is "whether the government agents persisted with their inducements to overcome the defendant's reluctance to commit the crime") and *Gardner*, 658 F. Supp. at 1574, 1577 (concluding that agent's persistence in inducing and persuading defendant to buy drugs for him through repeated requests and an offer to help repair defendant's car was a factor supporting dismissal of indictment).

Other courts have rejected threats as outrageous conduct but only where the evidence showed that the criminal enterprise under investigation was characterized by the routine use of vulgarity and "puffing." *See, e.g., United States v. Emmert*, 829 F.2d 805, 812 (9th Cir. 1987) (holding that implied threats by agent did not violate due process because they were "ordinary bargaining tactics in drug deals"); *United States v. Reynoso-Ulloa*, 548 F.2d 1329, 1340 (9th Cir. 1977) (concluding that agent's threat that he would kill defendant's friends if deal did not go through was not outrageous conduct when viewed in the context of the "vulgarity and 'puffing'" engaged in by all participants in the drug transaction at issue).

In the instant case, Morlandia's coercion of Ms. Forrest to participate in the bombing so far exceeded the degree of coercion in *Greene* that it should be independently sufficient to warrant reversal of the conviction. Ms. Forrest was reluctant to participate in the bombing and told Morlandia she did not think she could "do something like that." (R. at 42.) Morlandia then appealed to Ms. Forrest's environmental sympathies and even linked her participation to the future of her three-year-old daughter. (R. at 42.) When these persuasive tactics failed, he turned to threats. Specifically, after a dramatic pause he said, "I hope you'll make the right decision. You understand that we cannot take chances with defectors." (R. at 42-43.) Ms.

Forrest testified that she immediately feared for her safety and only then told Morlandia that she would "do what was required." (R. at 43.) Morlandia's use of the threat of death to procure Ms. Forrest's participation in the bombing offends fair play and decency just as surely as did the government's extraction of evidence from the defendant's stomach in *Rochin*. Indeed, it is more offensive since it was not directed merely at obtaining evidence of a preexisting crime but, in fact, coerced Ms. Forrest to commit the crime for which she has been convicted.

Notably, there is no evidence to suggest that Morlandia had to threaten Ms. Forrest in order to maintain his cover. Ms. Forrest was the only person present for the conversation. In contrast to the drug dealers involved in *Reynoso-Ulloa* and *Emmert*, Ms. Forrest was an assistant director of a nonprofit environmental action group whose worst infractions prior to her involvement in this crime were spray-painting an SUV and puncturing tires. (R. at 40, 41.) Moreover, Ms. Forrest's testimony that "[i]t never occurred to [her] before this that EARTH-ers might be dangerous" (R. at 43) reveals that violent threats were not a common practice among Crusaders. Thus, rather than necessary "puffing" characteristic of the criminal enterprise he was investigating, Morlandia's threat was clearly an effort to coerce Ms. Forrest to commit the crime for which the government now seeks to convict her. It was specifically designed to induce fear. Accordingly, the informant's conduct in this case shocks the conscience and requires reversal of the conviction.

C. The government's conduct in this case fails the five-factor test this Court has used to uphold convictions against claims of outrageous government conduct.

Even under the five-factor test upon which the government relies to justify its conduct, the government clearly exceeded due process limits.

This Court has established a five-factor test, which, when satisfied, will preclude claims of outrageous government conduct. *United States v. Bonanno*, 852 F.2d 434, 437-38 (9th

Cir. 1988). The factors are: (1) the defendant was already involved in a continuing series of similar crimes, or the charged criminal enterprise was already in process at the time the government agent became involved; (2) the agent's participation was not necessary to enable the defendant to continue the criminal activity; (3) the agent used artifice and stratagem to ferret out criminal activity; (4) the agent infiltrated a criminal organization; and (5) the agent approached persons already contemplating or engaged in criminal activity. *Id.* The use of "and" as a conjunction suggests all five factors must be satisfied by the facts of the case. In any event, the facts of this case fail to satisfy any of the five factors.

Factors one, three, four, and five are not satisfied in this case because, as explained in Section A.2 above, Ms. Forrest was not engaged in or planning criminal activity prior to the government's involvement with her and Morlandia's conduct created rather than infiltrated a criminal enterprise. In *United States v. Williams*, 547 F.3d 1187, 1200-01 (9th Cir. 2008), the court found factors one, three, four, and five of the *Bonanno* test were satisfied because the defendant was introduced to the agent as a drug dealer and was already planning a bank robbery before the agent convinced the defendant to rob a fictitious stash house instead. By contrast, Ms. Forrest was not planning any criminal activity prior to Morlandia's efforts to persuade her to participate in the car dealership bombing. Therefore, Morlandia created rather than "ferret[ed] out" criminal activity and created rather than "infiltrated" a criminal enterprise. *Bonanno*, 852 F.2d at 437-38.

The second factor is also not satisfied in this case because, as explained in Section A.1 above, Ms. Forrest was not capable of carrying out the bombing without Morlandia's assistance. In *Williams*, the second factor was satisfied because the defendant had already established detailed plans for a similar robbery and had an "experienced crew" that he represented was capable of handling the job. *Williams*, 547 F.3d at 1200. By contrast, in this case, Ms. Forrest had no plan, no explosives, and no experience to indicate she could have carried out the bombing without Morlandia's assistance.

Because the facts of this case do not satisfy the five-factor test and because they do, as explained in earlier sections of this brief, establish outrageous government conduct, this Court should reverse the conviction.

CONCLUSION

For the reasons explained above, the Court should reverse Ms. Forrest's conviction.

Dated: March 14, 2010

Respectfully submitted,

____

Jane Doe
Attorney for the Appellant

SAMPLE G. TRIAL BRIEF

JANE DOE
Doe & Allen LLP
3000 Main Street, Suite #1191
Santa Monica, California 90081
(310) 999-9999

Attorney For Defendant,
Reyna Forrest

UNITED STATES DISTRICT COURT
CENTRAL DISTRICT OF CALIFORNIA

	)	
UNITED STATES OF AMERICA	)	Case No.: ED CR 12-14183 CMW
Plaintiff,	)	
	)	Memorandum of Points and Authorities In
v.	)	Support of Motion to Dismiss Indictment
	)	
REYNA FORREST,	)	Hearing Date: November 23, 2009
Defendant	)	Time: 10:00 a.m.
	)	Place: Courtroom 950
______________________	)	Judge: Carron M. Warner

TABLE OF CONTENTS

TABLE OF AUTHORITIES

CASES

INTRODUCTION*

The Appellant, Ms. Forrest, seeks to dismiss her indictment on the ground that it was obtained in violation of her Due Process rights through outrageous government conduct.

Ms. Forrest was a nonviolent environmental activist whose worst transgressions were minor acts of vandalism that posed no risk of physical harm. However, on a day that would forever change her life, she detonated explosives at an auto dealership. At the heart of her progression from a nonviolent activist to an accomplice in a bombing is the government's reckless empowerment of its informant, a known terrorist who ultimately coerced, directed, and enabled Ms. Forrest to commit the crime. With the government's knowledge, its informant used threats to overcome Ms. Forrest's reluctance to participate in the bombing, located and surveyed the target, planned all logistics, obtained and stored explosives *provided by the government*, trained Ms. Forrest on how to detonate the explosives, and directed all of Ms. Forrest's actions.

The government's involvement in the bombing shocks the universal sense of justice and warrants dismissal of the indictment on Due Process grounds. This is a quintessential case of the government manufacturing a crime that would not otherwise have occurred. Dismissal of the indictment is necessary to preserve the integrity of our justice system. The government must adhere to some basic principles of fairness or be barred from invoking judicial process to sanction its misguided suspension of morality.

QUESTION PRESENTED

Do the dangers of overzealous police tactics that underlie the outrageous police conduct defense warrant dismissal of the indictment against Ms. Forrest for her limited role in a car dealership bombing on due process grounds where an FBI informant used a veiled threat to recruit Ms. Forrest to participate in the bombing on which her charges are based, Ms. Forrest had no prior intention of participating in a violent crime and no history of violent criminal activity, and the informant planned the bombing, obtained the explosives from the FBI, trained Ms. Forrest, provided explicit directions under which she was acting at every stage of the operation, and accompanied her to the crime scene?

STATEMENT OF FACTS

The defendant, Reyna Forrest, has been charged with terrorism in connection with the bombing of Lee King Autos. Forrest Decl. ¶ 59. She now moves to dismiss the indictment on the basis of outrageous government conduct.

Prior to her encounters with the government informant, Ms. Forrest pursued her passion for environmental causes solely through nonviolent advocacy. *Id.* ¶¶ 39-40. At age 18, Ms. Forrest witnessed the destruction of her hometown of Valdez, Alaska, due to the 1989 Exxon oil spill. *Id.* ¶ 39. Deeply affected by this experience, she joined an environ-

* Some courts may require double-spacing. Look up spacing requirements in your court's local rules. Students should follow professor instructions. When converting to double-spacing, leave headings single-spaced but with an extra line between the heading and the text underneath. Delete extra spacing between paragraphs.

mental organization called EARTH and eventually became the leader of the EARTH chapter at her college. *Id.* ¶ 40. The chapter engaged only in legal environmental advocacy. *Id.* After college, Ms. Forrest worked for a nonprofit organization devoted to advocating for environmental protection laws. *Id.* ¶ 39. Then, one day, a male member of EARTH asked to meet her for dinner. *Id.* Expecting a date, Ms. Forrest was surprised to learn that the purpose of the meeting was to recruit her to join the eco-terrorist branch of EARTH called the Crusaders. *Id.* ¶¶ 39-40. Ms. Forrest decided to join the Crusaders only after several months of deliberation. *Id.* ¶ 41. At that time, she was aware that the Crusaders used sabotage to promote its agenda but was not aware that the group resorted to violence as well. *Id.* ¶ 45. True to her understanding that the group's "extralegal" methods were strictly nonviolent, her participation was limited to two nonviolent missions. *Id.* ¶ 41. On one occasion, she and other Crusaders sprayed the phrase "Gas Guzzler" on an SUV. *Id.* On another occasion, they punctured the tires of construction vehicles at a new mall construction site. *Id.* After puncturing the tires, Ms. Forrest and the other Crusaders draped a large banner over the entrance to the site. *Id.* The purpose of the banner was to alert the construction workers not to use the vehicles so they would not be injured. *Id.* No one was hurt in either situation. *Id.* Indeed, in all of her years as a member of EARTH, she never met anyone she considered to be violent until Morlandia. *Id.* ¶ 43.

Morlandia's role as a government informant began after the FBI caught and arrested him for his involvement in a tree-spiking incident. Morlandia Dep. 14:3-15:1, Jan. 14, 2010. Morlandia identified himself as a Crusader, and the FBI agreed to release him in exchange for his service as an informant against the Crusaders. *Id.* 17:5-22. The FBI hoped he would gain the Crusaders' trust and work his way up the ranks of the organization so that the FBI could eventually take down the group. *Id.* 18:5-20. The FBI continued to trust Morlandia in this role even after they suspected him of participating in an arson at a housing development while he was an informant and without informing the FBI. *Id.* 19:15.

Morlandia and Ms. Forrest first crossed paths after a high-level Crusader assigned Morlandia to plan the bombing at issue in this case. *Id.* 31:14. The high-level Crusader specifically instructed Morlandia to recruit Ms. Forrest. *Id.* Morlandia understood that Ms. Forrest was a "very green" "rookie." *Id.* When Morlandia reported his assignment to the FBI, the FBI encouraged him to proceed with the plans for the bombing to earn the trust of the Crusaders' leadership. *Id.* 19:1-20:10.

Morlandia subsequently set out to obtain Ms. Forrest's participation. *Id.* 31:10. When Morlandia first communicated the plan to her, Ms. Forrest responded that she "didn't think [she] could do something like that." Forrest Decl. ¶ 42. She "had never done anything dangerous to others before" and "had no intent to do so." *Id.* Prior to her first conversation with Morlandia, she had attended a meeting where she was instructed on how to make incendiary devices, but she was "quite hopeless at it" and never intended to use the training. *Id.* ¶ 46.

In response to Ms. Forrest's refusal to participate in the bombing, Morlandia launched into a lengthy speech about the dangers of oil dependency, and the role of SUV companies in perpetuating it, and even commented that Ms. Forrest's three-year-old daughter faced an "uncertain future." *Id.* ¶ 42. Distressed by Morlandia's speech, Ms. Forrest stated that she needed to think about his proposal. *Id.* Morlandia, however, did not give her much time. *Id.* He called her back the same night. *Id.* In this second conversation, he questioned her loyalty and stated, "I hope you'll make the right decision." *Id.* He then warned her, "you do understand we cannot take chances with defectors." *Id.* ¶¶ 42-43. At that point, Ms. Forrest feared for her safety if she refused. *Id.* ¶ 43. As a result of her fear, she told Morlandia she would "do what was required." *Id.*

After Morlandia secured Ms. Forrest's involvement, he proceeded to plan the bombing, scope out the target, determine the appropriate time to strike, and procure the difficult-to-obtain explosives from the FBI. Morlandia Dep. 31:3-32:5. It is unclear whether the Crusaders would have otherwise been able to obtain such powerful explosives. *Id.* 32:1. Morlandia also secured a location to store them and trained Ms. Forrest. *Id.* 43:20-44:1. On the morning of the incident, Ms. Forrest obtained the explosives from the storage facility in which Morlandia had stored them, picked up Morlandia, and drove to the dealership. *Id.* 43:10. Morlandia waited at the crime scene while Ms. Forrest planted and detonated the explosives, and he drove the getaway car. *Id.* 12:13. At all times during the preparation and execution of the bombing, Ms. Forrest was acting under Morlandia's explicit instructions. Forrest Decl. ¶¶ 42-43. Ms. Forrest never wanted or expected to participate in this or any violent criminal activity and has stated that she will "regret it until the day [she] dies[s]." *Id.* ¶ 41.

ARGUMENT

The Court should dismiss the indictment because the government's investigative tactics exceeded due process limits.

This Court should dismiss the indictment because the government's conduct in this case exceeded due process limits.

The United States Supreme Court has recognized that the Due Process Clause of the Constitution imposes limits on the methods law enforcement may use to obtain convictions and, accordingly, convictions obtained through improper means are barred. *United States v. Russell*, 411 U.S. 423, 431 (1973) ("we may some day be presented with a situation in which the conduct of law enforcement agents is so outrageous that due process principles would absolutely bar the government from invoking judicial processes to obtain a conviction"). Unlike the defense of entrapment, a claim of outrageous government conduct may be successful even when the defendant was predisposed to commit the crime. *Hampton v. United States*, 425 U.S. 484, 495 (1976) (Powell, J., concurring); *id.* at 497 (Brennan, J., dissenting); *see also United States v. Bogart*, 783 F.2d 1428, 1432 (9th Cir. 1986) (explaining that the concurring and dissenting justices in *Hampton* comprised a majority to support the availability of an outrageous government conduct claim regardless of a defendant's criminal predisposition). The motion to dismiss the indictment raises a question of law for the Court to decide rather than the jury. *United States v. Gardner*, 658 F. Supp. 1573, 1577 (W.D. Pa. 1987).

The availability of a dismissal based on outrageous government conduct is necessary to guard against "'the dangers of overzealous law enforcement.'" *United States v. Twigg*,

588 F.2d 373, 380 (3d Cir. 1978) (quoting *Sherman v. United States*, 356 U.S. 369, 381 (1958) (Frankfurter, J., concurring)). This overzealousness is not merely theoretical but has warranted dismissals of indictments in several federal cases. *Twigg*, 588 F.2d 373, 380; *United States v. West*, 511 F.2d 1083, 1086 (3d Cir. 1975); *Greene v. United States*, 454 F.2d 783, 786-87 (9th Cir. 1971); *Gardner*, 658 F. Supp. at 1579; *United States v. Batres-Santolino*, 521 F. Supp. 744, 753 (N.D. Cal. 1981); *see also United States v. Luttrell*, 889 F.2d 806, 813-14 (9th Cir. 1989) (finding that indictment should be dismissed if government did not have reason to investigate defendants prior to presenting them with an opportunity to engage in criminal conduct and remanding for a factual determination of whether such a reason existed); *United States v. Archer*, 486 F.2d 670, 677 (2d Cir. 1973) (dismissing indictment on other grounds but stating it might have found government's authorization of crimes by government agents to be sufficiently outrageous to warrant dismissal on due process grounds).

The dangers of overzealous law enforcement that underlie the outrageous conduct theory are evident in this case. Ms. Forrest was a nonviolent environmental activist who had participated in only two minor acts of vandalism prior to becoming caught up in the criminal plan devised by the government's informant. The informant first coerced her into committing the crime by threatening her life and then directed every aspect of the plan. This case thus presents both of the main factual circumstances that have warranted dismissals of indictments on due process grounds: over-involvement in criminal activity and coercive tactics. Moreover, the government's conduct was improper even under the five-factor test on which the government relies to justify its tactics.

A. The government informant's role in planning and executing the bombing shocks the universal sense of justice.

The government's conduct requires dismissal of the indictment on due process grounds because the government's involvement in the bombing was excessive. This Court has held that an indictment must be dismissed when the government manufactured the crime to secure a conviction rather than to protect the public from ongoing criminal activity. *Bogart*, 783 F.2d at 1436, 1438. Ms. Forrest's indictment must be dismissed under this standard for the following three reasons. First, Morlandia completely manufactured the bombing from start to finish. Second, at the time Morlandia approached Ms. Forrest, she was not engaging in or planning any illegal activity. Third, Morlandia was motivated by pressure to obtain a conviction.

1. The government and its informant manufactured the crime from start to finish.

The degree of control the informant exercised over the bombing exceeds constitutional limits on government involvement in criminal activity.

The Due Process Clause limits the extent to which the government can involve itself in criminal activity. In *Greene*, for example, the court dismissed an indictment on bootlegging charges largely because of the government agent's role in setting up, supplying, and continuing the bootlegging operation. *Greene*, 454 F.2d at 786-87. Specifically, the agent had offered to find a still site, still equipment, and an operator. *Id.* at 786. In addition, the agent had actually provided two thousand pounds of sugar to ensure the continued operation of the still. *Id.* And the government agent was the only customer of the operation he had helped to create. *Id.* at 787. The court concluded that this conduct rose to a level of "creative activity" "substantially more intense and aggressive than the level of such activity charged against the government in prior entrapment cases." *Id.* It found that "when the government permits itself to become enmeshed in criminal activity, from beginning to end, to the extent which appears here, the same underlying objections which render entrapment repugnant to American criminal justice are operative." *Id.; see also Twigg*, 588 F.2d at 380 (basing dismissal of indictment in part on government's role in providing a location, supplies, and necessary expertise to enable the defendants' production of narcotics and on the court's conclusion that although defendants raised capital for the operation, the agent was "completely in charge" of the drug laboratory).

Extensive government involvement in criminal activity is particularly offensive when it enables crimes that would otherwise not have occurred. *Gardner*, 658 F. Supp. at 1567 (applying a four-factor test that includes consideration of whether the crime "would not have occurred but for the government's assistance"); *see also Bogart*, 783 F.2d at 1435 n.7 (recognizing the four-factor test without explicitly adopting it). Accordingly, the inability of the defendant to successfully commit the crime absent government involvement may support dismissal of the indictment. In *Twigg*, for example, due process prevented the government from obtaining a conviction for the manufacture of narcotics when the defendants lacked the expertise and may have lacked the ability to obtain a key ingredient to commit the crime absent the government's involvement. *Twigg*, 588 F.2d at 380. The court further found that the assistance provided by the defendants was "minimal and then at the specific direction of" the agent. *Id.* at 381. Similarly, the court in *Batres-Santolino*, 521 F. Supp. at 751, based its dismissal of a drug indictment partly on its conclusion that it was "inconceivable that [the defendants] could have entered the secretive world of international drug smuggling on their own" when they had never imported cocaine before and had no foreign source of supply of their own. Therefore, the court concluded that "government agents 'manufactured' a crime that . . . could not and would not have been committed if [the informant] had not inveigled defendants into it and offered to provide them with an otherwise unavailable source of supply of the illegal drug they were to import." *Id.*

Based on the case law explained above, the indictment should be dismissed because Morlandia manufactured the crime from start to finish. Like the agent in *Twigg*, Morlandia was "completely in charge" of the criminal enterprise. *Twigg*, 588 F.2d at 380. Not only did he plan the entire mission, but he also provided all the materials necessary to carry out the mission. Without any assistance from Ms. Forrest, Morlandia investigated the location of the crime, determined where and how to strike, and obtained the explosives from the FBI. Morlandia Dep. 31:3-32:4. In fact, Ms. Forrest's participation in the crime was even more minor than that of the defendants in either *Greene* or *Twigg*. Whereas the defendants in *Greene* manufactured bootleg alcohol, and the defendants in *Twigg* raised capital for the operation and arranged for distribution of the product, Ms. Forrest's participation in the crime was limited to following Morlandia's specific instructions. Forrest Decl. ¶¶ 43-44. In fact, Morlandia had to train Ms. Forrest in advance on how to set up the explosives. *Id.* ¶¶ 43-44.

Moreover, the bombing in this case could not have been committed without the government's involvement. Like the defendants in *Batres-Santolino*, who were novices incapable of engaging in drug smuggling without the government's assistance, Ms. Forrest similarly lacked the expertise to execute the bombing on her own. Although Ms. Forrest had been trained on how to make incendiary devices, Ms. Forrest explained that she was "hopeless at that kind of stuff." *Id.* ¶¶ 43-44. Therefore, it is unlikely she could have made the explosives necessary to carry out the bombing. Moreover, she did not have a source from which to obtain explosives. *Id.* ¶ 42. The government's provision of the explosives was critical to Ms. Forrest's ability to commit the crime. As in *Batres-Santolino*, *Twigg*, and *Greene*, the government's enablement of a crime that would otherwise not have occurred exceeds due process limits on government involvement in criminal activity and should result in a dismissal of the indictment.

2. The government's over-involvement in the bombing led Ms. Forrest to commit a crime she would not otherwise have committed.

The indictment should be dismissed because the Defendant was not planning to bomb a car dealership or commit any similar act until the government's informant approached her with the plan.

Courts have found that the government's involvement in initiating and directing criminal activity is particularly offensive when the "government generate[s] new crimes" by a defendant who was not otherwise engaged in or planning criminal activity. *Twigg*, 588 F.2d at 381. In *Twigg*, defendants Neville and Twigg challenged their convictions on charges of illegal drug manufacture. *Id.* at 374. The speed laboratory for which they were arrested had been originally proposed by an informant. *Id.* at 380. Although the informant had operated a speed laboratory with Neville more than three years earlier, neither Neville nor Twigg was engaged in any illegal activity at the time the informant contacted Neville to propose setting up a new laboratory. *Id.* at 375 n.2. Neville was immediately receptive to the idea and never expressed any hesitation. *Id.* at 376. Despite Neville's willing participation in the scheme, the court found that the government's role in originating the criminal plan and supplying the indispensable expertise needed to run the laboratory violated due process and required reversal of both defendants' convictions. *Id.* at 381. The court explained that "fundamental fairness does not permit [the courts] to countenance" the "generat[ion] of new crimes by the defendant . . . when, as far as the record shows, he was lawfully and peacefully minding his own affairs." *Id.*; *see also Bogart*, 783 F.2d at 1435 n.7 (recognizing ongoing criminal activity as a factor some courts have considered); *West*, 511 F.2d at 1086 (suggesting that whereas the government's provision of materials to make illegal drugs would not be outrageous where the government suspected the defendant was engaged in illegal drug activity, the result should be different where the defendant had not previously been engaged in drug transactions); *Gardner*, 658 F. Supp. at 1576 (considering absence of any ongoing criminal activity by defendant prior to his contact with government agent as one factor supporting dismissal of indictment).

The prior innocence of the defendant, however, does not appear to be a necessary element of establishing an outrageous conduct claim. In *Batres-Santolino*, for example, the court dismissed the indictment, 521 F. Supp. at 753, because even though at least one of the defendants had dealt cocaine on a small scale before, *id.* at 749, none of the defendants had ever imported cocaine prior to the encouragement of government agents, *id.* at 751.

Moreover, a vague, unrealized intent to engage in the type of crime at issue does not preclude an outrageous government conduct claim when the government's encouragement of the crime was central to its commission. In *Greene*, for example, the government reinitiated contact with the defendants at a time when they were released on bail after arrests that resulted from a successful sting operation that "terminated" their bootlegging operation. 454 F.2d at 784, 787. In response to the government agent's telephone call, which was intended merely to confirm that his cover had not been compromised, the defendants revealed that they were planning to get back into bootlegging. *Id.* at 785. They did not, however, have a still at the time and encountered various difficulties in getting their operation up and running again. *Id.* The government agent's subsequent involvement in the "creation and maintenance" of their bootlegging operation, including the supply of two thousand pounds of sugar, led the court to dismiss the indictment on due process grounds. *Id.* at 786-87.

In this case, as in *Twigg*, the defendant was not engaged in or planning any criminal activity. In fact, whereas defendant Neville was an enthusiastic participant in the crime conceived by the informant, Ms. Forrest was extremely reluctant to assist Morlandia in the bombing. She told Morlandia that she "didn't think [she] could do something like that" and acquiesced only after he warned her that EARTH could not "take chances with defectors." Forrest Decl. ¶¶ 42-43. Therefore, Morlandia's role in creating new crime by Ms. Forrest was even more pronounced than the government's role in *Twigg*.

Although Ms. Forrest was a member of the Crusaders and had committed two minor acts of vandalism prior to her contact with Morlandia, *id.* ¶ 41, neither her prior crimes nor her mere membership in a terrorist organization justifies Morlandia's solicitation and direction of her involvement in the bombing. Just as the minor drug transactions previously engaged in by one of the defendant's in *Batres-Santolino* did not indicate he would have engaged in the large-scale importation of drugs for which he was arrested, Ms. Forrest's minor acts of vandalism do not suggest she would have engaged in a bombing of a car dealership absent Morlandia's initiation and planning of the crime. Moreover, while her membership in EARTH might suggest a vague intent to someday engage in some type of sabotage in furtherance of EARTH's goals, she was neither engaged in nor planning any criminal act. Since the *Greene* defendants' hope of reestablishing a bootleg operation did not affect the availability of the outrageous conduct defense where the government's involvement was instrumental in their ability to realize that hope, Ms. Forrest's membership in EARTH should not bar her from asserting the defense. Morlandia's substantial role in creating and carrying out the plan for the bombing was even more egregious than the government's role in encouraging and supporting the bootleg operation in *Greene*. In this case, the government not only offered encouragement and supplies, but also decided all of the details of the plan for the bombing and directed Ms. Forrest's involvement. Accordingly, dismissal of the indictment is even more warranted here than it was in *Greene*.

3. The informant's eagerness to procure Ms. Forrest's involvement in the bombing resulted from the FBI's threat that it would arrest him for terrorism.

The informant's conduct in this case was outrageous because he was motivated solely by a desire to secure a conviction to avoid his own imprisonment.

It is unclear whether courts must address the motive of the government in inducing the crime. *See Bogart*, 783 F.2d at 1436, 1438 (stating initially that "criminal sanction is not justified when the state manufactures crimes that would otherwise not occur" but later adding "to secure the defendant's conviction rather than to protect the public from the defendant's continuing criminal behavior"). In any event, none of the decisions barring convictions on the ground of outrageous government conduct have discussed specific evidence of the government's motives. Instead, those courts that have considered motive a factor have found the factor satisfied by the lack of any criminal activity by the defendant at the time of the investigation. *See Twigg*, 588 F.2d at 381 (finding the government "generated new crimes by the defendant merely for the sake of pressing criminal charges" based on the lack of evidence that the defendants were engaged in criminal activity prior to the informant's proposal to create a speed laboratory); *United States v. Valdovinos-Valdovinos*, 588 F. Supp. 551, 556 (N.D. Cal. 1984) (holding that an undercover operation that circulated its telephone number in an unregulated manner and then advised callers from Mexico that it was acceptable to enter the United States without proper immigration papers constituted "the generation by police of new crimes merely for the sake of pressing criminal charges"), *rev'd on other grounds*, 793 F.2d 1436 (9th Cir. 1985); *Batres-Santolino*, 521 F. Supp. at 752 (concluding, based on the lack of any evidence that defendants were engaged in ongoing illegal activity when the government prompted them to import drugs, that the government "implant[ed] in the mind of an innocent person the disposition to commit the alleged offense and induce[d] its commission in order that they may prosecute") (quoting *Sherman*, 356 U.S. at 372).

Moreover, the motive of the government in inducing crime by someone who is not currently engaged in or contemplating criminal activity is suspect even when the government is not specifically targeting the particular defendant. In *Valdovinos-Valdovinos*, the undercover operation aimed to apprehend transporters of illegal aliens. 588 F. Supp. at 553. The government used its undercover telephone number to encourage Mexican citizens to cross the border illegally so that it could catch the aliens' transporters. *Id.* The defendant was arrested for transporting one of the Mexican citizens the government had encouraged to cross the border illegally. *Id.* at 554. Despite the legitimate goal of catching transporters, the court found that the generation of crimes by falsely telling Mexican citizens they could cross the border legally was a violation of due process. *Id.* at 556. Similarly, in *Twigg*, the court held that the agent's "specific direction" of defendant Twigg's actions in furtherance of the crime required reversal of his conviction even though Twigg was brought into the conspiracy by an acquaintance and not by the agent. 588 F.2d at 382.

As discussed above in Subsection 2, Ms. Forrest was not engaged in or planning criminal activity before Morlandia recruited her for the bombing. Therefore, as in *Twigg*,

Batres-Santolino, and *Valdovinos-Valdovinos*, the Court should infer that the government's role in the bombing was designed to secure a conviction rather than to protect the public from any ongoing criminal activity by Ms. Forrest. Moreover, such an inference has much greater support in this case because Ms. Forrest has provided specific evidence that Morlandia was motivated by a desire to secure a conviction. After an eight-year-long investigation of EARTH that produced relatively few leads or convictions, the FBI in this case exerted pressure on its agents to obtain convictions or face reassignment. Morlandia Dep. 22:10. In particular, Agent Tu threatened Morlandia that he might be arrested if his role as informant did not lead to some arrests. *Id.* 34:20-22. The FBI was so desperate to substantiate its operation that it encouraged overzealous law enforcement. This encouragement prompted Morlandia to lead Ms. Forrest, a relatively harmless environmental advocate, into a serious crime that claimed the life of an innocent man.

Although the FBI's undercover EARTH operation was designed to uncover important intelligence and thwart terrorist activities, *Valdovinos-Valdovinos* established that the broader purpose of a sting operation does not justify the generation of new crimes. 588 F. Supp. at 556. Just as it was wrong to induce aliens to cross the border illegally so that the government could catch their transporters in *Valdovinos-Valdovinos*, it was wrong to induce Ms. Forrest to commit arson in the attenuated hope that Morlandia's role in the mission might eventually enable him to gather some useful intelligence on EARTH's operations. In fact, the government's conduct in this case is even more outrageous than in *Valdovinos-Valdovinos* given the high likelihood of harm to the public that was inherent in the government's plan to intercept the bombing at the last minute. Moreover, as in *Twigg*, the government's specific direction of Ms. Forrest's actions in furtherance of the bombing is no less offensive merely because EARTH, rather than Morlandia, chose to bring her into the plan.

Because the government in this case involved itself in the generation of new crimes by Ms. Forrest in the absence of any evidence that she had been engaging in or planning criminal activity, the indictment should be dismissed.

B. The government's informant's use of coercion to convince Ms. Forrest to help him execute the bombing was fundamentally unfair.

The government informant coerced Ms. Forrest into participating in the bombing by threatening her life. The Due Process Clause forbids the government from inducing crime through coercion and therefore requires dismissal of the indictment.

In addition to the generation of new crimes by the government, unwarranted physical or mental coercion by the government independently requires dismissal of an indictment on due process grounds. *Bogart*, 783 F.2d at 1438. In *Rochin v. California*, 342 U.S. 165, 174 (1952), the Supreme Court reversed a conviction because it had been obtained through excessive physical coercion. Upon entering the defendant's home, the police saw some capsules. *Id.* at 166. The defendant then swallowed the capsules. *Id.* The police "jumped" on the defendant and tried unsuccessfully to extract the capsules. *Id.* They then brought him to the hospital and directed a doctor to forcibly pump his stomach. *Id.* The court found that the police conduct in obtaining the evidence of the defendant's drug possession offended principles of fair play and decency and, therefore, required reversal of his conviction on due process grounds. *Id.* at 173.

Although no court has yet relied exclusively on mental coercion to dismiss an indictment on due process grounds, the court in *Greene* did justify dismissal in part on mental coercion. *Greene*, 454 F.2d at 787. The court's finding of coercion rested on the following facts. When the defendants told the government agent they were having difficulty reestablishing their bootlegging operation, the agent, who was posing as a member of a drug ring, told them that "the boss [was] on [his] back." *Id.* at 785. Several months later, the defendants delivered alcohol from the new operation. *Id.* At trial, the defendants claimed that their discussions about the bootlegging operation were designed merely to impress the agent and that "they were reluctant to act and might never have produced any bootleg alcohol without the prodding of [the agent]." *Id.* at 786. The court found that the agent's statement "could only be construed as a veiled threat" and this threat was one of the reasons the court dismissed the indictment. *Id.* at 787. Mental coercion has similarly been recognized as a potential factor favoring dismissal in *Bogart*, 783 F.2d at 1435 n.7 (recognizing that one factor that courts have used to support dismissal is "whether the government agents persisted with their inducements to overcome the defendant's reluctance to commit the crime") and *Gardner*, 658 F. Supp. at 1574, 1577 (concluding that agent's persistence in inducing and persuading defendant to buy drugs for him through repeated requests and an offer to help repair defendant's car was a factor supporting dismissal of indictment).

Other courts have rejected threats as outrageous conduct but only where the evidence showed that the criminal enterprise under investigation was characterized by the routine use of vulgarity and "puffing." *See, e.g., United States v. Emmert*, 829 F.2d 805, 812 (9th Cir. 1987) (holding that implied threats by agent did not violate due process because they were "ordinary bargaining tactics in drug deals"); *United States v. Reynoso-Ulloa*, 548 F.2d 1329, 1340 (9th Cir. 1977) (concluding that agent's threat that he would kill defendant's friends if deal did not go through was not outrageous conduct when viewed in the context of the "vulgarity and 'puffing'" engaged in by all participants in the drug transaction at issue).

In the instant case, Morlandia's coercion of Ms. Forrest to participate in the bombing so far exceeded the degree of coercion in *Greene* that it should be independently sufficient to warrant dismissal of the indictment. Ms. Forrest was reluctant to participate in the bombing and told Morlandia she did not think she could "do something like that." Forrest Decl. ¶ 42. Morlandia then appealed to Ms. Forrest's environmental sympathies and even linked her participation to the future of her three-year-old daughter. *Id.* When these persuasive tactics failed, he turned to threats. Specifically, after a dramatic pause he said, "I hope you'll make the right decision. You understand that we cannot take chances with defectors." *Id.* ¶¶ 42-43. Ms. Forrest stated that she immediately feared for her safety and only then told Morlandia that she would "do what was required." *Id.* ¶ 43. Morlandia's use of the threat of death to procure Ms. Forrest's participation in the bombing offends fair play and decency just as surely as did the government's extraction of evidence from the defendant's stomach in *Rochin*. Indeed, it is more offensive since it was not directed merely at obtaining evidence of a preexisting crime but, in fact, coerced Ms. Forrest to commit the crime for which she has been convicted.

Notably, there is no evidence to suggest that Morlandia had to threaten Ms. Forrest in order to maintain his cover. Ms. Forrest was the only person present for the conversation. In contrast to the drug dealers involved in *Reynoso-Ulloa* and *Emmert*, Ms. Forrest was an assistant director of a nonprofit environmental action group whose worst infractions prior to her involvement in this crime were spray-painting an SUV and puncturing tires. *Id.* ¶¶ 40, 41. Moreover, Ms. Forrest's statement that "[i]t never occurred to [her] before this that EARTH-ers might be dangerous," reveals that violent threats were not a common practice among Crusaders. *Id.* ¶ 43. Thus, rather than necessary "puffing" characteristic of the criminal enterprise he was investigating, Morlandia's threat was clearly an effort to coerce Ms. Forrest to commit the crime for which the government now seeks to convict her. It was specifically designed to induce fear. Accordingly, the informant's conduct in this case shocks the conscience and requires dismissal of the indictment.

C. The government's conduct in this case fails the five-factor test the Ninth Circuit has used to reject claims of outrageous government conduct.

Even under the five-factor test upon which the government relies to justify its conduct, the government clearly exceeded due process limits.

The Ninth Circuit has established a five-factor test, which, when satisfied, will preclude claims of outrageous government conduct. *United States v. Bonanno*, 852 F.2d 434, 437-38 (9th Cir. 1988). The factors are: (1) the defendant was already involved in a continuing series of similar crimes, or the charged criminal enterprise was already in process at the time the government agent became involved; (2) the agent's participation was not necessary to enable the defendant to continue the criminal activity; (3) the agent used artifice and stratagem to ferret out criminal activity; (4) the agent infiltrated a criminal organization; and (5) the agent approached persons already contemplating or engaged in criminal activity. *Id.* The use of "and" as a conjunction suggests all five factors must be satisfied by the facts of the case. In any event, the facts of this case fail to satisfy any of the five factors.

Factors one, three, four, and five are not satisfied in this case because, as explained in Section A.2 above, Ms. Forrest was not engaged in or planning criminal activity prior to the government's involvement with her and Morlandia's conduct created rather than infiltrated a criminal enterprise. In *United States v. Williams*, 547 F.3d 1187, 1200-01 (9th Cir. 2008), the court found factors one, three, four, and five of the *Bonanno* test were satisfied because the defendant was introduced to the agent as a drug dealer and was already planning a bank robbery before the agent convinced the defendant to rob a fictitious stash house instead. By contrast, Ms. Forrest was not planning any criminal activity prior to Morlandia's efforts to persuade her to participate in the car dealership bombing. Therefore, Morlandia created rather than "ferret[ed] out" criminal activity and created rather than "infiltrated" a criminal enterprise. *Bonanno*, 852 F.2d at 437-38.

The second factor is also not satisfied in this case because, as explained in Section A.1 above, Ms. Forrest was not capable of carrying out the bombing without Morlandia's assistance. In *Williams*, the second factor was satisfied because the defendant had already established detailed plans for a similar robbery and had an "experienced crew" that he represented was capable of handling the job. *Williams*, 547 F.3d at 1200. By contrast, in this case, Ms. Forrest had no plan, no explosives, and no experience to indicate she could have carried out the bombing without Morlandia's assistance. Because the facts of this case do not satisfy the five-factor test and because they do, as explained in earlier sections of this brief, establish outrageous government conduct, this Court should dismiss the indictment.

CONCLUSION

For the reasons explained above, the Court should dismiss Ms. Forrest's indictment.

Dated: March 14, 2010

Respectfully submitted,

____

Jane Doe
Attorney for the Appellee

INDEX